OLYMPIA GUIDE

CZECHOSLOVAK

PRAGUE

OLYMPIA GUIDE

CZECHOSLOVAKIA
PRAGUE

CONTENTS

Contents

HOW TO USE THIS GUIDE

Czechoslovakia offers foreign visitors a very rich selection of interesting tourist sights and enough opportunities for everyone to enjoy several days or even weeks of active rest. One of the most attractive tourist destinations from the viewpoint of cultural and art history is Prague, the capital of the country. However, Czechoslovakia has scores of towns whose centre ranks among the gems of Central Europe. The objects of admiration include picturesque castles, châteaux and fortresses, now, naturally, often in ruins. Preserved buildings house museums and galleries, or serve the purposes of the most varied cultural institutions. In Czechoslovakia you will come across attractive folk architecture in its original environment and in skansens. Lovers of nature will find a wealth of opportunities to indulge their interests. National parks and protected landscape regions form the most valuable territorial wholes. Diverse forms and types of landscape — from high-mountain ranges to fertile lowlands — can be seen in the course of one-day excursions. This country has innumerable picturesque corners suitable for walking tours, skiing and bathing. Czechoslovakia is a big power also in the sphere of balneology.

The first part of this guide provides basic information about the natural features, history, culture, population, state administration and economy of Czechoslovakia. You can plan your itinerary on the basis of the information presented in the separate chapter headed **Tourist destinations.** In the dense surveys you will also find concrete possibilities for holidays at the waterside, for winter sports, for visits to special museums, and for watching outstanding sports and cultural events with international participation. The chapter headed **Practical information** contains valuable advice for travelling through the country.

A detailed text is devoted to the capital of Czechoslovakia, **Prague.** It contains instructions for several walks through the historical core of the city. Other places and also whole regions of interest are dealt with in alphabetical order in the **chapter Czechoslovakia A—Z (Topographical index).** Here greater attention is devoted to the capital of Slovakia, Bratislava, and the trade fair town Brno. The localization of all places relates to the co-ordinates on the enclosed map (e.g. Fulnek J-2 indicates that you will find the town in the square defined by the horizontal co-ordinate J and the vertical co-ordinate 2). Smaller places of interest are described in the environs of more important destinations with indication of their distance and the respective cardinal point (e.g. SW indicates south-west). You will find car camps and petrol stations on the enclosed map. You are recommended to reserve hotel accommodation in advance through the mediation of the Čedok Travel Office, which will send you its offer on request. The names of towns and communities are presented in Czech (Slovak), the names of mountain ranges, rivers and landscape wholes being used in the original language only in the items of the chapter Czechoslovakia A—Z. Otherwise names are translated where possible (e.g. the topographical item Vysoké Tatry appears in the rest of the text as the High Tatras). Orientation in the publication and the enclosed map is facilitated by an **index** of places at the end of the guide.

The numerous photographs contained herein will afford a more concrete idea of Czechoslovakia.

How to use
this guide

CHARACTERISTICS

OF THE COUNTRY

GEOGRAPHICAL POSITION

Czechoslovakia lies in the geographical centre of Europe. Its capital is Prague. The country spreads out between the 48th and the 51st degree of northern latitude and the 12th and the 22nd degree of eastern longitude, this meaning that in a straight line it covers a distance of 767 km in west-east direction and 276 km in north-south direction. Its total area is 127,877 sq. km. It lies 326 km from the Štětín Gulf of the Baltic Sea, 322 km from the Adriatic Sea and 678 km from the Black Sea. Czechoslovakia neighbours with the German Democratic Republic (common border 459 km) and Poland (1,391 km) in the north, with the Union of Soviet Socialist Republics (98 km) in the east, with Hungary (679 km) and Austria (570 km) in the south and with the Federal Republic of Germany (356 km) in the west.

A typical landscape in the
Bohemian Central Highlands
in North Bohemia

OROGRAPHY

The surface of Czechoslovakia is very heterogeneous. Its highest point is the peak Gerlachovský štít (2,655 m) in the High Tatras and its lowest point lies south of the River Bodrog (94 m) in East Slovakia. Elevations of 201—600 m above sea level prevail (62 %), 20.6 % being made up of elevations of 601—1,000 m, 13.7 % of elevations up to 200 m and 3.7 % of elevations exceeding 1,000 m. The biggest part of the Republic is divided by the Bohemian Highlands and the West and East Carpathians, the dividing line running approximately from Ostrava to Znojmo.

Practically the whole of Bohemia (the western part of Czechoslovakia) is bordered by mountain massifs: the border with Austria and the Federal Republic of Germany follows the Šumava Mountains (Plechý 1,378 m) with big areas of forests, a large part of the border with the German Democratic Republic is covered by the ridge of the Krušné (Ore) Mountains (Klínovec 1,244 m), the Jizerské (Jizera) Mountains (Smrk 1,124 m) and the biggest Czech range, the Krkonoše (Giant) Mountains (Sněžka 1,602 m) spread out along the Polish border in the north and the ridge of the Orlické (Eagle) Mountains (Velká Deštná 1,115 m) rises further eastwards. Bohemia and Moravia are separated by Českomoravská vrchovina (the Bohemian-Moravian Highlands; Javořice 837 m). The highest mountain range in Moravia (the central part of Czechoslovakia) is Hrubý Jeseník (Praděd 1,492 m), the more easterly situated Moravskoslezské Beskydy (Moravian-Silesian Beskids; Lysá hora 1,323 m) belonging in the Carpathian system. Rising steeply in the north of Slovakia (the eastern part of Czechoslovakia) are the rocky peaks of Vysoké Tatry (the High Tatras), the highest mountain range in Czechoslovakia as a whole (Gerlachovský štít 2,655 m), closely neighboured by Západné Tatry (the West Tatras; Bystrá 2,248 m) and Belianske Ta-

Orography

Veľký Rozsutec
and Malý Rozsutec
in the Little Fatra

try (the Belianske Tatras; Havran 2,152 m). The 80 km long ridge of Nízke Tatry (the Low Tatras; Ďumbier 2,043 m) runs in west-east direction in the south and running in parallel with it 600 m lower is the ridge of Slovenské rudohorie (the Slovak Ore Mountains; Stolica 1,476 m). Malá Fatra (the Little Fatra; Veľký Kriváň 1,709 m) and Veľká Fatra (the Big Fatra; Ostredok 1,592 m) also rank among Slovakia's best-known mountain ranges.

HYDROGRAPHY

Czechoslovakia is drained into the North Sea to the extent of 39 % (practically all waters are carried away from Bohemia by the River Elbe), into the Black Sea to the extent of 54 % (most of the waters from Moravia and Slovakia flow into the Danube) and into the Baltic Sea to the extent of 7 % (the northernmost territory of Bohemia and Moravia belongs in the basin of the River Oder, Slovakia in the basin of the

The border River
Dunajec at Pieniny

River Visla). In all, Czechoslovakia's rivers measure over 100,000 km. The longest are the Vltava (433 km) and the Váh (390 km), while Dunaj (the Danube; 2,291 m^3 . sec^{-1}), Labe (the Elbe; 306 m^3 . sec^{-1}) and the Váh (152 m^3 . sec^{-1}) have the most water. A cascade of dams has been built especially on the Vltava and the Váh (the biggest is Orlík — 90 m and the biggest reservoir is retained by Lipno dam — 4,870 hectares). The greatest number of lakes is situated in the High Tatras (110), the biggest of them being Veľké Hincovo (20.1 hectares). The biggest lake in Bohemia is Černé jezero in the Šumava Mountains (18 hectares). Particularly rich in ponds is South Bohemia (about 5,000), the biggest one being Rožmberk (489 hectares) near Třeboň. A considerable part of Czechoslovakia's natural wealth consists of mineral springs (there are some 3,000 of them) on which the renown of numerous spa towns is based (see also the chapter Spas).

CLIMATE

Czechoslovakia belongs in the zone with a mild climate. Its elongated territory lies on the border between the mainly oceanic and the mainly inland climate. The warmest region of the country includes the valley of the Danube (yearly average 10.7° C). Temperatures drop according to the height above sea level. The yearly average temperature on the peak Lomnický štít is −3.7° C. The highest temperature in Czechoslovakia has been measured at Komárno (+ 39.8° C) and the lowest at České Budějovice (−42.2° C). The biggest rainfall is again in the High Tatras (up to 2,130 mm annually at the chalet Zbojnická chata), the lowest being characteristic of the Žatec region (410 mm). The amount of yearly sunshine also increases approximately from west to east (1,450 hours yearly in the Cheb region and 2,150 hours in the Danube valley). On the average snow forms 20−50 % of the rainfall, the number of days on which snow falls in the mountains exceeding 80. The average yearly temperature in Prague is 9.7° C, in Brno 8.8° C and in Bratislava 10.3° C, the average yearly rainfall in these cities being 491, 531 and 642 mm respectively.

FLORA AND FAUNA

Over 3,500 species of tall **flowering plants** have been ascertained on the territory of the Czechoslovak Socialist Republic. A few of them are of an endemic nature, which means that they do not occur elsewhere, or are relics of the last Ice Age. The greater part of the territory of the Czech Socialist Republic belongs to the region of **Hercyn or Central European forest flora**, only the lowlands of South Moravia, the Upper Moravian Vale, the Elbe lowlands and the Ohře valley, including the Bohemian Central Highlands, are the domain of warmth-loving **Pannonian flora**. The East Moravian mountain ranges and the greater part of mountainous Slovakia are the home of **West Carpathian flora**, the lowlands of South Slovakia forming a part of the domain of Pannonian flora, whose origin lies in the lowlands of the Danube. A very small area of the mountains in north-east Slovakia acts as host to outstanding types of **East Carpathian flora**. Approximately one third of the territory of the Czechoslo-

vak Socialist Republic is covered with **forests** — the western part with fir and mixed trees and the eastern part mostly with deciduous trees. Apart from several remainders of original meadow forests, oak groves, mountain spruce forests and young fir and beech forests preserved in state nature preserves, Czechoslovakia's present vegetation cover is the result of human interventions in the countryside in the course of approximately the last 7,000 years.

In harmony with the varied geological structure and the diversity of the flora on the territory of the Czechoslovak Socialist Republic a wealth of different kinds of **fauna** also lives here — according to present estimates approximately 50,000 species, in particular, however, of insects and other invertebrates, including protozoans. Of the 80 species of mammals especially the bear, lynx and wild cat and, in the mountains, the chamois and marmot are remarkable for Central Europe. The European stag and the roebuck also occur in large numbers. In addition, 365 kinds of birds, 70 species of fish, 12 kinds of snakes and 18 types of amphibians have been ascertained on Czechoslovak territory. Over 200 species of flora and over 300 species of fauna are protected by law.

HISTORY

The territory of Czechoslovakia has been settled unceasingly since the oldest times. Finds document the existence of Neandertal primeval man here and the first people of our type lived in the basins of all big rivers (for example, finds from the times of mammoth hunters at Dolní Věstonice in South Moravia). **Celtic** oppida founded as long ago as 300 B.C. and then up to the beginning of our era (Závist near Prague)

Bukačka primeval forest
in the Orlické Mountains

were centres of a mature culture. In the 2nd century Roman legions penetrated as far as the present-day town of Trenčín.

The **Slavs** evidently settled the territory of present-day Czechoslovakia in the 5th century and in the 9th century they founded the first state formation of western Slavs — the **Great Moravian Empire.** Its focus lay in the basin of the River Morava (Mikulčice, Pohansko, Staré Město u Uherského Hradiště); the Nitra region was an important part of the empire and Bohemia also belonged to it.

The oldest churches on the territory of Czechoslovakia date from the first half of the 9th century, but greater spreading of the new religion was brought about by the Byzantine mission of Constantine and Method in 863. After the overthrowing of the Great Moravian Empire by the Hungarians the focus of state life was shifted to Central Bohemia, Slovakia forming a part of the Hungarian state until 1918. The **Přemyslid dynasty** ruled in Bohemia and Moravia.

In the 13th century the Czech kingdom ranked among the most powerful European countries. It underwent considerable economic development, mining activity flourished (Kutná Hora) and most of the towns of the present were founded — the period of reign of Přemysl Otakar I (1197—1230), Václav I (1230—1253), Přemysl Otakar II

History

Small Romanesque church
at Poříčí nad Sázavou

(1253—1278) and Václav II (1283—1305). After the Tartar invasion in the mid-13th century towns began to be founded in Slovakia as well and gold and silver mining developed (Kremnica, Banská Bystrica, Banská Štiavnica).

The peak period of the feudal state in Bohemia was the reign of **Charles IV** (1346—1378), who was also the Roman emperor. He attached Silesia, Lower Lusatia and Brandenburg to the Czech crown and brought about the development of culture. In 1348 he founded a university in Prague and had a number of monumental buildings erected. At that time Hungary also experienced a period of flourish, the ruler of that country from 1342 to 1382 being Louis I.

In Bohemia the results of the crisis which affected the whole of medieval Europe culminated in the **Hussite revolutionary movement** marked by the reformatory teaching of John Huss (Jan Hus) and his burning at the stake at Constance in Germany (1415). One of the most important centres of the Hussite revolutionary movement was the town of Tábor in South Bohemia. The Hussite armies were under the command of Jan Žižka and later of Prokop Holý. The radical Hussite movement was defeated in 1434 at the Battle of Lipany, but numerous consequences of the revolution survived for a long time. On the other hand, the power of the Catholic church was paralysed. Czech national self-confidence was strengthened. The Hussite movement also penetrated into Slovakia, where the whole of its eastern and a part of its central territory was under the rule of Hussite soldiers.

The Czech king **George of Poděbrady** (Jiří Poděbradský; 1458—1471) put forward a proposal concerning the formation of a peaceful union of European rulers. His death was followed by the period of the none too strong reign of the Jagiello dynasty. From 1490 Vladislav II (1471—1516) was also the king of Hungary, in 1526 the Hungarian and Czech armies were defeated by the Turks in the Battle of Mohács (during which King **Louis** also lost his life) and the border of the Turkish empire

Husinec in South Bohemia
— the birth-place
of Master John Huss

gradually shifted as far as South Slovakia. In 1526 Ferdinand I (1526—1564) of the **Hapsburg** dynasty was elected to rule as the Czech and Hungarian king. In the first half of the 16th century a big anti-feudal uprising broke out in Hungary (in 1514 the György Dózsa rebellion, in 1525—1526 a miners' revolt at Banská Bystrica) and in Bohemia the years 1546 to 1547 were marked by the first revolt of the Estates whose defeat resulted in the restriction of the power of towns. In 1618 the Estates rose up against the absolutistic endeavours of the Habsburgs, giving origin to the beginning of the **Thirty Years' War** throughout Europe. The troops of the Czech Estates were defeated in the Battle of the White Mountain in 1620, this opening the way for the Hapsburgs to assert strongly their policies of absolutism, centralization and forceful re-Catholization. Many people were compelled to emigrate (Jan Amos Komenský — Comenius). After the war a great part of the country was devastated and the population decreased by about one half. The feudal lords therefore raised the feudal taxes in all ways possible and bound the population to the soil, this giving rise to numerous **peasant revolts** (especially in the years 1680—1775). In the 17th and 18th centuries Slovakia, which was the core of Hungary (the greater part of which was occupied by the Turks), witnessed a number of uprisings of the Estates against the Hapsburgs (István Bocskay, Gabor Bethlen, Ferenc II Rákócsi).

The abolition of serfdom in the Czech Lands in 1781 and in Slovakia in 1785 consolidated the conditions for the development of capitalist relations. The **first factories** originated and modern transport developed (the Vienna — Bohumín railway line in the years 1836—1847). In the same period the so-called **national revival** brought the Czech and Slovak nations close together. The revolutionary movement of 1848 (a five-day battle at the Prague barricades in June) contributed to the collapse of the feudal system. The constitution of 1867 guaranteed basic civil freedoms and the Czech national culture underwent development. Industry developed (the consummation of the industrial revolution) and in 1878 the working class founded the **Social Democratic Party**. In Slovakia, where a strong process of Hungarization took place after the Austrian-Hungarian settlement, industrial development occurred later. From the eighties of the 19th century the class struggle between the bourgeoisie and the proletariat grew in strength, its strongest manifestation being a fight for general voting rights. In 1890 the workers celebrated May Day for the first time. Towards the end of the First World War a revolutionary situation developed. A military revolt broke out at Rumburk, a bloody anti-war demonstration took place at Prostějov and on 14 October, 1918 a general strike was waged on the whole territory of Bohemia and Moravia. The Austrian-Hungarian monarchy fell and on 28 October the **independent Czechoslovak Republic** was proclaimed. Tomáš Garrigue Masaryk was elected its first president.

The defeat of the Slovak Republic of Councils (1919) and the general strike in 1920 determined the bourgeois character of the new republic. Under the influence of the Great October Socialist Revolution the **Communist Party of Czechoslovakia** was founded in 1921. The bourgeois Czechoslovak Republic ranked among the developed countries with considerably developed parliamentary democracy. The world economic crisis of 1929—1934 (over one million unemployed in the Czechoslovak Republic) strongly shook its economy, however. The **Munich dictate** of 1938 attributed the border territory to Germany and in 1939 the rest of Bohemia and Moravia was occupied. Slovakia became a vassal state of Germany. The national liberation struggle of the Czechs and Slovaks culminated in the **Slovak National Uprising** in

1944—1945 and the **May Uprising of the Czech people** in 1945. Prague was liberated by the Red Army on 9 May, 1945.

The adoption of the Košice Governmental Programme on 4 April, 1945 made it possible for the nationalization of the key industry in October 1945. Political actions in February 1948 opened the way for the building-up of socialism. Communist politician Klement Gottwald became president. The leading role of the Communist Party of Czechoslovakia was fully manifested in the political and economic fields (Five-year Plans, the collectivization of agriculture). In 1960 a new constitution was approved and the country was renamed the Czechoslovak Socialist Republic. In 1969 the institutional law on the Czechoslovak federation became valid.

CULTURE

The beginnings of literature on the territory of Czechoslovakia date in the time of the Great Moravian Empire in the 9th century. Archeological excavations have revealed remainders of churches from that period (for example, the church at Mikulčice). Valuable historical sources include **Cosma's chronicle** of 1119—1125, written in Latin. In the 12th—13th century **Romanesque architectural** monuments originated — for example, St. George's Church at Prague Castle, the rotunda on the hill called Říp and at Znojmo (with valuable paintings), little churches at Poříčí nad Sázavou, churches at Spišská Kapitula, Doksany and Bíňa and castles at Přimda and Cheb. From the thirties of the 13th century **Gothic** art began to assert itself. **Dalimil's Chronicle**, written in the Czech language and in verse, was outstanding in the field of literature. The founding of **Prague University** in 1348 was an important event. One of its professors, later to become its rector, was **Master John Huss**. Architecture developed from the Early Gothic of the 14th century (Zvíkov and Bezděz

The memorial to the tragic
extermination of the community
Lidice

Castles) to the High Gothic of the mid-14th century. Outstanding among the architects of Charles IV's time was **Peter Parler**, who participated in the construction of St. Vitus's Cathedral, Karlštejn Castle and Charles Bridge. Worthy of mention among the painters of that time are Master Theodoric, originator of a number of paintings installed in Karlštejn Castle, the Master of the Vyšší Brod Altar, and the Master of the Třeboň Altar (paintings exhibited in the National Gallery in Prague). The Late (so-called Czech) Gothic left a number of architectural monuments behind it, particularly outstanding among which are the Vladislav Hall and the Powder Gate in Prague, St. Barbara's Cathedral at Kutná Hora, a church at Louny and Švihov water castle. These are connected with the names of the architects Matěj Rejsek and

---

Benedikt Ried. The best Gothic works in Slovakia include the cathedral at Košice, a church at Bardejov and Orava and Spiš Castles. One of the foremost Late Gothic sculptors — **Master Pavol of Levoča** — worked at Levoča.

In the **Renaissance period** comfortable noble seats were built instead of strong castles. The Belvedere Summer Palace originated at Prague Castle and outstanding among the châteaux of that time are those at Horšovský Týn, Litomyšl, Telč, Bučovice and Bytča. Then contemporary town houses and palaces were covered with graffito (Schwarzenberg Palace, the square Hradčanské náměstí in Prague). In the years 1579—1593 the **Kralice Bible** was published which was the source of the literary standard for long centuries.

Altar of
Master Pavol
of Levoča

After the Battle of the White Mountain in 1620 a number of the best artists and scientists was obliged to emigrate abroad, their ranks including in particular the brilliant founder of modern pedagogy, **Jan Amos Komenský** (Comenius). **Baroque** architecture contributed in a striking way to the appearance of Czechoslovak towns and villages — for example, St. Nicholas's Church and Wallenstein Palace in Prague, the episcopal château at Kroměříž, the hospital at Kuks, the palaces of the nobility in Bratislava. Outstanding among the architects of that period were Kilian Ignatius Dienzenhofer and Giovanni Santini. The most important personalities of Baroque sculpture were Matthias Bernard Braun, Ferdinand Maximilian Brokof and George Raphael Donner — see, for example, the statues at Kuks, on Charles Bridge and in Bratislava. Outstanding among Baroque painters were Karel Škréta, Václav Vavřinec Reiner, Jan Kupecký and Petr Brandl. Music also underwent considerable development (composers František Václav Míča, Jiří Antonín Benda, Josef Mysliveček).
The late 18th and the first half of the 19th century are referred to as the period of **national revival**. It was then that the foundations of modern Czech and Slovak literature, education, science and art were laid. Two of the first revivalists were Josef Dobrovský and Josef Kollár and an important role was played in the promoting of the Czech language by Josef Jungmann. Credit for the origin of literary Slovak belongs to the poet and politician Ľudovít Štúr. Karel Hynek Mácha stood out among the romantic Czech poets. The poet and journalist Karel Havlíček Borovský waged a fearless fight for Czech national rights on the pages of newspapers and books, the Czech village was portrayed in a masterly way by Božena Němcová and František Palacký dealt with the history of the Czech nation.
In the 19th century **Classicism** initially prevailed among architectural styles (Terezín, Františkovy Lázně), being followed by the **Empire** (Kačina Château) and the **Neo-Gothic** (Hluboká, Lednice, Bouzov, Smolenice and Bojnice Château). Outstanding among sculptors in the mid-19th century was Václav Levý (statues in the environs of Liběchov), while Josef Mánes is particularly noteworthy among the painters of that time.
Of the writers of the latter half of the 19th and the early 20th century mention should be made in particular of the author of numerous historical novels Alois Jirásek, and the poets Jan Neruda, Petr Bezruč and Pavol Országh Hviezdoslav.
The best Czech architects (Josef Zítek), painters (Mikuláš Aleš) and musicians (Bedřich Smetana) are connected with the building of the **National Theatre** (opened in 1883). Other members of this generation were the sculptor Josef Václav Myslbek (the statue of St. Václav in the square Václavské náměstí in Prague) and the composer Antonín Dvořák. Creative art of the Art Nouveau is chiefly represented by the painter Alfons Mucha and the sculptor František Bílek.
After the First World War the writers Karel Čapek and Jaroslav Hašek (author of the book The Good Soldier Švejk) as well as Marie Majerová, Stanislav Kostka Neumann, Ivan Olbracht and others wrote prolifically similarly as Ladislav Novomeský, Peter Jilemnický and Fraňo Kráľ and others in Slovakia. Remarkable works were created by the painters Emil Filla, Max Švabinský and Václav Špála and Jan Štursa was outstanding among sculptors. Testimony to the heroism of the fighters against fascism is provided by Julius Fučík's Reportage Written on the Gallows.
After the **Second World War** the writers Václav Řezáč and Jan Otčenášek and the poets Vítězslav Nezval and Jaroslav Seifert (Nobel Prize winner) — to name a few — were very active just as Rudolf Jašík, Vladimír Mináč, Pavol Horov and others in Slo-

vakia. Modern music is connected with the names of Leoš Janáček, Bohuslav Martinů, Eugen Suchoň and Ján Cikker, painting being represented by Karel Svolinský, Cyril Bouda, Jan Zrzavý, Vojtěch Sedláček, Cyprián Majerník and Ľudovít Fulla and sculpture by Vincenc Makovský, Karel Lidický and many others.

The library of Strahov monastery in Prague

POPULATION

On 1 January 1989 Czechoslovakia had a population of 15,620,000 of which 10,360,000 inhabitants live in the Czech Socialist Republic and 5,260,000 in the Slovak Socialist Republic. As regards the **minorities**, persons of Hungarian nationality make up the biggest of them 3.8 %. Scanty Polish, German and Ukrainian minorities also live on the territory of Czechoslovakia. A large part of the population lives in **towns**, the biggest of which are Prague (pop. 1,200,000) and Bratislava (pop. 435,000). Another 11 towns have a population exceeding 100,000 or closely approaching this number (Brno, Ostrava, Košice, Plzeň, Olomouc, Hradec Králové, České Budějovice, Pardubice, Liberec, Ústí nad Labem, Havířov).

The official **languages** are Czech and Slovak — two closely related Slav tongues. Men are in the minority. They form 48.7 of the population and their number in relation to women is slowly, but continually falling gently. The average life expectancy is 69 in the case of men and 72 in that of women. The number of employed women is very high: they form 45 % of the working population as a whole.

After the Second World War strong migration of the population came about in connection with the settlement of the border territory of the present Czech Socialist Republic as well as with the development of industry and the origin of industrial agglomerations. The former striking differences between certain ethnical groups and territories (the Chod region, the Wallachian region and the Hron valley) are gradually being wiped out.

STATE ADMINISTRATION

Since 1 January, 1969 the Czechoslovak Socialist Republic, whose capital is Prague, has been a federative state with two nations with equal rights — the Czechs and the Slovaks. It consists of the **Czech Socialist Republic** (ČSR, capital Prague, area 78,864 sq. km) and the **Slovak Socialist Republic** (SSR, capital Bratislava, area 49,013 sq. km). Both republics have their own government and national council (parliament). The supreme state organs of the Czechoslovak Socialist Republic are the **Federal Assembly** and the **government** of the Czechoslovak Socialist Republic. The **President** of the Czechoslovak Socialist Republic stands at the head of the state. From the administrative aspect Czechoslovakia is divided into **10 regions** (Central Bohemia, South Bohemia, West Bohemia, North Bohemia, East Bohemia, South Moravia, North Moravia, West Slovakia, Central Slovakia and East Slovakia) and the capitals Prague and Bratislava. It is further divided into 112 districts.

The **state flag** has a red lower field and a white upper one and inserted between them is a blue wedge running from the flagpole to the centre of the flag. The state emblem has the form of a red shield in the shape of a Hussite pavis with a five-pointed star in its upper part and a white double-tailed lion bearing a small shield with the blue outline of Kriváň and gold flames on its breast. The **national anthem** has two parts: the Czech part is the Czech song Kde domov můj (Where Is My Home) (from F. Škroup's scenic music to Tyl's play Fidlovačka of 1834) and the Slovak Nad Tatrou sa blýska (Lightning is Flashing Above the Tatras) (this text to the melody of a folk song probably originated in 1844).

ECONOMY

Czechoslovakia is a developed industrialized country with intensive agriculture. The extent of its industry ranks Czechoslovakia among the most industrial countries in the world. In the post-war period this production has registered a more than tenfold increase. Its share in the creation of the national revenue amounts approximately to 60 % and on the whole it is evenly scattered over the whole territory of Czechoslovakia.

One of the most industrialized regions is the part of North Bohemia lying between Ústí nad Labem and Chomutov (extensive brown-coal mining, power production, chemical industry), another being the Ostrava region (black-coal mining, metallurgical and chemical industries). The most important branch of Czechoslovak industry is the **engineering industry** (for example, production of machine tools, locomotives, trams, cars, tractors, agricultural machines, equipments for power plants and the chemical and food industries). Its share in Czechoslovakia's total industrial production amounts to about 23 % and its chief centres are, for·example, Prague, Plzeň and Brno. Bratislava has a developed chemical industry (oil refineries) and Košice is an important centre of metallurgy. The production of electric power depends on the mining of coal. The network of hydro-electric plants (cascades on the Vltava and the Váh) are relatively stabilized. The production of nuclear energy is gradually undergoing development (Jaslovské Bohunice near Trnava, Dalešice near Třebíč). The textile industry (North Bohemia) has a long-standing tradition similarly as footwear production (Gottwaldov), glass production (Karlovy Vary, Nový Bor, Železný Brod, Poděbrady), the ceramics industry and the food industry (export of Pilsner Urquell beer and Prague ham).

Agricultural land covers more than one half of the area of Czechoslovakia (69,000 sq. km), approximately 49,000 sq. km of this amount being arable land. It is cultivated to a great extent by Standard Farming Cooperatives (65 %), by state farms and, to a small degree, by private farmers. Approximately 10 % of the working people are employed in agriculture. Thanks to intensive farming, Czechoslovakia is self-sufficient in the production of the majority of foods. South Slovakia (the Danube valley), South Moravia, the Haná region (in the environs of Olomouc) and the Elbe valley (in Central Bohemia) rank among the most fertile regions where in particular wheat, maize and sugar-beet are grown. Hops from the environs of Žatec and Rakovník and also malt are important export items. Cattle-breeding (approx. 5 million pieces) and pig-breeding (approx. 7.5 million pieces) prevail in animal production. Fish-breeding, especially the breeding of carp in South Bohemia's ponds, is also an important branch.

Approximately 20 % of the total industrial production is **exported** abroad, machines and equipments being the main export items. Import is chiefly concentrated on raw materials (oil, natural gas, iron ore, non-ferrous metals). Trade is oriented to socialist countries to the extent of 75 %.

TOURIST DESTINATIONS

TOURIST REGIONS

The most popular destination of foreign visitors to Czechoslovakia is the capital, **Prague**, a city with a rich history and a lively present. The landscape in its environs is very diverse, especially the deeply cut valley of the River Vltava with a system of dam reservoirs (Slapy). A visit to ancient castles and châteaux — for example, Karlštejn, Křivoklát, Konopiště and Kokořín — is also worth while. Picturesque countryside with numerous ponds (the biggest is Rožmberk), glowing white farm buildings built in folk architectonic style, historical towns (Český Krumlov, Tábor, České Budějovice, Třeboň, Jindřichův Hradec and others) and unique castles and châteaux (Zvíkov, Orlík, Hluboká nad Vltavou, Červená Lhota) can be seen in **South Bohemia**. From the South Bohemian pond region the relief gradually rises to the ridges and plateau of the **Šumava Mountains**. Several popular tourist and skiing re-

Lower Gate
at the mining town
of Kremnica

sorts (Železná Ruda, Churáňov) can be found in this mountain range, but quiet corners just made for peaceful rest predominate. The neighbouring **Chod region** in the environs of the ancient town of Domažlice has preserved its characteristic folk culture to the present — for example, its special dialect, folk customs and architecture. And Chod folk costumes can still be seen in the villages. In the westernmost corner of Czechoslovakia the wealth of numerous mineral springs is exploited by the world-renowned **spa towns** of Karlovy Vary, Mariánské Lázně, Františkovy Lázně and Jáchymov.

The neighbouring region of **North Bohemia** below the slopes of the **Krušné Mountains** is one of the most industrialized parts of the country. In recent decades the landscape here has undergone substantial changes as a result of extensive brown-coal surface mining. Spreading out on the border with the German Democratic Republic in the place where the mighty flow of the River Elbe carries water away from Bohemia is the Elbe **Sandstone Region** abounding in sandstone rock formations, outstanding among which is the unique rock bridge called Pravčická brána. Rising directly from the suburban quarters of the industrial towns of Liberec and Jablonec nad Nisou (world-renowned for its fashion jewellery production) are the ridges of the **Jizerské Mountains**, which are richly used for recreation and tours on foot and on skis. In the east they are joined by the highest Czech mountain range, the **Krkonoše Mountains** (Sněžka, 1,602 m), which have been proclaimed a national park. The majority of summer and winter guests make their way to Špindlerův Mlýn, Pec pod Sněžkou and Harrachov. Attractive natural corners of the region called the Bohemian Paradise (**Český ráj**) — the sandstone rock towers of the rock formations called Prachovské skály, Hruboskalsko, the deeply hollowed valley of the River Jizera, the ruins of the castle called Trosky, built on rocks, and the Plakánek valley below Kost Castle — are visible from the ridges of the Krkonoše Mountains. The eastern border of Bohemia is lined with the forested zone of the **Orlické Mountains** with attractive folk architecture in the foothills. Situated nearby are the unique rock formations called Adršpašské and Teplické skály.

The biggest group of the Jeseníky mountain system is Hrubý Jeseník (Praděd, 1,492 m) with a partly bare ridge offering far-reaching views. Nestling below the mountains are the Lázně Jeseník and Karlova Studánka spa centres. The Moravian-Silesian **Beskids** (Moravskoslezské Beskydy) attract visitors with their forested mountain ridges and characteristic valleys with numerous recreation resorts. They are the background of the industrial Ostrava region (mining, metallurgy). Joining up with this mountain range in the south is the **Wallachia** (Valašsko) region with preserved folk architecture. The best structures are concentrated at the skansen at Rožnov pod Radhoštěm. **Moravian Slovakia** (Slovácko) is notable for its wealth of folk costumes, folklore ensembles and festivals and excellent wines.

The third biggest town in Czechoslovakia is **Brno,** known throughout the world for its trade fairs. Its environs are very attractive. A strong magnet for visitors is the **Moravian Karst** (Moravský kras) with a number of accessible caves, the Macocha Abyss and the underground River Punkva (boat trips).

The capital of Slovakia, **Bratislava,** lies on the Danube. Its landmark is an ancient castle. The mountain ridge of the **Little Carpathians** (Malé Karpaty) with vineyards at their foot stretches in the immediate vicinity of the city. Further north, on the River Váh, lies the world-renowned spa of **Piešťany. Trenčianske Teplice**, another spa, is also very popular.

The **Little Fatra** (Malá Fatra) in the north-western part of Slovakia offers an ideal ridge for walking tours with numerous far-reaching views. Excellent skiing grounds also exist here as well as charming karst passes. The main tourist centre here is Vrátna dolina.

Characteristic wooden folk architecture has been preserved in the valley of the **River Orava** (for example, at Podbiel). A dam reservoir near the Polish border is an excellent centre for recreation and water sports. Orava Castle is one of the most beautiful and the oldest castles in Slovakia.

The valley of the Orava is a starting point for the **West Tatras** (Západné Tatry) (Bystrá, 2,248 m), connecting up with Czechoslovakia's highest high-mountain range, the **High Tatras** (Vysoké Tatry) (Gerlachovský štít, 2,655 m) with the world-renowned resorts Štrbské Pleso, Starý Smokovec and Tatranská Lomnica. The whole territory has been proclaimed a national park. The high-mountain flora and fauna enjoy state protection. The mountain lakes (plesa) in this mountain range are unique. Sheer rock walls are reflected in their waters.

The **Low Tatras** (Nízké Tatry) are also a national park. Their 70 km long ridge stretches out between the valley of the Rivers Váh and Hron. The valley Demänovská dolina and the Tále region are the most highly frequented. A chair-lift runs across the main ridge at a height exceeding 2,000 m. The local karst caves are also valuable phenomena.

Tourist paths in the neighbouring **Slovak Paradise** (Slovenský raj) reveal enchanting sights to tourists in the form of deep passses, waterfalls, rock walls, karst rivers and surprising views. Lovers of cultural monuments come into their own in the **Spiš region.** Situated here are the historical towns of Levoča and Kežmarok, the biggest castle ruins in Czechoslovakia, Spiš Castle and a valuable Romanesque monument — the church at Spišská Kapitula.

In Czechoslovakia places practically untouched by tourism and negative influences of modern civilization can still be found. They include, for example, the region of the East Carpathians (Východné Karpaty) with the original growths of mixed forests, diverse fauna and valuable folk architecture (little wooden churches). The battlefield in the Dukla Pass was the scene of the bloodiest battles on the territory of Czechoslovakia during the Second World War.

Equally notable is the forested ridge of the Slovak Ore Mountains (Slovenské rudohorie), which stretch from Košice nearly to Banská Bystrica over a distance of 150 km. — The less frequented Bohemian-Moravian Highlands (Českomoravská vrchovina), the Slovak Beskids (Slovenské Beskydy) and other mountainous zones also have a charm of their own for tourism.

NATIONAL CULTURAL MONUMENTS

When travelling through Czechoslovakia the visitor comes across the sign National Cultural Monument (národní kulturní památka, NKP). This is used to indicate —*artistic and architectonic works forming important milestones in the history of Czech and Slovak culture* (for example, Devín Castle and the Academia Istropolitana in Bratislava, Karlštejn Castle, St. Elizabeth's Cathedral at Košice, the Italian Court at Kutná Hora, the high altar in St. James's Church at Levoča, the Přemyslid palace at

Olomouc, Prague Castle, Spiš Castle, the historical core of the town of Tábor, the castle rotunda at Znojmo and others);
— *works which bring the life and work of great personalities of both nations to mind:* the building of the former Matica slovenská organization and the National Cemetery at Martin, Bethlehem Chapel in Prague, or which were the scene of important historical events such as Bílá hora (the White Mountain) in Prague, the Laugaritio Roman camp below Trenčín Castle and the like;
— *works which originated from home, especially folk traditions:* Ratibořice — Babiččino údolí (Grandmother's Valley), connected with the Czech woman writer Božena Němcová, little wooden churches in East Slovak communities;
— *the most significant monuments connected with Czechoslovakia's most recent history, the revolutionary movement, the anti-fascist movement and so on:* Slavín in Bratislava, the Dukla Pass, Kalište (a memorable place of the Slovak National Uprising), Lidice, Ploština (a monument of the resistance movement), the Olšany cemetery of honour in which soldiers of the Red Army are buried in Prague) and the People's House in Hybernská Street in Prague, the Small Fortress with a cemetary at Terezín.

The mentioned monuments naturally represent only a small part of the national values protected by a collection of legal measures.

HISTORICAL TOWN RESERVES

In Czechoslovakia the post-war years were marked, among other things, by the wide-scale restoration of a number of historical towns, in particular of their preserved cores. These were then proclaimed — along with their whole environment, including buildings not necessarily of first-rank importance as ancient monuments — historical town reserves, i.e., as historically valuable wholes whose preservation is secured by a protection regime. In such places visitors admire, for example, preserved medieval town houses, town fortifications with walls, gates and bastions, church and monastery buildings and sometimes also châteaux. The following towns are historical town reserves:

Banská Bystrica, a Gothic mining town founded in 1255 with the area of the town castle.

Banská Štiavnica, a Late Romanesque mining town founded after 1230 with Renaissance monuments.

Bardejov, a Gothic town founded in the early 14th century on a right-angled ground-plan; among other things, its fortifications and an magnificent church have been preserved.

Bratislava, a city with a medieval ground-plan. Renaissance houses and Classical palaces; Bratislava Castle, St. Martin's Church and Michalská brána (Michal Gate) are its important historical landmarks.

Cheb, one of the oldest Czech towns with exceptionally valuable Romanesque monument (the castle palace) and Gothic architecture (frame-houses with high roofs and dormer windows).

České Budějovice, a medieval town with a chess-board ground-plan and an exceptionally big square.

Český Krumlov, whose town buildings with a landmark in the form of a castle squeezed in the space between two promontories of the River Vltava have been preserved in a rare state of completeness.

Domažlice, a medieval town of the street type with a picturesque, elongated square lined with arcades.

Františkovy Lázně, an Empire spa town.

Horšovský Týn, a medieval tributary town with a Renaissance château.

Hradec Králové, one of the oldest Czech towns, the dowry town of Czech queens, the Gothic Cathedral of the Holy Ghost in the triangular square.

Jičín, an example of Early Baroque urbanism whose typical manifestations are the square with arcading and a château built for Albrecht of Wallenstein.

Jihlava, a Gothic mining town with a chess-board groundplan surrounding a large square.

Jindřichův Hradec, a typical South Bohemian town with Gothic monuments which are now partly covered as the result of Renaissance reconstruction activity (the château and square with houses).

Josefov, a Late Baroque fortress.

Kadaň, a medieval town with a regular ground-plan surrounding a big oblong square whose most striking feature is the Gothic Town Hall with a tower.

Kežmarok, a royal town of the 13th century in the Spiš region with a Gothic castle reconstructed in the Renaissance.

Košice, a Gothic town with a spindle-shaped square with St. Elizabeth's Cathedral, the Michal Chapel and the Urban Tower.

Kremnica, the youngest Slovak mining town, founded in 1328, with a town castle and the preserved interiors of Gothic and Renaissance houses in the square.

Kroměříž, a town with a medieval urban structure; later a centre of the Anti-reformational Baroque characteristic of the architecture of the whole town, the

château, Květná Garden and other features.

Kutná Hora, an elementally developing medieval mining town with an irregular ground-plan; from the late 13th century it was the first economic centre of the Czech kingdom.

Levoča, a town with Gothic and Renaissance monuments.

Litoměřice, one of the oldest Czech towns with Renaissance and Baroque monuments (episcopal residence).

Litomyšl, a medieval town whose axis is formed by a street-type square; the burghers' houses and the château were lent their appearance chiefly by the Renaissance.

Loket, a town on a promontory protected by the River Ohře with the picturesque outline of a medieval castle; its burghers' houses of the frame type are a special feature.

Mikulov, a medieval tributary town nestling below a huge castle which was gradually converted into a luxurious Baroque château.

Moravská Třebová, a typical Gothic colonization town on a right-angled ground-plan; the castle, of earlier origin, was converted into a Late Renaissance château.

Nové Město nad Metují, a town on a castle headland surrounded by the River Metuje; it is an example of an exceptionally well-preserved urban formation of the turn of the Gothic and the Renaissance.

Nový Jičín, a historical town with a château and with Renaissance and Baroque houses in its regular square.

Olomouc, as regards monuments the richest Moravian town: the Romanesque palace of the Přemyslids, St. Wenceslas's Cathedral, a Gothic Town Hall and monuments from the Renaissance, Baroque and Classical periods.

Pardubice, an example of an organic symbiosis of a château and tributary

town with a number of mainly Renaissance burghers' houses.

Pelhřimov, an example of a medieval town with preserved fortifications.

Poprad, the part called Spišská Sobota; the former town was fortified already in 1240; characteristic Renaissance houses with wooden gables have been preserved on original Gothic lots.

Prague, from the 10th century the centre of the originating Czech state; an urban formation of European importance.

Prachatice, a Gothic town which underwent unique Renaissance reconstruction.

Prešov, a town with a Gothic church of the 14th century and picturesque burghers' houses.

Slavonice, a small medieval town on the southern border between Bohemia and Moravia which was reconstructed in the Renaissance at the time of its temporary period of economic flourish and which has been preserved in a rare unviolated state.

Spišská Sobota, see Poprad.

Spišské Podhradie, the part called Spišská Kapitula, originally the seat of the Spiš provost.

Štramberk, frame buildings on the outskirts of the older fortified Gothic township.

Tábor, a rarely preserved Gothic-Renaissance urban whole bearing traces of a Hussite military encampment in its ground-plan.

Telč, a town situated between two ponds and an example of the wealth and picturesqueness of South Moravian towns of the Renaissance period, a château and a square lined with houses with arcades.

Terezín, a town founded at the same time as Josefov in the late 18th century as a fortress.

Trenčín, a town with a castle.

Trnava, the town with the oldest town rights in Slovakia.

Třeboň, a town with a Gothic church,

*Historical
town reserves*

The square
at Telč

a Renaissance château and partly preserved fortifications; it is surrounded by a system of ponds.

Úštěk, a small town on a narrow rocky headland with partly preserved fortifications and a Gothic church and Renaissance houses in the square.

Znojmo, a town of early medieval origin; in the area of the local castle there is a Romanesque rotunda of the early 12th century with wall paintings.

Žatec, a town with Gothic burghers' houses, a Gothic gate and fortifications; the appearance of the present square is the result of later Baroque reconstructions.

Žilina, a town with a typical quadratic square.

CASTLES AND CHÂTEAUX

The information presented here about Czechoslovakia's castles and châteaux is of an orientation character only. The reader will learn more about them in the topographical part. Many of them form a part of historical town reserves and some have rich collections of weapons and trophies, or house expositions of paintings and sculptures or collections of old graphic sheets, furniture, vessels, glass and china, or gobelins. As a rule they are open to the public in April and October on Saturdays and Sundays only from 9—12 and 13—16 hours, in May and September daily from 9—12 and 13—16 hours and in June, July and August daily from 8—12 and 13—17 hours. The last tour of inspection usually begins one hour before closing time. With the exception of Karlštejn Castle, castles and châteaux are closed every Monday and in the winter months.

Antol, a Baroque-Classical château with a museum of forestry.

Banská Bystrica, the Old Château, a Romanesque-Gothic church converted into a fortress against the Turks in the 16th century; the New Château of 1564—1571.

Beckov, the ruins of a Gothic castle on the River Váh.

Betliar, an Early Baroque château with rich interior furnishings, a gallery and a library.

Bítov, a Gothic castle reconstructed in the Renaissance.

Bojnice, originally a Gothic castle which was later converted into a château after the model of French châteaux.

Bouzov, originally a Gothic, but now a Neo-Gothic castle; its collections are connected with the Order of German Knights (latter half of the 19th century).

Bratislava, a monumental castle in the style characteristic of the Theresian period; it has recently undergone a large-scale reconstruction.

Brno, Špilberk, an Early Gothic castle later converted into a Baroque fortress.

Bučovice, an especially notable Renaissance château with rich interior decoration.

Buchlov, a Gothic, later enlarged castle forming the landmark of its surroundings.

Buchlovice, a Baroque château-villa with a valuable park.

Bytča, a Renaissance fortified, four-winged château from 1571—1574; the so-called Wedding Palace is situated in its neighbourhood.

Cheb, the remainders of one of the oldest and the most important Czech Romanesque castle with its Black Tower and castle chapel in the outstanding historical town reserve.

Chlumec nad Cidlinou, a Baroque château called Karlova Koruna (Charles' Crown) with an outstanding and rich exposition of Czech Baroque art.
Čachtice, the ruins of a Gothico-Renaissance castle.
Častolovice, a Renaissance château with exceptionally valuable period furnishings.
Červená Lhota, a Renaissance water château with period furnishings.
Červený Kameň, a Renaissance château with a museum of furniture and collections of ceramics and china.
Český Krumlov, originally a castle which was later converted into a large Renaissance château, later reconstructed in the Baroque, in the exceptionally valuable historical town reserve.
Český Šternberk, a castle built in Late Gothic style with a collection of engravings from the time of the Thirty Years' War and with period furnishings.
Devín, the ruins of a castle on the confluence of the Rivers Morava and Danube.

Dolná Krupá, an Empire château with a music museum and a memorial hall devoted to Ludwig van Beethoven.
Helfštejn, the ruins of the biggest castle in Moravia.
Hluboká nad Vltavou, a monumental château rebuilt in English Windsor style in 1841—1871 with a notable gallery of Gothic and modern art.
Hradec nad Moravicí, a romantic château known for the sojourns of Ludwig van Beethoven, Paganini and others.
Hukvaldy, the ruins of a large castle.
Jaroměřice nad Rokytnou, a huge Baroque château with rich period interior decoration and an exposition of period musical instruments.
Jindřichův Hradec, a Renaissance château with a medieval core.
Kačina, an Empire château (1802—1822) with an exposition of an agricultural museum.
Karlštejn, a Gothic castle founded by Charles IV; it is the most outstanding Czech castle from the architectural and historical aspects.

---

*Castles
and châteaux*

The baroque château
at Jaroměřice nad Rokytnou

Kežmarok, a Renaissance château in the historical core of the town; a museum is installed in it.

Konopiště, an Early Gothic castle in the style of French castles, converted in the late 19th century into a luxurious château; valuable collections, among others of weapons and hunting trophies.

Kost, a very well-preserved Gothic castle with an exposition of Late Gothic art.

Krásna Hôrka, a Renaissance château, the family museum of the Andrássys.

Kratochvíle, a Renaissance château (built in the style of an Italian Renaissance villa with a garden) with an exposition of puppets and cartoon and animated film.

Kremnica, a town castle of the 13th—15th century with elements of Romanesque and Gothic architecture.

Kroměříž, a Renaissance château, reconstructed in the Baroque, in the particularly notable historical town reserve; it has richly decorated interiors, a gallery and unique gardens.

Křivoklát, a Gothic castle situated in deep forests; collections of Central Bohemian Late Gothic and Early Renaissance creative art are installed in it.

Kynžvart, a Classical château connected with the name of the Austrian Chancellor Metternich; it has rich interior furnishings and a valuable park.

Lednice, a Neo-Gothic château with a large park and a greenhouse.

Litomyšl, a huge Renaissance château with a Classical theatre and an exposition devoted to the development of Czech music culture.

Loket, an Early Gothic castle with a rich collection of china.

Mělník, a Renaissance château in a wine-producing region, later Barocized; it has a rich gallery of Czech Baroque painting.

Mikulov, a Late Baroque château in the town of the same name on the wine-producing territory of South Moravia.

Náměšť nad Oslavou, a Renaissance, Barocized château with an exposition of tapestries from the 16th—19th century.

Křivoklát
Castle

Nelahozeves, a Renaissance château of the latter half of the 16th century with an exposition of European art of the 12th—19th century (especially Spanish painting).

Nitra, a castle founded in the 11th century which now has the appearance of a Baroque fortress; the episcopal cathedral is situated on its area.

Opočno, an architecturally important Renaissance château with an armoury and a picture gallery of works by Italian and Netherlandish painters of the 16th century.

Orava Castle, an important monument of the 13th century, enlarged up to the 17th century.

Orlík nad Vltavou, a château whose last reconstruction was carried out in the style of the Romantic Gothic; it has exceptionally rich interior furnishings.

Pernštejn, a monumental Early Gothic castle rebuilt in the Renaissance.

Ploskovice, a Baroque château with rich furnishings and a small picture gallery.

Prague Castle, the biggest complex of castle and château buildings in the Czechoslovak Socialist Republic; it is a first-rank monument from the aspect of its role in the history of the country and that of the development of architectonic styles.

Rabí, the ruins of a big Gothic castle.

Rájec, a Late Gothic château with period furnishings and a picture gallery.

Slavkov u Brna, a Baroque château enlarged in Classical style with a picture gallery and a museum devoted to the Napoleonic Wars.

Spiš Castle, the biggest castle ruins in Slovakia; the castle was built gradually from the 13th—17th century.

Strážnice, a romantically rebuilt Renaissance château with expositions of folk ceramics, musical instruments and other artefacts.

Strečno, the ruins of a Gothic castle situated on a rock overlooking the River Váh in the foothills of the Little Fatra.

Šternberk, a Renaissance château modified up to the time of the Second World War; a clock museum is installed in the outer bailey.

Švihov, a Late Gothic water castle whose interiors are furnished in the typical style of a lordly mansion of the early 16th century.

Telč, a Renaisssance château in the notable historical town reserve.

Trenčín, a castle whose original Gothic appearance from the early 12th century has been preserved; it is the landmark of the region and has been reconstructed for museum purposes.

Trosky, the ruins of a Gothic castle, the landmark of the Bohemian Paradise.

Velké Losiny, a Renaissance château with rich interiors and a picture gallery.

Vranov, a Baroque château on a high rock overlooking the River Dyje with rich period interiors.

Zvíkov, the most important Czech Early Gothic castle with an exposition devoted to the history of the Czech state.

Zvolen, originally a Gothic castle built in the style of Italian castles and later converted into a Renaissance château; it now has a rich gallery.

SACRAL MONUMENTS

The development of architecture in past centuries is also documented by church and monastery buildings in which valuable sculptures and paintings are concentrated. Little country churches, especially those built in Gothic and Baroque styles, often still rank among the characteristic landmarks of small villages. Our ancestors

had a bent for building them on hilltops and the paths leading to them are usually lined with centuries old avenues of trees.

The outstanding **Romanesque** buildings include, for example, St. George's Church at Prague Castle, rotundas in Prague and the one on the hill called Říp, the tribune churches at Poříčí nad Sázavou, Neustupov and Kostoľany pod Tríbečom, the crypt of the monastery at Doksany and the church at Spišská Kapitula.

Magnificent **Gothic** buildings include St. Vitus's Cathedral at Prague Castle. Particularly outstanding monasteries are, for example, those at Osek, Vyšší Brod and Zlatá Koruna and equally noteworthy is the portal of the monastery called Porta Coeli at Předklášteří (Tišnov). The cathedrals in Košice, Bratislava and Brno also owe their appearance to the Gothic, while those at Kutná Hora, Louny, Most and Banská Bystrica feature the Late Gothic.

The **Baroque** left a strong mark on church architecture and the appearance of present buildings and seats. Mention should be made, for example, of St. Nicholas's Church in the Little Quarter in Prague, the church on Zelená hora near Žďár nad Sázavou, the hospital at Kuks and the monasteries at Kladruby, Jasov near Košice, Svatá Hora near Příbram and Kopeček near Olomouc.

The monastery at Kladruby
near Stříbro

Very often **folk artists** made good use of wood for the construction of little country churches. A valuable group of buildings of this type can be seen in East Slovakia and several similar structures also exist in the Moravian-Silesian Beskids.

Nowadays the most valuable monastery buildings are accessible as museum expositions with a sightseeing circuit. Churches are freely accessible when divine service is not in process. In view of the fact that their interiors often contain valuable paintings and sculptures they are often closed and visits must be agreed upon with the respective parish or dean's office. Some church steeples are exceptionally noteworthy. Their galleries, which are open to the public, afford a wide view of the surroundings (Domažlice, Hradec Králové, Prague, Prachatice and others.)

Sacral monuments

Small wooden church at Mirola near Svidník

TECHNICAL MONUMENTS

In recent years monuments documenting the technical skill of our ancestors have enjoyed deserved attention. They include, for example, **bridge structures.** The oldest of them (from the 13th century) stands at Písek. The most valuable from the artistic viewpoint is Charles Bridge in Prague (from the 14th century). There is a chain bridge of 1848 at Lužnice near Stádlec, a railway viaduct of 1870 at Ivančice in Moravia and a huge structure, Žďákov Bridge of 1965, spans the Vltava valley near Orlík. Roofed wooden bridges can also be seen (for example, at Lenora in the Šumava Mountains).

The oldest **horse-drawn railways** were in operation on Czechoslovak territory already in the twenties of the 19th century. They ran from České Budějovice to Linz and from Prague to Lány. Remainders of their viaducts, stations and other elements can still be seen.

Numerous ponds also testify to the skill of our ancestors. Some of them originated as long ago as the 13th century. Modern architects, on the other hand, are leaving numerous dam structures behind them. The biggest is Orlík dam (91 m).

At Kutná Hora, Příbram and Banská Štiavnica ore mines are accessible to visitors. Old water mills are still standing in the valleys of many streams and rivers. The one at Slup near Znojmo, which houses an exposition, is open to the public. Forges have gradually disappeared from villages. One of them (with an exposition) can still be admired by visitors at Těšany near Brno. A hammer-mill at Dobřív near Rokycany is accessible to the public. Windmills have been preserved at Kuželov near Hodonín, Ruprechtov near Vyškov, Choltice near Opava and other places.

A technical monument
at the Bardejovské Kúpele
skansen

There are nearly 350 museums, 150 memorial halls and 50 galleries in Czechoslovakia. Their opening hours differ greatly, but in nearly all cases their closing day is Monday.

Central museums are of a national character. They include the National Museum and the National Technical Museum in Prague and the Slovak National Museum in Bratislava and Martin. Also included in this category are the Moravian Museum in Brno and the Technical Museum at Košice. As regards Czech literature, the greatest number of exhibits is concentrated at the Museum of National Literature in Prague. The State Jewish Museum in Prague has unique collections to offer visitors.

All big, especially regional towns have well-equipped regional museums (the South Bohemian Museum at České Budějovice, the North Bohemian Museum at Liberec and others). Smaller museums can also be seen in district towns, their expositions usually being connected with the given district (history, nature, ethnography and so on).

Specialized museums and thematic expositions are of great interest to visitors. For example, the museum at Hostinné contains collections of Classical art and the museums at Třebechovice pod Orebem and Vysoké nad Jizerou have Bethlehem scenes. Bratislava and Šternberk have a clock museum, Nový Jičín an interesting hat museum, Vamberk a lace-making museum, Jablonec nad Nisou an exhibition of glass and fashion jewellery, Klášterec nad Ohří and Loket a china exhibition and Gottwaldov a unique footwear museum. At Velké Losiny near Šumperk a factory for the manual production of paper (with a museum) is still in operation. At Kratochvíle there is an animated film exposition, at Kámen Castle a motorcycle museum, at Kopřivnice a motor car exhibition and at Přibyslav fire brigade collections. The Krkonoše Museum at Vrchlabí is devoted to the only Czech national park and so we could continue.

A separate chapter is represented by museums, memorial halls and expositions acquainting visitors with the old and modern history of the country or given region, or devoted to events of special importance. They include in particular: monuments of the Hussite period (Tábor, Bethlehem Chapel in Prague, Kozí Hrádek, Husinec), monuments of peasant uprisings (Chlumec nad Cidlinou, Rtyně v Podkrkonoší — in the region below the Krkonoše Mountains, Újezd near Domažlice), monuments recalling the formation of the working class, big strikes and so on (the building called U kaštanu — At the Chestnut Tree — in Prague, the Duchcov viaduct, the Frývaldov strike, Rumburk), expositions illustrating these periods in newly originating industrial regions (Ostrava, Kladno, Čierny Balog, Podbrezová, Tisovec and other places) and finally monuments bringing to mind the tragic period of the Second World War (Lidice, Ležáky, Kremnička, Javoříčko, Banská Bystrica, Dukla, Ostrava, Hrabyně, Prague).

Some museums or memorial halls concentrate on a certain personality: in Prague there are museums devoted to Vladimír Ilyich Lenin, Klement Gottwald, Antonín Dvořák, Bedřich Smetana and Wolfgang Amadeus Mozart, in Bratislava a museum devoted to the composer Johann Nepomuk Hummel, in Brno a memorial hall devoted to Johann Gregor Mendel, at Teplice, Loket and Mariánské Lázně memorial halls recalling the sojourns of Johann Wolfgang Goethe, at Teplice and Hradec nad Mor-

avicí memorials recalling the sojourn of Ludwig van Beethoven, at Mariánské Lázně Maxim Gorký, at Horní Planá documents pertaining to Adalbert Stifter, at Slavkov u Brna documents concerning Napoleon and the Battle of the Three Emperors and at Přerov and Fulnek documents connected with the life and work of Jan Amos Komenský (Comenius). In a number of towns there are memorials or memorial halls connected with Czech and Slovak writers, painters, sculptors, musicians, inventors, scientists, etc.

Many other expositions can be found in the interiors of castles and châteaux (see the respective chapter) and visitors can also see open-air museums of folk architecture (skansens).

Picture galleries hold a great attraction for foreign visitors. The most important of them is the National Gallery in Prague. It has very rich collections which are often concentrated in an attractive environment such as the convents of St. George and the Blessed Agness. Other important galleries can be found in Bratislava, Brno, Hluboká nad Vltavou, Kroměříž, Gottwaldov, Ostrava, Mělník, Nelahozeves, Zvolen and Košice.

FOLK ARCHITECTURE, FOLKLORE

The rapid changes which came about in the Czechoslovak economy after the Second World War resulted in **folk architecture** speedily making way for new construction. In Slovakia in particular (sometimes as a consequence of war events) whole new villages originated so that even the formerly most backward regions (Kysuce) acquired an entirely new appearance.

The interior
of the Technical Museum
in Prague

Nowadays a number of **open-air museums** of folk architecture (skansens) are originating in the Czechoslovak Socialist Republic which are accumulating the most interesting still existing remainders of folk architecture and things connected with the former way of life of the country people for future generations.

Of the complexes of folk architecture and individual structures the attention of the foreign visitor is particularly deserved by the following:

— *Central Bohemian frame buildings,* preserved especially in the forested basin of the middle stream of the River Berounka (Hudlice, the house in which J. Jungmann was born) and also, for example, in the Sedlčany region

— *Central Bohemian stone village* architecture, represented by two open-air museums: at Třebíz to the west of Prague and at Přerov nad Labem to the north of the Prague—Poděbrady line. East of Prague there is also a skansen at Kouřim where buildings from beyond the boundaries of Central Bohemia are also concentrated

— *South Bohemian stone farmhouses* mostly with enclosed yards and Baroque elements particularly in the gables of the residential buildings (the so-called Rustic Baroque), but also of farm buildings (Zechovice near Volyně, Vlastiboř, Komárov, Plástovice — all to the north of České Budějovice)

— *the Alpine type of frame house* in the Šumava Mountains (the last remainders, for example, at Volary)

— *masonry folk structures,* sometimes with two storeys, in the west and the north of Bohemia (from Cheb over the Krušné Mountains to the foothills of the Krkonoše Mountains); examples can be seen, for instance, at the skansen at Zubrnice near Ústí nad Labem

— *the frame architecture of the Bohemian-Moravian Highland;* the best-preserved structures are concentrated in the skansen at Vysočina (to the west of Hlinsko) with several communities

— *the prevailingly clay house typical of Moravian-Slovakia* (with a decorated porch), for example, the Museum of Villages of South-East Moravia at Strážnice; similar buildings are frequently to be seen also in the more easterly valley of the Danube

— *the frame house of the north-east Moravian-Slovak border* (the Moravian-Silesian Beskids) and also of the Slovak-Polish border (the Slovak Beskids). A part of this very simple, but effective architecture has been preserved in the most remote mountain regions from Kysuce to Horehroní. Architecture of the Beskids is excellently preserved in the oldest Czechoslovak skansen, the Wallachian Skansen at Rožnov pod Radhoštěm, and the historical town reserve of Štramberk is also remarkable. In Slovakia this type of architecture is preserved at the Museum of the Kysuce Village at Nová Bystrica-Vychylovka (to the east of Čadca), the Museum of the Orava Village at Zuberec-Brestová (near Orava dam) and the Slovak National Museum of the Slovak Village on the south-east outskirts of Martin. Of the remarkable communities let us mention at least Štefanová (the Little Fatra), Podbiel (Orava), Vlkolínec (Ružomberok) and Čičmany

— *the folk architecture of the north-eastern part of Slovakia,* which those interested will find concentrated at the Museum of Folk Architecture at Bardejovské Kúpele and at the skansen below Stará Ľubovňa Castle. Worthy of a visit is also the community of Ždiar (to the east of the High Tatras). Specific examples of this preserved folk architecture are little wooden churches of East Slovakia which document in an exceptional way the formal refinement of folk architecture and which have been proclaimed a national cultural monument. These little wooden churches can be seen

---

Folk architecture,
folklore

in the districts of Bardejov, Humenné, Michalovce, Stará Ľubovňa, Prešov and Svidník.

Folk costumes have been preserved to a small extent only — in Bohemia only in the environs of Domažlice in the Chod region, in Moravia to the greatest extent in the environs of Uherský Brod and Uherské Hradiště in Moravian-Slovakia and in Slovakia on the upper stream of the River Hron below the Low Tatras, at Detva to the east of Zvolen and at Kysuce.

The tradition of **folk art production** continues to survive. Embroidery work, lace, glass adornments, ceramics, products made of reeds, decorative sticks, etc. can be purchased as valuable souvenirs. Painted eggs continue to mark the Easter holiday. Carved Bethlehem scenes are splendid works of art. The Bethlehem scene at Třebechovice pod Orebem near Hradec Králové is a unique example and others are on show at Třebíč and Jindřichův Hradec.

The biggest **ethnographical festivals** include the May Ride of Kings in Moravian-Slovakia, the June festival at Východná below the Tatras and, in August, the folk festival at Domažlice in the Chod region.

SPAS

In view of its more than 3,000 mineral and thermal springs Czechoslovakia can be regarded as a real balneological big power. A big power with a rich history, because curative springs were known on the sites of the present spas of Janské Lázně, Františkovy Lázně, Teplice, Piešťany, Sliač and Karlovy Vary in the period from the 11th—

Folk architecture
at Vlkolinec
in the Big Fatra

14th century. Their number was gradually increased by dozens of others with the most varied specifications and many-sided therapeutical effects.

Of the most important spas, usually of interest to foreign visitors also from the viewpoint of a short period of rest, the gaining of a knowledge of the local curative springs and facilities and tourism, we are presenting the following:

Bardejovské Kúpele (325 m) on the southern slope of the Low Beskids. In particular diseases of the alimentary tract are treated at this spa with a capacity of 900 beds, but patients can also receive treatment for diseases of the respiratory tract, metabolic disorders and other ailments.

Dudince (140 m) at the foot of the Štiavnica Hills in South Slovakia. At this newly built spa with 500 beds diseases of the motory organs and certain nervous diseases are treated.

Františkovy Lázně (450 m) in the westernmost corner of Czechoslovakia. Its architecture is Empire in style and its sanatoria have a total capacity of some 2,800 beds. Outstanding results have been achieved here in the treatment of cardiovascular disorders, gynaegological diseases and diseases of the motory organs.

Jáchymov (650 m), an ancient mining town in the heart of the Krušné Mountains, has over 1,000 beds. Its thermal radioactive springs condition the treatment of diseases of the motory organs and certain diseases of nervous origin.

Janské Lázně (670 m) on the southern slopes of the Krkonoše Mountains, has 400 beds. Its thermal springs and applied rehabilitation methods are of great benefit in the treatment of persistent nervous diseases, the consequences of poliomyelitis, etc.

Jeseník (650 m), originally called Grafenberg, is connected with the name of Vincenc Priessnitz (early 19th century). It now has 500 beds. Hydrotherapy and the climate of the mountain range called the Jeseníky provide good conditions for the loosening-up and tuning-up of the nervous system.

Karlovy Vary (380 m), the biggest and best-known Czech spa. It was founded by Charles IV in the mid-14th century and now has over 4,000 beds and 12 springs of a temperature ranging from 40–73°C. The local drinking cure has a favourable effect in the treatment of diseases of the alimentary tract, metabolic diseases and diseases of glands with internal secretion.

Luhačovice (300 m), the biggest Moravian spa (1,700 beds), situated near the town of Gottwaldov. Drinking cures based on acidulous waters, inhalation procedures and baths are used to treat diseases of the respiratory tract and alimentary tract and metabolic diseases.

Mariánské Lázně (628 m) in West Bohemia has 2,800 beds at its disposal for patients and over 40 curative springs with a favourable effect in the treatment of diseases of the kidneys and urinary tract, the respiratory tract, nervous diseases and diseases of the motory organs.

Piešťany (162 m) on the banks of the Váh has a proud history reaching back to Roman times. It now has 2,000 beds. The local thermal springs and mud are applied with great success in the treatment of diseases of the joints and the motory organs.

Poděbrady (188 m) in the flat region of the Elbe valley has some 1,600 beds. Its acidulous waters form a base for the treatment of cardiovascular diseases.

Sliač (373 m) in the valley of the Central Slovak River Hron has important curative springs with a favourable effect in the treatment of cardiovascular diseases and of post-infarct states.

Spas

dioactive springs have a therapeutical effect on diseases of the motory organs and circulatory diseases. It has 800 beds for patients.

Teplice nad Bečvou (254 m) lies in the valley of the River Bečva in Moravia and has a capacity of 800 beds. Its acidulous waters are used for the bath treatment of cardiovascular diseases.

Trenčianske Teplice (272 m) in West Slovakia has been known since the time of Roman settlement. It now has 1,300 beds. Its hydrogen sulphide thermal springs and mud serve for the treatment of diseases of the motory organs and nervous diseases.

Třeboň (430 m) in the South Bohemian pond region has a capacity of 500 beds. Sulphurous-ferrous mud is used to treat diseases of the motory organs.

If you are interested in taking a spa cure your travel agent will provide you with more detailed information or arrange it for you, or you can apply direct to **Balnea** (a specialized travel bureau) at Pařížská 11, Prague-Staré Město for the Czech Socialist Republic and **Slovakoterma**, Radlinského 13, Bratislava for the Slovak Socialist Republic.

Štrbské Pleso (1,351 m) on the south slopes of the High Tatras has an ideal high-mountain climate with favourable effects on bronchial asthma and catarrhs. It has 700 beds for patients.

Teplice (219 m) in the foothills of the Krušné Mountains is one of the oldest spas on the territory of the Czechoslovak Socialist Republic. Its thermal ra-

INTERESTING SIGHTS OF NATURE

Czechoslovakia is outstanding for its diverse scenery. Numerous types of landscape can be seen on its relatively small territory.

The most changeable and also the most attractive scenery is definitely to be seen in the **mountainous regions.** These are also the most popular destinations of home and foreign tourists. Many recreation resorts and mountain chalets have originated in the mountains. They are accessible by roads and funicular railways and numerous marked paths run to the highest peaks. However, the large number of visitors to these places carries numerous negative influences with it and therefore has to be limited in a number of localities.

The High Tatras and Krkonoše Mountains are particularly well-equipped for tourism. Excellent mountain resorts exist in the Šumava, Krušné and Jizerské Mountains, the Jeseníks, the Moravian-Silesian Beskids, the Little Fatra and the Low Tatras. Less frequented by visitors are, for example, Kralický Sněžník, the Rychlebské Mountains, the Slovak Beskids, the Slovak Ore Mountains, Vtáčnik and other peaks and ranges.

Piešťany
spa

Practically all important mountain complexes have been proclaimed national parks or protected landscape regions and thus you will find more detailed information in this chapter or in the separate items in the topographic index.

Rock towns, in which Czechoslovakia is especially rich, rank among this country's romantic natural formations. They have originated especially in the sandstone rock regions of the Bohemian Paradise, in the environs of Adršpach in East Bohemia and of Děčín (the Elbe Sandstone Region) in North Bohemia (with the well-known sandstone rock formation called Pravčická brána (Gate).

Czechoslovakia has also numerous karst regions with a total number of 23 accessible cave systems. Their biggest concentration is in the Moravian Karst near Brno (the well-known Punkva Cave with the River Punkva and the Macocha Abyss, 138 m in depth). Visitors can also see the Koněprusy Caves near Prague. The biggest cave systems in Slovakia are those called the Demänová Caves and Domica; the Dobšiná Ice Cave is another interesting sight.

River valleys attract the interest of tourists. The most attractive of them include the rocky valleys of the Vltava at Štěchovice, the Berounka at Karlštejn and Křivoklát and the Sázava at Jílové — all in the environs of Prague. Also popular are the valleys of the Elbe from Žernoseky to Děčín, the Ohře at Loket, the Metuje at Nové Město nad Metují, the Kamenice at Hřensko, the Váh at Strečno and the Dunajec at Červený Kláštor. Narrow passes with waterfalls, accessible only by ladders, can be visited in the Slovak mountains (the Little Fatra, the Slovak Paradise).

In Czechoslovakia, as a developed industrial country, the principles of the protection of nature and the landscape are being applied to an ever greater extent. The state participates in the endeavours exerted throughout Europe to prevent more profound disturbance of the state of balance between nature and human civilization and to realize the real needs of society, which include not only material welfare, but also a healthy, quality natural environment.

The first efforts to protect certain natural values were made just on the territory of present Czechoslovakia. The first two protected territories originated in 1838 — the South Bohemian Hojná Voda primeval forest and the Žofín primeval forest. Twenty years later the Boubín primeval forest was proclaimed a protected territory. Extra strict principles concerning visits to and sojourns on all these territories are applied. In the first place it is necessary to adhere to the regulations for visitors and to use public paths only. Camping and the lighting of fires are prohibited except in places reserved for the purpose, the making of excessive noise is forbidden, etc.

National parks are large areas of original, natural scenery, or natural territories which have hardly been violated by human interventions and are of special scientific and popular educational importance. The names of the individual parks and a short description of them follow.

The Krkonoše National Park (385 sq. km) manifests in particular traces of the fact that its area was once covered with ice (15 small glaciers) which left conspicuous glacial valleys with moraines as well as remains of Northern flora (e.g. the blackberry and the mulberry). Of the conspicuous types of present flora of this national park let us mention at least the wind-flower, the aconite, the pelagonia, the white hellebore, etc. In the 17th—18th century clusters of spruces were planted here which now show considerable damage caused by emissions. The original beech and mixed growths have survived on the lower elevations only. The territory of the Krkonoše National Park is used for excessive tourist and recreation activity.

The Tatra National Park (770 sq. km with a protected zone of 510 sq. km) includes the highest (2,655 m) mountain range in Czechoslovakia. It has a typical high-mountain relief with glacial valleys, moraines and over 100 glacial lakes. Its flora includes glacial relicts and of its fauna the rock eagle, the marmot, the bear and the chamois — to name a few examples — are protected. The forests mainly consist of fir trees above which a zone of dwarf and limbo pines stretches. It is necessary to regulate the high number of visitors to the mountains.

The Low Tatras National Park (811 sq. km) is formed by the long ridge part of the mountains. Large forests and, on its summit parts, Alpine grassy uplands are its specific features. The local stalagmite and stalactite caves (Demänovské jaskyne) are highly frequented. Big beasts of prey (the wolf, the lynx, the bear) and birds of prey continue to occur among the fauna of this national park.

The Pieniny National Park (21 sq. km) is covered with enchanting limestone mountains with a tourist attraction in the form of the breakthrough of the River Dunajec (navigated by rafts).

The Little Fatra (200 sq. km), a territory in the north-eastern part of the range of mountains of the same name rising to a height of 1,709 m with a varied mineral com-

Basalt organ
in the Panská skála
nature preserve

position (mainly granite, limestone and dolomites — Veľký Rozsutec, Sokolie, etc.) and rich flora ranging from warmth-loving to high-mountain types.

The Slovak Paradise (140 sq. km) consists of a limestone plateau articulated by erosions. It is characterized by canyon-type passes, gorges, waterfalls and numerous karst phenomena. (The breakthrough of the River Hornád, Kyseľ, Veľký Sokol, Piecky and the Dobšinská Ice Cave).

Other large territories have been proclaimed protected landscape regions. They are as follows:

The Beskids (1,160 sq. km), which comprise the Moravian-Silesian Beskids, a part of the Javorníky and the Vsetínské Hills. They attain a height of 1,323 m and are formed by several ridges situated behind one another and dislocated foothills. Remainders of primeval forests and quality mountain meadows can be seen here. The local folk architecture is an interesting sight. At Rožnov pod Radhoštěm there is a well-known skansen.

The Biele Carpathians (630 sq. km), flat mountainous country formed mainly by sandstone and slate. It links up with the protected landscape region of the White Carpathians in the Czech Socialist Republic. The north-eastern part is lined with a zone of cliffs with conspicuous limestone hills.

The Carpathians (730 sq. km) in the Slovak Socialist Republic rise to a height of 970 m and are covered with beech and oak growths. Submontane meadows with rare flora.

Blaník (40 sq. km), an example of the harmonious Central Bohemian landscape with the legendary peak (638 m) of the same name.

The Bohemian Central Highlands (1,070 sq. km), a region of cone- and heap-shaped hills which originated in the Tertiary period as the result of volcanic activity. It has the most varied flora in the whole of the Czech Socialist Republic. The River Elbe forces its way through the territory, creating the valley called Porta Bohemica.

The Bohemian Karst (132 sq. km), a region of limestone rocks with karst phenomena. It is very valuable from the paleontological and botanical aspects (rock-steppe flora).

The Bohemian Paradise (132 sq. km), a region of sandstone rocks which have created huge rock towns. Here nature is in a rare state of balance with human activity. Characteristic cottages and numerous castles and châteaux can be seen here.

Horná Orava (700 sq. km) covers the north-eastern part of the Slovak Beskids and includes the area of the Orava dam reservoir. Peat-bogs and remainders of primeval forests (Pilsko, Babia hora — 1,725 m).

The Jeseníks (740 sq. km) attain a height of 1,492 m and form a region of grassy mountain uplands and wild valleys. The glacial valleys Malá kotlina and Velká kotlina and the Rejvíz Peat-bog are remarkable, especially from the botanical viewpoint.

The Jizerské Mountains (350 sq. km) reach to a height of 1,124 m and now manifest considerable damage caused by emissions. On the central upper plateau there is a particularly notable peat-bog (Jizerka). Parts of the northern slopes are rocky and steep, while the southern ones are more gentle.

The Kokořín region (270 sq. km) is a territory of sandstone rocks and cliffs in which water has hollowed out a number of canyon-type valleys. The rock formations have bizarre shapes and another local feature are the so-called "lids", an example of the uneven disintegration of the rocks.

The Křivoklát region (630 sq. km) is a strongly forested territory whose axis is formed by the flow of the River Berounka. It is rich in natural growths consisting of deciduous and mixed forests. The yew tree also grows here. The whole natural environment is in an exceptionally good state of preservation and is a biospheric preserve of UNESCO.

Kysuce (654 sq. km) is a region in North West Slovakia (the Javorníks and the Slovak Beskids). It continues to preserve its typical landscape character with scattered settlement.

The Elbe sandstone region (300 sq. km), an only slightly inhabited region of huge rock towns, towers, pillars, wild gorges and passes with moisture- and shade-loving flora.

The Lusatian Mountains (350 sq. km) attain a height of 791 m and are composed of sandstone and volcanic rocks. They have charming folk architecture which is richly used for recreation purposes.

The Little Carpathians (655 sq. km) form a range of nearly 100 km in length. They reach to a height of 768 m and their border parts are characterized by karst formations, large forests and rich flora and fauna.

The Moravian Karst (92 sq. km) is an important karst territory with big cave systems, hollows , dips and springs. It is richly forested.

The Muráň Plateau (219 sq. km), a large territory consisting mainly of karst formations (e.g. 100 caves, 35 subterranean rivers, etc.). It reaches to a height of 1,409 m and endemic flora and big beasts of prey live on it.

The Orlické Mountains (200 sq. km) reach to a height of 1,115 m and form a long ridge with spruce forests and partly also with original beech forests. The range is divided by the deep valley of the River Divoká Orlice. Valuable folk architecture can be seen in the foothills.

Pálava (70 sq. km), a huge limestone barrier in a bend of the River Dyje. It attains a height of 550 m and has rich steppe flora. It is also notable from the archeological viewpoint (settlement of mammoth hunters). Biospheric preserve of UNESCO.

Podyjí (the valley of the River Dyje — 100 sq. km), a region with steep, rocky slopes through which the River Dyje flows.

Poľana (200 sq. km), the highest range of volcanic mountains in Czechoslovakia with a peak of the same name (1,458 m). On its summit there is a complex of primeval forests inhabited by rare beasts of prey, deer and birds.

Ponitrie (339 sq. km) is formed by the Tribeč Mountains (829 m) with valuable warmth-loving rock-steppe and forest-steppe flora and volcanic, mainly andezite rocks.

The Slavkov Forest (640 sq. km), a territory of a peneplain character with numerous peat-bogs (marsh pine). Gas effusions and mineral springs. Rare warmth-loving flora in some places (varieties of viper's bugloss).

The Slovak Karst (360 sq. km), the biggest and the best developed karst territory in the Czechoslovak Socialist Republic, formed by a typical system of karst plateaux separated by the deep canyons of rivers and streams. Numerous dips, abysses, caves and underground rivers. Rich flora and fauna. Biospheric preserve of UNESCO. It lies on both sides of the border with the Hungarian Republic, southwest of Košice.

The Štiavnické Hills (770 sq. km), forming one of the biggest volcanic ranges of the West Carpathians and attaining a height of 1,009 m. In the past it was an important metal-mining region.

The *Šumava Mountains* (1,630 sq. km), a territory of a peneplain character (approximately 1,000 metres above sea level, greatest height 1,378 m) with several small glacial lakes (Černé jezero and Čertovo jezero) and big summit peat-bogs.

The *Třeboň region* (700 sq. km), a harmonious pond region with a system of canals, peat-bogs and remains of meadow growths. Rich occurrence of water fowl. Biospheric preserve of UNESCO.

The *Big Fatra* (600 sq. km), identical with the range of mountains of the same name, characterized by a huge, continuous attaining a height of 1,592 m. Its higher parts are deforested.

Vihorlat (48 sq. km), a small volcanic range of the East Carpathians of a height of 1,076 m with sharp peaks and steep slopes in places. Its most interesting locality, the lake called Morské oko, lies below Sninský kameň. Big beech forests, partly of the character of a primeval forest, exist here.

The *East Carpathians* (668 sq. km), a range of mountains reaching to a height of 1,221 m and stretching from the Dukla Pass along the north-eastern border with Poland and the Soviet Union. The territory has numerous beech growths and its natural environment is in a universally good state of preservation. Bears, lynxes, wild cats, wolves, eagles, etc. live here.

The *Žďárské Hills* (715 sq. km), a naturally forested territory in the Bohemian-Moravian Highlands in the region of the sources of the Rivers Sázava and Svratka. Peat meadows with rare species of flora and numerous rock formations.

As previously mentioned, smaller territories have been declared state nature preserves. The best-known of them include the rock formations called Prachovské skály and the Adršpach-Teplice Rocks, the Boubín primeval forest, Kokořín Valley, Soos near Františkovy Lázně, proclaimed a protected territory of the lower category, which includes protected finding-places, protected parks and gardens, protected study areas, protected natural formations and protected natural monuments. In all Czechoslovakia has 1,679 protected natural territories of all categories, their total area of 17,272 sq. km representing approximately 13 % of the area of the state territory as a whole.

It should also be mentioned that very well-chosen and instructive nature study paths have been established on some protected territories. There are about 100 of them in all. They are usually marked with a white square with a diagonal green stripe and their individual halts provide detailed information about places and sights of interest along their routes.

BATHING

The chief motive of a foreign visitor's visit to the Czechoslovak Socialist Republic will rarely be bathing. This does not mean, however, that he or she would not take advantage of the possibility of becoming refreshed and rested after a fatiguing tour on foot or an exacting cultural and educational programme. We are therefore presenting at least some basic information.

At present the quality of the surface waters on the whole territory of the Czechoslovak Socialist Republic is not improving, this being connected with the growing industrialization of the country, intensive land cultivation and the economic exploitation of ponds, etc. For many years now flowing water has not been the most important source for bathing and recreation at the waterside. First place is now unquestionably held by reservoirs (valley dam lakes), due on one hand to the relatively high number of camps on their banks and, on the other hand, the possibility they offer of pursuing a whole complex of activities connected with water (swimming, rowing, windsurfing, yachting, fishing and sightseeing boat trips). In Bohemia and Moravia second place is occupied by ponds, in Central Slovakia by so-called lakes (reservoirs which originated in the course of ore-mining) and in South Slovakia by open-air thermal pools. Flowing water holds third place in both the Czech Socialist Republic and the Slovak Socialist Republic. Wholly pure (and very cold) are now only the uppermost sectors of rivers whose source lies in mountains, i.e. rather brooks and streams in which it is often impossible to swim or even wet the whole body.

Nowadays the Czech Socialist Republic has over 100 **reservoirs, including valley dam lakes.** Practically all of them are of power engineering importance. Many of them serve as reservoirs of drinking water and in these cases bathing and sojourns on their banks are prohibited. The biggest cascade of dams of recreative importance is on the River Vltava: Lipno (4,870 hectares), Orlík (2,730 hectares) and Slapy (1,400 hectares). Others of importance include Vranov in Moravia (760 hectares) and Seč (220 hectares) and Rozkoš (1,000 hectares) in Bohemia. Good possibilities are also afforded by the Jesenice dam lake near Cheb, the Hracholusky dam lake near Plzeň, Pastviny below the Orlické Mountains (all in Bohemia), Žermanice and Těrlicko in the Ostrava region, the Luhačovice dam lake and Bystřička in Wallachia and others. In Prague there are two small, highly frequented lakes: Džbán on the River Šárecký (18 hectares) and Hostivař on the River Botič (44 hectares); in Brno there is the Brno dam lake (250 hectares).

The Slovak Socialist Republic also has several big reservoirs affording recreation possibilities. These lie mainly in the north: the Orava dam lake (3,500 hectares) on the River Orava and the Liptovská Mara dam lake (1,800 hectares) on the River Váh. Then, in the east, there is the Zemplínská šírava dam lake (3,300 hectares) at Michalovce. The River Váh has several smaller reservoirs, the best-known of which is Sĺňava, situated to the south of Piešťany. Of the other reservoirs we are mentioning here Domaša on the River Ondava, Dedinky on the River Hnilec and Ružín on the River Hornád.

Ponds began to be built on the present territory of the Czechoslovak Socialist Republic from as long ago as the 14th century. The biggest number of them lies in the wide environs of the towns of České Budějovice, Třeboň and Jindřichův Hradec in South Bohemia. Particularly suitable for recreation (and car camping as well) are Bezdrev (south-west of Hluboká nad Vltavou), Dvořiště (at Lišov), Hejtman (Chlum u Třeboně), Knížecí (east of Tábor), Komorník (at Strmilov), Křivonoska and Mydlovarský (north of Hluboká nad Vltavou), Malý Jordán (Tábor), Osika (south-east of Albeř), Podroužek (south of Netolice), Staňkovský (south-east of Chlum u Třeboně) and Svět (Třeboň, Domanín car camp).

Car camps or at least camping sites can also be found on the banks of certain sought-after ponds in other parts of the Czech Socialist Republic, for example, Babylon (south-west of Domažlice), Bolevecké rybníky (north of Plzeň), Habr (south-west of Rokycany), Chmelař (on the Litoměřice — Česká Lípa route), Jinolické rybníky (north-west of Jičín), Kamencové jezero (north of Chomutov), Konopáč (south-west of Heřmanův Městec), Křišťanovický rybník (south-west of Prachatice), Máchovo jezero (at Doksy), Mlýnský rybník (south-west of Lednice), Valcha (east of Klatovy) and Velké Dářko (north-west of Žďár nad Sázavou).

Particularly attractive on the territory of the Slovak Socialist Republic are ponds and lakes lying in the vicinity of the capital (Bratislava): Zlaté piesky on the outskirts of the city, Slnečné jazero at Senec (north-east of the city), or the lakes in the vicinity of Štiavnické Bane: Počúvalské jazero, Evičkino and Richňovské jazero (south-west of Banská Štiavnica).

Thermal bathing-pools are of great importance for tourism. Let us mention at least Čalovo (south-east of Dunajská Streda), Diakovce (south-east of Galanta), Dudince (east of Levice), Kováčová (north-west of Zvolen), Liptovský Ján (south-east of Liptovský Mikuláš), Margita-Ilona (south-east of Levice), Nové Zámky, Piešťany, Šafárikovo, Štúrovo, Trenčianske Teplice and Vyšné Ružbachy.

SKIING

The **Czech Socialist Republic** has, as regards winter sports, several attractive mountain ranges with downhill runs and cross-country and tourist skiing grounds at altitudes of 400—1,400 m. As a rule the winter season lasts from Christmas to the middle and, on higher elevations, to the end of March. The **Krkonoše Mountains** are suitable for exacting downhill skiing as well as for cross-country and tourist skiing. Easier downhill runs are to be found in the **Šumava Mountains**, the **Jeseníks** and the **Beskids**. The **Jizera Mountains** and the **Bohemian-Moravian Highlands** offer grounds suitable rather for cross-country and tourist skiing. The Krušné and Orlické Mountains also have downhill runs and cross-country terrains.

The **Slovak Socialist Republic**, whose territory is of a highland and mountain character (over 300 m) to the extent of 60% and whose mountain slopes are mainly covered with meadows, has even more favourable conditions for skiing. One of the factors contributing to this is the good technical equipment of the skiing resorts. The best-equipped resorts are to be found in the **Low** and the **High Tatras** and in the **Little** and the **Big Fatra**. Good possibilities of skiing also exist, however, in the Slovak Beskids, on the peak called Čergov and other places.

As regards the funicular railways, chair-lifs and ski-tows, a certain disadvantage lies in their heavy use, especially at renowned resorts and at the height of the season. When spending a sojourn of several days in Czechoslovakia's winter mountains it is therefore advisable to be equipped also for cross-country or tourist skiing.

Downhill skiing

Basic information about the technical equipment of the biggest winter sports resorts (data given in the following order: elevation of resort; length of downhill runs; number of funicular railways, chair-lifts, ski-tows; total capacity/hour; number of hotel beds):

Krkonoše Mountains,
Harrachov, 660 m; 720—1,020 m; 1, 3; 2,650/hr.; 480.
Rokytnice nad Jizerou, 520 m; 630—1,310 m; 0, 8; 4,750/hr; 220.
Špindlerův Mlýn, 700 m; 700—1,300 m; 2, 9; 6,850/hr; 1,120.
Pec pod Sněžkou, 700 m; 700—1,300 m; 2, 9; 6,300/hr; 1045.

Šumava Mountains,
Železná Ruda-Špičák, 750 m; 780−1,210 m; 1, 13; 9,000/hr; 1,045.
Zadov-Churáňov, 880 m; 890−1,100 m; 1, 3; 2,500/hr; 310.
Krušné Mountains,
Klínovec (and Boží Dar), 1,244 m; 710−1,244 m; 1, 13; 7,000/hr; 42.
Bouřňák, 870 m; 0, 3; 2,000/hr; 300.
Jizerské Mountains,
Bedřichov, Severák, 600 m; 700−805 m; 0, 14; 8,300/hr; 180.
Špičák, 808 m; 530−808 m; 0, 7; 5,200/hr; 140.
Ještěd, 1,012 m; 660−1,012 m; 1, 8; 5,200/hr; 760.
Orlické Mountains,
Deštné, 650 m; 650−850 m; 0, 6; 3,500/hr; 350.
Říčky, 670 m; 750−980 m; 0, 2; 1,450/hr; 100.
Jeseníks,
Ramzová (Petříkov), 759 m; 730−1,300 m; 1, 5; 3,000/hr; 300.
Ovčárna 1,235 m; 1,235−1,440 m; 0, 3; 1,400/hr; 340.
Karlov pod Pradědem, 650 m; 700−936 m; 0, 6; 4,000/hr; 180.
Beskids,
Gruň, 840 m; 700−840 m; 0, 4; 2,400/hr; 240.
Pustevny-Radhošť, 1,018 m; 700−1,100 m; 1, 4; 2,200/hr; 460.
Portáš, 960 m; 690−955 m; 0, 6; 3,200/hr; 460.
High Tatras,
Štrbské Pleso, 1,350 m; 1,350−1,915 m; 2, 4; 2,500/hr; 600.
Smokovec, 850 m; 800−1,480 m, 1, 7; 5,100/hr; 1,030 + car camp.
Tatranská Lomnica, 850 m; 860−2,180 m; 5, 5; 3,800/hr; 1,450 + 3 car camps.
Ždiar, 800 m, 800−1,180 m; 1, 13; 8,500/hr; 2,000 (private accommodation).

Ideal skiing grounds
in the Krkonoše Mountains,
in the background Sněžka

Low Tatras,
Jasná (Chopok-north), 950 m; 950—2,005 m; 6, 12; 11,100/hr; 900.
Bystrianská dolina (Chopok-south), 600 m; 600—2,000 m; 2, 9; 900 + car camp.
Čertovica (and Bocianská dolina), 850 m; 850—1,450 m; 0, 9; 4,500/hr; 270.
Little Fatra,
Vrátna, 620 m; 620—1,500 m; 2, 12; 6,200/hr; 550.
Martinské hole, 1,200 m; 650—1,440 m; 1, 6; 5,800/hr; 170.
Big Fatra,
Málinô, 550 m; 550—1,350 m; 1, 3; 2,250/hr; 280.
Turecká, 580 m; 580—1,610 m; 1, 6; 2,250/hr; 110.
Donovaly, 860 m; 780—1,360 m; 1, 12; 6,350/hr; 150.
Slovenské Beskydy,
Veľká Rača, 1,236 m; 690—1,236 m; 1, 10; 4,800/hr; 260.
Čergov,
Drienica-Lysá, 550 m; 550—1,000 m; 1, 6; 4,700/hr; 260.

Cross-country skiing
Large areas for cross-country skiers have been established (and in some cases are regularly maintained with the aid of mechanization) at the following resorts (the figures indicate the length of the tracks in km):
Krkonoše Mountains, Horní Mísečky, 1, 2, 3, 4, 5, 7, 10, 15 km.
Benecko, 1, 2, 3, 4, 5, 7, 10 km.
Šumava Mountains, Zadov, Churáňov, 1, 2, 3, 4, 5, 7, 10, 15 km.
Krušné Mountains, Nové Město, 1, 2, 4, 5, 7, 10 km.
Jizerské Mountains, Jizerská arterial road beginning at Bedřichov (30 km).
Bohemian-Moravian Highlands, Nové Město na Moravě, 3, 5, 10, 15 km.
Jeseníks, Ovčárna, 1, 2, 3, 5 km.
Nová Ves u Rýmařova, 1, 2, 3, 5, 10 km.
Beskids, Pustevny, 1, 2, 3, 5, 7, 10 km.
High Tatras, Štrbské Pleso, 2 X 5; 7, 10 km.
Low Tatras, Jasná, 5, 10, 15 km.
Big Fatra, Donovaly, 3, 5, 10 km.
Slovak Beskids, Veľká Rača, 1, 2, 3, 4, 5, 10 km.

SPORTS AND CULTURAL EVENTS, TRADE FAIRS

Visitors who are active sportsmen or tourists can take part in a number of **sports and tourist events.** These include, for example, the exacting mass cross-country run for skiers, called the Jizera Fifty, held in January, and the skiing race for ten-member teams, called the Krkonoše Seventy, in February. In winter tourists organize camps, rallies and skiing trips along mountain ridges. March begins with the 100 Spring Kilometres event, held every year to open the tourist season for those fond of making tours on foot (even though it is opened with New Year ascents of a number of highly frequented mountains). A little later higher water levels are taken advantage of by watermen for their first river trips (for example, on the upper stream of the Vltava). April sees the season of tourist and long-distance walks (up to

100 km) in full swing. The best-known of them — the Prague—Prčice march — takes place in May with 20,000—30,000 participants on a number of short and exacting long routes (from 21—65 km). Other noteworthy events include the summer tourist rallies, walking tours across mountain ridges and, in August, the international ascent of youth of Mount Rysy (in the High Tatras). In September the Běchovice—Prague Run is organized for both the wide public and active sportsmen and in November the Grand Kunratice field run takes place. Orientation races are also very popular. Those interested can gain information from travel agents, in particular from Sportturist and Slovakoturist, or directly from the organizers of the individual events. Most of these sports events are run by the Czechoslovak Union of Physical Culture (Praha 1, Na poříčí 12, Postal Code No. 115 30).

Sports fans are attracted by a number of events with international participation. Held in the course of every year are, for example, the ski-jumping contests at Frenštát pod Radhoštěm (ski-jumping contests on a structure with a plastic surface take place here in September) and Štrbské Pleso and especially the Bohemia tournaments at Harrachov and Liberec in January. Equally attractive are the downhill run contests held on Hrebienok or at Skalnaté Pleso (in the High Tatras), or at Jasná (in the Low Tatras). Events of this kind held in the Czech Socialist Republic usually

Gymnasts
at the Czechoslovak
Spartakiade

53

take place at Špindlerův Mlýn. Young skiers compete in a similar way at Říčky in the Orlické Mountains (the Interskikritérium event), or at Vrátna dolina in the Little Fatra. The World Cup events in cross-country skiing take place at Zadov in the Šumava Mountains and at Nové Město na Moravě. Deštné in the Orlické Mountains is the frequent meeting-place of skibob racers. Every year in May stages of the Peace Race for cyclists pass through Czechoslovakia. In August the attention of visitors is attracted by the motor car race held on the Brno circuit. In September Prague is the scene of the notable event held under the name of the **Rudé právo Run** and organized by the daily newspaper Rudé právo (Red Rights) and in October Košice acts as host to the **International Peace Marathon.** Another attractive event held in October is the **Grand Pardubice Steeplechase** held at Pardubice, yet another being the Golden Helmet speedway motor-cycling race. Czechoslovakia is often the scene of world and European championships in various sports disciplines.

The summit of physical culture events are the **Czechoslovak Spartakiades,** held every five years. The next one will take place in 1990. Approximately 15,000 gymnasts appear in each of the mass performances held on the large area of the Strahov Stadium in Prague.

As regards **cultural events** we are presenting in particular those which could hold an attraction also for foreign guests. They include in the first place the International **Prague Spring Music Festival** in May — June in Prague and the Bratislava Music Festival held in September in the Slovak capital. In the course of the main tourist season concerts and theatre performances take place in Prague's gardens and historical interiors under the name of The Prague Cultural Summer. Performances by historical fencing ensembles and period concerts take place at many castles and châteaux. In February the Festival of Political Songs takes place at Sokolov and in May — June the international competition of singers and composers of popular

---

Sports and cultural
events, trade fairs

A typical Moravian Slovak
folk costume

songs, the Bratislava Lyre, takes place in Bratislava. Another type of musical gathering is represented by the international brass band festival held under the name of Kmoch's Kolín at the town of Kolín.

In the sphere of special-interest and folklore performances great response is aroused by the International Folklore Festival at Strážnice, the Rožnov Festivals in June and the Chod Festivals held in August in Domažlice. In August visitors also have the possibility of attending amateur theatre performances held under the name of Jirásek's Hronov (with foreign participation). In September visitors can attend the International Bagpipe Festival at Strakonice, which takes place, however, only every second or third year.

In June, likewise every second year, Karlovy Vary is the scene of the **International Film Festival** and, in September, of the festival held under the name of **Tourfilm** at which films concerned with tourism compete. Entries are submitted for projection from the whole world.

As regards **trade fairs**, let us mention at least the International Engineering Trade Fair held in Brno (September), the Incheba International Chemical Trade Fair (June, Bratislava) and the International Consumer Goods Fair (March, Brno). Of home events of this kind mention should be made of the international Salima food salon (February, Brno), the Garden of Bohemia exhibition of fruit, vegetables, flowers, etc. (September, Litoměřice), the Slovak agricultural exhibition held under the name of Agrocomplex (August—September, Nitra) and the Czech exhibition The Land Our Nourisher (September, České Budějovice).

PRACTICAL INFORMATION

In order to cross the Czechoslovak border visitors must be in possession of a valid passport and an entry visa (a sojourn or transit one). A Czechoslovak visa can be obtained from all Czechoslovak consulates abroad on presentation of a passport, duly completed application forms and photographs. A visa can also be obtained at the border crossings Rozvadov, Horní Dvořiště, Hatě and Petržalka. After arriving in Czechoslovakia a tourist must exchange a certain amount of foreign currency for Czechoslovak crowns. If he fails to do so his visa will become invalid. This regulation naturally does not apply in the case of sojourns organized by travel agents, whose price is higher than the sum of the obligatory exchange. If a foreigner does not reside at a public accommodation facility he must register at the respective District Department of Passports and Visas in the place of his sojourn within 48 hours after crossing the state border (in Prague: Olšanská 2, Prague 3). Drivers of motor vehicles must see that they are provided with the international registration letters of their country of origin and also possess a so-called green card certifying payment of the compulsory insurance.

Travel
documents

A new hotel building
at Opava

Czechoslovakia can be entered by means of over 90 border crossings, most of which are road or rail ones. An experienced traveller will tell you that their busiest times are Friday and Sunday morning and that they are relatively far less busy in the middle of the week.
In the following survey we are presenting selected border crossings only, omitting in particular those intended exclusively for citizens of socialist countries on the basis of bilateral agreements.

From the German Democratic Republic:
road crossings: Zinnwald — Cínovec (international road E 55 from Berlin to Prague), Bad Brambach — Vojtanov (E 49 Plauen — Cheb — West Bohemian spas). — Seifhennersdorf — Varnsdorf, Schmilka — Hřensko (in the tourist region of the Bohemian-Saxon Switzerland), Bahratal — Petrovice (from Dresden to Ústí nad Labem), Reitzenhain — Hora Svatého Šebastiána (the shortest route from Leipzig and Karl-Marx-Stadt to Prague) and Oberwiesenthal — Boží Dar (one of the holiday resorts of the Krušné Mountains) road crossings are intended solely for use by citizens of socialist countries;
rail crossings: Bad Schandau — Děčín (Berlin — Prague line), Bad Brambach — Vojtanov (trains from Leipzig to Karlovy Vary);

from the Federal Republic of Germany:
road crossings: Schirnding — Pomezí nad Ohří (E 48 from Marktredwitz to Cheb and the West Bohemian spas), Waidhaus — Rozvadov (E 50 from Nuremberg to Prague), Furth im Wald — Folmava, Bayerisch Eisenstein — Železná Ruda (E 53 in the Šumava region, Munich — Prague route) and Philippsreut — Strážný (from Passau to Prague);
rail crossings: Schirnding — Cheb (express trains Paris—Frankfurt—Nuremberg—Prague), Furth im Wald — Domažlice (express trains Munich—Prague);

from Austria:
road crossings: Weigetschlag — Studánky, Wullowitz — Dolní Dvořiště (E 55 from Linz to Prague), Gmünd N. Ö. — České Velenice, Neu Nagelberg — Halámky (E 49 the shortest route from Vienna to Prague), Grametten — Nová Bystřice, Klein Haugsdorf — Hatě (E 59 from Vienna to Znojmo and Jihlava), Laa an der Thaya — Hevlín, Drasenhofen — Mikulov (E 461 from Vienna to Brno) and Berg — Petržalka (from Vienna to Bratislava);
rail crossings: Gmünd N. Ö. — České Velenice (Vienna — Prague line), Summerau — Horní Dvořiště (from Linz to České Budějovice), Hohenau — Břeclav (express trains on the Vienna — Ostrava — Warsaw line) and Marchegg — Devínská Nová Ves (Vienna — Bratislava line);

from Hungary:
road crossings: Rajka — Rusovce (E 75 and E 65 from Budapest to Prague), Vamosszabadi — Medveďov (from Györ to Bratislava), Komárom — Komárno, Parassapuszta — Šahy (E 77 from Budapest to Banská Bystrica), Balassa Gyarmat — Slovenské Ďarmoty, Banréve — Král (from Miskolc to the Tatra region), Hidasnemeti — Hraničná pri Hornáde (E 71, from Miskolc to Košice) and Sátoraljaújhely — Slovenské Nové Mesto;
rail crossings: Rajka — Rusovce (trains from Budapest to Bratislava), Komárom —

Komárno (express trains on the Budapest — Bratislava — Prague line), Szob — Štúrovo (express trains on the Budapest — Bratislava — Prague line), Somoskoújfalu — Fiľakovo and Hidasnémeti — Čaňa (express trains on the Budapest — Cracow line);
from the Soviet Union:
road crossing: Uzhgorod — Vyšné Nemecké;
rail crossing: Chop — Čierna nad Tisou;
from Poland:
road crossings: Barwinek — Vyšný Komárnik (area of the Dukla Pass battlefield), Lysa Poľana — Javorina (in the High Tatras), Chyzne — Trstená (E 77 from Cracow via Banská Bystrica to Budapest), Cieszyn — Český Těšín (E 75 and E 462 from Warsaw to Brno and Vienna), Chalupki — Bohumín, Kudowa Zdroj — Běloves (E 67 from Warsaw and Wroclaw to Náchod and Prague) and Jakuszyce — Harrachov (E 65 from the Baltic to Prague);
rail crossings: Muszyna — Plaveč (express trains from Cracow to Budapest), Zebrzydowice — Petrovice u Karviné (express trains from Warsaw to Prague) and Miedzylesie — Lichkov (express trains from Warsaw via Wroclaw to Prague).

DUTY

According to Czechoslovak custom regulations the foreign visitor can import valuable things intended for his or her personal needs into Czechoslovakia. Visitors of over 18 years of age may also import 2 l of wine, 1 l of spirits, 250 cigarettes or the corresponding amount of other tobacco products. In the case of a short stay (up to two days) one half of the above-mentioned quantities may be imported. In the case of hunting requisites, 1,000 cartridges for shot-guns and 50 cartridges for rifles may be imported. Articles for personal use also include cameras, radios and the like, their import naturally being permitted on the assumption that they will be exported on departure.

With the exception of pure spirit and things which propagate ideas out of keeping with the interests of Czechoslovakia's socialist society everything may be imported into the country. Visitors may bring the necessary amount of fuel and lubricating materials for their vehicles into Czechoslovakia.

Goods to the value of 1,000 Czechoslovak crowns, calculated in accordance with the valid prices in Czechoslovakia's retail network, may be imported duty-free. Duty is collected on a sum exceeding 1,000 Czechoslovak crowns.

When leaving Czechoslovakia visitors may export duty-free gifts to the value of 500 Czechoslovak crowns per person providing goods whose export is either prohibited or restricted are not concerned. For example, the export of foods (with the exception of Czechoslovak spirits and wines), plush, corduroy, stockings, footwear, leather gloves, products made of gold and silver, tyres and inner tubes, feather products, sewing machines, etc. is prohibited. In the case of certain articles the visitor must possess an export permit (tents, sports requisites, bed-linen, various types of craft instruments, etc.) necessitating an administrative charge to the value of 150% of the respective retail price. In the case of articles whose price exceeds 500 Czechoslovak crowns the administrative charge amounts to 30% only. Articles purchased with freely convertible currency (at Tuzex shops, etc.) are exempt from duty, but the bill for their purchase must be presented.

Duty

In Czechoslovakia the right-hand drive principle applies. The maximum speed limits are as follows: 110 km/hr on motorways and 90 km/hr on other roads, and 60 km/hr in built-up areas providing there is no sign indicating a different speed.

The consumption of alcohol (including beer) is prohibited before and during a drive. Czechoslovakia's traffic code and signs are similar to those valid throughout Europe. Trams have priority when turning to the right. Buses have priority when leaving stops providing the driver signals his intention by means of his direction indicators.

The network of petrol stations (the Benzina Concern Corporation in the Czech Socialist Republic and Benzinol in the Slovak Socialist Republic) suffices the needs of motorists. Special petrol with the octane number 90 (8 Czechoslovak crowns per litre) and super petrol with the octane number 96 (9 Czechoslovak crowns per litre) are sold. Selected petrol stations also sell leadless petrol with the octane numbers 91 (8 Czechoslovak crowns per litre) and 95 (Eurosuper 9, Czechoslovak crowns per litre). As a rule oil and other necessities (distilled water, lubricants, etc.) can be purchased at petrol stations. With the exception of big petrol stations on the motorways, the purchase of other necessities such as tyres, tubes, spare parts, road maps, refreshments, etc. cannot, as a rule, be counted with.

A number of petrol stations provides round-the-clock service, for example, in regional towns, on motorways and on main roads. On the other hand, visitors must count with the fact that these services are not available on Saturdays and Sundays in less frequented places. Although we do not wish to say that drivers run the risk of being stranded, we nevertheless advise them not to leave the purchase of petrol to non-working days. By adhering to this recommendation they will, to say the least, avoid possible queues, anxiety caused by a search for an accessible petrol station, etc.

The self-service system exists at all big petrol stations.

Car and tyre repair shops can be found in practically all towns. In the summer tourist season selected car repair shops are open on Saturdays and Sundays (information about their opening hours can be obtained from petrol stations). Czechoslovakia also has emergency road services (the so-called Yellow Angels in view of the yellow colour of the emergency repair vehicles) which render drivers first aid in the case of sudden unforeseen defects. They can be called by telephone (a dense telephone network exists on the motorways). The basic expressions necessary to cope with such a situation are presented in the chapter Czech and Slovak.

Information about the location of car repair shops, petrol stations and car camps, including their opening times, is contained in the road atlas for motorists, usually available especially at bookshops.

In the Czechoslovak Socialist Republic a network of public (sometimes also guarded) car parks is systematically being built up, particularly in large towns, tourist resorts, spas, etc. In less frequented places it is in essence possible to park everywhere where parking is not specifically prohibited, i.e. in front of hotels, in squares, in front of railway stations, in shopping centres, etc. Car parks are marked with the letter P.

As regards parking, the situation is more complicated in Prague. For example, visiting motorists are forbidden to enter the square Václavské náměstí and the adjoining streets. This prohibition naturally does not apply in the case of guests accommodated at hotels in these parts of Prague. In the so-called blue zone, i.e. in the historical centre of the city, parking is permissible only on a limited number of car parks. Motorists who park their cars elsewhere run the risk of their vehicle being towed away — and this involves a considerable charge. It is therefore advisable to leave your car on marked car parks on the outskirts of the city.

The previously mentioned car parks in the centre of the city operate on a progressive charge system: 1 Czechoslovak crown up to 30 min., 4 Czechoslovak crowns up to 2 hours and 10 Czechoslovak crowns for every further started hour. (Automatic parking machines do not exist in the Czechoslovak Socialist Republic.)

TRANSPORT

Czechoslovakia's railway network measures 13,186 km and ranks among the densest in Europe. Passenger and goods transport is the concern of Czechoslovak State Railways (ČSD). Trains are differentiated into the passenger, fast and express categories. First-class travel is possible on fast and express trains. Smoking is permissible in specially marked carriages of fast and express trains only. Rail transport is very cheap. For example, a journey in a 2nd class carriage of an express train from Prague to Košice (708 km) costs 89 Czechoslovak crowns and a 1st class ticket 133.50 Czechoslovak crowns.

Roads and motorways cover over 73,000 km in Czechoslovakia and they are used by over 3,000,000 motor vehicles. The most frequented is the motorway connecting Czechoslovakia's three biggest cities (Prague — Brno — Bratislava). Other motorways are under construction, the individual completed sectors gradually being put into use. There are also roads for motor vehicles which, similarly as the motorways, have four lanes. They differ only in certain technical parameters. The network of 1st class roads connecting the majority of towns is also of a high quality and 2nd class roads link up with it. Roads of the 3rd class run to even the smallest villages.

Public road transport is secured by over 4,000 bus lines (operated by Czechoslovak Automobile Transport — ČSAD), running to even the smallest villages. In some cases bus transport is quicker than rail transport and in recent years the number and extent of use of long-distance lines (for example, Prague — Brno) have increased. Bus transport is somewhat more expensive than rail transport.

The importance of air transport has decreased somewhat with the construction of motorways. The most frequented home lines connect in particular Prague, Bratislava, Košice and Ostrava. Other airports are situated at Karlovy Vary, Brno, Piešťany, Sliač and Poprad. They are operated by Czechoslovak Airlines (ČSA).

Navigable sectors of the Rivers Elbe, Vltava and Danube are mainly used for goods transport, passenger boats being used chiefly for sightseeing trips.

Municipal transport is secured in Prague by the 3 lines of the underground, trams and buses. Tram and bus and sometimes trolley-bus transport also exists in other big towns. The self-service system is applied on all these transport media. Tickets can be purchased mainly at hotels, tobacconists', newspaper stalls, underground stations (automatic machines), etc.

Transport

All large towns have a taxi service. Apart from fixed taxi ranks, it is usually possible to order a taxi by telephone. The basic tariff is 6 Czechoslovak crowns. As a rule the charge for 1 km is 3 to 3.40 Czechoslovak crowns according to the cubature of the respective vehicle. A charge of 7.50 Czechoslovak crowns in made for every 15 minutes of waiting time. Czechoslovak crowns.

EMBASSIES

The address of the British Embassy in Prague is Thunovská 14, Prague 1 — Malá Strana, Tel. 533347, 533370.
The address of the American Embassy is Tržiště 15, Prague 1 — Malá Strana, Tel. 536641.
The address of the Canadian Embassy is Mickiewiczova 6, Prague 6, Tel. 326941.

CURRENCY

The currency unit is the Czechoslovak crown (Kčs) consisting of 100 hellers (hal.). Banknotes to the value of 1,000, 500, 100, 50, 20 and 10 Kčs and coins to the value of 5, 2 and 1 Kčs and 50, 20, 10 and 5 hal. are in circulation. It is prohibited to export

Entrance to the underground
railway at the Main Station
in Prague

Czech currency. (Currency exchange bureaux in non-socialist countries are not authorized to either purchase or exchange Czechoslovak currency.)
In Czechoslovakia currency can be exchanged at the exchange offices of banks, at the reception desks of Interhotels and at the border crossings.

POSTAL RATES

	Letters and large postcards	Postcards
In Czechoslovakia and to European socialist countries	1 Kčs (up to 20 g)	50 hal.
Other European countries	4 Kčs (up to 20 g)	3 Kčs
Overseas air mail	6 Kčs (up to 10 g)	5 Kčs

TRAVEL BUREAUX

Czechoslovak travel bureaux offer their services to home and foreign visitors. They secure board and accommodation, transport, spa sojourns, standard sightseeing tours, sightseeing tours of towns and tickets for cultural and sports events. They also organize hunting trips, congresses and symposia and offer the services of guides and interpreters.
Czechoslovakia's biggest travel bureau is Čedok, whose main seats are in Prague (Na příkopě 18) and Bratislava (Štúrova 13). It also has branches in all large towns (about 150 in all). Čedok also has agents abroad:
Bundesrepublik Deutschland, ČEDOK Reisen GmbH., Spezialbüro für Reisen in die Tschechoslowakei, Kaiserstrasse 54, 6000 Frankfurt am Main, Tel. 232975—7
Österreich, ČEDOK, Tschechoslowakisches Reisebüro GmbH., Parkring 12, A-1010 Wien, Tel. 5120199, 5132609
Great Britain, ČEDOK, London Ltd., Czechoslovak Travel Bureau, 17—18 Old Bond Street, London W1X 4RB, Tel. 01-6296058
Belgique, Rue d'Assaut 19, 1000 Bruxelles, Tel. 5116870, 5116247
Bulgaria, Bul. Alexander Stambolijski 27, 1000 Sofia, Tel. 877713, 874245
Denmark, Vester Farimagsgade 6, 1606 Kobenhavn V, Tel. 120121
Deutsche Demokratische Republik, Strausberger Platz 8/9, 1017 Berlin Friedrichs-hain, Tel. 4394135, 4394113
France, 32, Avenue de l'Opéra, 75002 Paris, Tel. 47428773, 47421811
Italia, Via Piemonte 32, 00187 Roma, Tel. 483 406
Jugoslavija, Strahinjića bana 51/III, 11000 Beograd, Tel. 629543, 628416
Magyarország, Kossuth Lajos tér 18, 1055, Budapest V, Tel. 128233, 119855
Nederland, Leidsestraat 4, 1017 PA Amsterdam, Tel. 020—220101
Polska, ul. Nowogrodzka 31, 00-511 Warszawa, Tel. 267076, 217955

Postal
rates

Romania, Str. Visarion 9 A, Bucuresti, Tel. 596860
SSSR, 4. Tversko-Jamskaja ul. 35/39, 125 047 Moskva, Tel. 2588932
Sverige, Sveavägen 9-11, 11157 Stockholm, Tel. 207290, 210790
Schweiz, Urania Strasse 34/2, 8025 Zürich, Tel. 2114245—6
USA, 10 East 40th Street, New York N. Y. 10157, Tel. (212) 689 9720
Services for young people are secured by the Travel Bureau for Youth (CKM — Žitná
12, Prague 1). The Rekrea cooperative travel bureau has its seat in Prague (Revoluční
13) and the Tatratour cooperative travel bureau in Bratislava (Martanovičova 18).
Sport-turist is the travel bureau of the Czech physical culture organization (Národní
třída 33, Prague 1) and similar services are offered by Slovakoturist (nábrežie L.
Svobodu 7 a) in Bratislava. Balnea (Pařížská 11, Prague 1) and Slovakotherma (Radlinského 19, Bratislava) secure spa sojourns. Services for motorists in particular are
secured by Autoturist, the travel bureau of Svazarm (the Union for Cooperation with
the Army), whose address is Ječná 40, Prague 1.

ACCOMMODATION

In Czechoslovakia hotels are divided into 5 classes marked with stars (*) and the original system of classification into A* de Luxe, A*, B*, B and C is also used, especially
in the case of older hotels. The prices of accommodation are fixed on the basis of
these categories, a surcharge being made in the case of foreign guests (approximately 100% of the basic price). Čedok's Interhotels, which in most cases offer services of the highest quality, are intended particularly for foreign visitors. In view of
the considerable interest in hotel accommodation (especially in Prague, Brno, Bra-

Intercontinental Hotel
in Prague

tislava, spas and mountain resorts) visitors are recommended to reserve accommodation in advance, best of all through the mediation of the Čedok travel bureau (see
also the separate item Travel Bureaux). Quality services are offered by certain mot-
els and in Prague there are 3 botels, anchored in the River Vltava. Less exacting
guests can find accommodation at inns, tourist chalets and tourist hostels. Chalet
communities and car camps, intended in particular for motorized visitors, offer their
services especially in the summer period. A list of Interhotels and other information
can be obtained from Čedok Travel Bureaux. Lists of accommodation facilities and
car camps as well as clear maps of car camps, included, for example, also in the
map enclosed in this guide, are published in Czechoslovakia.

CATERING, CZECHOSLOVAK CUISINE

Catering facilities offering hot meals throughout the whole day exist particularly in
towns and tourist resorts and along the main road communications. Restaurants are
classified into 4 classes according to the quality and assortment of their services.
Meals can be obtained at snack-bars, certain espressos, self-service dining-rooms
and buffets. As a rule country pubs offer drinks and cold dishes only. Foreign visitors seek stylish catering facilities serving various local specialities (these are called,
for example, "koliba", "šenk"), or typical ale-houses.
At all Czechoslovak catering facilities, restaurants, ale-houses, etc. the reward for
service is always included in the price of a meal. Quality service can be rewarded
with a tip to the maximum value of 10% of the bill.

Catering,
Czechoslovak
cuisine
64

A car camp on the bank
of the Orlík valley
reservoir

Modern Czechoslovak cuisine is very diverse. The normal menu of the 2nd price group does not differ from the European average to any great extent. Here and there dishes are prepared according to real (i.e., Old) "Czech" and "Slovak" cuisine in small towns and the countryside, or, on the contrary, in new, so-called stylish restaurants. However, such dishes are usually heavier and richer in calories, although it must be said that they are very tasty. A smaller selection is usually possible when it comes to fresh vegetables (sterilized ones are often served even in summer), poultry and fish.

Czech cuisine is characterized rather by heavy dishes with which side dishes made with the use of flour are served. Not in vain is the typical Czech dish made up of pork, sauerkraut and dumplings. Lighter kinds of meat are "improved" in the same sense with, for instance, cream sauce (undercut of beef sirloin, hare, lights). Another Czech speciality consists of sweet fruit dumplings. Dumplings are also served as a separate dish (a very cheap one) with eggs. And potato dumplings are regarded as a real delicacy.

Slovak cuisine differs from Czech cuisine mainly due to the fact that it employs more spices, especially red pepper (the influence of Hungarian cuisine). Slovak goulashes are usually more piquant than Czech ones. Potatoes and potato dishes also appear on the menu more frequently. Game plays a far more important role in Slovak cuisine and Slovakia is more inventive in combining various types of meat.

A considerable number of simple, tasty dishes (including soups), based on potatoes, cabbage and spices of home origin (or mushrooms) has, on the territory of the whole country, been taken from the menus of poor submontane regions, now enjoying general popularity.

A popular soup of this kind is made from potatoes and mushrooms and another favourite dish is the so-called "bramborák", a kind of potato pancake which, together

Obří sud (Giant Barrel) Restaurant
at Lázně Libverda
below the Jizera Mountains

with sausages and the internationally known hamburger, represents the most frequent offer of street stalls.

Buns, tarts, apple rolls, scones, pancakes, differently flavoured cream cakes and the
like are offered in a rich selection by both Czech and Slovak cuisine.

As regards drinks, beer is consumed to the greatest extent. It is usually tapped into
half-litre vessels. Light beer (10°, 11° or 12°) is very popular and in special restaurants dark beer (14°) is served. The best-known brands of beer include Pilsner Urquell, Budweiss from České Budějovice and Old Spring, brewed in Prague. Moravian
and Slovak wines (from the environs of Mikulov, Znojmo, Bzenec, Pezinok and Modra, for example) are of a high quality. Czechoslovak liqueurs known abroad include
the Becher brand of the herb type from Karlovy Vary, Moravian "slivovice", made
from plums, and a Slovak juniper liqueur called "borovička", very similar to gin.

FISHING

Organized fishing has a long-standing tradition in Czechoslovakia. The fish stocks
are continually supplemented. As a rule small and big mountain streams and rivers
and similar flows in the foothills are marked as trout waters. According to their
character, other waters and reservoirs contain pike, carp, tench, barbel, pike-perch,
perch, sheat-fish and bream. However, a fishing permit for angling in certain waters
is necessary. Fishing is not permitted in breeding waters. More detailed information
can be obtained from the Čedok Travel Bureau and the Czechoslovak Fishing Union,
Žitná 13, Praha 1, or its local branches.

HUNTING

In Czechoslovakia it is possible to hunt in many places. Huntsmen can shoot roe-
bucks, wild boars, moufflons, bears, pheasants, hares and wild ducks. Czechoslovak
travel bureaux will provide those interested with information about hunting permits
and the charges involved. In general it can be said that better conditions for hunting
— especially for the more exacting — exist in Slovakia than in Bohemia and Moravia.

SHOPS, SOUVENIRS

In Czechoslovakia shops are open throughout the whole day from Monday to Friday
and on Saturday morning. All shops are closed on Sunday with the exception of certain food and confectionery shops. In big towns the visitor will find Prior department
stores which are usually open from 8—18 (19) hours. Food shops are open from 6—8
hours and closed from 16—18 hours and in small towns, similarly as small shops,
have a noon break. Other shops open at 9 hours. Foreign visitors usually purchase
Bohemian glass, china, fashion jewellery, works of art, products of folk art, Pilsner

Fishing

Urquell beer, etc. In Czechoslovakia's biggest towns there are Tuzex shops where goods can be purchased in a wide assortment for foreign currency or special vouchers.

WORKING HOURS, HOLIDAYS

In Czechoslovakia a working week consists of 42 1/2 hours per week, i.e. from Monday to Friday. Saturday and Sunday are days of rest. State holidays include 1 January (New Year), Easter Monday, 1 May (Holiday of Work), 9 May (the liberation of Czechoslovakia in 1945), 28 October (Independence Day) and 25 and 26 December (Christmas holiday). As a rule a work day begins between 6 to 8 hours and ends between 14 and 17 hours. Central European time (+ 1 hour in comparison with Greenwich time) is used in Czechoslovakia, so-called summer time being in force from April to September (i.e. East European time, + 2 hours in comparison with Greenwich time).

PHOTOGRAPHING

Photographing is forbidden in places where there is a sign with a crossed-out camera, or where there is a board bearing the inscription "Fotografování zakázáno" (Photographing Prohibited).

MEDICAL CARE

In the case of accidents or sudden illnesses foreign visitors can seek help at any small medical facility (out-patient departments), policlinic or hospital. Medical aid will be rendered free of charge. Citizens from socialist countries are exempted from paying for medical remedies, a stay in hospital and transport to their home country.

TOURIST SIGNS, MAPS

The network of marked paths in Czechoslovakia is very dense and reliable. The total length of these paths is 70,000 km. All tourist paths are marked in the same way, i.e. with two white stripes with a stripe of the main colour between them (red, blue, green or yellow). Situated along all marked paths are panels containing data concerning distances to important places (elevation points, crossroads, villages and so on) on the next part of the route. In Bohemia and Moravia distances are indicated in kilometres and in Slovakia in hours. Furthermore, tourist maps illustrating the wide environs are situated at all important crossroads and tourist resorts.

Short side turnings (approximately up to 1 km in length) are marked with pictorial signs (for example, castle ruins, sources of drinking water, caves, observation towers, etc.). On some excursions the visitor comes across signs indicating a nature study path (a white square with a green diagonal stripe). These are accompanied by clear charts and useful information. Some sightseeing routes round car camps and recreation spa routes are also usually marked in their own way.

Tourist maps with delineations of the routes followed by marked paths are on sale in Czechoslovakia. They can be obtained from Kniha (Book) shops and sometimes also at railway station stalls, large hotels, etc. The most recent edition depicts practically the whole territory of the Czech Socialist Republic on 42 pages and the territory of the Slovak Socialist Republic on 29 pages. The scale is usually 1 : 100,000. In most cases tourist maps are published as summer ones, but in the case of the most frequented winter resorts winter maps are also available (for example, the Krkonoše Mountains, the High Tatras).

Also on sale is a series of car maps, scale of 1 : 200,000 consisting of 17 pages and coverting the whole territory of Czechoslovakia in a comprehensive way. A very good aid for motorists are the car maps contained in the publication Autoatlas ČSSR which appears in many editions in the Czech Socialist Republic and the Slovak Socialist Republic. The scale used in this case is 1 : 400,000.

CZECH AND SLOVAK

Two equal languages are used in the Czechoslovak Socialist Republic — Czech and Slovak. Their mutual understanding by the two nations does not cause any great problems. In the interest of simplification only one of the two languages, Czech, is used in this guide, because two thirds of the population speak it. The names of Slovak mountains, museums, streets, etc. are naturally presented in Slovak.

Basic expressions and phrases

Good day — *Dobrý den;* Good evening — *Dobrý večer;* Good bye — *Na shledanou;* Happy journey! — *Šťastnou cestu!;* Thank you — *Děkuji;* I don't understand — *Nerozumím;* Yes — *Ano;* No — *Ne;* I don't know — *Nevím;* Where? — *Kde?;* When? — *Kdy?;* Who — *Kdo?;* What? — *Co?;* How much?, How many? — *Kolik?;* Which way? — *Kudy?;* Men's (women's) toilets — *WC*; My name is . . . — *Jmenuji se . . .;* I come from . . . — *Jsem z . . .*

Time

What is the time please? — *Kolik je, prosím, hodin?;* It's one o'clock — *Je jedna hodina;* It's four o'clock — *Jsou čtyři hodiny;* It's five o'clock — *Je pět hodin;* Morning — *Ráno;* At noon — *V poledne;* Afternoon — *Odpoledne;* Evening — *Večer;* Night — *Noc;* Day — *Den;* Yesterday — *Včera;* The day before yesterday — *Předevčírem;* Tomorrow — *Zítra;* The day after tomorrow — *Pozítří.*

Week — *Týden;* Monday — *Pondělí;* Tuesday — *Úterý;* Wednesday — *Středa;* Thursday — *Čtvrtek;* Friday — *Pátek;* Saturday — *Sobota;* Sunday — *Neděle.*

Month — *Měsíc*; January — *Leden;* February — *Únor;* March — *Březen*; April — *Duben;* May — *Květen;* June — *Červen;* July — *Červenec;* August — *Srpen;* Sep-

tember — *Září;* October — *Říjen;* November — *Listopad*; December — *Prosinec.*
Cardinal points — *Světové strany;* North — *Sever;* South — *Jih;* West — *Západ*;
East — *Východ.*
Seasons of the year — *Roční období;* Spring — *Jaro;* Summer — *Léto;* Autumn —
Podzim; Winter — *Zima.*
Numbers — *Čísla*; One — *Jedna;* Two — *Dvě;* Three — *Tři;* Four — *Čtyři*; Five —
Pět; Six — *Šest*; Seven — *Sedm;* Eight — *Osm;* Nine — *Devět;* Ten — *Deset;* Twenty — *Dvacet*; Thirty — *Třicet;* Forty — *Čtyřicet*; Fifty — *Padesát;* Sixty — *Šedesát;*
Seventy — *Sedmdesát;* Eighty — *Osmdesát;* Ninety — *Devadesát*; One hundred —
Sto; One thousand — *Tisíc*; One million — *Milión.*

Travel

Passport — *Cestovní pas;* Have you anything to declare? — *Máte něco k procleni?;*
Personal needs — *Osobní věci;* Timetable (bus, train, air) — *Jízdní řád;* Waiting-room — *Čekárna;* Left luggage office — *Úschovna zavazadel;* Smoking prohibited!
— *Kouření zakázáno!;* Excuse me, where is the station (the square?, the Post Office?, a dental surgery?, the Police Station?) — *Promiňte, kde je nádraží? (náměstí?,
pošta?, zubní lékař?, policie?)*; Information Office — *Informační kancelář;* I need
some information — *Potřebuji informaci;* On the right — *Vpravo*; On the left — *Vlevo;* Straight ahead — *Rovně;* You must go back — *Musíte zpátky;* Does this road
lead to . . .? — *Vede tato cesta do . . .?;* How many kilometres is it to . . .? — *Kolik je
kilometrů do . . .?;* Must I turn left (right)? — *Musím odbočit?*

Shopping, Meals

I want to buy some bread (butter, milk, meat, smoked meat, fruit, vegetables, sugar,
cheese, cottage cheese, rolls, cigarettes, matches) — *Chtěl bych chléb (máslo, mléko, uzeniny, ovoce, zeleninu, cukr, sýr, tvaroh, rohlíky, cigarety, zápalky).*
Café — *Kavárna;* Restaurant — *Restaurace;* Ale-house — *Hostinec;* Wine tavern —
Vinárna; Night bar — *Noční bar;* Milk bar — *Mléčný bar.*
May I have the menu, please? — *Prosím o jídelní lístek;* Is this seat vacant? — *Je zde
volné místo?;* What do you recommend? — *Co mi doporučujete?;* Have you a speciality? — *Jakou máte specialitu?*
Breakfast — *Snídaně;* Lunch (dinner) — *Oběd;* Dinner (supper) — *Večeře;* Vacant
— *Volno;* Engaged — *Obsazeno.*
Knife — *Nůž;* Spoon — *Lžíce;* Fork — *Vidlička;* Plate — *Talíř;* Glass — *Sklenice.*
Tea — *Čaj;* Coffee — *Káva;* Mineral water — *Minerální voda;* Soda water — *Sodová
voda;* Beer — *Pivo;* Wine — *Víno;* Spirits — *Lihoviny.*
Cold dishes — *Studená jídla;* Hors d'oeuvre — *Předkrm;* Soup — *Polévka;* Fish —
Ryby; Beef — *Hovězí;* Pork — *Vepřové;* Veal — *Telecí;* Mutton — *Skopové;* Stewed
meat — *Dušené maso;* Boiled meat — *Vařené maso;* Fried meat — *Smažené maso;*
Roasted meat — *Pečené maso.* Salad — *Salát;* Vegetable side dish — *Zeleninová
příloha;* Compôte — *Kompot;* Potatoes — *Brambory;* Fried potatoes (chips) — *Opékané brambory;* Dumplings — *Knedlíky;* Nocci — *Noky;* Rice — *Rýže;* Dessert —
Moučník; Icecream — *Zmrzlina;* Fruit cup with whipped cream — *Šlehačkový pohár.*
Can I have my bill, please? — *Zaplatím;* Waiter — *Číšník;* Head waiter — *Vrchní
číšník;* Waitress — *Servírka.*

Accommodation

Hotel — *Hotel;* Motel — *Motel;* Botel — *Botel;* Tourist hostel — *Turistická ubytovna;* Hostel — *Noclehárna;* Mountain chalet — *Horská chata;* Inn — *Ubytovací hostinec;* Car camp — *Autokempink;* Public camping site — *Veřejné tábořiště;* To reserve a hotel room — *Zamluvit hotel;* Bathroom — *Koupelna;* Shower — *Sprcha;* Balcony — *Balkón;* Facing the street — *Do ulice.*

First aid

First Aid Post — *Stanice první pomoci;* Health Centre — *Zdravotnické středisko;* Pharmacist's — *Lékárna;* Physician (doctor) — *Lékař;* Specialist in internal diseases — *Internista;* Dental surgeon — *Zubní lékař;* Eye specialist — *Oční lékař;* Children's doctor — *Dětský lékař;* Injection — *Injekce;* Tablets — *Tabletky;* Drops — *Kapky.* Medical Examination — *Lékařská prohlídka;* I don't feel well — *Není mi dobře;* I've got a headache — *Bolí mne hlava;* I've got a pain in my arm — *Bolí mne ruka;* I've got a pain in my leg — *Bolí mne noha;* I've got a pain in my back — *Bolí mne v zádech;* I've got a pain in my neck — *Bolí mne v krku;* I've got toothache — *Bolí mne zub;* I fell over — *Upadl jsem;* I bumped into . . . — *Narazil jsem se.*

Phrases and expressions for motorists

Where is the nearest petrol station? (repair garage?, service?, tyre repair shop?) — *Kde je nejbližší benzínové čerpadlo? (autoopravna?, servis?, vulkanizační dílna?);* I need to fill up my radiator (battery) — *Potřebuji doplnit vodu v chladiči (baterii);* I need to check the pressure of my tyres — *Potřebuji zkontrolovat tlak v pneumatikách;* I need to have my brakes (valves, carburator, the geometry of the wheels, the steering system) checked — *Potřebuji seřídit brzdy (ventily, karburátor, geometrii kol, řízení);* I've got an engine (dynamo, ignition, starter) defect — *Mám poruchu motoru (dynama, zapalování, startéru);* My brake fluid has escaped — *Vytekla mi brzdová kapalina;* I want the lamp (safety valve, Veebelt, spark plug) changed — *Potřebuji vyměnit žárovku (pojistku, klínový řemen, zapalovací svíčku);* The inner tube needs mending — *Potřebuji svařit duši;* The gear box (petrol pump, water pump, radiator) needs repairing — *Potřebuji opravit rychlostní skříň (benzínovou pumpu, vodní čerpadlo, chladič);* When will my car be repaired? — *Kdy bude vůz opraven?;* How much will the repair cost? — *Kolik bude stát oprava vozu?*

Travelling

Town — *Město;* Capital — *Hlavní město;* Village — *Vesnice;* Square — *Náměstí;* Street — *Ulice;* Castle — *Hrad;* Château — *Zámek;* Palace — *Palác;* Fortress — *Pevnost;* Gate — *Brána;* Tower, Steeple — *Věž;* House — *Dům.*

PRAGUE — THE CAPITAL

OF CZECHOSLOVAKIA

Prague (Praha), the capital of the Czechoslovak Socialist Republic and the Czech Socialist Republic, is the most important political, economic and cultural centre of the country and the seat of the President of the Republic, the Federal and the Czech Government, the Federal Assembly, etc. It covers an area of nearly 500 sq. kilometres and its population numbers 1,200,000. The city's height above sea level fluctuates between 180 m (the surface of the River Vltava) and 391 m (Kopanina, Prague 5). Prague is divided into 10 districts. The historical centre of the town, which comprises the Old Town (Staré Město), Josefov, the Little Quarter (Malá Strana), Hradčany, the New Town (Nové Město) and Vyšehrad, collectively form a historical town reserve of European importance.

In Prague there are many outstanding and, for foreigners, very interesting **national cultural monuments.** They include in particular Prague Castle and St. Vitus's Cathedral and the whole complex of Old Town Square with the Town Hall, Týn Church and Kinský Palace. The third important historical area is Vyšehrad. The foremost secular buildings and structures are Charles Bridge, the Carolinum, the National Theatre and Tyl Theatre, the National Museum and the New Town Hall. Out-

View
of Prague Castle
and Charles Bridge

standing among Prague's church buildings and complexes are the Convent of the Blessed Agnes, Bethlehem Chapel and the Monastery "Na Slovanech" (Emmaus). Other places and buildings are connected with our national history: the scene of the tragic Battle of the White Mountain, the People's House in Hybernská Street, the National Monument in Žižkov, the Burial-ground of Honour of Red Army Soldiers in Olšany Cemetery, and others.

Prague is an important **industrial town** and transport cross-road. Since the end of the war dozens of housing estates have sprung up here. The decisive industrial branch is the engineering industry, followed by the food (meat, milk and brewing) industry, the ready-made garment, chemical and polygraphic industries, and others. Prague's share in the total volume of industrial production in the Czechoslovak Socialist Republic amounts to nearly 9%.

In the course of its history Prague has been the point of intersection of Eurepean **cultures** for whole centuries. One of the bearers of this tradition is, for example, Charles University, the oldest institution of its kind in Central Europe (it was founded in 1348). The roots of Prague's musical life date back to the Middle Ages — from the Hussite chorals and Baroque organ music to the compositions of the great representatives of Czech music Bedřich Smetana and Antonín Dvořák. The National Theatre, built from collections accumulated by the Czech nation, has outstanding traditions. Prague has rich collections of creative art, exhibited, for example, in Šternberk Palace, the Convent of the Blessed Agnes and St. George's Convent. The New Palace of Culture affords numerous opportunities for cultural entertainment. The best-known orchestral body is the Czech Philharmonic Orchestra. Every year the Prague Spring International Music Festival takes place in May — June in Prague. Expressed simply, every lover of art comes into his own in Prague.

Prague is also an important centre of **physical culture and sports** events of the whole country. Every five years Strahov Stadium is the scene of the Czechoslovak Spartakiade, marked by mass performances of physical culture enthusiasts. Prague is often the scene of top European as well as world sports events.

HISTORY

A legend connects the founding of Prague with Princess Libuše, the first mother of the Přemyslid dynasty. As her consort she chose Přemysl, a ploughman from a village situated north-west of Prague. Endowed with the gift of prophesy, Libuše foretold the future glory of Prague, which would "touch the stars".

The oldest settlement of the region of present-day Prague dates back 25,000 years. It has been proved historically that the Slavs arrived on the present territory of Prague during the 5th century of our era. In the latter half of the 9th century a historically documented castle site stood on the area now covered by Prague Castle and the first Christian church originated at the end of the same century. In the latter half of the 10th century St. Vitus's Rotunda, a prince's palace and a convent with a church consecrated to St. George were built on the Hradčany headland. And in the same period a bishopric was founded in Prague (973).

Prague's other castle, Vyšehrad, came into the foreground in the latter half of the 11th century and for a time it was even the seat of Czech rulers.

Prague

In the latter half of the 12th century the intersecting point of trade routes, situated somewhere on the area now occupied by Old Town Square, became the centre of Prague's economic life where the walled-in merchants' court called Týn spread out. Approximately 75 of the stone houses which stood on the territory now occupied by the Old Town at that time have been uncovered. The whole ground-floors of the original buildings have been preserved in the cellarages lying 4—7 m below the present ground level. In the same period a Premonstratensian monastery was built at Strahov and a Johannite monastery in the Little Quarter. Other smaller churches also originated and the River Vltava was spanned by the first stone bridge, called Judith's Bridge (1172).

Approximately in the mid-13th century German colonists also began to arrive in Prague. By then Prague was a really big and significant town of Central Europe as we know it today. The colonists were summoned by King Přemysl Otakar II (1253—1278), who in 1257 founded in the sparsely populated outer bailey the Lesser Town (Menší Město) of Prague, later to be called Malá Strana — the Little Quarter, for them. The upsurge of the town reached its peak in the mid 14th century, when Prague became the imperial residence of Charles IV (1346—1378). The bishopric was raised to an archbishopric (1344), Charles University (1348) and the New Town (Nové Město 1348), one of whose axes was the Horse Market (now Wenceslas Square — Václavské náměstí) and the other the Cattle Market (now Charles Square — Karlovo náměstí), were founded. Charles also gave the impulse for the construction of other secular and church buildings such as St. Vitus's Cathedral and Charles Bridge (erected on the site of Judith's Bridge). Thus Prague was made up of three towns with a total population of approximately 40,000.

After the death of Charles IV the town lost its social and particularly its economic importance. The results of the many years of reform endeavours prepared the soil for the Hussite revolutionary movement. The sermons of John Huss (1371—1415, burnt at the stake as a heretic at Constance) in Bethlehem Chapel aroused especially great response. After Huss's death, the popular movement against the church practises and the rich continued. In 1419 the defenestration of the counsellors from the windows of the New Town Hall took place. In 1420 Jan Žižka defeated the first anti-Hussite crusade on Vítkov Hill. After the execution of the radical Hussite leader Jan Želivský in 1422 the citizens and their moderate Hussite programme permanently prevailed in Prague. The town was one of the leading centres of the Hussite revolutionary movement and held one of the most important places in the political life of the country. In 1458 George of Poděbrady was elected in Prague as the Czech king.

At the turn of the 15th and 16th centuries a great deal of construction work was carried out in Prague in the so-called Czech Gothic style. For example, King Vladislav II of the Jagiello dynasty (1471—1516) had the Vladislav Hall built in the framework of the reconstruction of the Royal Palace at the Castle, the fortifications strengthened and other works carried out. However, from the political aspect Prague's position became still weaker and Vladislav II and Louis I often sojourned in Buda in Hungary. The resistance movement against Ferdinand I of the Hapsburg dynasty (1526—1564) in 1547 was severely punished. Prague was rid of its town freedoms and property. At the end of the 16th century, however, Prague's importance as the Hapsburg residence grew once again. During the reign of Rudolph II (1576—1611) it was the seat of the Hapsburg monarchy and many artists and scientists of that time were concentrated at the imperial court. In 1618 the Czech Estates rose up against the Haps-

burgs and Fridrich of the Palatinate was elected king, these events also being the beginning of the Thirty Years' War throughout Europe. After the elapse of two years the Czech Estates were defeated at the Battle of the White Mountain, this having an influence on the whole of the future history of the country. The defeat of the Czech Estates was the symbol for the end of Czech independence and the beginning of the bondage of the Czech nation for three centuries.

All this was also reflected in the development of Prague. The town suffered confiscations and fines and was recatholized. A considerable number of the inhabitants deserted Prague and the town also lost its economic significance. From 1631—1632 it was occupied by the Saxons and in 1648 it was besieged by the Swedes. However, the Baroque building-up of the town at that time proved to be of permanent artistic and historical importance, that period lending the historical core of the town the greater part of its present appearance (the architects K. Dienzenhofer, K. I. Dienzenhofer and J. B. Mathey, the sculptors M. B. Braun and F. M. Brokof and others). It was not until the end of the 17th century that a certain cultural enlivenment of life in Prague came about.

An important milestone in Prague's development was the year 1784, when the four

---

Prague

Horologe
on the Old Town Hall

towns of Prague were combined to form one single administrative whole. At that time Prague had about 80,000 inhabitants and a number of manufactories. Moreover, it gradually became the centre of the Czech national revival. This development continued until the mid-19th century, when the revolution of 1848 made way, in spite of its political defeat, for the development of capitalism and thus the formation of the bourgeoisie and the proletariate. Prague then gradually became one of the most industrialized towns of the Austrian-Hungarian monarchy. This led to the development of the workers' movement. In 1878 the Czechoslovak Social Democratic Party was founded. In 1912 the People's House in Prague was the scene of a conference of Russian social democrats, attended by V. I. Lenin.

In 1918 Prague became the capital of the newly formed state — the Czechoslovak Republic. The working-class of Prague took part in the mass social struggles waged to determine the character of the republic. Apart from other things, these resulted in the institution of the Communist Party (1921). In 1922 Greater Prague was formed by means of the attachment of the 38 independent suburban communities. In the twenties and thirties the population of Prague increased in number and extensive construction work was carried out, especially on the outskirts of the city. In 1938 big manifestations took place for the purpose of securing the defence of the republic and in 1939 Prague was occupied by German troops.

During the occupation it was an important focus of the resistance movement. In 1942 its inhabitants were strongly persecuted after the assassination of the deputy protector, Reinhard Heydrich. Organized resistance culminated in May 1945 with the Prague Uprising, when barricades were built in the streets. On 9 May, 1945 Prague was liberated by the Red Army (now a state holiday of the Czechoslovak Socialist Republic). Prague was the main scene of the political struggle of the years 1945 to 1948 and a witness to the gathering of the working people of Prague in Old Town Square on 21 February, 1948. In the late fifties the extensive construction of new housing estates on the outskirts of the city was started and in 1967 the construction of the underground was commenced. In the seventies and eighties the present agglomeration of Prague originated on the basis of the inclusion of other suburban communities in the city boundaries. New housing estates with hundreds of thousands of inhabitants have sprung up to the north and south and, most recently, to the south-west of the city.

GUIDE THROUGH PRAGUE

A big, historically significant and **artistically rich** city like Prague can hardly become wholly acquainted with during the few days which the foreign visitor usually devotes to it. Pragues has, moreover, its own **typical environments** (including hospitable ale-houses) and **intimate corners** (for example, on the embankments of the Vltava, in the gardens nestling below the Castle, in the narrow little streets of the Old Town). This guide will help tourists to get to know the most essential features of Prague, summarized in the introductory characterization of the city.

As the axis of an **individual sightseeing tour** of Prague we recommend you to choose the so-called **Royal Route.** It begins at the Powder Gate and in the distant past the coronation processions of Czech kings passed along it to the Old Town and the Little Quarter on their way to Prague Castle. Lying on this route are Celetná Street (Walk No. 1), Old Town Square (2), Karlova Street (3), Charles Bridge (6), Mostecká Street (7), Nerudova Street (8) and, finally, Prague Castle (11). A part of the Royal Route now forms a section of Prague's pedestrian zone. If desired, it is possible to turn off in order to see other significant monuments and interesting sights in Prague. These include in the first place Josefov — the Jewish Town with the nearby Convent of the Blessed Agnes (4), a walk through the narrow little streets of the Old Town in the vicinity of the Carolinum and Bethlehem Chapel, finally ending at Křižovnické náměstí (Knights of the Cross Square; 5) and a stroll through the Little Quarter outer bailey, ending up on Petřín Hill (8). Worthy of attention are Vyšehrad (12) and a number of monuments in the New Town (13—14) as well as others situated outside the boundaries of the historical town reserve. These are dealt with in Part 15, at the end of the guide through Prague.

In order to gain a picture of Prague in a nutshell during a stay of one or two days advantage can be taken of the **organized sightseeing tours** laid on by the Čedok Travel Bureau (Bílkova 6, Prague 1, Tel. 2316619). These are of about three hours' duration and their place of departure is the bus park adjoining the Intercontinental Hotel. Other sightseeing tours are run by the Rekrea and Bohemiatour Travel Agencies. Their purpose is to acquaint participants with the biggest gems of the city. On certain days evening or night sightseeing trips, connected with an evening programme and dinner, are organized. Furthermore, a special programme can also be ordered and for this purpose a coach or a passenger car for one to three persons is used. Such a programme can take up a whole day, or be centred on Prague's Romanesque, Gothic, Renaissance or Baroque monuments, or devoted to the city's musical past, etc.

A sightseeing tour of Prague is facilitated by the **municipal mass transport system** comprising trams, buses and the underground. The price of a ticket for travel on all media is 1 Czechoslovak crown (Kčs) regardless of the distance to be covered. However, a new ticket must be purchased when changing from one medium to another. Tickets can be bought at newspaper stands, tobacconists' and hotel reception desks, from automatic machines on the stations of the underground, etc. The main lines operate throughout the night (at intervals of 40 minutes). Otherwise the underground is in operation from 5.00 hours to 24.00 hours. Travel tickets must be invalidated immediately on entering a transport medium and on the underground they must be punched with the time on an automatic machine. On the underground a travel ticket is valid for 90 minutes. Any number of changes of train can be made in that period, but it is not permitted to leave and return to a station. Single- or multiday tickets for use on all mass transport media are available.

Information and purchases in the pedestrian zone. In recent years Prague has been enriched by the establishment of the first part of the pedestrian zone, concentrated on the so-called **Golden Cross**, Václavské náměstí (Wenceslas Square) and 28. října Street and the street called Na příkopě linking up with it at right angles. However, the pedestrian zone also includes Old Town Square and some of the adjoining streets (Celetná Street, Melantrichova Street, Železná Street). Four stations of Prague's underground are situated in this locality: the Muzeum Station (lines A and C) at the upper end of Václavské náměstí, Můstek (lines A and B) at the lower end of Václavské náměstí, the Národní Station (line B) and the Náměstí Republiky Station (line B) lying 100 metres from the street called Na příkopě. — Three banks with **currency exchange offices** are situated in this street: the State Bank of Czechoslovakia opposite the Powder Gate (No. 28), the Živnobanka (No. 20) and the Czechoslovak Trade Bank (No. 14). Situated in the building No. 20 in the street Na příkopě is also the **Prague Information Service** (PIS), which affords information about Prague orally, in writing and by telephone (Tel. 544 444) and also provides the services of individual guides (Tel. 223 411).

Accommodation is secured for foreign tourists in Prague by Čedok, Panská 5, Prague 1, or Pragotur, U Obecního domu 2, Prague 1. Other services are concentrated in the Čedok building at Na příkopě 18.

In the square náměstí Republiky (a continuation of the street Na příkopě) visitors will find Prague's modern and biggest department store, **Kotva** (Anchor). making it possible, for example, to make various purchases under one roof. The square Václavské náměstí, 28. října Street and the streets Národní třída and Na příkopě abound in shops which satisfy the individual interests of visitors to Prague. Suitable souvenirs, folk art products, glass and so on — to mention a few of the available goods at random — can be purchased at them .

St. Vitus's
Cathedral

1. Celetná Street — from the Powder Gate to Old Town Square

The **Powder Gate (Prašná brána)**, a notable monument of the Czech Late Gothic, stands on the outskirts of Prague's new pedestrian zone to which visitors are chiefly drawn, as said previously, by the most varied practical interests. One of the thirteen gates of the fortification system of the **Old Town of Prague** originally stood here, i.e. already in the late 13th century. The locality was the starting point of the coronation processions of Czech kings, which ended in front of St. Vitus's Cathedral at Prague Castle. The Powder Gate has been called such since the late 17th century, when it was used for the storing of gunpowder. Its present appearance dates from the last quarter of the 19th century, when its architecture was completed in the pseudo-Gothic style. It is 65 m high and a splendid view of Prague can be obtained from its gallery. Standing next to the Powder Gate is Prague's noted cultural and social centre called **The Municipal (Representative) House** of Prague. It was built in the years 1905—1911 and is one of the most beautiful Art Nouveau buildings in Prague. It has a big concert hall, named after the Czech composer Smetana, and five other halls (used mainly for balls and exhibitions), a coffee-house, a restaurant and a wine tavern. The interior decoration of the building represents the best Czech creative art of its time. A memorial tablet on the Municipal House recalls the fact that its site was once occupied by the so-called **Court of Kings** which served between 1383 and 1483 as the seat of Czech kings, among them also the provincial administrator and, later, Czech king George of Poděbrady (1458—1471).

Situated opposite the two previously mentioned outstanding buildings is the **House of Exhibition Services**, known rather by the name of The House At the Hybernians. It was once a custom-house, built in the period of High Classicism from 1808—1811. The interiors of the building were adapted to meet its present purposes from 1940—1942. **Celetná Street**, which connects the square náměstí Republiky with Old Town Square, is now intended for use solely by pedestrians. It is one of the oldest streets in Prague. A number of historical buildings, mostly of Gothic origin, can be seen in it. The foundations of many of them are of even earlier origin. — At the very beginning of the street attention is attracted by the tripartite Baroque portal with statues by I. F. Platzer of the building of a former mint (coins were minted here in the years 1539—1784), now a court building (No. 36). Also situated at the beginning of the street is an outstanding example of cubistic architecture by J. Gočár in the form of the house called **(At the Black Mother of God** — No. 34). It was erected in the years 1911—1912. And on the right, in the short adjoining street called U obecního domu, stands the Art Nouveau **Paříž Hotel**, which has recently been renovated. — Of the historical buildings in Celetná Street let us mention: house No. 25 with a memorial tablet recalling the fact that the philosopher and mathematician Bernard Bolzano (1781—1848) lived and died in it; the house of the Schönpflok family (No. 23) with a statue of the Madonna from M. B. Braun's workshop (c. 1730) on its façade; house No. 22 of Gothic origin, now housing an ale-house called At the Vulture (U supa); house No. 20, formerly Buquoy Palace, purchased in the mid-18th century for Charles University, which has recently had it adapted; Menhart's House (No. 17), originally

Gothic, outstanding for its portal bearing the date 1700, an attractive passageway and a courtyard; the wine tavern called At the Spider (U pavouka) is now housed in it; Millesimo Palace (No. 13), now called the House of Political Education, built in Baroque style in 1750 with the use of the masonry of a Gothic house of the 14th century. The most valuable building in Celetná Street as regards architecture is **Hrzán Palace** (No. 12, now used for residential purposes) with the remainders of a Romanesque house. Its present appearance dates from the early 18th century. — A great attraction for foreign tourists will certainly be house No. 11 with the wine tavern called At the Golden Stag (U zlatého jelena), built in the original banquet hall of one of medieval Prague's stone houses.

2. Old Town Square — Staroměstské náměstí

Apart from Prague Castle, the historically most important place in Prague. From the 11th century several trade routes intersected at this point and there was also a market-place here. The site of the square was the scene of many tragic events, for example, the execution of 27 leading participants in the uprising of the Czech Estates against the Hapsburgs (1621). However, it also witnessed the election of George of Poděbrady as Czech king (1458), the big demonstrations of 1918 calling for a new, free state and, in May 1945, the new struggle for national freedom. And, finally, in February 1948 the most significant assembly of the people took place in the square.

Nowadays perhaps all visitors to Prague make their way to Old Town Square at all times of the day and on the stroke of every hour admire the run of the **horo-**

Old Town
Square

loge situated on the Old Town Hall. It is controlled by a very complicated mechanism from the Middle Ages. It seems that it gained its oldest form as long ago as 1410, when it was made by the clockmaker Mikuláš of Kadaň. The horologe was reconstructed at the end of the 15th and again in the mid-16th century. The clock also underwent later repairs (for example, its statuettes were destroyed by fire in 1864 and after 1945 they were renewed. A part of the horologe was damaged by gunfire from Nazi tanks in May 1945, but its mechanisms and outer appearance have still their original medieval form. The lowest part of the horologe, the calendarium, is also the youngest part. The course of village life (12 outer medallions) and the signs of the Zodiac (12 inner medallions) are depicted on it. Situated on the sides of the calendarium are statuettes of burghers and an angel.

The middle part of the horologe is occupied by a complicated sphere (a term of medieval astronomy indicating that the Earth is the centre of the universe). It measures time and shows the movement of the Moon and the Sun between the signs of the Zodiac.

In the two small windows in the uppermost part of the horologe a procession of the Apostles can be seen on the stroke of every hour and before them a skeleton, the symbol of death, tolls a passing-bell by means of a rope and raises an hour-glass. After the Apostles a cock shakes its wings and crows in a niche above the small windows. Another part of the horologe is an allegorical statue of a Turk, obviously recalling the Turkish invasion of Europe in the 16th and 17th centuries, and two figures representing human miserliness and vanity.

The horologe is, however, only a small part of the present **Old Town Hall**, which originated gradually from a whole complex of buildings. Originally the Gothic corner house, to which a square tower was added in 1364, was the seat of the Town Council from 1338. The oriel of a chapel was adjoined to its eastern side and the horologe was placed on its southern side. In 1470—1480 this façade was provided with a decorative Gothic portal which now serves as the main entrance to the Town Hall.

In the latter half on the 14th century the Town Hall was enlarged by the addition of another house, decorated in 1520 with a Renaissance window above which we can read the Latin inscription Praga — caput regni (Prague, the capital of the kingdom). After the mid-15th century a third house, reconstructed in Neo-Renaissance style in 1878, became the property of the community. And, finally, the house called At the Cock, of Gothic origin with an Empire façade, became the last part of the Town Hall complex. A Romanesque room has been preserved in the basement of this house, while Renaissance ceilings and wall paintings can be seen in a preserved state on its first floor. In 1610 the complex of Town Hall buildings of the present was enlarged still further by the building-on of the Renaissance house called U minuty (At the Minute), whose façade is decorated with graffito with biblical and classical motifs.

During the Prague Uprising, on 8 May, 1945, one day before the end of the war, the Old Town Hall was severely damaged by gunfire and later by fire during which the whole of the Neo-Gothic eastern and northern wings were destroyed.

Of special interest in the Town Hall itself is the second floor with the original Gothic councillors' room of 1470. The sculpture of Christ dates from the early 15th century. To be seen in the big assembly hall are two historic canvasses by the Czech painter Václav Brožík. One depicts John Huss standing in front of the Constance Council and the other the Election of George of Poděbrady as Czech king. Also situated on this floor is the Late Gothic Jiřík Hall. The gallery of the Old Town Hall affords a fine view of the Old Town.

A Wedding Hall and an exhibition hall are situated in the Old Town Hall.

The Old Town Hall Tower, affording fine views of the city, is open to visitors. Also worthy of particular attention in Old Town Square is its eastern side with the **Gothic Church of Our Lady Before Týn**. It has three naves and was founded in 1365, its twin towers of a height of 80 metres dating from the latter half of the 15th century. The reformatory ideas of John Huss's predecessors were avowed in the church already in the 14th century and the church belonged to his followers until 1621. In 1689 the church was damaged by a great fire and thus it now has a Baroque vault. The tympanum of the northern portal with the theme of The Suffering of Christ dates from about 1390. In the interior of the church: a Gothic pulpit, a Gothic Madonna and Calvary on the altar in a side nave, recesses with pews (so-called sedile) in both side naves and a tin font — all of the early 15th century. The Late Gothic stone baldachine is from the late 15th century and the Baroque paintings by Karel Škréta on the altars date from 1648—1660. On the right, in front of the high altar, can be seen the tombstone of the Danish astronomer Tycho Brahe who towards the end of his life, in the years 1599—1601, worked in Prague and Benátky nad Jizerou in the services of the Emperor Rudolph II.

The recently reconstructed house called At the Bell — U zvonu — No. 13 represents a monumental Gothic tower house. It was built in the second quarter of the 14th century as a town palace, most likely for King John of Luxembourg. It now serves cultural purposes (exhibitions, concerts). A house sign in the form of a stone bell is situated on the corner of the building.

Standing on the right of the house At the Bell is **Týn School** (No. 14), rebuilt in Renaissance style. Its Gothic arcading dates from the 14th century and the gables on its façade feature the style of the Venetian Renaissance. It also serves as an entrance to Týn Church.

Still further to the right stands the house called At the White Unicorn — No. 15. It is an Early Classical building in whose cellar can be seen a Romanesque room from the turn of the 12th and 13th centuries. In the 19th century its height was raised by the addition of a new floor.

Situated to the left of Týn Street, on the same front of Old Town Square, is the remarkable building of the former **palace of the Golz-Kinský family**. It ranks among the most attractive Late Baroque buildings in Prague and gained its present appearance in 1755—1765. Below the palace are the foundations of a Romanesque and Early Gothic house. On 21 February, 1948 Klement Gottwald, later the first working-class president of Czechoslovakia, addressed the historic assembly of the people of Prague from the balcony of the palace. This fact is recalled by a memorial tablet situated on the façade of the building. It is planned to use the palace for museum purposes.

On the northern side of Old Town Square attention is attracted by **St. Nicholas's Church**, built in Baroque style in 1732—1735 after a project by K. I. Dienzenhofer. Its southern façade with the main portal and two steeples is decorated with statues by A. Braun. Although the church now has only a small part of its original interior furnishings, its architecture is exceptionally outstanding. It serves the Czechoslovak

Hussite church, which was founded in 1920.

The **houses on the southern side of the square** also have a rich past. For example, the house called At the Golden Angel (No. 29) is Gothic in origin. It has a preserved oriel (a part of the former chapel) with a Gothic net vault. Its present façade is Late Baroque. The house called At the Ox (No. 27) is now Baroque. House No. 25, called At the Blue Star houses the renowned wine tavern U Bindrů. House No. 20. called At the Golden Unicorn, has a Baroque façade and a passageway with a ribbed net vault. The house called At the Stone Ram (No. 17) has a Renaissance portal and gable. Štorch's House, No. 16, is Neo-Renaissance and dates from 1897. It is decorated with paintings executed after designs by Mikoláš Aleš. Standing in the centre of Old Town Square is the John Huss memorial, sculptured by L. Šaloun in 1915.

An interesting building behind the eastern front of Old Town Square is **Týn**

St. Nicholas's
Church
in the Old Town

(The Ungelt). It was a framed merchants' court which stood here already in the 11th century. It was the gathering place of foreign merchants who came to Prague for trading purposes. Up to the end of the 16th century duty was also paid here. The original form of the framed court with two relatively narrow gates has been preserved to the present. Certain buildings of Týn also have their own historical value. In this respect particular mention should be made of the **Granovský House,** a Renaissance building of the palace type with an open loggia on its first floor. At present adaptations are being carried out in the Týn area in order to make the complex of buildings suitable for cultural purposes and for the needs of tourism.

The environs of Old Town Square: From Celetná Street it is possible, by passing through a passage on the right, to enter **Malá Štupartská Street** in which the noted Baroque building of **St. James's Church** stands. The present appearance of the church dates from the late 17th century (the church itself was, however, founded already in the early 13th century). The interior of the church is very imposing. It has 22 altars and very rich decoration in the form of paintings, for example, the altar paintings by Petr Brandl (c. 1710) and the painting by V. V. Reiner on the high altar (1739). To be seen in the left nave of the church is the most beautiful Baroque tombstone in Prague. It belongs to Count Jan Václav Vratislav of Mitrovice and is the work of J. B. Fischer of Erlach and F. M. Brokof. Concerts of church music now take place in the church in view of the exceptionally good acoustics of the building.

Running from the northern front of Old Town Square towards the embankment of the River Vltava is **Pařížská Street**. It is of great architectural interest due to the mainly Art Nouveau buildings from the turn of the century which line it on both sides. It leads to the monuments of the former Jewish town. The offices of air companies and travel bureaux, to mention only a few enterprises, are situated in the street.

In the neighbouring street called **U radnice** stands the pseudo-Renaissance building (No. 5) in which the writer Franz Kafka was born in 1885.

Small Square (Malé náměstí), one of the oldest parts of the Old Town and a community of French merchants in the 12th century, lies in westerly direction from the Old Town Hall. Here particular attention is attracted by the ironmonger's shop called U Rotta (**At the Rott's**) housed in the building called At the Three White Roses (No. 3), originally a Romanesque house rebuilt in Neo-Renaissance style in 1890. However, there are several historical buildings in the little square whose cores are of Romanesque origin. They have Gothic portals or Renaissance graffito. According to their house signs they are called At the White Lion (No. 2), At the Black Pony (No. 14) and At the White Lily — (No. 12). Standing in the centre of the square is a fountain with a Renaissance metal grill — of 1560. The figure of the lion on it is 100 years younger in origin.

Melantrichova Street runs off the southern side of Old Town Square and has retained its original medieval ground-plan. It contains a number of small shops and catering facilities. For example, in the ancient cellerage of house No. 20, called U zlaté konvice (At the Golden Jug), the visitor will find a stylish Old Prague wine tavern whose original stone masonry dates from the 13th—14th century. The building bearing No. 17 with St. Michael's Church of Gothic origin, later Barocized, affords access to **Michalská Street** where attention is deserved by building No. 19

with the right of way through its yard. Of Gothic origin, it was reconstructed in Renaissance style and its name is Železné dveře (The Iron Door). The portal in Michalská Street is Gothic and the portal and façade facing Jilská Street are Renaissance. A Baroque reconstruction (including the iron gate bearing a painting of Samson) was carried out in the period preceding the mid-18th century. In the seventies of the 19th century the building housed the editorial offices of the first Czech magazine for the working class. A stylish wine tavern is now situated in the building. — In nearby **Kožná Street** the visitor will find house No. 1 called At the Two Golden Bears, now a remarkable Renaissance building with arcades in its courtyard. In 1885 the journalist Egon Ervin Kisch, known as the "wild reporter", was born in the house.

3. Karlova Street

This street runs from Malé náměstí to Charles Bridge and will gradually become a part of the pedestrian zone. Walk No. 3 intersects Walk No. 5 near the building of the Central Bohemian Gallery. The most valuable houses are concentrated opposite the area of the Clementinum, namely the house called At the Golden Well (No. 3). It has a Renaissance oriel and a roofed gallery. The stucco reliefs of saints on the façade most likely originated in 1701 after the plague epidemic. The building has been restored in recent years and a wine tavern is now situated in it. The house called At the Blue Pike (No. 20) was the domain of Prague's first cinema in 1907. On the corner with Liliová Street stands house No. 18. called At the Golden Snake. Of Gothic origin, it was reconstructed in the Renaissance and in 1714

an Armenian street coffee vendor lived in it. The restaurant U zlatého hada is now situated in it. From here we shall pass a shop selling folk art products. In house No. 10 there is a stylish ale-house called U Malvaze. Pötting Palace (No. 8), originally Gothic, was rebuilt in the Renaissance and now has a Baroque façade. Apart from other things, the Disk theatre studio of the State Conservatory is housed in it. The last interesting buildings to be seen here include the former Colloredo-Mansfeld Palace (No. 2, now used partly for residential purposes and partly to house archives. It is a Baroque building (remainders of Romanesque and Gothic masonry), erected after 1735. Standing in its courtyard is a fountain with a statue of Neptune from the same time and in the court tract there is an oval hall. Karlova Street ends here in Křižovnické náměstí (Knights of the Cross Square; see Walk No. 5).

4. Josefov — The Jewish Town and the Convent of the Blessed Agnes

The monuments in this locality can be seen when walking through the little streets surrounding Pařížská Street. Already in the late 12th century the Jewish communities, linking up with Old Town Square, formed an isolated enclave where the Jews established their own autonomy, schools and synagogue. Due to conflicts with the home population pogroms took place even in the Old Town on several occasions. In 1541 and 1744, for example, the Jews were banished from the whole of Bohemia, but they soon returned to Prague. The exclusion of the Jews from political and economic life and their social isolation from the rest of the population conditioned the development of a characteristic culture on the territory of Josefov. Life in the Jewish Town was centred round the synagogues. The core of the principal synagogue, the Old-New Synagogue (**Staronová synagoga**) in Červená Street, originated as long ago as the mid-13th century. In the last quarter of the 13th century it was enlarged by the addition of the main hall. It has been preserved in this form and is now the oldest documented synagogue in Central Europe. It is built in Early Gothic style. Its oldest part is its Early Gothic entrance, a hall with a vault supported by two centrally situated pillars. The synagogue has brick gables of the latter half of the 15th century whose surface is articulated with panelling. In the centre of the hall there is a Gothic grill from the late 15th century. Situated on the eastern side is a tabernacle with the original Early Gothic tympanum. Several bronze chandeliers from the 16th – 19th century hang from the ceiling.

Standing in short **Červená Street** is also the **High Synagogue (Vysoká)**. It was built in the latter half of the 16th century and originally formed a part of the Jewish Town Hall. At the end of the 17th century it was enlarged. Its present façade dates in the 19th century. Nowadays this synagogue serves as an exhibition hall containing the exposition of textiles of the State Jewish Museum. By making our way through the little street called **U starého hřbitova** we come to the **Klaus Synagogue**. It was built in the late 17th century in Baroque style and modified in a modern way in 1884. Its name is derived from the word "klause", the designation for the small buildings such as tabernacles or Talmud schools which once occupied its site. The expositions of Hebrew manuscripts and old prints of the State Jewish Museum are installed in the synagogue. The street U starého hřbitova also af-

fords access to the second most important monument of the Jewish Town, i.e. the **Old Jewish Cemetery**, which ranks among the rarest Jewish cemeteries in general. In the Middle Ages the cemetries of the Jews were situated in the Little Quarter and on the territory of the later New Town. However, about the mid-15th century the Jews purchased new plots of land on the boundaries of their town and founded a cemetery there. It was used for burials up till 1787 and some 12,000 gravestones have been preserved in it to the present. They have the form of flat panels with sculptural and architectonic decoration, or of whole stone tombs. The area of the cemetery was firmly fixed and so new earth and new gravestones and panels were placed on already existing graves. The old ones were raised to the level of the new layers of earth, thus giving rise to groupings of graves which at first sight appear quite incomprehensible and which are so typical of the Old Jewish Cemetery.

The Hebrew inscriptions and relief symbols on the gravestones express the origin of the deceased, his name or his profession. The oldest gravestone in the present cemetery is that of Abigdor Kar. It is from 1439 and lies to the north of the Pinkas Synagogue. Also buried here are Mordechaj Maisel (1601), Jehuda ben Bezalel, called Rabbi Löw (the alleged creator of the legendary Golem, 1609), the historian and mathematician David Gans (1613) the astronomer, philosopher and physican Joseph del Medig (1655) and others.

The pseudo-Romanesque hall of 1906 which forms a part of the cemetery contains a permanent exhibition devoted to the period of the Second World War (the Terezín concentration camp in Czechoslovakia).

It is also possible to gain access to the **Pinkas Synagogue** from the Old Jewish Cemetery. It was founded in 1479 by

Rabbi Pinkas and enlarged in 1535. The Late Gothic ribbed net vault of the hall dates from that time. The southern wing and the women's empora were added in the early 17th century. A memorial hall to the Czech and Moravian Jews tortured by the fascists has been established in the synagogue.

In **Maislova Street,** running parallel to Pařížská Street, there stands the **Maisel Synagogue** (No. 10), founded in the late 16th century by the previously mentioned mayor of the Jewish Town. The Renaissance building was destroyed during a fire which occurred in the Jewish Town. Its later Baroque appearance was later concealed by a Neo-Gothic reconstruction carried out in 1892—1905. An exposition of synagogal silver from the collections of the State Jewish Museum is now installed in the building.

Maisel also had the **Jewish Town Hall** (No. 18) built in the same period. Its present appearance dates in the mid-18th century, when it was supplement-

---

ed with a small wooden turret with a clock, the figures of which are Hebrew.

Finally, in **Dušní Street,** there stands the **Spanish Synagogue** (No. 12). It occupies the site where Prague's oldest synagogue, called the Old School, once stood. The present Spanish Synagogue was built in the mid-19th century in pseudo-Moorish style and a little later it was decorated with stucco ornaments in the style of the interiors of the Spanish Alhambra.

By walking through Dušní Street, in the direction of the River Vltava, and turning off into the street called U milosrdných on the right we shall come to one of the most valuable and the oldest Early Gothic monuments of Czech Christianity — the **Convent of the Blessed Agnes** (Anežská Street No. 12), which lies outside the boundaries of the Jewish Town, however. Its construction was started before the mid-13th century on the incentive of Anežka Přemyslovna, sister of King Václav I. She introduced the Franciscan side Order of the Poor Clares and after the founding of the convent she became its Abbess.

A monastery of the Minorite Order with St. Francis's Church was founded in the neighbourhood of the nuns' convent with a church and St. Mary Magdelene's Chapel. The monastery was abolished in the late 18th century and fell into a state of ruin. After thorough archeological research in the seventies of the present century reconstruction of the whole area was started under specialized supervision.

In its first phase the former convent of the Poor Clares was chiefly reconstructed, after which the two churches and the Chapels of Mary Magdalene and St. Barbara were reconstructed.

In 1985—1986 St. Francis's Chapel, in whose presbytery the tomb of the Czech king Václav I, who founded the church, was revealed, was provided with a new roof. In the interior of the building there is a hall in which lectures, concerts and various literary programmes take place. Concerts are also held in the cloister of the convent of the Poor Clares.

The chapter and ceremonial hall on the ground-floor contains an exposition of applied art of the 19th century (glass, china, stoneware, textile, furniture). — In the former kitchen and in the refectory there is an exhibition which acquaints visitors with the history and restoration of the Convent of the Blessed Agnes. — On the first floor, especially in the former convent hall, there is the main exposition of Czech painting of the 19th century — landscapes, portraits, still lifes, a number of paintings with social themes and others.

In this part of the Old Town nearby **Haštalské Square** with its Gothic church (side naves and sacristy with Gothic wall paintings form its oldest part), rebuilt in Baroque style after the fire in 1689, is worth visiting.

---

5. **Through the Old Town streets round the Carolinum and Bethlehem Chapel to Křižovnické náměstí**

From Old Town Square it is possible to reach Charles Bridge by following another route, equally remarkable from the historical aspect. The most important sights to be seen on the way are the Carolinum, Bethlehem Chapel and the square Křižovnické náměstí. The route in question runs through **Železná Street,** another lively Old Town street where trade with iron was carried out in the Middle Ages. The attention of the visitor is immediately attracted by two very significant Prague monuments.

The first of them is the **Carolinum**, a building of Charles University, while the second is the Tyl Theatre neighbouring with it. **Charles University** was founded on 4 April, 1348 as the first institution of its kind in Central Europe. The core of the Carolinum is formed by the so-called Rothlev's House of the first half of the 14th century. It was gained by King Václav IV, who presented it to Charles College, founded for 12 masters of free art by Charles IV in 1366. The college used the building as its seat from 1386. Later practically the whole life of the university was concentrated here. Master John Huss also held the function of rector here and after his death the university became one of the centres of the Hussite revolutionary movement. After the defeat at the Battle of the White Mountain the Carolinum was handed over to the Jesuits in 1622. Law and medical faculties were situated in the building. In 1718 the Carolinum was rebuilt in Baroque style — with a Baroque portal leading to Železná Street. The main entrance to the building was formerly situated here. Now, however, the main entrance is in Fruit Market (Ovocný trh), where there is a new entrance building designed by the architect J. Fragner and completed in 1969. In front of the building there is a cour d'honneur with a fountain with lions. A Baroque window with the inscription Lex civium dux (Law is the leader of the citizens, let Law be decisive for the citizens) had already previously been built in the front facing Železná Street. — The building was not maintained in the 18th—19th century. The restoration of the Carolinum was carried out from 1934—1950. Today the building has a Baroque character, partly marked by Gothic elements. The core of the building is formed by the great hall of the late 14th century, newly enlarged and modified, in which graduation ceremonies and assemblies take place. The present **Tyl Theatre** (No. 11) stands opposite the longitudinal side of the Carolinum. It is a Classical building from 1781—1783. It was originally called the Nostic Theatre and performances were staged in German and Italian at it. In 1787 the theatre was the scene of the world premiére of Mozart's opera Don Giovanni. From 1797 the theatre was the property of the Czech Estates and from that time it was called the Estates Theatre. From 1785—1862 afternoon performances in the Czech language were also staged at the theatre on Sundays and holidays. In 1834 the song Kde domov můj (Where Is My Home, now a part of the Czechoslovak anthem) from J. K. Tyl's play Fidlovačka was heard here for the first time. After the opening of the so-called Provisional Theatre in 1862 performances were given at the theatre in the German language only. In 1920 it fell into Czech hands and since 1945 it has borne its present name. The theatre is currently undergoing reconstruction.

Our route continues through **Rytířská Street** round the **House of Soviet Science and Culture** (No. 31) and the **Klement Gottwald Museum** (No. 29), named after the president of the Czechoslovak Republic from 1948—1953. Other notable buildings: the Old Town Magistrate's house (No. 12) the seat of the royal magistrate in the Middle Ages, later reconstructed in the Renaissance and the Baroque. Discovered in the rear wing of the building was the walled-up Gall Gate, the only one of the Old Town's 13 large and small gates to have been preserved. — The Old Town market (No. 10) with a spacious hall from 1893—1894 has recently been restored.

Running in parallel (on the right) with Rytířská Street is **Havelská Street** with arcades lining one of its sides. Vegetable, fruit and flower markets used to take place here. Standing in the street is Baroque **St. Galls' Church**, founded as long ago as the 13th century, with a number of preserved architectural elements. The reformer Konrád Waldhauser preached here from 1363—1369 with great success, followed later by John Huss. The well-known Czech Baroque painter K. Škréta (1604—1676) is buried in the chapel on the right side of the church. Worthy of mention among the burghers' houses standing here are those with an Early Baroque and Renaissance façade and Gothic arcading — At the Golden Scales (No. 3), with a painting of the Archangel Michael on its façade, and At Bruncvík's (No. 5), one of the best-preserved Renaissance houses in Prague.

Rytířská Street and Havelská Street served as a market-place in the Middle Ages. They were divided by a stone building containing small stalls serving as the shops of craftsmen and merchants. After the demolition of the stalls before 1800 the passage of this exceptionally long building was changed into the little street called **V kotcích** where cheap and poor-quality textile goods were sold.

Rytířská Street and Havelská Street run into the ancient environment called **Coal Market** (Uhelný trh) with historical buildings only on its southern side now. The most remarkable of them is the house called At the Three Golden Lions (No. 1). Of Gothic origin, it was later Barocized. Its façade bears a memorial tablet recalling the fact that W. A. Mozart stayed in the house in 1787. — On the left of this building is the house called **Platýz**, which originated as the result of the Empire reconstruction of the Renaissance palace of the Platýz family of Plattenštejn in the early 19th century. It was the first apartment house of its time in Prague and is alleged to have brought the biggest profit. For this reason it was called The Golden Mother-hen. Its rear tract faces Uhelný trh and bears a bust of F. Liszt, who gave concerts in the building. — In the next house, called Malý Platýz (Little Platýz), there is a popular old, ale-house called At the Two Cats (U dvou koček). Short **Martinská Street** runs round the **Church of St. Martin in the Wall**. On the outer side of the presbytery there is a memorial tablet bringing to mind the fact that members of the Brokof family of sculptors, among them the renowned F. M. Brokof (1688—1731), were buried in the adjoining cemetery. From here a few dozen steps to the right brings us to the street **Na Perštýně** and from here it is possible to proceed to the square **Betlémské náměstí** with **Bethlehem Chapel**, a noted medieval monument. The original building dated in the late 14th century. The chapel was founded in 1391 by the royal courtier Hanuš of Mühlheim and a counsellor by the name of Kříž in order that sermons might be given in the Czech language in it. The chapel was able to hold three thousand people. From 1402—1413 John Huss preached here and in 1521 sermons were given in the chapel by the German reformer Thomas Müntzer. After the Battle of the White Mountain the Jesuits purchased the chapel and still later it was abolished with the exception of three of its peripheral walls and a residential building was built-in into it. From 1950—1954 it was reconstructed by the architect Jaroslav Fragner. The interior walls bear remnants of Master John Huss's tracts. Also to be seen here are new paintings executed after the Jena Codex.

The **Náprstek Museum**, installed in a building once called U Halánků (At the Haláneks — No. 1), is interesting for quite different reasons. It is situated in the square to the left of Bethlehem

Chapel. The complex of buildings originated at the turn of the 16th and 17th centuries through the joining-up of three old houses and two hundred years later it underwent reconstruction. In the 19th century it became the property of the well-known patrons of the arts and public functionaries V. Náprstek and his wife, who founded a specialized library in it as a result of which the house was one of Prague's centres of literary and scientific life. Nowadays a museum of native African, Asian and American cultures is installed in it.

Situated in **Karolína Světlá Street** is one of the oldest preserved Romanesque buildings in Prague — the **Rotunda of the Holy Rood** — of the early 12th century. It was restored over one hundred years ago. The cast iron grill surrounding the rotunda is Neo-Romanesque (of 1865). In the seventies of the present century the building was subjected to general repairs.

From Bethlehem Chapel we can make our way to the street Na Perštýně and by turning to the left enter **Husova Street**. Situated on the right is **St. Giles's Church,** converted from what was originally a small Romanesque church in 1339—1371. The well-known reform preacher J. Milíč of Kroměříž preached here from 1364—1374. Later the church was Barocized. It has rich inner furnishings and a valuable Baroque confessional. The frescoes on the vaults and the painting of St. Wenceslas on the altar are the work of V. V. Reiner.

Running into Husova Street from the left is short **Řetězová Street** with **the house of the lords of Kunštát** (No. 3), one of the most valuable Romanesque monuments in Prague. From 1453—1458 the house was the main seat of the provincial administrator George of Poděbrady, up to the time of his election as Czech king. The whole ground-floor of a Romanesque residential palace building of the 12th century has been preserved on the level of the present cellerage.

Let us now return to Husova Street. In No. 19, a Renaissance house of the latter half of the 16th century, is the **Central Bohemian Gallery** and interesting Romanesque interiors can be seen below the building.

Not far from the cross-road with Karlova Street stands **Clam-Gallas Palace** (No. 20), in which the archives of Prague are housed. Jan Václav Gallas had the building erected from 1715—1730 after plans designed by the Viennese court architect J. B. Fischer of Erlach. Its two portals bear statues of giants hewn, in addition to other sculptural decorations (e.g. the triton on the fountain in the first courtyard) by M. B. Braun. The monumentality of these entrance portals is characteristic of the whole composition and the individual details of the building. According to the original project, a space was to be freed in front of the palace for a square which would allow the monumentality of the building to stand out well. This aim was never realized, however.

Mayor Vacek Square (**Náměstí primátora dr. V. Vacka**) has two new buildings. The first is the **Municipal Library** (No. 1) of the twenties of the present century. It has lecture and concert halls. — Standing on the right front is the **New Town Hall** (No. 2) in which the National Committee of Prague and the Mayor of Prague have their seat. Opposite it is the entrance to the rear tract of the **Clementinum**. This building, the second biggest in Prague after Prague Castle, was built from 1653—1726 on a site formerly occupied by more than 30 houses, 3 churches and other buildings, nearly all owned by the Jesuits, who arrived in Prague in 1556. The theological and philosophical faculties of

Charles-Ferdinand University also had their seat here. Rising above the third courtyard is an astronomical tower in which the astronomer Josef Stepling established an observatory which has regularly recorded meteorological data for over two hundred years. Nowadays the State Library of the Czech Socialist Republic, of which, for example, the Univeristy Library, the State Technical Library, the Slavonic Library and others are important parts, is installed in it. Apart from three million volumes, the library also contains thousands of medieval manuscripts and incunables. Among the rarest of them is the Vyšehrad Codex of 1085. The complex of buildings contains a number of interesting rooms (in particular the library hall on the first floor, the Rococo Mozart Hall and others). A statue of a Prague student stands in the first courtyard, bringing to mind the assistance rendered by students during the defence of Prague against the Swedes in 1648. After leaving the Clementinum (and also Karlova Street) we find ourselves in **Křižovnické náměstí** (Knights of the Cross Square). Actually it is a very small and unfortunately, very busy square. Standing opposite us is the **Old Town Bridge Tower,** built on the first pier of Charles Bridge. The construction of the tower was completed in the early 15th century after a plan by Peter Parler. In those days the tower formed a part of the town's fortification system. It is one of the most beautiful gateways in Europe. The whole sculptural decoration of the tower and the portrait sculptures on its eastern façade are also the work of Peter Parler's workshop. Of these let us note in particular the seated figures on the sides. They represent Charles IV (on the left) and Václav IV (on the right). Situated between them is a statue of St. Vitus. A wall of the tower bears a memorial tablet set in place in 1650. It brings

to mind the conquering of Prague by the Swedes in 1648, when, apart from other things, the decoration of the western wall of the tower was destroyed. From 1621 the heads of twelve Czech lords who were executed for their participation in the uprising of the Estates against the Hapsburgs (twenty-seven were executed in all) were displayed on the tower as a warning for a full ten years.

The Church of the Holy Saviour. standing next to the exit from the Clementinum, is a valuable Renaissance and Early Baroque building in whose origin the outstanding architects C. Lurago, F. Caratti and F. M. Kaňka participated. The church belonged to the Jesuits and formed a part of the Clementinum.

Situated on the right of the Old Town Bridge Tower is **St. Francis's Church** and the monastery of the **Knights of the Cross with a Red Star,** a Baroque building with a magnificent dome, built from 1679—1689. In the dome there is a fresco The Last Judgment by V. V. Reiner, dating from 1722, and on the altar in the side chapel there is a Late Gothic Madonna of the late 15th century. In 1847 a Baroque vintners' column with a statue of St. Wenceslas by J. J. Bendl (1676) was placed in front of the church. Standing in the square is a Neo-Gothic memorial to Charles IV, cast in iron in 1848 and placed here to mark the 500th anniversary of the founding of Charles University.

Before crossing Charles Bridge we can turn to the left and follow the tram lines in order to take a short walk along the **Smetana Embankment.** It was built from 1841—1845 and it affords a beautiful view of the **Hradčany panorama.** Of the interesting buildings which line it let us mention in particular the **Bedřich Smetana Museum,** devoted to the Czech national composer (1824—1884), in the short street called the **Novotný Footpath** leading off the embankment. The museum has been situated here since 1936. The building originally housed the city's waterworks of 1885. A memorial to the composer stands in front of the building. House No. 16 features the style of the Netherlandish Renaissance and was built in 1895. It is now the seat of the Union of Czechoslovak-Soviet Friendship. Lažanský Palace, No. 2, built from 1861—1863, is now the seat of the Academy of Fine Arts (from 1863—1869 Bedřich Smetana lived here and, among other works, wrote his classical opera The Bartered Bride here). The Neo-Gothic architecture on the left side of the embankment is a part of the Franz I memorial, called Homage of the Czech Estates. The statue itself is housed in the lapidarium of the National Museum. On reaching the cross-road, on whose opposite side stands the National Theatre, we shall make our way back again.

6. Charles Bridge

This bridge is a unique technical and art monument and one of Prague's most remarkable tourist sights. It connects the Old Town with the Little Quarter. Already in the early 12th century a wooden bridge stood practically in the same place, being replaced after the mid-12th century with a stone bridge called Judith's Bridge. Both bridges were destroyed by floods. The new bridge was founded by Charles IV in 1357, its construction being entrusted to Peter Parler, then twenty-seven years of age. However, the building of the bridge was completed in the following century. After the bridge at Regensburg it is the oldest bridge in Central Europe. It is 520 m long and 10 m wide and it is term-inated with Gothic towers on both banks of the river. Charles Bridge gradually became one of the lively centres of life in Prague. Trade was carried out here, justice was administered here (delinquents were dipped in the Vltava in wicker baskets) and tournaments took place here. The bridge was adorned with a popular group of statues whose number grew to the present thirty in the course of the passing centuries. Their sculptors were outstanding masters such as Matthias Braun and Jan Brokof and his two sons. The following pairs of statues can be seen on the bridge in the direction away from the Old Town Bridge Tower (first of all always on the right and then on the left in the direction of our walk):
1—2 The Madonna and St. Bernard (M. V. Jäckel, 1708) — St. Ives, the patron of lawyers (M. B. Braun, 1711).
3—4 The Madonna, SS. Dominic and Thomas Aquinas (M. V. Jäckel, 1708): SS. Barbara, Margaret and Elizabeth (F. M. Brokof, 1707).
5—6 Calvary, a group of statues (sculp-

Little Quarter bridge towers from Charles Bridge

tured after the model of sculptures for a bridge in Dresden, gilded bronze, cast in 1629). It is alleged that the Hebrew inscription on the cross had to be paid for in the 17th century by a Jew as a fine for mocking the cross. Two stone statues by E. Max of 1861. — Pietá (E. Max, 1859).

7—8 St. Anne (M. V. Jäckel, 1707) — St. Joseph (J. Max, 1854).

9—10 SS. Cyril and Method (K. Dvořák, 1938) — St. Francis Xavier (F. M. Brokof, 1711).

11—12 St. John the Baptist (J. Max, 1857) — St. Christopher (J. Max, 1857).

13—14 SS. Norbert, Wenceslas and Sigismund (M. Max, 1853) — St. Francis Borgia (F. M. Brokof, 1710).

15—16 St. John Nepomuk (this bronze statue is from 1683 and is thus the oldest sculpture on the bridge; it was cast after a model by J. Brokof) — St. Ludmila (M. B. Braun's workshop, 1730).

17—18 St. Anthony of Padua (J. Mayer, 1707) — St. Francis of Assissi (E. Max, 1855).

19—21 St. Jude Thaddeus (M. Mayer, 1708) — SS. Vincent Ferrarius and Procopius (F. M. Brokof, 1712) — Standing on the bridge pier below the group of statues is a copy of the torso of a Late Gothic sculpture (Bruncvík) of 1884 by L. Šimek (20).

22—23 St. Augustin (F. Kohl, 1708) — St. Nicholas of Tolentino (J. F. Kohl, 1708).

24—25 St. Theatin (Cajetanus) (F. M. Brokof, 1709) — St. Luitgarde (M. B. Braun, 1710).

26—27 St. Philip Benitius (M. B. Mandl, 1714) — St. Adalbert (J. M. Brokof, 1709).

28—29 SS. Vitus (F. M. Brokof, 1714) — St. John of Matha, Felix de Valois and Ivo with the figure of a Turk guarding arrested Christians (F. M. Brokof, 1714). This group of statues is an expression of thanks to the Trinitarian Order, which

KARLŮV MOST

redeemed Christians from Turkish captivity.

30—31 A group of statues of SS. Cosmas and Damian with Christ in the cen-

tre (J. Mayer, 1709) — St. Wenceslas
(J. M. Böhm, 1858).
32 Old Town Bridge Tower.
33 Malá Strana Bridge Towers.
In the course of the passing ages the
sandstone bridge has had to be repaired on several occasions. The most
extensive repairs were carried out on it
in the seventies of the present century.

---

7. Mostecká Street and the square Malostranské náměstí

We shall now pass through the Malá
Strana Bridge Towers and Mostecká
Street and make our way to the square
Malostranské náměstí. This small sector
offers rich possibilities of becoming
acquainted with the wealth of art and
historical monuments of **Malá Strana**
(the Little Quarter), which, after Staré
Město (the Old Town), was Prague's
second town, founded by Přemysl Otakar II.
The **Malá Strana Bridge Towers** are
themselves notable historical monuments. The smaller of them, situated on
the left, formed a part of the Romanesque fortifications of Judith's Bridge already in the late 12th century and is
thus one of Prague's oldest historical
monuments in general. Its outer appearance is younger, dating from the
late 16th century. In the latter half of the
15th century the second, larger tower
was built which was intended to corre-
spond to the Old Town Bridge Tower at
the other end of the bridge. The gallery
of this higher tower is accessible for
sightseeing and observation purposes.
The gate with battlements built-in between the two towers was built in the
early 15th century, but it belonged to
the Old Town similarly as Charles
Bridge, the two towers and the whole of
the Malá Strana bridgehead.

Mostecká Street was clearly an important communication already in the
Middle Ages. After all, it was here (from
the present house No. 16 on the right up
to the square Dražického náměstí) that ·
the Bishop's Court, the seat of the bishops of Prague who moved here from the
Castle at the end of the 12th century,
spread out. During the Hussite battles
the court was destroyed, after which it
was never renewed.
In Mostecká Street No. 1 there used to
be a custom-house, a Renaissance
building from the late 16th century.
House No. 4, At the Holy Saviour's, is
a Baroque building called At the Black
Bear. Also to be seen in this locality is
the former Kounic Palace, No. 15, which
is now the seat of the Yugoslav embassy. It is a Rococo building with Classical
elements.
Several buildings in the old streets running off from the left side of Mostecká
Street are worthy of note.
Particularly noteworthy in Lázeňská
Street is the **Church of Our Lady Below
the Chain,** the oldest church in the
Little Quarter. Its site was originally occupied by a Romanesque basilica of the
12th century. The present church was
Barocized (C. Lurago) in the mid-17th
century. Inside the church there are two
paintings by the Czech painter Karel
Škréta. House No. 6, called In the Baths,
is an interesting secular building, where
baths were really situated in the Middle
Ages. In the 19th century it was one of
Prague's well-known hotels which accommodated a whole number of eminent personages (the Tsar Peter the
Great, Chateaubriand and others).
House No. 11, called At the Golden Unicorn, was also a foremost hotel at
which Ludwig van Beethoven stayed in
1796.
Lying somewhat to the right is the
square **Maltézské náměstí** with a group
of statues depicting St. John the Bap-

tist by F. M. Brokof. Building No. 1, Nostic Palace, an Early Baroque structure of about 1660 which was subjected to modifications in the 18th century, is now the seat of the Netherlandish embassy. The Rococo Turba Palace, No. 6, now houses the Japanese embassy. From 1622 building No. 8 was the seat of Prague's Post Office for a whole century and building No. 11 contains a well-known wine tavern named U Malířů (At the Painters) after the house, which be-

longed to the painter Jan Šic in the 16th century.

In the direction towards the Vltava the square **Velkopřevorské náměstí** (Grand Prior Square) joins up with the previously described square. Here building No. 1 is the former Hrzán Palace. No. 2 houses the French embassy (Buquoy Palace), while No. 4 was once the palace of the Maltese Grand Prior. This building is one of the most beautiful samples of the Baroque in the Little

Roofs of the Little Quarter
with the dome
of St. Nicholas's Church

Quarter. It was built from 1726—1731. The sculptural decoration of the portals and staircase are the work of M. B. Braun's workshop. Musical performances take place in the adjoining garden in the summer months.

Those who wish to take a rest at this point can make their way round Prague's last typical mill, called the Grand Prior Mill (No. 6) to the Vltava, cross the romantic branch of the river called Čertovka (the Devil's Stream), whose water once drove a number of mills, and thus reach Kampa Park. Until the outbreak of the Second World War pottery markets took place here and this custom has recently been renewed. From the embankment wall fine views can be obtained of Charles Bridge and the Smetana Embankment. By walking in northerly direction it is possible to pass under the arches of Charles Bridge, where a particularly romantic sector of the Čertovka, flowing through a group of houses, begins. This locality is popularly called the Prague Venice. Now let us return to Mostecká Street and continue to the square Malostranské náměstí with a number of interesting Renaissance and Baroque buildings. Since ancient times the square has been divided into the so-called Lower Square (the part where trams now run) and the Upper Square (the so-called Italian Square) formed by the part above St. Nicholas's Church. Baroque buildings make this division even more striking.

The most outstanding building here is St. Nicholas's Church, the peak work of the Prague Baroque. Its construction was started at the very beginning of the 18th century and took 60 years to complete. The best architects of the Prague Baroque, Kryštof Dienzenhofer and his son Kilián Ignác, who also designed the decoration of the interior of the church, participated in its construction. A magnificent ceiling fresco portrays the life of St. Nicholas (it is one of the biggest frescoes in Europe) and is the work of J. L. Kracker. The pulpit with sculptures by R. and P. Prachner (c. 1765), several paintings by K. Škréta and other works of art are of great value. Near the entrance to the church stands a plague column with a group of statues of the Holy Trinity of 1715.

Standing in the right-hand lower corner of the square is the Little Quarter Town Hall (now known rather as the Malostranská beseda), a Renaissance building from 1617—1622 in which social and cultural gatherings now take place. Those who long to enjoy a rest will find a suitable place for this purpose in the Little Quarter Café, situated in the Rococo Grömlingor Palace near the tram stop.

8. The Outer Bailey and Petřín

North-east of Malostranské náměstí, in the place which once formed the outer bailey, there is still a number of historical gems which should definitely be seen. All we have to do is to make two loops through two adjoining streets, each of which is 1 km long. The first begins behind the Little Quarter Town Hall in Letenská Street. At its very beginning our attention will be captured by St. Thomas's Church, erected gradually from the late 13th to the late 14th century along with a monastery and a brewery. In the twenties of the 18th century it was Barocized by K. I. Dienzenhofer. On the high altar there are copies of two paintings by Rubens of 1637: The Torture of St. Thomas and St. Augustine (the originals are in the National Gallery). In the church there are also valuable altar sculptures (F. M. Brokof, J. A. and O. F. Quitainer). — Further along the left side of the street, in building No. 12, is the brewery called U Tomáše (At Thomas's), founded in 1358, with a garden. A special brand of beer is tapped here. After continuing another hundred metres or so — still on the left — we come to the inconspicuous entrance to Wallenstein Garden where we are especially attracted by the remarkable Sala terrena, built from 1623—1627 after a plan by G. Pieroni. Standing in front of it is a bronze fountain of 1630 with a copy of a statue of Venus (the original of 1599 is housed in the Arts and Crafts Museum). The row of bronze statues by Adrian de Vries are also copies. The originals of 1625—1626 now stand in the royal château at Drottningholm in Sweden. In the summer months concerts and theatre performances take place in the garden. This peaceful environment is intended to serve as a place of rest. At the end of the street we turn to the left and after covering about 30 metres pass through the architectonically interesting exterior and interior of the Malostranská Station of the underground railway. A special attraction in its vestibule is a copy of the Baroque statue called Hope by M. B. Braun and also a tripartite sliding grill in the entrance to the atrium. Lining the former Wallenstein riding-school is a group of copies of statues which likewise came from M. B. Braun's workshop. Ten steps further on we turn left once again, this time into Valdštejnská Street. Building No. 2 at the very beginning of the street is the former riding-school of Wallenstein Palace, which now serves as an exhibition hall. — Building No. 8 is Fürstenberg Palace, now the Polish embassy. Built in the Renaissance, it was Barocized in the mid-18th century. — Building No. 10 is Kolovrat Palace, a Late Baroque architectonic work. Next to the palace is the entrance to the palace gardens below the Castle (Ledebourg, Pálffy and Kolovrat Gardens), now mutually connected. Their foundation was started from the 16th century according to Italian models. They are usually open to the public in the summer months. Apart from being suitable for resting purposes, they also offer a number of unique views of Prague. Cultural programmes and the like take place here. The most significant building in the square Valdštejnské náměstí is Wallenstein Palace, Prague's first Baroque palace. Its construction was commissioned by the imperial Generalissimo Albrecht of Wallenstein to serve as his seat, intended to be comparable with the royal palace.

Albrecht of Wallenstein was a historical figure worthy of a Shakespearian tragedy. Originally he attained the rank of colonel in the army of the Czech Estates, but later he became a traitor and went over to the side of the Emperor Ferdinand I of the Hapsburg dynasty. As a result of gaining immense wealth from confiscated properties he was able to maintain his own army. The emperor raised him to the rank of generalissimo and bestowed the title of Duke of Frýdlant on him. During the Thirty Years War he served the emperor, but secretly negotiated with the Swedes. In his grandiose plans he even counted with gaining the Czech crown. When the sovereign learned of his traitorship, he had him murdered at Cheb in 1634 and confiscated all his property.

The main hall in the interior of the palace passes through two floors. Its ceiling fresco shows Albrecht of Wallenstein as Mars, the god of war, in a triumphal chariot. A considerable number of Flemish tapestries can be seen in the other interiors of the palace. The building now serves as the seat of the Ministry of Culture and the J. Amos Komenský (Comenius) Pedagogical Museum. Another palace in this square is Ledebourg Palace, built in Late Baroque style in the late 18th century.

The atmosphere of Valdštejnské náměstí is also created by the old Wallenstein Ale-house, building No. 7. This Empire building is called At the Three Storks and bears a house sign. It occupies a site which can boast of having had catering traditions ever since the 14th century, when the monks of the Augustian Monastery of St. Thomas brewed beer here.

From Valdštejnské náměstí we shall now proceed to **Tomášská Street**. Especially worthy of attention is house No. 15 called U Klárů, Barocized in the first half of the 18th century. The sketcher of views of Prague, Vincenc Morstadt (1802—1875), lived and died in the house. — On the façade of house No. 4, called At the Golden Stag and built by K. I. Dienzenhofer, there is a house sign in the form of a group of statues of the patron saint of huntsmen, St. Hubert, with a stag, the work of F. M. Brokof. — This street also has an ale-house. It is called U Schnellů (At the Schnells) and is situated in building No. 2. Pilsner Urquell beer is served in it.

Our next walk takes us through **Karmelitská Street** on the left of Malostranské náměsti. **Vrtba Palace** (No. 25), built in Late Renaissance style, has a unique atmosphere. Its terraced garden, laid out about 1720, has a Baroque character. Its sculptural decoration is of great value and came from M. B. Braun's workshop. The upper terrace affords a picturesque view of Prague Castle and the Little Quarter.

Another remarkable building in Karmelitská Street is the **Church of Our Lady Victorious** on the right-hand side. It was built in the early 17th century by the German Lutherans after a plan by M. Filippi and after 1636 it was Barocized. Four paintings by Peter Brandl can be seen in its interior. The church is known outside Czechoslovakia (especially in Spain, Italy and South America) for the statuette of the Prague Child Jesus — Bambino di Praga — a work of Spanish origin.

We shall now return to Vrtba Palace and make our way to the slope of **Petřín Hill** (318 m). First of all through the street **Tržiště** on whose left side stands the Early Baroque Schönborn Palace (No. 15), now the embassy of the United States of America, with a large garden and then through **Vlašská Street** where Lobkovic Palace stands (No. 19), the embassy of the Federal Republic of Germany, likewise with a large garden. Further on we come to the building of Pod Petřínem Hospital and the Church of St. Charles Borromaeus.

On the slopes of Petřín Hill there is a 2 km long **observation path** with a number of observation points affording views of historical Prague. Perhaps the most important feature on Petřín Hill is the 60 m high **observation tower**, built in 1891 after the model of the Eiffel Tower in Paris. At present it is undergoing reconstruction. Situated near the observation tower is a maze, an ancient attraction of small and big children, which dates in the same year. To be seen in this pavilion is a diorama creating the illusion of the battle of the people of Prague against the Swedes on Charles Bridge in 1648. — A popular observatory is also situated on Petřín Hill. Another interesting feature here is the Hunger Wall, a Gothic fortification element of the Little Quarter, built from 1360—1362 on the command of Charles IV. The wall is more than 1 km long, about 8 m high and 1.70 m thick.

Those who are good at walking can extend this sightseeing tour to include a walk from Petřín Hill to the Strahov sports area whose biggest, we may even say world rarity is the **Spartakiade**

Stadium for mass physical culture performances. They are held once in every five years (the next Spartakiade will take place in June 1990). As many as 16,000 persons can participate simultaneously in the individual parts of the Spartakiade, which take place on an area of 300 × 200 m, and there is accommodation for as many as 220,000 spectators. Situated nearby is the Evžen Rošický Stadium with accommodation for nearly 50,000 spectators. It is suitable for big events in the sphere of light athletics and for football matches. The adjoining students' hostels with a capacity of 5,000 beds provide accommodation for persons participating in the programmes of the Spartakiade and for visitors to Prague in the summer period. True, the ancestors of Prague's present inhabitants were, on the average, good cultivators of physical culture and movement (this is best documented by the Museum of Physical Culture and Sport, situated in building No. 40 in the street Újezd, called Tyrš House), but many of them gladly allowed themselves to be transported to the summit of Petřín Hill by the **funicular railway,** whose lower station was — and still is — situated near the Újezd crossroad. (It was in operation in the years 1891—1965). After undergoing general repairs it now covers a distance of approximately 500 m and a difference in height of 100 m. And thus Prague has renewed one of its interesting tourist attractions.

9. Through Nerudova Street
   to Prague Castle

Nerudova Street was named after the classic of Czech realistic poetry and journalist Jan Neruda (1834—1891), who lived in the house called U dvou slunců No. 47 (At the Two Suns).

Many of the houses in this street are decorated with **house signs,** most of which originated in the period of the High Baroque. Some of them are executed in stone or plaster, some are painted on plaster, while still others are made of metal, sheet or wood. Very often they indicate the profession of the original owner of the house, his social status, his patron saint, or a certain event, or perhaps a legend connected with the given house. In some cases, on the contrary, the new owner of a house adopted a surname derived from the house sign.

Of the notable houses in Nerudova Street let us mention Morzini Palace, now the Rumanian embassy (No. 5). It is one of the most beautiful Baroque buildings in Prague and was built in the early 18th century by G. Santini. The sculptural decoration on its façade is the work of F. M. Brokof: the balcony is borne by the figures of Moors, above the portals there are allegorical busts Day and Night and on the attic there are statues of the four parts of the world. Other Baroque houses (sometimes with cores of earlier origin) include the following: No. 6 At the Red Eagle, No. 12 At the Three Fiddles, No. 16 At the Golden Goblet and No. 18 At St. John Nepomuk's. — Thun-Hohenštejn Palace (No. 20) now houses the Italian embassy. This palace also has an artistically rich portal, the work of M. B. Braun in the form of the coat-of-arms of the Kolovrat family and the figures of two Roman gods — Jupiter and Junona. — Immediately following the palace is the former monastery of the Theatin Order (No. 24), later converted to meet residential purposes, and the Church of Our Lady at the Theatins. Building No. 33 is the former Bretfeld Palace of Rococo origin with a relief of St. Nicholas.

Building No. 34 is called At the Golden Horseshoe and has a painting of St. Wenceslas.

Such a notable street as Nerudova Street naturally cannot lack Old Prague ale-houses in which the history of the Little Quarter was also written. They include those called At the Cat (U kocoura) and At Bonaparte's (U Bonaparta). In the house called At the Three Fiddles (U tří housliček) there is also a pleasant wine tavern which from 1667 housed Otto's violin-building school. Instruments were built here for another two centuries by violin-builders, their ranks including Tomáš Edlinger of Augsburg. The street continues to rise, finally turning sharply to the right. From here we shall walk through the street Ke Hradu to the square Hradčanské náměstí.

10. Hradčany

The square **Hradčanské náměstí** has preserved its medieval ground-plan. Of interest here are the cast iron candelabras which originated 120 years ago.

A number of remarkable palaces can be seen here.

Most visitors halt first of all by the **main building of the National Gallery in Šternberk Palace** (No. 15), dating in the early 18th century. Of particular interest in the gallery is the collection of old world art. Let us mention a few of the exhibited paintings: The Assumption of the Virgin Mary (P. Veronese), David with the Head of Goliath (J. Tintoretto), The Rosary Celebration (A. Dürer) and Haymaking (P. Bruegel). Also displayed here are works by L. Cranach, P. Rubens, H. Rembrandt van Rijn and other painters.

Among the representatives of French art of the 19th and 20th centuries are E. Delacroix, H. Daumier, C. Corot and G. Courbet. Most widely represented, however, are the impressionists: C. Monet, A. Sisley and C. J. Pissaro and works by G. Seurat, P. Signac, H. Rousseau, P. Cézanne, P. Gauguin, V. van Gogh, H. Toulouse-Lautrec and H. Matisse can also be seen. Of the greatest value, however, are the paintings by M. Chagall and particularly rich is the collection of paintings by P. Picasso.

Military history is documented by the historical collections installed in the Museum of Military History in **Schwarzenberg Palace** (No. 2). Originally called Lobkovic Palace, this building ranks among the gems of the Prague Renaissance, having been built in the mid-16th century. The façade of the palace has rich graffito decoration, recently restored. — The other **Schwarzenberg Palace** (originally Salm Palace — No. 1) was built in the early 19th century on the site of two Renaissance houses. — Standing on the opposite side of the Castle is the huge Early Baroque building of **Tuscany Palace,** whose attic is decorated with a number of statues by J. Brokof. Situated next to the Gallery is the **Archbishop's Palace** (formerly Gryspek Palace), built in the 16th century. It has undergone several reconstructions and its present Rococo façade dates from 1764—1765. The most interesting buildings in the square include the former **Martinic Palace** (No. 8) of the mid-16th century. It is richly decorated with graffito and some of its interiors have old wooden, richly painted ceilings. The Department of the Chief Architect of Prague is now housed in the building. Those who wish to devote full attention to all the individual parts of the Castle will obviously have to resign themselves to another deviation from our route, to a tour of **Hradčany,** founded about 1320 as the third town of Prague. Originally

the nearest environs of the Castle belonged to it, by which we mean the area surrounding the square Hradčanské náměstí. However, Charles IV enlarged Hradčany by the addition of **Pohořelec, Strahov** and a part of **Petřín**. A considerable part of Hradčany and the Castle was destroyed by fire in 1541. Half a century later Rudolph II raised Hradčany to a royal town.

The little houses of the poor of that time, originally of 16th century origin, now have an appearance dating from the 18th-19th century. The little street called **Nový Svět** (The New World) in particular has preserved its charm. Special mention should be made of No. 3 — At the Golden Pear and No. 5 — At the Golden Cluster. A memorial tablet on No. 1 recalls the stay of the German astronomer Johannes Kepler here. On house No. 5 in adjoining Černínská Street there is a statue of St. John Nepomuk.

Our walk now takes us from the Castle to **Strahov Monastery**. First of all we must walk through gently rising **Loretánská Street** on whose left side stands the former Town Hall of Hradčany (No. 1), a Renaissance building of the late 16th century with decoration in the form of graffito, and, further on, Hrzán Palace (No. 9). The nearby square **Loretánské náměstí** originated at the very beginning of the 18th century. Facing us is **Černín Palace,** a monumental building whose façade is 150 m long. It was built by Italian architects and artists. From 1928—1934 it was restored and enlarged for the Ministry of Foreign Affairs, which still has its seat here. The decoration of the interior of the palace is from the 17th—18th century.

The right-hand side of the square is formed by the **Loretto.** This church was built after the model of the well-known Casa santa in the Italian Loretto. The Prague "Holy Stable" is the central building of the Loretto, built from 1626—1631. As the Loretto was unable to accommodate a large number of believers, it was enlarged by the addition

Loretto

of a cloister which enclosed the whole of its immediate environs on all four sides. The façade part of the church complex is Baroque, having been built in 1721 by K. I. Dienzenhofer. However, it is dominated by the older, Early Baroque steeple bearing, apart from a clock, a carillon dating from 1694. The play of bells now has several song variants and can be heard on the stroke of every hour. Standing in the middle of the eastern side of the cloister is the Church of the Nativity of Our Lord, built from 1734–1735. Nowadays the most attractive part of the Loretto is the church treasury. It is situated on the left of the entrance to the courtyard. Its most valuable exhibits include a diamond monstrance of 1699, made by Viennese jewellery-makers of gilded silver. It is set with 6,222 diamonds and weighing 12 kg; a Gothic chalice of 1510, the oldest item in the treasure, made of gilded silver, a cross of the early 17th century, made of ivory, and another six monstrances.

Our tour continues through the street above Černín Palace to the square **Pohořelec**. It was founded in 1375 and in the period of the 15th to the 18th century its houses were really burned to the ground, as the name of the square implies. By walking up the road running from Pohořelec we come to the courtyard of Strahov Monastery on the left. Standing near the gate on the left is the Church of St. Roch, built in the Gothico-Renaissance, and further on the oldest part of the monastery, the originally Romanesque Church of the Assumption of Our Lady, built in the latter half of the 12th century. As was usually the case, it was later subjected to several reconstructions, first in the Gothic, then in the Renaissance and finally in the Baroque. Numerous valuable paintings and sculptures can be seen in its interior. The big organ in the church is from

1736. In 1787 W. A. Mozart played on it. Strahov Monastery was founded in 1140 by Prince Vladislav II. Originally it was a provisionary wooden building, but after the elapse of several years it was rebuilt, along with the church, of stone. The whole history of the monastery was very moving. In the mid-13th century the Romanesque building was destroyed by fire and the Hussite Wars, the Thirty Years War, the conquering of Prague by the Prussians and other events all left their mark on the monastery buildings. The core of the whole Strahov area is formed by the monastery with a library. It bears numerous traces of the original Romanesque buildings, but in essence it is Baroque. The entrance is now formed by the former chapter hall, but the most interesting of the interiors is the monastery library. It is Early Baroque of the latter half of the 17th century and was once called the Theological Hall. Theological literature is kept in it as well as libri prohibiti (forbidden books) in special cabinets. The centre of the hall is occupied by geographical and astronomical globes and a number of illuminated manuscripts, the oldest of which is the Strahov Evangeliary of the 9th century. In the late 18th century a new building containing the so-called Philosophical Hall was built to supplement the old library. Of the greatest historical value are its cabinets and shelves, transferred here from the Moravian monastery at Louka (Znojmo), and the magnificent ceiling painting (The History of Mankind) by F. Maulbertsch.

From the monastery windows and garden it is possible to gain exceptional views of historical Prague.

Soon after the end of the last war the **Museum of National Literature** was established here as a permanent exhibition illustrating the development of Czech literature.

11. Prague Castle

History: Prague Castle was founded after the year 880 by the first historically documented Přemyslid prince, Bořivoj, as the main seat of the ruling prince. About the year 884 he had the Church of Our Lady, the second Christian church to originate in Bohemia, built here. In 921 St. George's Church was founded and after 925 Prince Václav (later St. Václav — Wenceslas) founded St. Vitus's Rotunda. Fifty years later the permission of the Pope was gained for the founding of the Prague bishopric (in 973). In the 11th—12th century a Romanesque basilica was built to replace St. Vitus's Rotunda and in the same period St. George's Church was reconstructed. The prince's palace was rebuilt as a walled building and a bishop's house and stone fortifications were built.

The Castle experienced its greatest period of flourish during the reign of Charles IV. In 1344 the construction was started of St. Vitus's Cathedral for the then newly founded archbishopric. Charles IV's successor, Václav IV, deserted the Castle and took up residence at the King's Court in the Old Town. George of Poděbrady and, at first, also Vladislav of Jagiello also resided there. However, the latter supported the construction of new buildings in the style called the Vladislav Gothic.

The Hapsburg sovereign Ferdinand I (1526—1564) founded the Royal Garden behind Stag Moat and then had the Renaissance Royal Summer Palace built in it. — During the reign of Rudolph II the Castle became a notable centre of culture and art. True, the emperor was more interested in art, astrology and alchemy than in ruling the country, but for the Castle this meant that outstanding collections of art and curiosities began to be accumulated at it. And the Spanish Hall and the Rudolph Gallery were built to house them.

After the defeat of the Czech resistance movement (1620) the Hapsburgs ceased to reside at the Castle, travelling to it for occasional visits only. Building activity therefore stagnated here even after the Thirty Years War.

The Castle gained its present appearance in the latter half of the 18th century in accordance with a design by the Viennese architect N. Pacassi.

After the year 1918 the castle became the seat of the head of the new state, the President of the Czechoslovak Republic. Systematic archeological research of its area was started and numerous architectonic modifications were realised after designs by J. Plečnik. These activities have continued since the end of the Second World War.

Sightseeing tour

The main entrance to Prague Castle for the purpose of a **sightseeing tour** is gained from the square Hradčanské náměstí. Passenger cars and buses can find **parking space** in Jelení Street (3—5 minutes from here). — **Approach on foot:** from Nerudova Street in the Little Quarter; from Klárov from the Malostranská Station of the underground railway via the Old Castle Steps 10 minutes (uphill); from the Hradčanská Station of the underground railway 10 minutes; from the Pohořelec tram stop 10 minutes (mildly downhill); from the Hrad tram stop 2 minutes; from the upper station of the funicular railway on Petřín Hill 20—25 minutes (fine views!). The **individual buildings** are open daily except Mondays — in summer from 9—17 hours and in winter from 9—16 hours. The southern gardens are open on Saturdays and Sundays in the summer months only.

The **Information Centre** at No. 37 Vikářská Street has the same opening hours as the Castle buildings. Apart from other things, it secures the services of guides for a complete sightseeing tour as well as for its individual sectors. — A Post Office is situated in the Third Courtyard and toilets are situated in the Third Courtyard, below the Riding-school, near the Golden Lane, in the Royal Palace and, in summer, in the garden called On the Ramparts.

PRAŽSKÝ HRAD

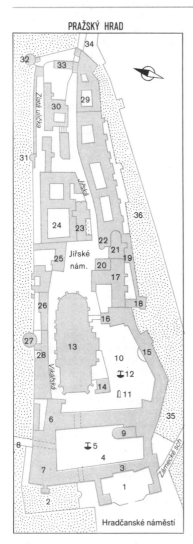

1. The First Castle Courtyard.
2. Garden on the Bastion (Zahrada Na Baště).
3. Matthias Gate.
4. The Second Castle courtyard.
5. Kohl's fountain.
6. Rudolph Gallery.
7. Spanish Hall.
8. Prašný most (Powder Bridge).
9. Chapel of the Holy Rood.
10. The Third Castle Courtyard.
11. Monolith.
12. Equestrian statue of St. George.
13. Cathedral of St. Vitus.
14. Old Provost's Residence.
15. Municipal tract (south side of the courtyard).
16. Old Royal Palace.
17. Vladislav Hall.
18. Louis Wing.
19. Theresian Wing.
20. Diet Hall.
21. All Saints' Church.
22. Institute of Gentlewomen.
23. Basilica of St. George.
24. Convent of St. George.
25. New Provost's Residence.
26. Old Deanery.
27. Mihulka Tower.
28. Vikárka Restaurant.
29. Lobkovic Palace.
30. Burgrave's House.
31. White Tower.
32. Daliborka Tower.
33. Black Tower.
34. Observation terrace.
35. Garden of Paradise (Rajská zahrada).
36. Garden on the Ramparts (Zahrada Na valech).

Shops selling souvenirs, works of art and books can be found in the Golden Lane, in the street U Daliborky and in Vikářská Street.

Before making a tour of Prague Castle we shall halt for a few moments on the **Castle ramp** from where there is a very attractive view of Prague. From here we shall then enter the Castle grounds through a **Baroque grill gate** of the sixties of the 18th century. Above the gate are copies of the sculptures Battling Giants by I. F. Platzer.

Situated directly opposite the main gate is the **Matthias Gate** affording entry to the Second Castle Courtyard. This gate resembles the old Roman arches of triumph. It was the first Baroque structure to originate at Prague Castle and dates in 1614.

On the left of the First Courtyard there is a grill gate leading to the garden called On the Bastion. Its name was derived from the heaped bastions of the time of the last Přemyslids. The present layout of the park-like garden dates from 1930.

Running directly from the Matthias Gate on the right is Pacassi's staircase from 1765—1766, from where access is gained to the representative interiors of the Castle which are not accessible to the public. They include, for example, the Throne Room, serving for official audiences, the Hapsburg Hall, named after the dynastic gallery, and others.

The **Second Courtyard** originated in the latter half of the 16th century on the site where the original castle ditch was filled in. (The chambers of the President of the Czechoslovak Socialist Republic are now situated in the southern wing on the right, where Rudolph's palace once stood.) Standing in the centre of the courtyard is **Kohl's Baroque fountain of 1686.** Situated near the fountain is a well provided with a forged grill. Also standing here is the extremely noteworthy **Chapel of the Holy Rood with the treasury.** The present appearance of the chapel dates from 1852—1856. Its ceiling is decorated with frescoes on biblical motifs by V. Kandler and on its altar there are sculptures by I. F. Platzer. Since 1961 the St. Vitus cathedral treasure has been housed in the chapel. It originated from the time of Prince Václav. Valuable relics of the then Christian world were accumulated here by Charles IV and others date in the Late Gothic and Baroque periods.

Standing near the chapel is a stone fountain with a lion by J. Fragner and V. Makovský of 1966.

Running on the western side of the courtyard is the tract dating from the time of Maria Theresa. Its ground-floor part along with the stables in the northern wing were converted into the **castle picture gallery,** accessible to the public, in 1965. These sites were once occupied by very old buildings. The masonry of the foundations of the previously mentioned little **Church of Our Lady** was revealed here and is now preserved in the castle picture gallery. In the entrance chamber of the picture gallery several samples from the collections of Rudolph II, stolen by the Swedes from 1648—1649, are accumulated. Installed in other rooms are works from the collections of Ferdinand III (mid-17th century) and others gained on a purchase basis. They include in the first place paintings by the Italian masters Tizian, J. and D. Tintoretto and P. Veronese as well as works of Czech Baroque art — paintings by J. Kupecký and P. Brandl and sculptures by M. B. Braun. Unfortunately, most of the original collections were sold to Dresden, Vienna and other places with the passing of time.

The space above the stables is occupied by two magnificent halls, now inaccessible to the public. The first of them, the

Spanish Hall, was built at the very beginning of the 17th century, reconstructed by K. I. Dienzenhofer and A. Lurago in the mid-18th century and finally pseudo-Barocized from 1866—1868 for the prepared coronation of Franz Joseph I, which finally did not take place here. The other hall, **Rudolph's Gallery** (originally the Picture Gallery and also called the German Hall), was built in the late 16th century. Collections and rarites accumulated by Rudolph II, a well-known patron of the arts and sciences, were installed in it. This hall was also provided for the previously mentioned coronation with eclectic stucco decoration. Nowadays both halls serve representative purposes and various important assemblies.

The **Third Courtyard** is dominated by **St. Vitus's Cathedral with St. Wenceslas's Chapel.** The cathedral is the biggest of all Prague's churches. It is 124 m long and its greatest width is 60 m. The height of the cathedral up to the vault is 33 m, the façade steeples are 82 m high and the height of the main steeple attains nearly 100 m. The site of the cathedral was originally occupied by a rotunda built about 926 and in the latter half of the 11th century this was replaced with a triple-naved Romanesque basilica. In 1344 Charles IV founded a Gothic cathedral on its site and summoned Matthias of Arras from Avignon to build it. And with the wreath of chapels round the choir and the complicated supporting system the building really does resemble a French cathedral. After Matthias' death in 1352 the building works were continued by P. Parler of Gmünd in Swabia and his sons. The Hussite revolutionary movement brought building activity to a halt here for a number of years and it was not until the mid-16th century that a Renaissance helmet was set in place

on the main steeple and one hundred years later a new Baroque, onion-shaped roof. Not until the years 1873—1929 did the cathedral finally gain its present appearance — especially its Neo-Gothic western part.

By walking through the central part of the cathedral we shall come to the **royal mauseoleum** immediately behind the cross nave. This work by the Netherlandish sculptor A. Collin, realized in the latter half of the 16th century, has the form of a marble tomb on whose upper panel lie the figures of the Emperor and King Ferdinand I of the Hapsburg dynasty, his consort and his son Maxmilian II, whose remains lie at rest in the sepulchre. The tomb is surrounded by a valuable Renaissance iron grill of the mid-16th century. On the walls of the mausoleum there are medallions containing the busts of Charles IV, his four consorts and his successors.

The mausoleum actually forms the above-ground part of the **royal tomb** to which access is gained from the Chapel of the Holy Rood (on the right). The tomb contains the remains of the kings and the members of their families, placed in new sarcophagi (the modification was carried out 60 years ago). The Czech king and Roman emperor Charles IV (1378) is buried in the centre of the tomb, Ladislav the Posthumous (1457) on the right and George of Poděbrady (1471) on the left. The second row contains the remains of Václav IV (1419) and the common sarcophagus with the remains of the four consorts of Charles IV. At the rear of the crypt stands the Empire coffin of the daughter of Maria Theresa, Maria Amelia (1804), the original tin coffin of the Emperor Rudolph II (1612) and, finally, the granite sarcophagus with the remains of the children of Charles IV. — Remainders of the masonry of the original rotunda of the 10th century and the later Romanesque basi-

lica are visible in the underground part. Standing next to the Chapel of the Holy Rood (when walking back towards the west) is the Martinic Chapel and, further on, the **Gothic Chapel of St. Wenceslas** (the first chapel behind the transverse nave). It is the most notable chapel in the cathedral. It was built by P. Parler from 1362—1367 on the site of the original grave of St. Wenceslas. The chapel was the centre of the St. Wenceslas cult, in whose tradition Charles IV also followed, and was thus a really holy place for all visitors. The lower zone of the walls below the cornice is faced with over 1,300 pieces of semi-precious stones of Czech origin — amethysts, jaspers, chalcedonies, cornelians, etc. — which are set in gilded plaster. They fill the space between the individual paintings of the cycle called The Suffering of Christ (the Passion cycle) from 1372—1373 by a Czech master. The walls above the cornice are covered with scenes from the life of St. Wenceslas and are the work of the

St. Vitus's
Cathedral

Master of Litoměřice of 1509. Also situated here is Václav's tombstone of the 14th century, somewhat modified in the recent past. Also to be seen in the chapel is a Gothic cretaceous marly limestone statue of St. Wenceslas, a work of P. Parler's workshop (1373), with remainders of its original polychrome. Mounted in the southern wall of the chapel is a forged door, only 120 years old, which leads to the **Crown Chamber**. It has 7 locks whose keys are deposited in the safe-keeping of 7 institutions. The St. Wenceslas coronation jewels are housed in the chamber. They include the St. Wenceslas crown, a work executed in gold in the 14th century with scores of spinels, sapphires, emeralds and pearls, a sword of the first half of the 14th century, a Renaissance gold sceptre and the imperial orb of the first half of 16th century and a cloak and stoles of the 18th century. Copies can be seen in the exposition Monuments of the National Past.

The **high altar**, built of cretaceous marly limestone, is Gothic from 1868—1873. On its right side, neighbouring on the Chapel of the Holy Rood, is the oratory of 1493 with a Late Gothic ornament in the form of dry twigs and with the monogram of Vladislav Jagiello, who commissioned the building of the oratory. The emblems of the countries over which he reigned can also be seen here. Situated in the individual chapels on the gallery of the cathedral are the Gothic stone tombs of Czech kings, the work of P. Parler's workshop from 1370—1375. The present century has contributed to the decoration of the cathedral with, among other things, a series of original **coloured windows** created by leading Czech artists. The first window on the right in St. Ludmila's Chapel was designed by M. Švabinský, the second window on the right in the Chapel of the Tomb of God by K. Svolinský, the third

on the right in Thun Chapel by F. Kysela and the fifth on the right in Házmburg Chapel by C. Bouda. A window designed by M. Švabinský can also be seen in the transverse nave. — The window in the first chapel of the cathedral from the left, that of the Bartoň family of Dobenín, was designed by F. Kysela, in neighbouring Schwarzenberg Chapel by K. Svolinský and in the third chapel, the New Archbishop's Chapel, by A. Mucha. Standing next to it since 1929 is a remarkable work of modern art in the form of an altar sculptured by F. Bílek in 1899. It has a wooden relief The Crucifixion.

Worthy of our attention is also the coloured window in a rosette in the western façade, designed by F. Kysela. Running round the whole cathedral above the pillared arcades is a triforium, the **inner gallery** with 21 busts of the last quarter of the 14th century portraying members of the family of Charles IV, the Archbishops of Prague, the supervisors of the construction of the cathedral and the two architects concerned in its building. To be seen in the new part of the gallery are busts of outstanding personalities of the 20th century who participated in the construction and decoration of the cathedral. — The Gothic masonry of the **main steeple** reaches approximately to a height of 58 m. Its top part is built of bricks. On the first floor of the steeple there is a Renaissance bell called Sigismund (1549). It weighs 18 tons and is about 2 m in height. On the second floor are the bells called Wenceslas, John the Baptist and Joseph. The horologe was built in Magdeburg in 1597.

Situated next to the steeple is the ceremonial entrance to the cathedral, called the **Golden Portal**. Above it there is a mosaic on the theme of The Last Judgment from 1370—1371. Kneeling in the centre field are the donor Charles IV and his consort Elizabeth. — The grill of the portal is decorated with figural symbols of the twelve months of the year (J. Horejc, 1954).

Standing in the Third Courtyard is a Gothic **statue of St. George** of 1373 and also a 16 m high **granite monolith**, set in place in the course of the tenth year of the existence of the Czechoslovak Republic — 1928 — to commemorate the victims of the First World War. — Next to the cathedral stands the building of the **Old Provost's Residence,** originally the Romanesque bishop's palace. In the 18th century the building was Barocized. — On its corner there is a sandstone statue of St. Wenceslas of 1662.

The present appearance of the southern side of the Third Courtyard dates from the time of the reconstruction commissioned by Maria Theresa and carried out from 1755—1761. In its main façade there is the entrance to the offices of the Bureau of the President of the Czechoslovak Socialist Republic and other reception rooms.

The eastern side of the Third Courtyard is closed by the **Royal Palace,** the seat of Czech princes and kings up to the end of the 16th century.

Standing by the entrance staircase is the Baroque **Eagle Fountain** of 1664. It indicates the original level of the courtyard. We shall pass through the **antechamber** where, on the left, there is the entrance to the **Green Chamber** where various courts assembled from the time of Charles IV and which was later also used as an audience hall. Connected with it by means of a staircase is the so-called **Vladislav's Bedchamber,** richly decorated with emblems and also the **archives of the court rolls.**

Now let us return to the antechamber and enter the **Vladislav Hall.** It is 62 m long, 16 m wide and 16 m high. Its construction by the architect B. Ried from

1493—1502 was commissioned by Vladislav Jagiello when he decided to move back to Prague Castle from the King's Court. The hall was the Hall of Homage of Czech kings in which diets of the Estates also assembled. During the reign of Rudolph II various social events and markets where rare goods and works of art, etc. were sold took place here.

Since 1934 the elections of the presidents of Czechoslovakia have taken place in the hall and since 1945 it has also been used for scores of other events of national importance.

From the Vladislav Hall we shall pass into the **Louis Wing** on the right, specifically into the two rooms of the so-called **Czech Chancellery** which served as the offices of the Czech governors for two centuries. They assembled here in the absence of the king. It was also from here that two governors — hated reactionaries — and their secretary were thrown from the window in 1618. This event was actually the beginning of the uprising of the Czechs against the Hapsburgs and is referred to as the Prague defenestration.

On the second floor of the Louis Wing there is the **Hall of the Imperial Court Council** where assemblies took place during the reign of Rudolph II and also later. The furniture and paintings are from the 16th—18th century and hanging on the walls are portraits of the Hapsburgs and other persons.

From the Vladislav Hall we can also gain access to the choir, from where it is possible to view the interior of **All Saints' Chapel.** It was built by P. Parler from 1370—1387 and rebuilt and enlarged in the Renaissance. Later, in the mid-19th century — in connection with the building of the Institute of Gentlewomen — it was attached to it as a private chapel. On the high altar there is a painting All Saints by V. V. Reiner.

Housed in the northern part of the Baroque altar are the remains of St. Procopius (d. 1053), the first Abbot of the Sázava monastery, and on it are 12 paintings depicting scenes from his life by K. Dittmann (1669). Below the choir there is a triptych by the Rudolphian painter Hans von Aachen of the late 16th century.

We shall now descend several steps in order to return to the Vladislav Hall and, on the right, come to the **Diet Hall**, which formed a part of Chárles IV's palace. It was rebuilt about 1500 and wholly destroyed by fire in 1541. It was renewed from 1559—1563. The architect concerned deliberately copied the Late Gothic vault of the Vladislav Hall. The Diet Hall served for the assemblies of the Provincial Court and the diets of the Estates. The royal throne of the mid-19th century is situated here and on its right there stand the chair of the archbishop and the benches of the supreme clerks and the clergy. There is also standing room once used by representatives of the royal towns. The whole arrangement is in full accord with the customs of the time. Portraits of the Hapsburg rulers hang on the walls.

From the Vladislav Hall it is possible to descend a staircase leading to the rooms of the **New Land Rolls**. A cabinet with carved decoration of 1562 in which documents were deposited can be seen in the rear room.

Leading off from the Vladislav Hall is also the entrance to the so-called **Riders' Steps**. If we glance backwards from the steps we can see the remains of the Gothic portal of the Royal Palace of about 1355. There is a valuable crest vault above the first part of the steps. On the left there are the rooms of the so-called **New Appeals** where courts of appeal took place in the 18th century. The shape of the steps corresponds to the requirements of the time — they

were used by knights on horseback in order to enter the hall, where tournaments were held.

From the staircase, with a vault by B. Ried (c. 1500), we can gain access through a Renaissance exit door on the right of the square U Sv. Jiří, or make our way down to the **Gothic palace** below the Vladislav Hall. The first interior, the room of the Old Land Rolls of the time of Přemysl Otakar II, was destroyed by the known fire. It acquired its present appearance during the last few decades.

We then come to an arcaded passage, also of the time of Přemysl II (three of the arcades are open). One of the open arcades affords access to a gallery from which the remainders of a Romanesque room with a fireplace and the remainders of two small portals can be seen. From here we pass on to so-called Charles' Hall, to the Old Registry and to the Hall of Columns of Václav IV (its vault originated in the early 15th century).

On our way back from the palace courtyard we shall make a steep descent to the uderground part of the Royal Palace with remainders of the fortifications of the late 9th century and to the hall of Soběslav's Romanesque prince's palace in which fragments of Romanesque architecture are now installed. — Our tour of the Old Royal Palace ends with the entrance to the square U Sv. Jiří. The square **náměstí U Sv. Jiří**, attracts attention due especially to the presence of two of the most valuable Castle buildings, the **Basilica and Convent of St. George**, which form the eastern side of the square. The church was founded here in the early 10th century by Prince Vratislav I and in 973 the very first convent in Bohemia — a Benedictine convent for nuns — was built by it. Many of the later abbesses were members of the ruling family. The church

gained its present appearance of a twin-steepled basilica after a fire which occurred in 1142. Like most of Prague's churches, it was finally Barocized — its main façade is from 1677—1678. During the reign of Joseph II the convent was abolished and the building was adapted to serve various purposes, particularly as a barracks. In the seventies it was newly adapted to house a **permanent exhibition of Old Czech art** from the Gothic to the Baroque (a part of the National Gallery). Most outstanding from the artistic aspect are the works forming the cycle of the Master of Vyšší Brod (9 panels of the mid-14th century) and the works of the Master of the Třeboň Altar, now regarded as the greatest Czech artist of the Middle Ages. (The only known painter of that period was Master Theodoric, who worked for Charles IV at Karlštejn Castle). Also to be seen here is a remarkable group of so-called beautiful Madonnas from the turn of the 14th and 15th centuries. The Late Gothic is represented by the Masters of St. James's Altar, St. George's Altar and the Litoměřice Altar. Art of the 17th and 18th centuries is represented by K. Škréta, P. Brandl, J. Kupecký and V. V. Reiner.

The present appearance of St. George's Basilica is the result of an extensive puristic restoration carried out at the turn of the 19th and 20th centuries and of later modifications. Inside the basilica are the tombs of the Czech princes Vratislav I, the founder of the church, and Boleslav II. Below the double-branched staircase leading to the choir there is the crypt of the 12th century. From the mid-17th century the vault of the abbesses was also situated here. On the right, on the altar table, stands a naturalistic Baroque statue of St. Bridget, called Vanitas (Vanity). It is alleged to have been carved by an Italian stone-

The interior
of St. Georges's Basilica
at Prague Castle

mason in the early 18th century as a form of penitence for an act of violence which he had committed in the church. The square choir has a hemispherical apse. Visible in the vault of the choir are the remains of Romanesque ceiling paintings of the early 13th century. — In the adjoining Chapel of St. Ludmila there is the cretaceous marly limestone tomb of the saint, the work of P. Parler's workshop of the late 14th century. — Facing Jiřská Street is an Early Renaissance portal from B. Ried's workshop (after 1500). — Neighbouring on the basilica is the Chapel of St. John Nepomuk, built in the early 18th century on its southern side. The painting of the saint on the altar and the decoration of the cupola are the work of V. V. Reiner. Especially worthy of our notice in **Jiřská Street** is **Lobkovic Palace** (No. 1), in which a permanent **museum exposition Monuments of the National Past** is installed. The exposition depicts Czechoslovak history from the time of the arrival of the Slavs up to 1848. The palace was built after 1570 and after the mid-17th century it was reconstructed after a plan by C. Lurago. Its present appearance dates from 1791. Building No. 6 was the **Old Burgrave's House,** the seat of the king's deputy. In the early sixties of the present century it was restored in order to serve as the House of Czechoslovak Children. Jiřská Street terminates with the **Black Tower,** a part of the old Romanesque castle fortifications of the 12th century. Later the tower served as a prison for debtors. By passing through the gateway we can descend to the Old Castle Steps and from there to the Malostranská Station of the underground railway.

On the way back it is possible to turn to the right from Jiřská Street and enter the **Golden Lane** with picturesque little houses forming an environment which is one of Prague's chief tourist attractions. The lane was named after the medieval craftsmen who settled here and built their dwarf-like houses on both sides of the street in such a way that the passage between them was hardly one metre wide. Rudolph II reserved the lane for the 24 marksmen who guarded the castle gate and the prisons. In time, however, the Golden Lane became a refuge for the poor. As their way of life disturbed the nuns at the nearby convent, a part of the lane was abolished. The legend connecting the lane with Rudolph II's alchemists originated in the romantic 19th century.

From the Golden Lane there is a view of **Stag Moat,** which in combination with the fortifications formed the orginal northern defence system of the Castle. Later stags and fallow deer were kept here. — Standing at the eastern end of the Golden Lane is the tower called **Daliborka,** a round defence tower which ended the fortifications built by Vladislav II Jagiello in the late 15th century. It was named after Dalibor of Kozojedy, a knight who was imprisoned in it at the very end of the 15th century because he supported the serfs from the neighbouring estate when they rose up in rebellion. His fate inspired the well-known classic of Czech opera composition B. Smetana to write his opera Dalibor. Standing at the opposite, western end of the Golden Lane is the **White Tower,** also used as a prison. One of those imprisoned in it, for example, was the English alchemist E. Kelley. After the Battle of the White Mountain representatives of the Czech Estates were also held in captivity in the tower as well as imperial officers after lost battles, etc. The last prisoners were imprisoned here in the mid-18th century. Many of their inscriptions and drawings can still be seen on the walls.

We shall now walk back along Jiřská Street to the square náměstí U Sv. Jiří

and alongside St. Vitus's Cathedral turn right into **Vikářská Street.** Building No. 37 is the former Old Deanery.

The neighbouring buildings were adapted for the restoration of the **Vikárka Restaurant**, where the Czech poet and prosaist S. Čech set the plot of his satire about the excursions of a Prague burgher, Mr. Matěj Brouček, to the Moon and to the 15th century. Contrary to the motivation of modern science fiction, the cause of Mr. Brouček's excursions was Czech beer. The present alehouse called Sklípek pana Broučka (The Little Cellar of Mr. Brouček) is situated in the original Gothic cellar. However, not beer, but wine is served here.

Behind Vikárka Street, separated by a parkan, is the tower called **Mihulka,** originally a cannon bastion. Nowadays a permanent museum exposition devoted mainly to the culture of Prague Castle in the 16th and 17th centuries, but also to then contemporary metallurgy, Rudolph II's alchemists, etc. is installed in it. A modern horologe is situated above the entrance.

On this route access can also be gained from the right of the Castle to **Prašný most** (Powder Bridge), which was built as a wooden bridge on stone piers before the mid-16th century. Later it was replaced with a heaped path. In the street U Prašného mostu we pass by the **Riding-school** on the left side. It was built at the end of the 17th century. After being modified in the late fifties of the present century it began to serve as an exhibition hall in which notable exhibitions of creative art are held.

Opposite the Riding-school, on the other side of the street. we come to the beginning of the **Royal Garden.** Ferdinand I started to build it and his successors made it quite unique for its time. A number of exotic trees, fig-trees and even then rare tulips were cultivated in it. There is now a park here which, together with the big **Ball-game Hall**, now serves representative purposes.

From the Riding-school we shall proceed on the right through the street called Mariánské hradby, first of all passing round the so-called **Lion Court**, once the private zoological garden of the sovereign.

After walking approximately 200 m we shall come to the **Summer Palace**, the

Golden Lane
at Prague Castle

gem of the Royal Garden in which small, but noteworthy art exhibitions are held. The summer palace was founded in 1538 and nearly 30 years passed before it was wholly completed. It is perhaps with full right said that it is the purest manifestation of the Italian Renaissance north of the Alps. For example, the original Renaissance copper truss of the summer·palace is unique and its arcaded gallery has rich figural and ornamental relief decoration.

The garden of the summer palace also has preserved Renaissance elements. Standing in its centre is the renowned **Singing Fountain,** the model for which was created by an Italian master. It was cast by the court bell-founder T. Jaroš from 1564—1568. It got its name due to the ringing sound of the drops of water falling into the bowls. — The modern statue called Victory is the work of J. Štursa.

In the interest of a few moments of rest and leisure it should be added that on Saturdays and Sundays in the summer months visitors to Prague Castle can sit in the **southern gardens,** or look down on Prague. The gardens are accessible from the ramp near the square Hradčanské náměstí, from the Third Courtyard and from the bastion by the Black Tower.

12. Vyšehrad

Formerly Vyšehrad was one of Prague's towns, situated on a rock overlooking the River Vltava in a very conspicuous position. The easiest way to reach the Vyšehrad area is from the Palace of Culture (the Gottwaldova Station of the underground railway C). Vyšehrad is the landmark of the southern part of Prague and an interesting observation point. It is unquestionably one of Prague's oldest and most significant monuments, for it was originally the castle site of the Přemyslids, only a little younger than Prague Castle. In the latter half of the 11th century and the first half of the 12th century Vyšehrad served as the residence of the Přemyslid princes. However, the importance of Vyšehrad was marked by a strong decline already after the mid-12th century. Although Charles IV renewed its royal palace, practically all the buildings were demolished during the Hussite revolutionary movement. The site then became a small town of craftsmen, which also disappeared after the mid-17th century, when Vyšehrad was advantageously changed into a Baroque fortress. After the mid-19th century, however, it was abolished.

The old cemetery was later transformed into the so-called **National Cemetery** with the graves of eminent personalities in the spheres of culture, science and politics (for example, the writer K. Čapek, the composer A. Dvořák, the co-creator of the polarograph, J. Heyrovský, winner of the Nobel Prize, and others). A place of honour in the cemetery is occupied by Slavín (the Pantheon), where the graves of outstanding representatives of the Czech nation are buried. Their gravestones form an art gallery (works by J. V. Myslbek, F. Bílek, B. Kafka and others).

Well-preserved monuments at Vyšehrad include **St. Martin's Rotunda,** whose original appearance of the latter half of the 11th century has been preserved. — Another interesting monument is the **Leopold Gate** dating from the time of the Baroque fortifications of Vyšehrad. — The site which was perhaps the centre of the former royal Vyšehrad is now occupied by parks, paradises of peace and quiet. Situated here is a small, but interesting monument of Ancient Slavonic origin, the so-called **Devil's Column**, which perhaps served to determine the solstice. — The original Romanesque **Church of SS. Peter and Paul** now has a Neo-Gothic appearance of the end of the 19th century. It is lent a striking form, visible from far and wide, by its twin towers. There are two ancient monuments in its interiors: a stone Romanesque coffin, most likely that of a prince, and a panel painting of the Madonna of the latter half of the 14th century.

Extensive archeological research and reconstruction work are now being carried out at Vyšehrad.

---

13. From Václavské náměstí through Národní Street to the National Theatre

---

This area plus the street called Na příkopě form the so-called **Golden Cross of Prague**, the city's shopping and social centre. It is a part of the **New Town** (Nové Město), founded in 1348 by Charles IV in order to relieve the older part of the town somewhat of the noise from craftsmen's workshops and bustling commercial activity, because it was rather intended that the sciences should flourish, rich palaces be built and other similar activities carried out here. At the very time of its foundation the New Town was composed of a number of older communities which even contained, for example, small Romanesque churches. With its area the new part of the town was bigger than all three already existing quarters of Prague together. The development of trade naturally involved sacrifices. A number of old monuments was demolished, so that ancient buildings remained only in unique cases.

The centre of the New Town, St. Wenceslas Square (**Václavské náměstí**), is

actually a large boulevard of approximately 750 m in length and 60 m in width. It is accessible from the Můstek and Muzeum Stations of the underground railway. — The square was originally called the Horse Market and it was the biggest market-place of the New Town. A number of events in the most recent history of Czechoslovakia has taken place here. Nowadays there is a continuous zone of greenery in the central part of the square, which serves as a place of rest. In the upper part of Václavské náměstí our attention is attracted in the first place by the **statue of St. Wenceslas** by J. V. Myslbek, variants of which this classic of Czech monumental sculpture created for whole decades — in the years 1884—1924. On the pedestal of the statue there are sculptures of Czech patrons — in the foreground St. Ludmila and St. Procopius and at the rear St. Agnes and St. Adalbert.

The area behind the statue of St. Wenceslas is dominated by the **National Museum** (Národní muzeum), whose ramp affords the most beautiful view of the square. Although this institution itself was founded already in 1818, it was not until the years 1885—1890 that its outstanding building was finally built in Neo-Renaissance style (its site was previously occupied by the so-called Horse Gate). Above all the Museum has valuable collections pertaining to history and natural science. It also has a library with a million volumes, including rare medieval manuscripts. — On the right side of the Museum (when viewing the square from the ramp) stands the modern building of the **Federal Assembly**. Once the stock exchange, it was wholly reconstructed from 1967—1972. Situated beyond it is the **Smetana Theatre** a Neo-Renaissance building from 1886—1888. Originally a German theatre, it has been the second opera house of the National Theatre since 1948. — Further on is the **Main Station** (Hlavní nádraží), an Art Nouveau building from 1901—1909. Its basement part was wholly reconstructed in connection with the building of the underground railway.

Of the most outstanding buildings in Václavské náměstí let us mention (on the right side of the square) the Zlatá husa (Golden Goose) Hotel (No. 7), the Ambassador Hotel (No. 5) and the more recent Koruna Palace (No. 1) with a big popular dining-room and buffet. To be seen on the left side is the Art Nouveau Lucerna Palace (No. 38) with a typical Prague arcade, the Neo-Renaissance building called Wiehl's House (No. 34) of 1896 with a façade painted after sketches by the Czech painter Mikoláš Aleš, and constructivistic Alfa Palace, likewise with an arcade (No. 28).

The point of intersection between Václavské náměstí and 28. října Street and the street Na příkopě forms the crossroad **Můstek** and the little street called **Na Můstku** after the small stone bridge which, in the Middle Ages, ran from the Gall Gate, remains of which can be seen in the courtyard of the Old Town Magistrate's Residence (No. 12, Rytířská Street), over the ditch of the Old Town fortifications to the area now occupied by Václavské náměstí. We can find them along with the remains of a medieval well in the vestibule of the subway affording access to the underground railway station. Můstek is one of the liveliest places of Prague's commercial and social life.

Of the interesting buildings lining the busy shopping street **Na příkopě** let us mention the modern ČKD Prague building (No. 1) with a café on the fifth floor (view of the historical centre of the city); the House of Elegance (No. 4), Prague's oldest department store (1868—1871) with a façade in the style

of the Italian Late Renaissance; the Baroque Sylva-Taroucca Palace (No. 10)., built from 1743—1751 after plans by K. I. Dienzenhofer and with sculptures by I. F. Platzer; the Neo-Romantic façade of the house called U černé růže (At the Black Rose — No. 12), originally Gothic, which in the early 15th century was the place of work of German reformers whose teaching was close to that of Master John Huss. No. 15 on the opposite side is the constructivistic building of the House of Children of 1927—1929. Of the other buildings here we shall mention the Classical Church of the Holy Rood of the early 19th century, the building of the State Bank, whose present appearance dates in 1938, and the building called Moskva (Moscow) with a restaurant providing Russian cuisine and the self-service restaurant Arbat.

When walking from Václavské náměstí in the opposite direction we shall make our way through the short street called **28. října.** From here access can be gained to the Old Town Market from 1893—1894.

An outstanding historical monument on this route is the Gothic **Church of Our Lady of the Snows** standing in the small square Jungmannovo náměstí. It was founded by Charles IV in 1347. Its vault is Late Renaissance. It played an important role in Czech history as a place of assembly of the radical Hussites and the work place of the revolutionary preacher Jan Želivský. Particularly valuable among its interior furnishings is the painting The Annunciation of Our Lady by V. V. Reiner (1724, on the left-hand side altar).

On the opposite side of Jungmannova Street let us notice the Adria Palace (No. 40), built from 1923—1924. On the façade facing **Národní Street** there is a bronze sculpture Adria by the leading Czech sculptor J. Štursa. Situated in the

basement of the building is the Laterna magica, the experimental studio of the National Theatre. — No. 37 is formed by a complex of buildings called Platýz (with a passageway leading to the area called Uhelný trh (Coal Market). Among other things, a sales gallery is now situated in the building. — In building No. 36, built in 1935, there is a shop which sells folk art products. — Standing by the Perštýn cross-road is the House of Children's Book (Albatros) of 1970 and, on the other side, the Máj (May) department store (1975). Further along is the Dunaj Palace (No. 10) from 1928—1930 with the cultural and information centre of the German Democratic Republic, the Art Nouveau building of the former F. Topič publishing house from 1907—1908, now the Czechoslovak Writers' publishing house (No. 9), and St. Ursula's Church with a former convent. The convent was built for the Ursuline Order after a project by M. A. Canevale in the years 1674—1578 and the church originated from 1702—1704 (on the altar

there is a painting The Assumption by P. Brandl).

The **National Theatre** in Prague is considered to be the most beautiful sample of Czech architecture of the latter half of the 19th century. It was built in the style of the North Italian Late Renaissance from public collections — twice in succession. Before its ceremonial opening in 1881 it was severely damaged by fire and in the course of the next two years it was rebuilt. Practically all the leading Czech artists of that time (the so-called National Theatre generation) participated in its decoration. In the main foyer there are paintings by M. Aleš and F. Ženíšek and the curtain was painted by V. Hynais. In the recent past — in 1977 — a costly renovation of the whole building was commenced and up to 1983 three other administrative and social buildings, including the so-called **New Stage,** were erected in its nearest environs.

Across the street, opposite the National Theatre, stands the building of the

The square Václavské náměstí
from the ramp
of the National Museum

Czechoslovak Academy of Sciences, built in Neo-Renaissance style from 1858—1861. — The site of the present **May Day Bridge** (1. máje) connecting the New Town with Smíchov on the opposite bank of the River Vltava was occupied up to the end of the 19th century by a chain bridge named after Franz I, after Charles Bridge the second oldest bridge in Prague from 1839—1841. — Situated in line with the centre of May Day Bridge is **Marksmen's Island** (Střelecký ostrov) the site of the training ground of Prague marksmen up to the mid-15th century. — The other nearby island in the River Vltava, directly opposite the National Theatre, is called **Slavonic Island** (Slovanský ostrov). In the 19th century it was an important centre of then contemporary cultural, social and political life.

---

14. The square Karlovo náměstí and its environs

From the Perštýn cross-road we shall now proceed along Spálená Street leading to Prague's biggest square, **Karlovo náměstí,** with a large park. It was founded in 1348 by Charles IV and was originally called the Cattle Market, because cattle markets really took place there. The square acquired its present appearance in the mid-19th century. Its short northern side is lined by the **New Town Hall,** originally Gothic, founded after the mid-14th century. The so-called Prague Defenestration in 1419, during which the Hussites threw New Town councillors from the windows of the Town Hall, was the signal for the outbreak of the Hussite revolutionary movement. The present appearance of the building dates in the early 20th century. The building is currently undergoing extensive reconstruction and reno-

vation. — There are several memorials and sculptures in the square and its park. A plague column with a statue of St. Joseph of the late 17th century and a bronze memorial to the Hussite preacher Jan Želivský stand in front of the Town Hall. — On the southern side of the square there is another monument in the form of the Renaissance, later Barocized **Faust's House** (No. 40), whose name is connected with the legend about Dr. Faust, who sold his soul to the devil. Already in the 16th century the house was resided in by the English adventurer and alchemist E. Kelley, who promised Rudolph II that he would produce artifical gold. Standing near the house is a bronze group of statues portraying the botanist B. Roezl. On the eastern side of the square (on the corner of Ječná Street) stands the once notable Jesuit **Church of St. Ignatius.** A statue of the saint, a work of 1671, projects from the gable of the church. From Ječná Street we can turn left into Štěpánská Street, where Gothic **St. Stephen's Church** is worth seeing. Its inner furnishings include a valuable Gothic Madonna and three paintings by K. Škréta. In the nearby street called **Na Rybníčku** there is **St. Longinus's Rotunda** of the late 11th century. On the right we shall turn from Ječná Street into the street **Ke Karlovu** with a remarkable building representing the work of K. I. Dienzenhofer — the **summer palace of the Michnas of Vacínov,** also called the Villa Amerika. The **Antonín Dvořák Museum** is now housed in it. In the garden of the building we can find valuable sculptures from M. B. Braun's workshop. — In the neighbouring street called Na bojišti stands the ale-house called U kalicha (At the Chalice) whose constant guest was the chief character from J. Hašek's novel The Good Soldier Švejk. The main connection between the square Karlovo náměstí and the Vltava embankment (Jirásek Embankment and Jirásek Bridge) is **Resslova Street.** Standing on its left side is the Gothic **Church of St. Wenceslas Na Zderaze** of the 14th century and situated almost opposite it is the Baroque **Church of SS. Cyril and Method** (built by the architect K. I. Dienzenhofer from 1730—1736), which now belongs to the orthodox church. The parachutists who assassinated Reinhard Heydrich, the deputy protector in Bohemia, in 1942 hid and died in its crypt.

Not far from Faust's House, on the right side of **Vyšehradská Street,** a complex of modern design and administrative building was built in the years 1970—1974 next to which there stands the **Monastery Na Slovanech** (Emmaus) which was founded by Charles IV for the Slavonic Benedictines and soon became an important cultural centre. Its cloister was decorated with Gothic wall paintings. During an air raid in the spring of 1945 the monastery and the Church of Our Lady were heavily damaged, but they have since been reconstructed. The church was provided with a modern façade which brings the former Gothic gable to mind. The profile of the national cultural monument stands out particularly well when viewed from the Vltava embankment.

Good walkers can prolong the previously described walk through the street Ke Karlovu by continuing round the **Karlov** area (the Gothic building of the Church of Our Lady and Charles the Great, completed as late as 1575) to the **Klement Gottwald Bridge,** Czechoslovakia's biggest prestressed concrete structure (built from 1965—1973). The bridge, which is nearly 500 m long, serves as an arterial road leading to the Prague — Brno — Bratislava motorway and trains of the C line of the underground railway pass through its body. In 1976—1981 the

Palace of Culture, Prague's biggest cultural and social centre, was built on the more distant side of the bridge. With the **Forum Hotel,** built later (1988), it forms one of the landmarks of new Prague and an excellent observation point. From here it is possible to return easily to the centre of the city.

15. Other Prague monuments and places of interest

Bertramka, the newly restored monument recalling W. A. Mozart and F. Dušek and his wife (Smíchov, Mozartova 2), is a suburban homestead of the 17th century where Wolfgang Amadeus Mozart stayed during his sojourns in Prague in 1787 and 1791. His hosts and close friends were the owners of the seat, the composer František Xaver Dušek and his wife Josephine, a well-known singer at her time. The interiors of the building now bring the end of the 18th century to mind and they contain a number of exhibits, among others the piano and clavicembalo on which Mozart gave concerts in Prague. Concerts of classical music now take place in the villa and its garden in the summer season.

Břevnov Monastery (Břevnov, Markétská Street 28), a former Benedictine monastery, founded already in 993 as the first monastery for monks in Bohemia. It gained its present Baroque appearance in the years 1700—1720 after a plan by K. Dienzenhofer. Valuable paintings of about 1740 can be seen in the interiors. K. Dienzenhofer built another outstanding building, St. Margaret's Church (1708—1715), in the immediate environs of the monastery. A few years ago a pre-Romanesque crypt of the early 11th century was discovered below the choir of the church.

The Hvězda (Star) Summer Palace (Liboc) in an enclosure of the same name was built, soon after its foundation, from 1555—1556 in Renaissance style on a ground-plan in the form of a six-sided star. The tragic battle of Czech history, the Battle of the White Mountain (1620), took place near the enclosure. In the 19th century the enclosure was converted into a park. Since 1951 a museum devoted to the leading Czech writer of historical novels Alois Jirásek (1851—1930) and the outstanding painter of Czech history Mikoláš Aleš (1852—1913) has been installed in the summer palace. Nowadays the park is used not only for rest purposes, but also for recreative sport (jogging).

The **Julius Fučík Park of Culture and Rest** (Holešovice) was proclaimed such on the area of a former exhibition ground in 1952. It is the scene of displays, markets, exhibitions and various sports and cultural events and it also has a number of attractions for children. For example, in early spring every year the Matthew Fair traditionally takes place here. The main building in the park is the pseudo-Baroque iron structure of the Congress Palace of 1891 in which, apart from congresses, exhibitions also take place. The modern sports hall, with a seating capacity for 17,000 spectators, serves mainly for winter sports. To be seen in a separate round pavilion is a panoramatic painting The Battle of Lipany (the tragic battle of 1434 in which the radical wing of the Hussite troops was definitely defeated), covering an area of 1,000 sq. m. It is the work of the painter and graphic artist L. Marold (1865—1898). — In the nearby building of the former Trade Fair Palace of 1924—1928 (in the street Dukelských hrdinů), which was severely damaged by fire in 1974, an exhibition of Czech creative art of the 20th century is to be installed.

The **V. I. Lenin Museum** (formerly the People's House, Praha 1, Hybernská Street No. 7) is an Early Baroque building from 1651—1657. In 1907 the Social Democratic Party gained it from its original owners, the Kinský family. In 1912 the building was the scene of the so-called Prague Conference of the Social Democratic Workers' Party of Russia, chaired by V. I. Lenin. The struggle waged for the People's House between the right-wing socialists and the revolutionary workers in 1920 anticipated the founding of the Communist Party of Czechoslovakia in 1921. A museum devoted to V. I. Lenin's heritage is now situated here.

Letná, Letná Park in Prague 7 was founded in the mid-19th century. — It provides a number of opportunities for rest and offers excellent views of historical Prague. An interesting view can be gained from the Praha Expo 58 Restaurant, transferred to the park from the World Exhibition in Brussels, where it reaped exceptional success. Fine views can also been seen from the area from where a group of statues with J. V. Stalin was removed. — An unusual building in Letná Park is the Art Nouveau Hanava Pavilion, built for the Jubilee Exhibition held in Prague in 1891 and later transferred to its present site. — An attraction for many visitors is the National Technical Museum in adjoining Kostelní Street No. 42 whose most interesting exhibits include historic cars and motorcycles as well as astronomic and optical apparatuses and so on.

Olšany Cemeteries (Vinohradská Street) — since 1784 these cemeteries have been Prague's main place of burial. They contain the graves of numerous outstanding personalities of Czech culture and so on. In the Second Municipal Cemetery there is the Burial-ground of Honour containing the graves of soldiers of the Red Army who lost their lives during the liberation of Prague in May 1945.

Stromovka, also called the Royal Enclosure (Bubeneč), was founded already in 1266 during the reign of King Přemysl Otakar II. Since the early 19th century this large, natural park has served as a place of recreation for the citizens of Prague. — Particularly attractive among the buildings in the Royal Enclosure is the Governor's Summer Palace, reconstructed in Neo-Gothic style in 1811. Until 1919 it served as the summer seat of the Czech governor. The department of periodicals of the library of the National Museum is now housed in it.

Troja, a château and a zoological garden. — Troja Château was the first Baroque summer residence to be built in Prague. It was erected in the years 1679—1685 after a plan by J. B. Mathey. Its huge exterior staircase is decorated with a group of statues by the Dresden sculptors J. J. and P. Heermann. Now a gallery. — The nearby zoological garden, founded in 1931, is situated in a very suitable and attractive natural environment. The rare exemplars housed in the zoo include the Przewalski horse, the wild ancestor of the domestic horse. It is a world rarity.

U kaštanu (At the Chestnut Tree), a former inn situated in Bělohorská Street No. 150 which in April 1878 was the scene of the founding congress of the Czechoslovak Social Democratic Workers' Party, which at that time was actually a part of the Austrian Social Democratic Party. It now serves cultural purposes.

Zbraslav, until recently a community lying to the south of Prague on the confluence of the Vltava and Berounka, but now a part of Prague 5. A former monastery complex founded in 1292 by Václav II (its Latin name is Aula regia) is situated here. The last Přemyslids were buried in the Church of Our Lady of the monastery. The monastery ceased to exist during the Hussite revolutionary movement, but it was renewed after the Thirty Years War. It was definitely abolished by Joseph II. Its present appearance dates in the first half of the 18th century and was designed by J. B. Santini and F. M. Kaňka. A collection of Czech sculpture of the 19th and 20th centuries is installed in the former convent. Sculptures are also situated in the courtyard and in the garden.

Žižkov — the **National Monument on Žižkov** Hill, situated in the place where, under the command of Jan Žižka, the Hussites defeated the considerably more numerous crusaders in 1420. The bodily remains of the presidents Klement Gotwald, Antonín Zápotocký and Ludvík Svoboda and leading representatives of the Czechoslovak working-class are housed in it. After the Second World War the Monument to Soviet Soldiers with the Hall of the Soviet Army was built on to it. In 1950 a bronze memorial to Jan Žižka, 9 m high, the work of B. Kafka, was unveiled in front of the monument.

Theatres

The National Theatre (Národní divadlo) (Národní Street 2), the leading theatre — chiefly presents performances of classic Czech and world plays, but also operas
The New Stage (Nová scéna) *of the National Theatre* (Národní Street 4) — presents works of more recent origin
The Tyl Theatre (Tylovo divadlo) (Železná 11) — presents mainly plays
The Smetana Theatre (Smetanovo divadlo) (Vítězného února Street 6), presents opera and ballet performances
The Laterna Magika (Národní Street 40), a great attraction at the World Exhibitions in Brussels and Montreal. It makes polyphonic use of all the technical possibilities offered by theatre, film and music
The Theatre on the Balustrade (Na zábradlí) (Anenské náměstí 5) — presents Czech and world plays and pantomime performances
The Music Theatre in Karlín (Křižíkova 10) — presents classical operettas and musicals

Music

The House of Artists (Dům umělců, Krasnoarmejců 10) — presents mainly serious music, for example, concerts of the Prague Spring Music Festival held every year from 12 May to 3 June
The Smetana Hall of the Municipal House (náměstí Republiky 5) — presents a similar programme
The Palace of Culture (5. května) — presents a very wide range of programmes

Concerts of *chamber music or choral singing* are organized in the Convent of the Blessed Agnes, in St. George's Convent at Prague Castle, in Bethlehem Chapel and in the Hall of Mirrors of the Clementinum. Concerts on the staircase of the National Museum, in the Bedřich Smetana Museum, in the halls of the Municipal Library and other places are also well-known.
A common attraction for foreign visitors are concerts of mainly organ music held in *Prague's biggest churches,* for example, in St. Vitus's Cathedral, in St. James's Church, in Týn Church, in St. Nicholas's Church in the Little Quarter or in the Loretto.
Concerts held on summer evenings *in Prague's gardens* (the Maltese and Wallenstein Gardens in the Little Quarter, the Garden on the Ramparts at Prague Castle and at Bertramka in Smíchov) afford an unusual experience. Programmes of *light entertainment* take place in the big hall of Lucerna Palace (Štěpánská Street 61), of jazz music in Reduta (Národní Street 20) and so on.

Galleries and exhibition halls

Below are listed several important galleries in the vicinity of Prague Castle:
Šternberk Palace (Hradčanské náměstí 15) — collections of old and modern European art and French art of the 19th and 20th centuries
The Convent of St. George (Prague Castle) — a collection of old Czech art
The Picture Gallery of Prague Castle (Second Courtyard) — a collection of selected works forming a part of the royal collection of paintings

The Convent of the Blessed Agnes (Anežská Street) — an exposition of Czech painting of the 19th century
The Trade Fair Palace (třída Dukelských hrdinů) — a collection of modern Czech art to be opened in 1990
Especially valuable *monothematic exhibitions* can be seen in the Wallenstein Riding-school (Valdštejnská 4), in the Riding-school of Prague Castle, in the Royal Summer Palace, in the Arts and Crafts Museum in the square náměstí Krasnoarmejců, in the U hybernů exhibition hall (náměstí Republiky 4) and other places.

Museums

The National Museum (třída Vítězného února 74) with the following expositions: zoology, mineralogy, paleontology, archeology and others
Monuments of the National Past (Prague Castle, Lobkovic Palace)
The Náprstek Museum of Asian, African and American Cultures (Betlémské náměstí 1)
The Ethnographical Museum (Petřínské sady 98, the Kinský Villa) with collections from the whole territory of the Czechoslovak Socialist Republic
The Museum of Physical Culture and Sport (Újezd 40) with a permanent exposition
The Museum of Czech Music (Novotného lávka 1) with the Bedřich Smetana exposition; the Antonín Dvořák exposition (Ke Karlovu 20 — Villa Amerika); the W. A. Mozart Memorial at the Bertramka Villa (Mozartova 169); an exposition of musical instruments (Lázeňská 2), one of the most valuable European collections
The National Technical Museum (Kostelní 42) with a particularly big exposition of historic road vehicles, but also of aircraft, locomotives, astronomical historic apparatuses, exhibits representing time-measuring technology and so on
The Museum of National Literature (Strahovské nádvoří 132)
The State Jewish Museum (Jáchymova 3) with unique collections installed in several buildings in the former Jewish Town
The Arts and Crafts Museum (17. listopadu 2) with collections of glass, ceramics, china and so on
The Museum of Military History (Hradčanské náměstí 2) with a historical exposition
The V. I. Lenin Museum (Hybernská 7)
The Klement Gottwald Museum (Rytířská 29)

Restaurants

The Municipal House (náměstí Republiky), a restaurant in an Art Nouveau interior
Staročeská rychta (The Old Czech Magistrate's House — Václavské náměstí 7), specialities of old Czech cuisine
Paříž (U Obecního domu)
Moskva (Na příkopě 29), Russian cuisine
Chinese Restaurant (Vodičkova 19)
Zlatá Praha (náměstí Curieových) — an exclusive restaurant on the 8th floor of the Intercontinental Hotel
Valdštejnská hospoda (Tomášská 16)
Vikárka (in the area of Prague Castle)
U kalicha (At the Chalice — Na bojišti 12), typical for its atmosphere of J. Hašek's novel The Good Soldier Švejk

Ale-houses

U dvou koček (At the Two Cats —
Uhelný trh 10)
U Fleků (At the Fleks — Křemencova 11)
U medvídků (At the Little Bears — Na
Perštýně 7)
U Pinkasů (At the Pinkases — Jungman-
novo náměstí 15)
U Schnellů (At the Schnells — To-
mášská 2)
U supa (At the Vulture — Celetná 22)
U svatého Tomáše (At St. Thomas's —
Letenská 12)

Wine Taverns

U pavouka (At the Spider — Celetná 17)
U zelené žáby (At the Green Frog —
U radnice 8)
U zlaté konvice (At the Golden Jug —
Melantrichova 20)
Viola (Národní 7) — with a programme
of new and classical poetry and the like
Klášterní vinárna (The Monastery Wine
Tavern — Národní třída 8)
U Malířů (At the Painters' — Maltézské
náměstí 11)
U mecenáše (At the Patron's — Malo-
stranské náměstí 10)
U tří housliček (At the Three Little Fid-
dles — Nerudova 12)
U labutí (At the Swan — Hradčanské
náměstí 11)
Sklípek pana Broučka (Mr. Brouček's
Cellar — in the area of Prague Castle,
Vikářská Street)
Lobkovická vinárna (The Lobkovic Wine
Tavern — Vlašská 17)

Hotels (selection, marked according to price categories)

Alcron, A* de luxe, Štěpánská 40
Ambassador, A*, Václavské náměstí 5
Atlantic, B, Na Poříčí 9
Belveder, B*, Obránců míru 19
Beránek, B*, Bělehradská 110
Družba, B*, Václavské náměstí 16
Esplanade, A*, Washingtonova 19
Evropa, B*, Václavské náměstí 25
Flora, B*, Vinohradská 121
Forum, Kongresová
Intercontinental, A* de luxe, náměstí
Curieových
International, A*, náměstí Družby 1
Jalta, A* de luxe + A* a B*, Václavské
náměstí 45
Merkur, B, Těšnov 9
Meteor, B, Hybernská 6
Olympic, A*a *Garni* B*, Invalidovna
Palace, A*, Panská 12
Panorama, A*, Milevská 7
Parkhotel, A*, Veletržní 20
Paříž, B, U Obecního domu 1
Savoy, B, Keplerova 6
Tatran, B*, Václavské náměstí 22
Albatros Botel, B*, nábřeží Ludvíka Svo-
body
Admiral Botel, B*, Hořejší nábřeží

Car Camps (according to direction of approach)

Ústí na Labem and Teplice: Dolní Cha-
bry camping-site, Obslužná; Na Vla-
chovce chalet camp, A, třída Rudé armády 217
Plzeň, Karlovy Vary, Chomutov: Cara-
vancamp, A, Plzeňská; Sportcamp,
V podhájí; TJ Aritma camping site, Nad
lávkou 3 (near the Džbán dam lake)
Mladá Boleslav, Poděbrady, Kolín: Cara-
van, A, Kbely, Mladoboleslavská 72;
Xavercamp, A, Horní Počernice,

Božanovská; Sokol Dolní Počernice, A, Nad rybníkem

Brno — Prague motorway: Kotva Braník, A, U ledáren 55

The underground railway

At present Prague's underground railway has three lines of a total length of 27.8 km:

Line A: Leninova — Hradčanská — Malostranská — Staroměstská — Můstek (forms a junction with line B) — Muzeum (forms a junction with line C) — Náměstí Míru — Jiřího z Poděbrad — Flora — Želivského — Strašnická. Line A is 8.5 km long.

Line B: Sokolovská (forms a junction with line C) — Náměstí Republiky — Můstek (forms a junction with line A) — Národní — Karlovo náměstí — Moskevská — Smíchovské nádraží. Line B is 5 km long.

Line C: Fučíkova — Vltavská — Sokolovská (forms a junction with line B) —

Hlavní nádraží — Muzeum (forms a junction with line A) — I. P. Pavlova — Gottwaldova — Pražského povstání — Mládežnická — Budějovická — Kačerov — Primátora Vacka — Budovatelů — Družby — Kosmonautů. Line C is 14.3 km long.

ENVIRONS

Flowing to Prague through a deeply cut valley is the River Vltava on which there are several dams. **Slapy dam** retains a 40 km long lake which is used for recreation purposes. From the left the Berounka empties into the Vltava after flowing through the forested territory of the **Křivoklát** protected landscape region. Below Beroun it cuts its way through the limestone rocks of the **Bohemian Karst** (situated nearby are the Koněprusy stalagmite and stalactite caves). The Berounka also flows in the immediate vicinity of two of Bohemia's

---

Typical Prague
ale-house — U Fleků

most beautiful castles — **Karlštejn** and **Křivoklát**. The right tributary of the Vltava is the Sázava whose deep, forested valley is a popular place of recreation among the inhabitants of Prague. The attractive landscape extends an invitation for excursions and their destination can also be **Český Šternberk** Castle and the monastery at **Sázava** with a museum of Old Slavonic literature. Situated to the south of the Sázava valley is **Konopiště** Château, another popular tourist destination.

Spreading out to the north of Prague is the most fertile part of Bohemia — the lowlands of the Elbe. Here the Vltava flows below **Mělník** Château with the Elbe, standing on which are the ancient towns of Nymburk and Kolín and Poděbrady spa. South of the Elbe lies the town of **Kutná Hora**, the richest in monuments after Prague. The chief industrial centre of Central Bohemia is Kladno, in whose vicinity lies **Lidice**, a village exterminated by the German Nazis during the Second World War.

CZECHOSLOVAKIA

A – Z

General view
of the centre
of the town of Tábor

romantically grouped **sandstone rocks** in East Bohemia forming rock towns of an area of 25 sq. km. The more northerly situated Adršpach Rocks are separated from the Teplice Rocks by the Wolf's Gorge (Vlčí rokle). The rock towns originated as the result of the uneven process of erosion in the sandstone rocks formed by deposits of the sea which once reached this locality from the north. The region is a nature preserve to which tourist paths lead from Teplice nad Metují and Dolní Adršpach.

BANSKÁ BYSTRICA   L 3—4

a regional town (pop. 78,000) and the administrative, industrial and cultural centre of the Central Slovak region. It is picturesquely situated in the immediate vicinity of the Kremnica Hills, the Big Fatra and the Low Tatras. Wood-working, engineering and textile industries, cement works and others. Theatre, symphony orchestra and universities. In 1255 Banská Bystrica became a free royal mining town, silver having been mined here and from the 14th — 16th century especially copper (on the territory of the present community of Špania Dolina), which was exported to the whole of Europe. In 1525 a big uprising of the miners took place and the miners occupied the town for a time. In the late 18th century and especially in the mid-19th century the town was the centre of the Slovak national movement. In 1850 the first Slovak gymnasium (secondary school) was founded here. The workers' movement and the endeavours of the Communist Party of Czechoslovakia to raise Slovakia from the economic, so-

cial and cultural aspects gained in strength especially after the First World War. On 29 August, 1944 the **Slovak National Uprising** broke out and Banská Bystrica was for two months the seat of the Slovak National Council and political and military representatives of the resistance movement and broadcasts were transmitted from a free transmitter in the town. Nazi units occupied the town on 27 October, 1944; it was liberated by Soviet troops on 26 March, 1945. The historical core of Banská Bystrica is a **historical town reserve** with a striking landmark in the form of a former medieval castle with a clock-tower situated in its neighbourhood. The Late Gothic Matejov dom (i. e., the house of King Matthias), the Romanesque-Gothic parish church, a Gothic Slovak church, the former Town Hall (the so-called Praetorium, now a gallery), the Parish, the Miners and the Pisárská Bastion and a tower with a barbican are parts of the castle complex. In the square there is a number of Gothico-Renaissance and Renaissance burghers' houses with graffito decoration and courtyards with arcaded galleries. So-called Thurz's

Adršpašsko-teplické skály

The Adršpach Rocks

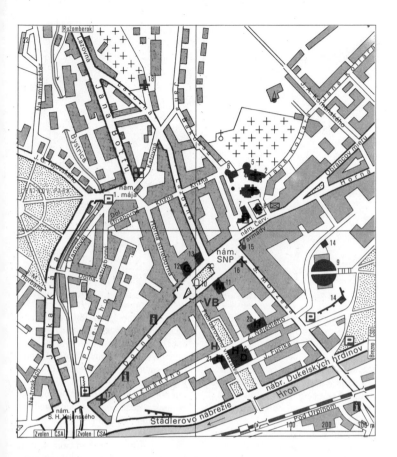

BANSKÁ BYSTRICA

1. Parish Church (b). **2.** Pisárska Bastion (b). **3.** Slovak Church (b). **4.** Matejov dom (b). **5.** Hornická (Miners') Bastion (b). **6.** Farní (Parish) Bastion (b). **7.** Castle tower with barbican (b). **8.** Former Town Hall (now the Regional Gallery) (b). — Buildings Nos. 1—8 form the complex of the town castle. **9.** Monument and museum of the Slovak National Uprising (d) **10.** Red Army memorial (d). — **11.** Thurz's House (Central Slovak Ethnographical Museum) (d). **12.** Benický's House (House of Art) (c). **13.** Bishop's palace (c). **14.** Bastions of the town fortifications (d). **15.** Clock tower (d). **16.** Jesuit church (d). **17.** Hospital Church of St. Elizabeth (c). **18.** Evangelic church (a). **15.** National House (hotel and J. G. Tajovský Theatre) (d). **20.** Urpín Hotel (d). **21.** Junior Hotel (d). **22.** Amphitheatre (a).

House (now the Central Slovak Museum — history, natural history) and Benický's House are the most valuable of them.

The town is dominated by the modern **Monument and Museum of the Slovak National Uprising** with expositions documenting the anti-fascist movement and displays of arms and military equipment. Audiovisual programmes. In the square there is a memorial to the Red Army. Numerous memorial tablets from the time of the uprising. The Workers' House with the Klement Gottwald memorial hall (Klement Gottwald worked here from 1921—1922) and the Free Slovak Transmitter memorial hall.

BANSKÁ ŠTIAVNICA   K 4

a town on the slopes of the Štiavnické Hills. At the turn of the 12th and 13th centuries a **mining town** originated near the rich deposits of silver and gold ores and soon attained European im-

portance. In the 17th—18th century it headed world development in the sphere of mining technology: in 1627 gunpowder was used for the first time in mines, in 1763 the Academy of Mining originated here and in 1786 the first international society of mining and metallurgical specialists was founded here. In the latter half of the 18th century the population of the town numbered 25,000, making it the third biggest town in Hungary. In the 19th century mining suffered a gradual decline, but it has now been renewed (non-ferrous metals).

A **historical town reserve,** nearly 350 historical monuments, including in particular Starý zámok (Old Château), a Renaissance fortress against the Turks of 1546—1559, converted from an original Romanesque-Gothic church, and Nový zámok (New Château), a Renaissance fortress from 1564—1571. St. Catherine' s Church of Late Gothic origin with wall paintings from the turn of the 15th and 16th centuries. The so-

Banska
Štiavnica

The square námestie
Slovenského národného povstania
at Banská Bystrica

130

called Klopačka, a Baroque towered building of 1681 from which the miners were called to work by the sound of blows made by an oak hammer on a wooden panel. In the square Trojičné námestie there is a number of Gothic and Renaissance burghers' houses. The **Slovak Mining Museum** is housed in the old Château and an exposition documenting the battles waged against the Turks in Slovakia can be seen in the New Château. In the Renaissance building of the former mining court (Berggericht) entrance to a mine can be gained (the original adit is 76 m long). Near Lake Klinger there are an open-air mining museum covering an area of 20 hectares, head frames and the Bartholomew adit leading underground.
Environs: the protected landscape of the **Štiavnické Hills.** — 9 km S **Počúvalské Lake,** bathing and camping. — 4 km SE **Antol,** a Baroque-Classical château of 1744. It stands on the edge of a large forest park and museum expositions devoted to forestry, woodworking and hunting are installed in its interiors.

St. Catherine's Church
and Town Hall
at Banská Štiavnica

Town Hall and church
in the square
at Bardejov

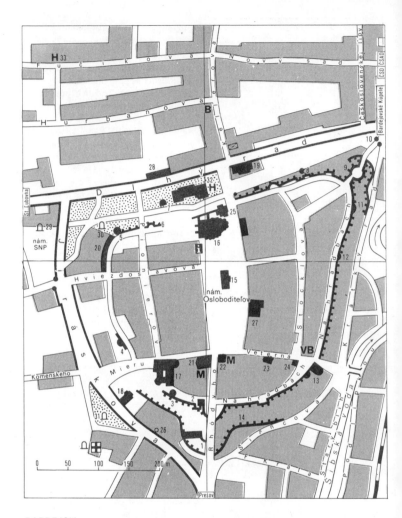

BARDEJOV

1. Gate (with barbican and bridge) (c). 2. Prašná Bastion (c). 3. Kláštorná (Františkanská) Bastion (c). 4. Školská Bastion (c). 5. Nárožná Bastion (a).
6. Semicircular bastion (a). 7. Archívní (northern) Bastion (a). 8. Renaissance bastion (b). 9. Stone bridge (b). 10. Gate (easter barbican) (b). 11. Červená Bastion (b).
12. Velká Bastion (b). 13. Hrubá and Malá Bastions (d). 14. Moat (d). 15. Old Town Hall (Šariš Museum) (d). 16. Parish Church of St. Egidius (b). 17. Former Franciscan monastery with church (c). 18. Greek-Catholic church (c). 19. Evangelic church (b).
20. Salt-house (a). 21. Gründlovský House (museum) (c). 22. Šariš Museum (history of the workers' movement) (d). 23. Former house of the town executioner (d).
24. Former town prison (d). 25. Humanistic school (b). 26. Gothic lamp standard (c).
27. Former town house (Municipal National Committee) (d). 28. District National Committee (a). 29. Memorial Gratitude and Friendship (a). 30. Georg Winter memorial (a). 31. Alois Jirásek memorial (c). 32. Dukla Hotel (a—b). 33. Topľa Hotel (a).

a district town (pop. 28,000) in the valley of the Topľa. Footwear, leather, woodworking, engineering and other industries. A town from the 14th century, characterized in the 15th and 16th centuries by a period of economic and cultural flourish (linen production, two printing works and a gymnasium).
The centre of the town is now a **historical town reserve** representing the best-preserved medieval town complex in Slovakia. Its oblong square is surrounded by Gothic and Renaissance houses, most of which were later modified. Standing in the square is the Gothic parish Church of St. Egidius of the mid-15th century with 11 Gothic folding altars. In the centre of the square stands the former Gothico-Renaissance Old **Town Hall** from 1505—1511, now serving as the Šariš Museum (collection of icons, the biggest in Slovakia).
A number of old burghers' houses can also be seen in Rhodyho, Veterná and Stöcklova Streets. The historical core is surrounded by very well-preserved fortifications of the 14th—15th century with a number of bastions and 2 gates.
Environs: 6 km N **Bardejovské Kúpele** spa, where diseases of the alimentary tract and metabolic diseases are treated. New, modern construction (balneotherapy with a policlinic and an indoor swimming-pool). Museum of folk architecture (some 30 exhibits). — Small **wooden churches** in the communities of Hervartov (8 km SW). Krivé (9 km W), Lukov (14 km W) and others.

a town and peat spa. Ceramics industry with a specialized school of European repute. — On a high promontory overlooking the River Lužnice stands a castle of the 12th century, rebuilt in the Late Gothic, and a Renaissance château enlarged in the latter half of the 16th century. — Monastery church with a valuable Gothic diamond vault. — *Environs:* the valley of the River **Lužnice** (used by watermen). — 5 km N the ruins of Dobronice Castle. — 2 km S the romantic valley called Židova strouha.

a district town (pop. 24,000) on the River Berounka in the Bohemian Karst. — Two Gothic **town gates** (the Plzeň and the Prague Gate) and remains of the town's fortifications of the early 14th century have been preserved in the historical core of the town.
Environs: starting point for the **Bohemian Karst** protected landscape region. — 5 km S the **Koněprusy** stalagmite and stalactite Caves, the biggest Czech cave system where the bones of primeval animals and a coiners' workshop have been found. — 9 km SE Karlštejn Castle. — 15 km SW **Točník** Castle (the royal palace of the 15th century is accessible) and Žebrák Castle (in ruins).

The — see Moravskoslezské Beskydy

a district town (pop. 20,000) on the River Svitava. Centre of the **iron industry** whose iron production history dates back to the Middle Ages. Turbine production. The building of the reconstructed château houses the Museum of the Moravian Karst with expositions documenting the local artistic cast iron tradition.

Environs: the **Moravian Karst,** the starting point for an excursion to which is Skalní Mlýn (3 km E) with an information centre.

BLATNÁ   C 3

a town lying in a district of ponds. Traditional rose cultivation, big plantations. A **château,** originally a water castle, re-Gothicized in the 19th century, with valuable interiors, a park and an enclosure. Valuable late Gothic church.
Environs: 2 km NE **Paštiky,** a Baroque church (K. I. Dienzenhofer 1747—53). — 10 km W **Lnáře,** Baroque château, monastery and monastery church.

BOJNICE   K 3

a spa and château on the upper stream of the River Nitra. Springs with water of a temperature of up to 47 °C gush forth in several places here. Their waters are trapped in 5 pools. In particular rheumatism and nervous diseases are treated here. — An originally Gothic **castle** rebuilt in the style of French romantic castles from 1899—1909. A museum is installed in the building. A sightseeing tour includes a visit to the stalagmite and stalactite caves called Prepoštské Caves below the château.

BOUZOV   G 2

a **castle** 25 km NW of Olomouc, founded after 1300, rebuilt in the late 19th century in the Romantic Gothic for the Order of German Knights. Rich collections.
Environs: 4 km SE the community of **Javoříčko** which was burned by the Nazis on 5 May, 1945; 38 men were shot at the same time. — 5 km S the big stalagmite and stalactite **Javoříčko Caves** hollowed out by an underground river. Total length of the system 5 km; the biggest cave is called The House of Giants (18 m high).

BRANDÝS NAD LABEM —   D 2
STARÁ BOLESLAV

a double town (pop. 16,000) on both banks of the River Elbe. A Přemyslid castle stood in historically important

Blatná

Bojnice
Château

Stará Boleslav already in the early 10th century. The Romanesque crypt of St. Wenceslas's Church of 1046 now forms a part of a Baroque church. Originally it was a part of the basilica in front of whose entrance Prince Václav (St. Wenceslas), the fourth historically proved Czech ruler, was, according to a legend, murdered in 929. Also standing here is a Gothic town gate, rebuilt in the Baroque, and a museum with a former church of pilgrimage of the 17th century. — At Brandýs nad Labem there is a Renaissance château.

---

the capital of the federative Slovak Socialist Republic and the West Slovak region (pop. 435,000) and the second biggest city in the Czechoslovak Socialist Republic. The seat of central Slovak political, state and economic organs. The city spreads out on both banks of the Danube, which helps to determine its character to a great extent. The nearness of border crossings to Vienna and Budapest underline its importance as a transport cross-road. Practically one sixth of all Slovak **industry** (engineering, metallurgical, chemical and rubber industries) is concentrated in it. Extensive housing estate construction, now especially on the right bank of the Danube, at Petržalka.

Bratislava is the most important Slovak centre of scientific research and the seat of the Slovak Academy of Sciences and many scientific institutions and research institutes. The city has seven universities, six theatres, a number of museums and several exihibition halls. The historical core of the city, the area of Bratislava Castle and Podhradie (Outer Bailey), form a **historical town reserve**.

The territory of the present city was settled already from the mid-10th century before our era. In the 2nd — 1st century before our era the Celts minted coins here and later, in the 1st — 4th century of our era, the Romans had military fortresses and camps here. The oldest Slav monuments date in the 9th century, in the time of the Great Moravian Empire. Bratislava was granted town privileges in 1291. In 1465 the first university on Slovak territory was founded in Bratislava for the whole of Upper Hungary — the Academia Istropolitana. In the years 1536—1784 Bratislava was the capital of Hungary. It enjoyed its greatest importance during the reign of Maria Theresa (1740—1780). From the 18th century Bratislava was an important centre of the Slovak national liberation and cultural endeavours. Since the origin of the Czechoslovak Republic in 1918 its significance as the centre of Slovak political, economic and cultural life has continually grown.

We shall begin our *sightseeing* tour of Bratislava in the very centre of the city, by the only preserved city gate, **Michalská**. In front of the gate, in the direction of the square Hurbanovo, we can see remainders of the old defence walls of the town and a stone bridge with a fortification ditch. The gate was built in the 14th century. Its original Gothic tower was lower than the present one, which gained its appearance as the result of a Renaissance reconstruction caried out in the early 16th century. Its Baroque roofing is from the mid-18th century. An exposition of medieval arms and town fortifications is installed in the tower of the gate. The gate was protected from cannon fire by barbicans. From the 17th century dwelling-houses directly linked up with them. Among others, they include Bratislava's oldest pharmacy called The Red Crab, in which a **pharmaceutical museum** is now in-

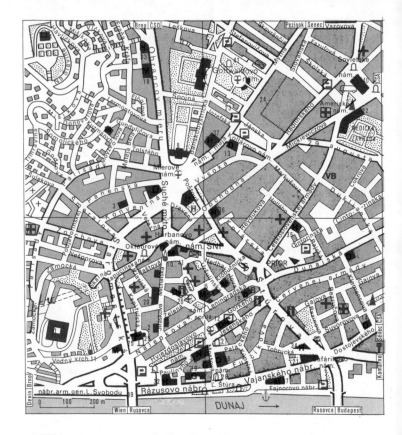

BRATISLAVA

1. Castle (c). 2. Former Academia Istropolitana — Academy of Fine Arts (c).
3. Former Evangelic Lyceum (a). 4. Slavín (a). 5. Old Town Hall (Municipal Museum)
(c). 6. Primatial palace. 7. Former archbishop's summer palace (seat of the
presidium of the government of the Slovak Socialist Republic) (b). 8. Grassalkowich
Palace (a). 9. House At the Good Shephherd's (c). 10. Michalská Gate (c).
11. Sigismond Gate (c). 12. Slovak National Theatre (opera) (d). — 13. New Stage
(b). 14. Small Stage (d). 15. P. Országh Hviezdoslav Theatre (d). 16. Reduta Theatre
(d). 17. Slovak National Museum (d). 18. V. I. Lenin Museum (a). 19. Slovak National
Gallery (c). 20. Former palace of the Hungarian Chamber (University Library) (c).
21. J. Amos Komenský University (d). 22. Aspremont Palace (medical faculty) (b).
23. Slovak Technical University (b). 24. Engineering faculty (b). 25. St. Martin's
Cathedral (c). 26. Roland's Fountain (c). 27. Statue Victory (d). 28. Ľ. Štúr memorial
(d). 29. A. Bernolák memorial (c). 30. Országh Hviezdoslav memorial (c).
31. Franciscan church (c). 32. Carlton Hotel (c). 33. Devín Hotel (c). 34. Krym Hotel
(d). 35. Kyjev Hotel (d). 36. Palace Hotel (b). 37. Tatra Hotel (b). 38. Manderla
skyscraper (d). 39. Slovak National Uprising Bridge (c). 40. Avión (b).

stalled (No. 24), and the city's narrowest house (No. 10). In the street of the same name, i.e., **Michalská Street**, there is a small Gothic chapel of 1311, consecrated to St. Catherine, which now has a Classical façade. Opposite it is a Renaissance yeoman's house (curia) of 1648 (No. 7). In 1704 the pioneer of hydraulics, J. A. Segner (d. 1777 in Halle), was born here. Further on stands the Baroque palace of the former **Hungarian Royal Chamber** of 1753—1756 (No. 1). In 1802—1848 the Diet of the Hungarian Estates assembled in it. After adaptations of the fifties, it now serves as the University Library. In the palace garden there is a small music pavilion in which nine-year-old Ferenc Liszt gave concerts.

Lying to the east of Michalská Gate is the attractive **square námestie Slovenského národného povstania,** whose outstanding feature is a group of statues unveiled to mark the 30th anniversary of this event, the most important in modern Slovak history.

To the west of the gate is the **square Októbrové námestie** which acquired its appearance in the 18th century. Particularly interesting here is the oval ground-plan of the Baroque **Church of the Holy Trinity** from 1717—1727, similarly as the painting of illusive architecture on the ceiling of the dome of the nave and on the lunette vault of the presbytery. After 1848 the present building of the Slovak National Council served as an administrative building and before that a monastery stood here. The centre of the square is occupied by a Baroque **plague column** of 1723, erected after the plague epidemic of 1712—1713. Behind the column stands a Capuchin church of 1707—1711. From the square there is an ever fresh view of Bratislava Castle. From the square Októbrové námestie we can continue through Kapucínská Street on the left to **Klariská Street** with the former **Gothic church and convent of the Poor Clares** of the latter half of the 14th century. Its Gothic stone steeple is of the early 15th century. It is interesting that it is built on a peripheral wall and not on the main nave of the church. The principles of the Order prohibited churches to be built with steeples.

Continuing on our way, we come to **Ji-**

General view
of the historical core
of Bratislava

ráskova Street in which, as No. 3, there stand the buildings of the Bratislava and Slovak humanistic university — the Academia Istropolitana — founded by King Matthias Corvin in 1465. The buildings were constructed in Late Gothic style with Renaissance elements. The university had four faculties. Its development was interrupted by the death of its founder in 1490. (The Theatre Faculty of the Academy of Fine Arts is now situated in its interiors.) Also located in this street are the former palaces of Count Erdödy — Rococo (No. 1), Count Zichy — Classical (No. 9) and Count Pálffy — Baroque (No. 10 — among others, W. A. Mozart also performed here as a child).

Several palaces of the former nobility are also to be seen in Nálepkova Street, which crosses Jiráskova Street. Building No. 13 was the Baroque palace of Count Eszterházy and building No. 15 the Rococo palace of the Ballas family. Building No. 19 was the palace of the Pálffy family. After their restoration expositions of the Gallery of the City of Bratislava were installed in them. The Baroque palace bearing No. 27 belonged to the Kelgevich family (concerts were given here by, for example, L. van Beethoven) and the palace with No. 33 belonged to Count Csáky. — On the façade of house No. 28 the remains of a former city gate can be seen and next to it there are the remains of the city walls.

Nálepkova Street ends in the small square námestie Rudnayovo. One of Bratislava's noteworthiest church monuments, St. Martin's Cathedral, is situated here. Its construction was started in the early 14th century on the site of an older Romanesque church. The cathedral has three naves of equal height. Its 85 m high steeple formerly served defence purposes. On its summit there is a copy of the royal crown of St. Stephen. The additions to the cathedral date in the 15th — 18th century; in the 19th century it was re-Gothicized. St. Martin's Cathedral has exceptionally valuable interior decorations: a bronze font of 1403, an epitaph of 1470, a Baroque lead equestrian statue of St. Martin by G. R. Donner, etc. The decoration of the altar is Neo-Gothic. Nine Hungarian kings and eight queens were crowned in the cathedral. A list of them can be seen by the side of the presbytery. — In the square we can finally see three statues: a Baroque one of the sculptor Georg Rafael Donner, who lived and worked in Bratislava for ten years, of Ferenc Liszt and of Anton Bernolák (1762—1813), who was the first to try to codify a literary Slovak language. — Opposite the cathedral, in the direction of the castle hill, but beyond the bustle of the transport artery, we can see Bratislava's most beautiful Rococo house. It is called At the Good Shepherd's and is situated in Židovská Street (No. 1). Nowadays a small historical exposition of clocks is installed in it. From Nálepkova Street we shall continue in south-easterly direction, to the Danube, to the square Hviezdoslavovo námestie where the most notable building of the Slovak National Theatre from 1884—1886 stands. In front of the theatre we can see Ganymede's s Fountain of 1888. In the park stands a memorial to the outstanding Slovak poet Pavol Országh Hviezdoslav (1849—1921) and also one to National Artist Andrej Bagar (1900—1966), a leading personality in the sphere of Slovak theatre. From the theatre let us now make our way through the street called Rybárská brána to the square námestie 4. apríla, once the main square of old Bratislava where markets, popular assemblies — and also executions — took place. Standing in the centre of the square is Roland's Fountain of 1572. The noteworthiest and also the most valuable building is the **Old Town Hall,** a Gothic building of the 14th—15th century, adapted to serve public purposes. Further adaptations were necessitated by a fire which occurred in 1733, e.g., a Baroque reconstruction of the tower, in which fanfare concerts of classical music take place in summer. By passing through the passageway with a Gothic portal we shall find ourselves in the courtyard with two Renaissance loggias of 1581. Unfortunately, only the northern one has been preserved in its original likeness. Here, too, concerts and performances by amateur dramatic groups take place in the summer months. The coffered ceilings in the Hall of Councillors of 1577 in the Old Town Hall have been preserved and the Courtroom has rich stucco decoration and frescoes of 1695. Most of the interiors of the building contain expositions of the Municipal Museum. Standing next to the Old Town Hall is a Late Renaissance **Jesuit church** from 1636—1638 with valuable Baroque furnishings. In front of the church there is a **Marian column** of 1675. — The square is lined with old houses and palaces. No. 2 is an originally Gothic house of the mid-15th century and the Baroque palace at No. 4 is also of Gothic origin. House No. 5 is of Art Nouveau origin, No. 7 was the Rococo palace of Count Eszterházy, etc. The next building, No. 10, houses the wine tavern Velkí Františkáni, mentioned for the first time in 1347.

From here our walk through Bratislava continues in northerly direction to the **square Dibrovovo námestie.** Let us take note of the Gothic **Franciscan church and monastery.** The church is actually the oldest preserved building in the historical core of the town. It was consecrated in 1297. The monastery was built in the course of the 14th and 15th centuries and rebuilt in the 18th

century. Near the church is the two-storeyed **Gothic Chapel** of St. John the Evangelist of the latter half of the 14th century, one of the most beautiful Gothic buildings in Slovakia. This burial chapel belonged to the family of the magistrate Jakob — like the house which was later converted into the Old Town Hall. Opposite the church is Bratislava's most beautiful palace of all, the Rococo **Mirbach Palace** from 1768—1770 (No. 11). After undergoing a costly renovation, its interiors now serve as exhibition halls of the Municipal Gallery.

From the square Dibrovovo námestie we shall continue through Pugačevova and Uršulínská Streets to the **square Primaciálne námestie** on whose left side stands the notable architectonic monument in the form of the **Primatial Palace.** This building from 1777—1781, built in the style of French Classicism, originally served as the winter seat of the Bishop of Esztergom. It inscribed itself in history due to the fact that the so-called Bratislava Peace of 1805 be-

Rococo house
At the Good Shepherd's
in Bratislava

tween Napoleon and the Austrian Emperor Franz I was signed in it. From 1903 it was used as the Town Hall.

From the square Primaciálne námestie let us now make our way to **Klobučnícka Street** where, in the court of house No. 2, the outstanding Baroque composer and pianist Ján Nepomuk Hummel (1778–1837, museum) was born. He is buried in Weimar.

The final part of our walk takes us to the square námestie Slovenského národného povstania, or perhaps from here back to Michalská Street, from where we set out on our sightseeing tour. The appearance of historical Bratislava is also contributed to by the **Evangelic Lyceum,** situated in Konventní Street (in houses Nos. 13 and 15), north-west of the gate Michalská brána. It was of exceptional importance for the Slovak national revival, especially at the time when Ľudovít Štúr, its leading personality, came here, i.e., after 1829. The building is now a national cultural monument. — Grassalkovich Palace, situated nearby in the square Mierové námestie, is a Rococo building of 1765 ranking among the summer palaces built for members of the nobility in the latter half of the 18th century outside the historical core of the city. The more northerly situated **summer palace of the archbishop** from 1761–1765 in the square Gottwaldovo námestie, now the seat of the presidium of the government of the Slovak Socialist Republic and other organs, belongs to it. Thirdly, here we can see the former **palace of Count Aspremonte** which now serves as the seat of the dean of the medical faculty of Komenský University (in the street Československej armády 52).

When making a sightseeing tour of Bratislava we must naturally devote attention to the city's biggest monument — **Bratislava Castle** — on whose site remainders of the oldest settlement of the town have been excavated. In the 12th century a Romanesque stone castle stood here which in the years 1431–1434 was converted into a Gothic fortress and provided with two gates and its present square ground-plan. In the years 1552–1570 it was reconstructed to serve as a base against the Turks and in the period of 1635–1646 it acquired a third storey and four corner towers. The last reconstruction of the castle was carried out on the order of Maria Theresa from 1751–1766, when the building became a representative royal seat. When central offices were shifted to Budapest or Vienna the castle lost its importance and, furthermore, in 1811 it was severely damaged by fire. It was not until the post-war period that, from 1953, its Theresian appearance was restored to it. Nowadays the castle is the seat of the Slovak National Council; the historical expositions of the Slovak National Museum are installed in it and a concert hall, etc. are situated here. The eastern terraces afford a good **view** of the city and its wide environs. Access to the castle from the western side is gained through the Classical Vienna Gate (Viedenská brána), while from the old town the castle can be reached through the Gothic Sigismond Gate (Žigmundova brána).

Another important landmark in Bratislava is the **Slavín area** (252 m), lying north-west of the historical core of the city. This memorial was built to commemorate the Soviet army and its 6,847 soldiers who lost their lives during the liberation of Bratislava in the spring of 1945. The memorial is composed of three parts: an entrance staircase decorated with a relief and a group of statues of girls carrying ribbons and flowers of thanks, then six common graves of fallen soldiers and groups of statues called After the Battle and Above the Grave of a Fellow-Fighter which lead the visitor to the dominant of the memorial — the Hall of Piety with a 42 m high pylon on which there is a sculpture of a victorious soldier with a raised flag. In Bratislava we can find numerous buildings representing **modern architecture**. One of the exceptionally impressive buildings which catches the eye at first sight is the **Bridge of the Slovak National Uprising** spanning the river, whose restaurant opens up new views of the city on the Danube. Mention is also deserved by the building of the **Slovak National Gallery** on Rázusovo Embankmet, the building of the Czechoslovak Radio in Mýtná Street, the building of the House of the Revolutionary Trade Unions in the square námestie Františka Zupku, the fountain called Friendship in the square Gottwaldovo, the statue of a lion with the Czechoslovak state emblem in front of the Slovak National Museum, erected in honour of the proclamation in 1918, several modern hotels (the Forum, the Kyjev), etc.

A steamboat trip along the Danube, which starts from the passenger harbour on Fajnorovo Embankmet near the Slovak National Museum and lasts one to two hours, finally presents Bratislava from an unusual angle. It also acquaints visitors with Bratislava's four **bridges:** the Bridge of the Dukla Heroes by the Winter Harbour, completed in 1985, the Red Army Bridge of 1945, the oldest bridge spanning the Danube in Bratislava, the previously mentioned Bridge of the Slovak National Uprising, completed in 1972, and the youngest of the four, the Bridge of Youth at the mouth of the valley Mlynská dolina, currently in the course of construction.

Bratislava Information Centre, Rybárska brána (on the corner of Nálepkova Street)

Theatres:

Slovak National Theatre, opera and ballet, Gorkého Street 2

P. O. Hviezdoslav Theatre, play theatre of the Slovak National Theatre, Gorkého Street 17

The Small Stage, play theatre of the Slovak National Theatre, Dostojevského rad Street 7

The New Stage, operettas and plays, Živnostenská Street 1

The Studio of the New Stage, plays, Suché mýto 17

The Poetic Stage, currently in the House of the Revolutionary Trade Unions Movement, námestie Fr. Zupky

Reduta

State Puppet Theatre, Dunajská Street 36

Music:

Slovak Philharmonic Orchestra, Palackého Street 2, Reduta

Mirbach Palace, Dibrovovo námestie 11 (Sunday matinée)

Music Hall of Bratislava Castle

Courtyards of Baroque palaces in summer

Cultural events and exhibitions:

Bratislava Music Festivals, October, serious music with notable international participation

Bratislava Lyre, May, international festival of popular songs

Cultural Summer, June — September, the most varied spheres of art at a number of places

Flora, April, international flower exhibition held every even year

Bratislava Biennial of Illustrations, September, every odd year

Incheba, June, international chemical trade fair

P-T-S (Pravda — Television — Slovnaft), international light athletics competitions

Galleries:

Slovak National Gallery, Rázusovo nábrežie 2, old European art, Slovak Gothic, Baroque and 20th century art

Bratislava Gallery, Mirbach Palace, painting and sculpture of the 17th—19th century, Slovak art of the 20th century, etc.

C. Majerník Gallery, Hurbanovo námestie, occasional exhibitions

Exhibition halls:

Dielo, House of Art, námestie SNP and Obchodná Street 27, 29, 33

Laco Novomeský Exhibition Hall, Leningradská Street 2

Union of Slovak Creative Artists, Dostojevského rad Street 2, Gorkého Street 11

House of Czechoslovak-Soviet Friendship, nám. Ľ. Štúra 2

D. Jurkovič Exhibition Hall, nábřezie arm. gen. L. Svobody 3

Museums:

Slovak National Museum, Vajanského nábrežie 2, in particular exposition of natural history; Bratislava Castle, history of Slovakia and Bratislava, etc.

Municipal Museum, history of Bratislava and exposition devoted to feudal rights, Old Town Hall; exposition of arms and town fortifications, Michalská Tower; viniculture, Apponyi Palace, Radnická Street 1; J. N. Hummel Museum, Klobučnícka Street 2; pharmaceutical, Michalská Street 28; arts and crafts, Beblavého Street 1; Bratislava's historical clocks, At the Good Shepherd's, Židovská Street 1

Lenin Museum, Street Obrancov mieru 25

Museum of Vajnor Folklore, Roľnícka Street 97

Hotels:

Devín, *****, Riečna 4

Forum, ****, Vysoká

Carlton, ****, Hviezdoslavovo nám. 5

Kyjev, ****, Rajská 2

Car camp Zlaté piesky, Senecká cesta 10

Environs: on the NW outskirts of the city **Železna studienka** — a bus of the municipal mass transport system runs to this popular recreation place. After walking through the valley of the River Vydrica, a forest environment with romantic lakes, it is possible to travel by chair-lift to the summit of **Kamzík** (440 m) with a TV transmitter and a view of Bratislava and its wider environs. From here a marked path leads to the **Koliba** trolley-bus station. — Beyond the NE outskirts of the city lies the lake **Zlaté Piesky** covering an area of 52 hectares and offering good possibilities for bathing and water sports. This recreation area is situated on the road to Senec and has board and accommodation facilities. — 10 km W lies **Devín,** the ruins of a border castle of the 9th century. Easily accessible by municipal mass transport media. The castle, situated on a rock on the confluence of the Morava and the Danube, already enjoyed importance as a Roman fortress. It preserved its strategic importance up to the end of the Turkish wars and was finally destroyed by Napoleon's troops in 1809. At present archeological research is being carried out at the castle and at the same time its ruined walls are being conserved and partially reconstructed. From here more energetic tourists can make their way to **Devínská Kobyla** (514 m), a nature preserve with warmth-loving flora lying to the N of the castle. — Spreading out in NE direction from the city is the vinicultural region on the slopes of the **Little Carpathians.** A one-day car trip takes the tourist first to the vinicultural regions Jur pri Bratislave, Pezinok and especially Modra. Interesting ceramics also come from this, perhaps the best-known **vinicultural region** in Slovakia. **Modra** has other interesting features as well: preserved parts of the town fortification of the first half of the 17th century, a number of burghers' houses and the Ľudovít Štúr Museum. Ľudovít Štúr (1815–1856) was a leading personality of the Slovak national revival, a scientist and a politician who lived here after the revolution of

Bratislava

1848 and also died here. From Modra it is possible to turn off 8 km to the NW to **Zochova chata**, a mountain chalet in a recreation locality in the Little Carpathians. From Modra also via the community of Častá to **Červený Kameň** Castle from 1220—1235 with a furniture museum and collections of ceramics and china. Return to Bratislava in SE direction via Blatné to **Senec** with the Slnečné jazera lakes and bathing possibilities.

BRNO G 3

the historical centre of Moravia, now the capital of the South Moravian region and the third biggest city in the Czechoslovak Socialist Republic (pop. 390,000). It has developed industry, especially in the engineering, electrical engineering and textile branches. In 1928 the core of an exhibition ground was built and since 1959 it has been the scene of the **International Engineering** **Trade Fair** and later also of the International Consumer Goods Fair and a number of specialized exhibitions. The city has a very rich, historically important cultural background, several universities, theatres, museums and other cultural and educational institutions. Due to its advantageous position, the territory of present-day Brno was settled already from the most ancient times. In the 5th century of our era the Slavs arrived here. In the first third of the 11th century a residential castle of the Přemyslid apanage princes originated here. In 1243 Brno became a town, from 1349 it was the seat of the Moravian margraves and from 1641 the capital of Moravia. From the mid-17th century to the early 19th century it was an important provincial fortress. From the mid-18th century textile manufactories, which formed the base of the later industrial works, began to develop in Brno. The city was strongly damaged during the battles which took place at the end of the Second World War. The

Brno,
in the foreground the Cathedral
of SS. Peter and Paul

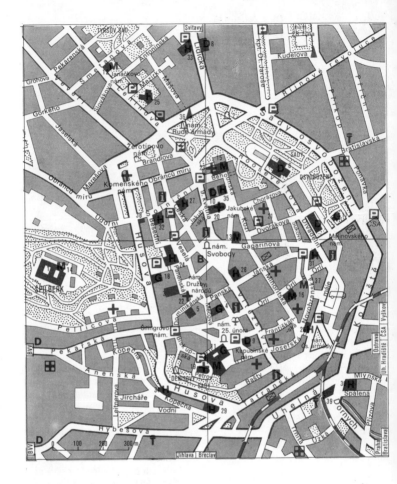

BRNO

1. Fortress and Špilberk Castle (c). **2.** Liberation memorial (b). **3.** New Town Hall (c). **4.** Old Town Hall (gallery) (d). **5.** House of the lords of Kunštát (c). **6.** Janáček Theatre (b). **7.** Mahen Theatre (b), **8.** Brothers Mrštík Theatre (a—b). **9.** Reduta Theatre (d). **10.** Večerní Brno Theatre (b). **11.** Moravian Museum (Dietrichštejn Palace) (d). **12.** Moravian Museum (music department) (a). **13.** Moravian Museum (ethnographical department) (b). **14.** Museum of the City of Brno (casemates) (c). **15.** Museum of the Workers' Movement (b). **16.** Technical Museum (d). **17.** House of Arts of the City of Brno (b). **18.** Moravian Gallery (c). **19.** Cathedral of SS. Peter and Paul (c). **20.** St. James's Church (b). **21.** Church of the Assumption of Our Lady (b). **22.** Dominican Church of St. Michael (c). **23.** St. Thomas's Church (b). **24.** International Hotel (c). **25.** Continental Hotel (a). **26.** Grandhotel (d). **27.** Avion Hotel (a). **28.** Evropa Hotel (d). **29.** Korso Hotel (d). **30.** Metropol Hotel (d). **31.** Morava Hotel (d). **32.** Slavia Hotel (a)., **33.** Slovan Hotel (a). **34.** Tatran Hotel (c). **35.** Hotel U Jakuba (b). **36.** Group of statues Communists (a). **37.** Museum of the City of Brno (Měnínská Gate) (d). **38.** House Besední dům (a)

BVV = Brno Exhibitions and Trade Fairs

post-war period was marked by the growth of the city and its intensive development as the centre of an important industrial region.

Our sightseeing tour of Brno begins in the centre of the city, in its biggest square, **náměstí 25. února**. It originated in the course of the founding of the town in the 13th century and it is still called Zelný trh (Cabbage Market — market sale of vegetables, fruit, flowers, etc.). At first sight our attention is captured by the Baroque **Parnas Fountain** of the late 17th century and **Reduta** (a theatre where operettas and musicals are presented). Dating in the late 18th century, it is Brno's oldest theatre building. The interiors of the former **Dietrichštejn Palace,** an Early Baroque building of the early 17th century (its substantial reconstruction has recently been completed), of the so-called **Bishop's Court**, a complex of buildings with a medieval core (the historical building dates in the 14th century) and of other neighbouring buildings serve as exhibition halls and work places of the **Moravian Museum,** founded in 1818. The neighbouring square **Kapucínské náměstí**, the former Coal Market, has a triangular shape given by the system of medieval streets; charcoal was sold here already in the 14th century. From the square there is an interesting view across the courtyard of the Moravian Museum to Petrov Hill. The Petrov terraces, reconstructed in the first half of the eighties, serve for recreation and in the summer months cultural programmes are also presented on them. The **Capuchin monastery** with the Church of the Finding of the Holy Rood originated in the mid-17th century. Below the church there is a crypt, open to the public, containing the mummified bodies of members and benefactors of the monastery, among them also the leader of the Pandours, Baron von Trenck, who was imprisoned in Špilberk Castle.

From the square náměstí 25. února we continue to **Radnická Street** with the **Old Town Hall**, Brno's oldest secular building whose core with a tower dates in the first half of the 13th century. On the first floor, for example, a rib vault and painted ashlar masonry can be seen which date from that time. In the early 16th century an entrance was driven in the tower. It has a stone portal with a characteristic, bent central pinnacle and an allegory of justice. In 1660 a gable with the new town emblem was set in the portal. In the seventies and eighties the building was subjected to an extensive reconstruction as a historical monument. The portal is closed by the original Late Gothic gate. The Town Hall tower with an **observation gallery** is open to visitors in the summer months. Chamber concerts and other programmes are held in the historical halls and the rear tract serves exhibition purposes. At the entrance to the Town Hall there are two interesting features in the form of the "Brno dragon" (a crocodile) and a cart wheel. A legend is attached to both of them.

Let us return to the square náměstí 25. února again. Houses Nos. 12 and 13 with medieval cores form here the architectonically remarkably unified **Malý (Small) Špalíček** (last reconstruction carried out in the years 1969-1973). From here we shall make our way upwards through **Petrská Street**, where in the near future the unconventional building of the Theatre on a String will originate, and then ascend the steps leading to the **Cathedral of SS. Peter and Paul** on **Petrov Hill.** Some historians maintain that the original Brno castle of princes, about which a written report of 1091 exists, was situated here. A Romanesque basilica also clearly stood here. The present appearance of the Gothic church, built from the 14th century, is influenced by a reconstruction carried out in the mid-18th century. The presbytery was puristically re-Gothicized in the late 19th century and it acquired two new steeples in the years 1904-1905. The oldest object in the interior of the cathedral is a stone statue of the Madonna and Child (c. 1300) with which the modernly designed Ways of the Cross forms an effective contrast. The high altar is Neo-Gothic.

From Petrov Hill, from where there is a fine view of the city, it is possible to descend to **Denis Park**, where remains of medieval and Baroque walls with bastions have been preserved and where a Classical obelisk, built in 1818 to commemorate the end of the Napoleonic Wars, stands. From here we shall make our way through Biskupská Street to the square **Šilingrovo náměstí** and from there through **Dominikánská Street**. The **House of the Lords of Kunštát**, a noble seat with a Renaissance courtyard, converted in the early 18th century into a market-place, has been adapted to serve as an exhibition hall with departments of graphic sheets, photographs and models of buildings and concerts and chamber theatre performances take place in its courtyard. The whole area between Dominikánská, Starobrněnská and Mečová Streets, the so-called **Velký (Big) Špalíček**, is undergoing reconstruction and its buildings will later mainly serve cultural purposes. Worthy of attention in the square **náměstí Družby národů** (originally the Fish Market) is the Early Baroque **Church of St. Michael** of the latter half of the 17th century. On its terrace there is a gallery of stone sculptures which originated before the mid-18th century. Of particular interest here, however, is the complex of buildings forming the **New Town Hall**, the original seat of the

Moravian provincial administration which now serves as the seat of the National Committee of the City of Brno. The Town Hall was reconstructed in the thirties of the present century. The oldest part is the cloister of the former Dominican monastery, built in the 13th—15th century. The Renaissance annex with a staircase dates in the late 16th century and most of the buildings in the first and second courtyards in the 17th—18th century. Of the bigger halls let us mention the Diet Hall, the Hall of Knights (now a Wedding Hall) and the Hall of the Land Rolls.

From the New Town Hall let us make our way through Zámečnická Street to the square **náměstí Svobody**, Brno's oldest square, once called the Lower Market. In our century it has been the scene of the most important revolutionary popular assemblies (in 1917 and 1948). Of the remarkable buildings let us mention **Klein Palace** (No. 15), a Neo-Renaissance residential building of the mid-19th century, and the Renaissance **Schwartz House** (No. 13) of the late 16th century, whose graffito decoration dates in 1938. In the corner of the square, Gagarinova (No. 13) and Běhounská Street stands the "house of gentlewomen", now the seat of the **ethnographical department** of the Moravian Museum. It was built in the late 17th and adapted in the 18th and 20th centuries. Running from the square is the most important street in Brno's pedestrian zone, **Česká Street**. Worthy of attention in it are the burghers' house No. 5 (now undergoing reconstruction) and No. 8 (a house with a Renaissance core), a Neo-Renaissance apartment house of the gallery type (No. 6) and especially the constructivistic building of the Avion Hotel (No. 20).

In the first third of Česká Street we shall turn right and walk through Jakubská Street to **St. James's Church** standing in the picturesque square of the same name. The church was founded in the twenties of the 13th century and rebuilt from the late 14th to the late 16th century, when its steeple was erected. The Neo-Gothic high altar, sacristy, etc. date in the late 19th century. In the church there is a stone pulpit of 1525 with reliefs of the late 17th century. Two Late Gothic stone reliefs (Lamentation, The Crucifixion) of the early 16th century are built-in in the modern Ways of the Cross. On the gallery of the choir there are Gothic, Renaissance and Baroque tombstones (also of Raduite de Souches, defender of Brno against the Swedes). On a peripheral wall there is a wooden cross of the latter half of the 14th century.

Our sightseeing tour of the city now takes us from the church through 9. května Street to the square **náměstí Rudé armády**. Situated on the right is **St. Thomas's Church**, a part of a former Augustinian monastery founded in the 14th century. Its Gothic nave was rebuilt in the latter half of the 17th century. A stone pieta, a part of its original furnishings of the same period, has been preserved. Next to the church stands the **Museum of the Workers' Movement**, originally the prelature of the mentioned church complex and later the house of the Moravian governor and the provincial offices. In December 1920 a big workers' manifestation took place in front of the building.

We shall now follow the former castle circuit to the **Janáček Theatre** (opera and ballet) of 1960—1965 and then to the **Mahen Theatre** (plays) of 1881—1882 and the originally Art Nouveau building of the **House of Art of the City of Brno**, reconstructed in 1946. We shall now return through the park to the square **Rudé armády**, to the memorial The Victory of the Red Army Over Fascism (Vincenc Makovský) and the group of statues called Communists (Miloš Axman). By the so-called university library of 1924 we shall turn off shortly into Leninova Street (on the right the Continental Hotel of 1961—1964 and the Institute of the History of Music of the Moravian Museum with the Leoš Janáček Memorial Hall). From here we now return to the square **Žerotínovo náměstí** where the Regional National Committee has its seat in Nos. 3—5, and then pass round the Municipal Committee of the Communist Party of Czechoslovakia of 1974—1976 to the architectonic uniformly designed square **Komenského náměstí** with the Neo-Gothic Evangelic Church of Jan Amos Komenský (Comenius) of 1863-1865 and the Neo-Renaissance buildings of the medical faculty, the Janáček Academy of Fine Arts and the building called **Besední dům**, originally the cultural and social centre of Czech Brno, where performances are given by the Brno State Philharmonic Orchestra (all these buildings date in the sixties and seventies of the 19th century).

Now we shall continue through Husova Street round the **International Hotel** of 1960—1962 to the Neo-Renaissance Moravian Gallery, built in 1882—1883 for the museum of applied art. The International Biennial of Applied Graphic Art takes place here similarly as a number of short-term exhibitions. From here let us turn right and walk up the path to the memorial to five Italian carbonaros who died in the castle prison and from here make our way to **Špilberk Castle.**

Brno castle was built in the third quarter of the 13th century. It was subjected to several reconstructions, especially in the 17th century, when it became, apart from other things, a prison. About the year 1740 it was converted into a fortress. It gained notoriety especially in the first half of the 19th century when it served as a prison for Polish, Italian and

Hungarian revolutionaries. The prison was abolished in 1853 and the castle was converted into a barracks. During the Second World War opposers of fascism were imprisoned in the cells of Špilberk Castle. The casemates are now accessible as well as other expositions of the **Museum of the City of Brno**, including the Gallery of the City of Brno. A panoramatic view of the city and its environs can be gained from Špilberk Castle.

The importance of Brno as a leading industrial and commercial centre is enhanced by the previously mentioned trade fairs. If we have time, let us descend from Špilberk Castle and make our way through the main gate to the orthodox church and then continue down the street called Úvoz to the square **Mendlovo náměstí** with the Gothic **Church of the Assumption of Our Lady** and the former **convent of the Poor Clares**. It has a Baroque high altar whose most interesting part is the so-called Silver Altar of 1734-1736 with an Italian-Byzantine ikon. Of the original convent, founded in 1323, the core of the residential buildings, the torso of the cloister and the chapter hall have been preserved. Extensive adaptations and the construction of new buildings were carried out in the 15th—17th century. In the late 18th century the building with the library hall (valuable Baroque shelves of the mid-18th century) was added. The library stock is very rich, especially in the spheres of natural history and social sciences. Among others, the genetician Johann Gregor Mendel (1822—1884), whose life and work are brought to mind by a memorial hall, worked here.

From the square Mendlovo náměstí we can cover the short distance to the **Brno exhibition ground** by walking through Rybářská or Výstavní Street. The first exhibition, devoted to contemporary Czechoslovak culture, took place here in 1928. A grandly designed area (headed by Pavilion A) was built for it as a formally compact manifestation of Czechoslovak modern architecture of the period of constructivism and functionalism. In the latter half of the fifties the dozens of preserved buildings, protected as monuments, were added to by the construction of new structures in connection with the Exhibitions of the Czechoslovak Engineering Industry, later with trade fairs and specialized exhibitions (these include in particular Pavilions B, C and Z, later the administration building, Pavilions D, O and others). The eighties were marked by another important wave of building activity (the trade fair centre, the exhibition pavilions of Tuzex, Houses of Technology, the Czechoslovak Scientific and Technical Society, the commercio-business centre, etc). The exhibition ground covers an area of 76 hectares, its roofed exhibition area amounting to 100,000 and its open-air exhibition area to 111,000 sq. m. Every year some 5,000 exhibitors from 50 countries of the world take part in 10—15 trade fairs and international exhibitions which are attended by some 1 1/2 million visitors. In adjoining Křižkovská Street interesting sights are the summer palace of the Mitrovský family of the late 18th century and the complex of buildings of the **Voroněž Hotel** (1978—1987).

A velodrome for cycling events is wedged in the exhibition ground. In view of its mission it corresponds to the multipurpose hall of the Rondo Stadium Na náplavce.

The place locally called **Pisárky** is situated on the River Svratka. It was once an excursion destination of the inhabitants of Brno, but now it serves for short-term recreation as the so-called Riviéra. To the west of the exhibition ground, on the right bank of the river,

stands the **Anthropos** exhibition pavilion with an exposition documenting the evolution of Man. And in still more westerly direction there is an attractive panoramatic view of the exhibition ground and the whole of Brno from the terrace of the **Myslivna Restaurant**, which in 1987 was enlarged by the addition of an accommodation part. An even wider radius is offered by the Grand Prix Café on the nearby Kohoutovice housing estate. Its name is connected with the automobile and motorcycle races for the **Grand Prix** of the Czechoslovak Socialist Republic, for which a new track corresponding to world parameters was built in the mid-eighties.

A view of the exhibition ground from the Jirásek quarter is also opened up by the terrace of the Horizont Restaurant in Barvičova Street. Further on in the direction of our view we can see before us the big vinicultural region with its own characteristic charm and, in southeast direction, also with the folklore of Moravian Slovakia, still alive.

Theatres:

Janáček Theatre, mainly opera and ballet, Rooseveltova Street 1—7

Mahen Theatre, plays, Malinovského náměstí 1

Reduta, operettas and musicals, náměstí 25. února 4

Brothers Mrštík Theatre, Lidická Street 14/16

Theatre on a String (Divadlo na provázku), Malinovského náměstí 2 (under construction in Petrská Street)

Evening Brno (Večerní Brno), satirical theatre, Jakubské náměstí 5

Joy (Radost), puppet theatre, Bratislavská Street 32

Music:

Brno State Philharmonic Orchestra, Besední dům, Komenského náměstí 8

House of the Lords of Kunštát, chamber concerts, Dominikánská Street 9

House of Art of the City of Brno, Malinovského náměstí 2

Cultural events and exhibitions:

10—15 *trade fairs* and exhibitions every year

Exhibition ground
in Brno

Grand Prix of the Czechoslovak Socialist Republic, automobile and motorcycle races

Galleries and exhibition halls:

Moravian Gallery, Czech and European art, collections of works of applied art, Husova Street 14

House of Art of the City of Brno, the biggest exhibition institution in the Czechoslovak Socialist Republic, Malinovského náměstí 2

House of the Lords of Kunštát, departments of graphic art, photography and architecture, Dominikánská 9

Gallery of the City of Brno, creative art of the 20th century, Castle

Museums:

Moravian Museum, náměstí 25. února 8; the Ethnographical Institute, Gagarinova Street 1, the Anthropos Pavilion with an exposition depicting the evolution of Man, Pisárky 9, the genetic department at the J. G. Mendel Memorial Hall, Mendlovo náměstí 1 and the Institute of the History of Music, Smetanova Street 14 all belong to it

Museum of the City of Brno, Castle

Museum of the Workers' Movement, náměstí Rudé armády 1a

Hotels:

Continental****, Leninova 20

Grandhotel, A*, 1. máje 18—20

International, A*, Husova 16

Voroněž, A*, Křížkovského 47; B*, Křížkovského 49

Avion, B*, Česká 20

Slavia***, Solniční 15/17

Slovan, B*, Lidická 23

Car camps:

Obora, Brněnská přehrada, 635 00 Brno

Bobrava, Modřice u Brna (in the direction of Mikulov)

Environs: On the NW outskirts of the city lies the **Brno dam lake,** Brno's biggest recreation facility, in the midst of forests. It is accessible by tram and, in the season, also by express buses. The

dam wall was built in the years 1935—1939, it is 34 m high, its crest is 120 m long and the length of its backwater is 9 km. A boat transport service operates on the lake. By the lake there are beaches, restaurants and a camp. In the immediate Bystrc quarter there is also a zoological garden. — Rising above the narrowest part of the lake is **Veveří Castle** of the mid-13th century, later rebuilt (it is not open to the public). — 10 km SE of Brno lies Slavkov Battlefield. It can be reached by travelling along road No. 51, turning off to the left to Sokolnice and then continuing to the community of Prace. For description see Slavkov. — 23 km NW **Předklášteří** (part of Tišnov), one of the noteworthiest sacral monuments on the territory of historical Moravia, the former Porta coeli (The Gate of Heaven) monastery and its church including a valuable portal from the time of the transition of the Romanesque to the Gothic. The church has a ground-plan in the form of a cross and an Early Gothic cross vault. Another 14 km NW **Pernštejn** Castle. — North of Brno, near the district town **Blansko,** lies the **Moravian Karst** with numerous caves and the Macocha Abyss.

Brno

Portal
of the Porta coeli monastery
at Předklášteří near Tišnov

BRUNTÁL   H 2

a district town (pop. 18,600) in the foot-hills of the Jeseniks. An ancient mining town documented already in the early 13th century. A Baroque **château** with valuable interiors stands in the north-west part of the core of the town. In its courtyard there is a two-storeyed arcade. The town has a regular ground-plan, a quadratic square and remains of its former fortifications.
Environs: 2 km SW the extinct quater-nary volcano **Uhlířský vrch** (672 m) on whose summit there is a Late Baroque church of pilgrimage. — 20 km NE the town of **Krnov** (pop. 26,000), world-fam-ous for its organ production. Monumen-tal parish church and Renaissance châ-teau.

BYTČA   K 3

a town (pop. 12,000) in the valley of the River Váh, W of Žilina. Four-winged Renaissance **château** (1571—1574) with corner towers, a central tower above the entrance and an arcaded courtyard on the site of a Gothic water castle. In the 17th century so-called Sobášný Pal-ace with rich graffito decoration was built by the château.
Environs: 8 km S the **Súľovské skaly** rock formations; huge conglomerates form bizarre, stage-set shapes, for ex-ample, the Gothic Gate, the Súľovská Gate and a rock Town. — 10 km SW **Manínska tiesňava**, a limestone canyon between the hills Veľký (Big) Manín (891 m) and Malý (Little) Manín (812 m).

CHEB   A 2

a district town (pop. 31,000) in the westernmost part of Czechoslovakia. Its historical core forms a notable **historical town reserve**. Bicycle pro-duction, textile industry, railway junc-tion. Theatre.
From 1179—1188 a Romanesque castle (falc) was built by the Emperor Fridrich Barbarossa on the site of an old Slavon-ic castle and in the first half of the 13th

The group of houses
called Špalíček
at Cheb

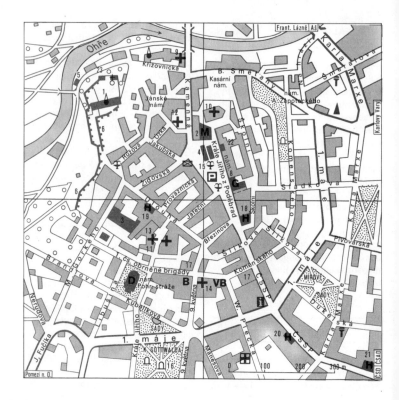

CHEB

1. Castle (a). 2. Municipal House (museum) (a—b). 3. Municipal armoury (granary) (c). 4. Špaliček (a). 5. Písečná Gate (a). 6. Remains of the town fortifications (a). 7. West Bohemian Theatre (c). 8. Town Hall (Gallery of Creative Art) (b). 9. Former Church of St. Bartholomew (gallery) (a). 10. St. Nicholas's Church (b). 11. Former Church of St. Clare (concert hall) and Convent of the Poor Clares (district archives) (c). 12. Former Dominican monastery with church (museum) (a). 13. Former Franciscan monastery with church (c). 14. Evangelic church (c—d). 15. Roland and Hercules Fountain (b). 16. Border Guard memorial (c). 17. District National Committee (c). 18. Hvězda Hotel (d). 19. Hradní dvůr Hotel (c). 20. Slávie Hotel (d). 21. Chebský dvůr Hotel (d). 22. Schirndinger's House (b). 23. Mill Tower (a).

century a town was founded below it. In 1322 Cheb with its environs was pledged to the Czech king. From then on it was a permanent part of the state and possessed a certain degree of auto- nomy until the 18th century. During the reign of King **Sigismund** it was the starting place of campaigns against the Hussites. In 1634 the imperial generalis- simo Albrecht of Wallenstein was mur-

Cheb

dered here. After the mid-17th century the town was a Baroque fortress. In 1871—1872 a railway was put into operation here and industry developed. Overlooking the River Ohře are the **ruins of a castle** with the 21 m high Black Tower of basalt block (observation point) and a Romanesque imperial palace of the 12th century (Baroque chapel), destroyed by fire during the French siege in 1742. — The old burghers' houses have roofs running systematically in parallel with their façade with the result that they have neither gables nor attics. The two rows of little houses of Jewish shopkeepers of the 16th century, called **Špalíček**, in the square are a sample of framed architecture. Also standing in the square is the Baroque Town Hall built by G. B. Alliprandi (before 1726); a gallery of Czech art of the 20th century is now installed in it. The parish Church of St. Nicholas from 13th—15th century, a concert hall in the former Baroque Church of St. Clare (1707—1711, K. Dienzenhofer) and a gallery of Cheb Gothic art in the Gothic Church of St. Bartholomew.

J. W. Goethe paid several visits to Cheb and in 1791 F. Schiller stayed here when he prepared his trilogy about the Wallenstein tragedy.

Environs: in the neighbourhood of the town the **Skalka dam** reservoir, bathing. — 7 km E the **Jesenická dam** reservoir, bathing, fishing, boat trips.

CHOD REGION, The   B 3

---

a historically significant region near the western border of Bohemia and the FRG. Originally a part of the border territory reaching from Nýrsko and Domažlice as far as Tachov and Planá; its protection was entrusted to the free border guards — the Chods. The inhabitants of 11 villages concentrated round the town of Domažlice retained their autonomy for the longest period. It is in this demarcation on the territory stretching in the 30 km long zone from Pocinovice to Postřekov that we understand the Chod region also from the viewpoint of the present visitor.

Rising here in parallel with the state border is the forested ridge of the Bohemian Forest which culminates with Čerchov (1,042 m, inaccessible) and the Haltrava ridge (852—888 m). The local, once impenetrable forests formed a natural source of protection of the country against foreign attacks; for example, in 1040 the troops of the German emperor Heinrich III were defeated at Brůdek similarly as the attack of the crusaders on the Hussites at Domažlice in 1431. At that time the border was guarded by the Chods, who were granted numerous privileges by the Czech kings and who had a dog's head in their emblem. In the 17th century, after the Thirty Years War, the Chods lost their historical rights and in 1692 an armed struggle against the lord of the estate broke out. The leader of the rebellion, Jan Sladký-Kozina, was executed in 1695. Folk costumes, a special dialect, old local customs and folk architecture still characterize the Chod region. The ethnographical Chod Festival takes place at Domažlice every year (August). The centre of the Chod region is the town **Domažlice**. — Lying 4 km W is the village **Újezd**, the place of birth of Jan Sladký-Kozina. There is a memorial hall commemorating him at so-called Kozina's Farm. Above it, on the hill called Hrádek (595 m), stands the Jan Sladký-Kozina memorial. A far-reaching view of the Chod region can be seen from here. Nearby a typical Chod cottage. — At the village of **Draženov** 5 km NW of Domažlice samples of characteristic Chod farms (Nos. 2, 5, 8). — SW, below Hrá-

dek, the village of **Trhanov** with a Baroque château, once the seat of the owners of the estate comprising the Chod villages. Inside the J. Špillar (a painter of the Chod region — 1869—1917) picture gallery. — Below the slope of Haltrava the small town of **Klenčí pod Čerchovem** with a Baroque church, an old post office (of 1546) and a museum devoted to the writer of the Chod region J. Š. Baar (1869—1925). The Chodovia Cooperative produces folk ceramics. — 2 km above the town, near the roadside, the Výhledy (705 m) observation point with a memorial to J. Š. Baar affords a far-reaching view of the Chod region. — 7 km SW of Domažlice the village of **Babylon**, a recreation resort surrounded by forests with a big pond (13 hectares, bathing), a car camp and hotels. — 10 km SE of Domažlice the town of **Kdyně**, overlooked by the ruins of Rýzmberk Castle with an observation tower, Nový Herštejn Castle and the hill Koráb (773 m) with an observation tower. — 11 km NE of Domažlice the small ruins of **Netřeby** Castle with a nature preserve with yew

trees which, on the average, are about 600 years old. — 3 km further NE the community of **Koloveč,** known for its ceramics. — On the northern border of the Chod region lies the town of **Horšovský Týn.**
Recommended car route: Domažlice — Draženov — Újezd — Hrádek — Trhanov — Klenčí pod Čerchovem — Postřekov — Výhledy — Babylon — Domažlice. — Total length 41 km.

CHRUDIM F 2

a district town (pop. 20,000) in East Bohemia. Originally a Slavonic fortified settlement, later a Přemyslid castle and, from 1263, already a Royal town. — Its historical core has a regular groundplan and a quadratic square lined with mainly Baroque burghers' houses. The original Renaissance Town Hall was Barocized about 1721. Plague column from the early 18th century. — The most valuable of the town's several rare church buildings is the Church of the

---

Chrudim

The interior of a Chod cottage in the museum at Domažlice

Assumption of Our Lady of the 14th century. — A well-known **puppet museum** is now installed in the former Renaissance Mydlář House. A puppet festival takes place in the town every year.

Environs: 4 km S **Slatiňany**, a château with a hippological museum, an English park and a horse stud. Horse races take place here. — 5 km E in the village **Kočí** a small Gothic church of the 14th century, folk ceiling paintings, a wooden bridge of 1721 and a wooden belfry of 1666. — 13 km SE **Ležáky**, a former community of stonemasons. Destroyed by the German fascists 2 weeks after the liquidation of Lidice (24 June, 1942) as retribution for its hiding the secret transmitter of a group of parachutists sent from London to assassinate Heydrich. The adult population was shot. Memorial and museum devoted to the resistance movement against fascism. — 18 km SW the **Seč** valley reservoir, a summer recreation resort with an international pioneers' camp, overlooked by the ruins of Oheb Castle.

ČERVENÁ LHOTA   E 3

a small Renaissance **château**, converted from a Gothic fortress after 1530 and later modified. It stands in the middle of a pond. This four-winged, two-storeyed building with an advanced façade tower is accessible by means of a stone bridge. Recently reconstructed and supplemented with valuable interior furnishings. The château is surrounded by a park.

ČERVENÝ KAMEŇ   H 4

a Renaissance fortress from 1533—1537, converted fifty years later into a **château**. Several valuable expositions are installed in its interiors: furniture, arms, majolica and so on. Starting point for the forested range of the Little Carpathians.

ČERVENÝ KLÁŠTOR   M 3

a community on the bank of the River Dunajec. The **former monastery** with a church founded in the 14th century was the important cultural and economic centre of the region. The whole building has now been restored and a museum with historical, ethnographical and pharmaceutical expositions is housed in its interior. — The seat of the administration of the Pieniny National Park. Raft navigation on the Dunajec.

ČESKÉ BUDĚJOVICE   D 3

a regional town (pop. 955,000) and the administrative, industrial and cultural centre of the South Bohemian region. Situated in a large pond basin. The historical part of the town has been proclaimed **a historical town reserve.** Food industry and brewery producing Budweis beer since 1894, Koh-i-noor pencil factory (formerly Hardtmuth) founded in 1847, Sfinx enamelware factory, engineering industry. Pedagogical faculty, Agricultural University. Scientific institutes. Theatre.

The town was founded in 1265 as a royal town intended to restrict the expansion tendencies of the feudals. In the 16th century it experienced a period of great

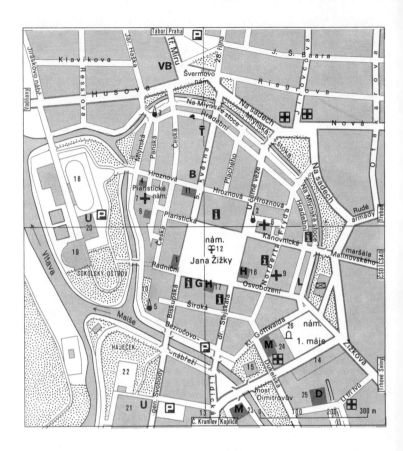

ČESKÉ BUDĚJOVICE

1. Town Hall (c). 2. Black Tower (b). 3. Rabenštejn Tower (a). 4. Salt-house (armoury) (a). 5. Iron Maiden (c). 6. St. Nicholas's Cathedral (b—d). 7. Church of the Sacrifice of Our Lady (a). 8. Former Dominican monastery (a). 9. Former St. Anne's Church (concert hall) (d). 10. Bishop's Garden with remains of fortifications (c). 11. Meat shops (a). 12. Samson's Fountain (d). 13. Regional National Committee (c). 14. House of Culture of the Revolutionary Trade Unions Movement (d). 15. Municipal House of Culture (d). 16. Zvon Hotel (d). 17. Slunce Hotel (d). 18. Stadium (a). 19. Swimming stadium (c). 20. Sokolovna (accommodation) (a—c). 21. Winter stadium (c). 22. Summer cinema (c). 23. Museum of the Workers' and Revolutionary Movement of South Bohemia (d). 24. South Bohemian Museum (d). 25. South Bohemian Theatre (d). 26. V. I. Lenin memorial (d).

prosperity (ponds, beer, storehouse of salt transported from Austria, own mint). The Thirty Years War also brought about its decline. In 1641 a great fire occurred in the town. From 1832 České Budějovice was the starting point of the Budějovice—Linz **horse-drawn railway** (the first in Europe). The centre of the town is formed by the large **quadratic square Žižkovo náměstí** of a size of 133 x 133 m. It has a number of Renaissance and Baroque houses with arcades. Standing in the square is Samson's Fountain of 1727 and the Renaissance **Town Hall** from 1727—1730, later Barocized. — In the NE corner of the square stands a striking landmark — the Gothico-Renaissance **Black Tower**, 72 m high (panoramatic view) — and next to it **St. Nicholas's Cathedral**, Gothic of 1625 and Barocized from 1641—1649. — A number of other historical monuments can be seen in the centre of the town: a salt-house, originally an armoury of 1531, in the NW corner, the Renaissance Meat Shops of 1554 with an Empire gable, adapted in 1953 and now a restaurant. Also to be seen in this part of the town is the Church of the Sacrifice of Our Lady and a former Dominican monastery of the 13th century. — In the SW part of the town centre stands the so-called Iron Virgin, a castle tower with a defence gallery, and in the E part the former Renaissance St. Anne's Church (concert hall) from 1615—1621. A number of outstanding modern buildings: for example, the House of Culture of the Revolutionary Trade Unions Movement, the Building of the Museum of the Workers' and Revolutionary Movement of South Bohemia, the university centre at Čtyři Dvory, the sports stadium on Sokolský Island, the exhibition ground (the national Earth Our Nourisher exhibition held every year in August) and others.

Environs: 9 km N Hluboká nad Vltavou and the nearby Ohrada hunting château, built in Baroque style. — 8 km NW **Bezdrev** Pond, the second biggest pond in Bohemia.

Samson's Fountain
and the Black Tower
at České Budějovice

ČESKÉ STŘEDOHOŘÍ (The Bohemian Central Highlands) C—D 1

a diversely shaped range of **volcanic origin**, divided by the valley of the Elbe (picturesquely hollowed out, especially below Litoměřice — the so-called Porta Bohemica) into two halves. In the west part the highest peak **Milešovka** (837 m), the windiest mountain in the Czech Socialist Republic (meteorological station). Protected landscape region. Its warm climate and nutrious soil determined the mainly forest-steppe character of its flora and fauna. There are 21 preserves on its territory. The region is one of the driest and the mildest in the Czech Socialist Republic. — The slopes facing the south afford conditions for the growing of fruit, vines and less hardy vegetables. The region is called the "Garden of Bohemia". — **Starting points:** Most, Louny, Ústí nad Labem, Litoměřice.

ČESKOMORAVSKÁ VRCHOVINA
(The Bohemian—Moravian Highlands), E—G 2—3

a large, hilly region spreading out along the whole border between Bohemia and Moravia. Rising in its southern part are the Jihlava Hills with **Javořice** (837 m) and in its western part the Žďárské Hills with the Devět skal rock formations (836 m) and the mountain Žákova hora (810 m). Stretching out in the north-west are the Železné (Iron) Mountains (Pešava, 697 m). These are suitable mainly for unexacting excursions in a quiet and undisturbed environment without any overcrowded tourist centres. A number of **rivers, ponds and lakes** attract tourists to this region. The first include, for example, the Rivers Sázava, Chrudimka,

Svratka and Jihlava and their tributaries and of the ponds special mention should be made of Velké Dářko (206 hectares) and Řeka. Also worthy of special note is the Seč valley reservoir (very good conditions for bathing and water sports).

The region is very rich in **architectonic monuments.** It has four historical town reserves: mining Jihlava, "white" Telč, Renaissance Slavonice and Pelhřimov with two gates. Other monuments include, for example, Dačice Château, the ruins of a castle at Lipnice nad Sázavou, the former monastery at Žďár nad Sázavou, Pernštejn Castle and others. Folk architecture has been preserved, for example, in the environs of Nové Město na Moravě and a complex of folk buildings can be seen in the skansen called Veselý kopec near Hlinsko. Nature is protected particularly in numerous preserves and in the protected landscape region of the Žďárské Hills.

The Prague — Brno motorway runs through the centre of the Bohemian-Moravian Highlands and so the region is easily accessible from the west and the east.

Starting points: Chrudim, Hlinsko, Havlíčkův Brod, Žďár nad Sázavou, Nové Město na Moravě, Jihlava, Pelhřimov, Telč, Dačice and Slavonice.

České středohoří

Folk buildings at the Veselý kopec skansen in the Bohemian-Moravian Highlands

ČESKOSASKÉ ŠVÝCARSKO
(Bohemian-Saxon Switzerland),

see Labské pískovce

ČESKÝ KRUMLOV D 4

a district town (pop. 14,000) in the southern foothills of the Šumava Mountains. One of the most important **historical town reserves** in Czechoslovakia with a number of Gothic, Renaissance and Baroque monuments.
The town originated below a castle of the Vítek family in the first half of the 13th century and was mentioned for the first time in 1253. From the early 14th century, after the Vítek family had died out, it was the administrative, economic and cultural centre of the estate of the lords of Rožmberk, who until 1602 were the biggest landowners in Bohemia. The period of flourish of Český Krumlov culminated in the 16th century, at the time of Vilém of Rožmberk. After the Rožmberks the estate was in the hands of the Emperor Rudolph II for a time and then, from 1622, it was owned by the Eggenbergs and, from 1719, by the Schwarzenbergs.
The **château** building is the landmark of

General view
of Český Krumlov
with the château

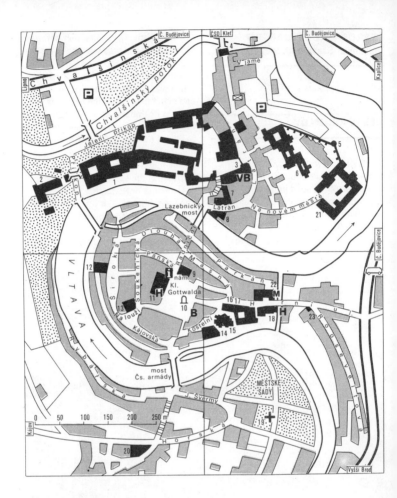

ČESKÝ KRUMLOV

1. Château (a). **2.** Château theatre (a). **3.** Former Latrán Town Hall (b). **4.** České Budějovice Gate (b). **5.** Novoměstská Bastion (b). **6.** Former convent of the Minorites and Poor Clares (b). **7.** House No. 15 with Gothic wall paintings (b). **8.** Former Church of St. Jošt (b). **9.** Old Town Hall (Municipal National Committee) (c). **10.** Marian plague column (c). **11.** Krumlov Hotel (c). **12.** House of the alchemist Michael of Ebersbach (c). **13.** House of Jakub Krčín of Jelčany (No. 54) (c). **14.** Old Latin school (d). **15.** Prelature Church of St. Vitus (d). **16.** Kaplanka (d). **17.** Prelature (d). **18.** Former Jesuit college (Růže Hotel) (d). **19.** St. Martin's Chapel (d). **20.** Renaissance house (c). **21.** Former armoury of the Rožmberks (brewery) (b). **22.** Former Jesuit seminary (museum) (d).

Český
Krumlov

the town and after Prague Castle it is the biggest of its kind in Bohemia. On a rock overlooking the Vltava stands a round tower of the latter half of the 13th century, later rebuilt in the Renaissance. It is a remainder of the oldest part of an original castle called Hrádek. Linking up with it is the Upper Castle of the first half of the 14th century, grouped round two courtyards. Renaissance and Baroque reconstructions lent the whole complex the character of a château. Other notable buildings are the burgrave's house of the seventies of the 16th century, an exceptionally well−preserved theatre from 1766−1767, connected by a bridge with the château, and a riding-school. In the château park a summer palace called Bellarie and a fountain from 1706−1708. In 1958 a summer theatre with a revolving auditorium was built in front of the summer palace. The most valuable château interior is the Hall of Masks, richly decorated with frescoes (illusive paintings by J. Lederer of 1748). Other interiors contain collections of wall carpets, paintings and furniture.

The oldest part of the settlement, the **Latrán** outer bailey with Renaissance buildings, lies below the château on the left bank of the river. Of the fortifications the České Budějovice Gate of the late 16th century and Novoměstská bastion have been preserved. Behind it is the building of the former Rožmberk armoury, now a brewery. A number of valuable Renaissance houses, a Town Hall and the large area of a former monastery of the Minorites of the mid-14th century with Baroque annexes and of the Poor Clares with Gothic cloisters. The **old town**, whose most notable building is the Late Gothic Church of St. Vitus from 1407−1439, lies on a headland round which the Vltava flows on three sides. In the interior of the church the net vault of the main nave, the

mausoleum of Vilém of Rožmberk and remains of Gothic paintings. In the square a Renaissance Old Town Hall with an attic of 1580, a complex of burghers' houses and a Marian plague column (1716). A number of other valuable houses in the adjoining streets (Horní, Kostelní, Kájovská, Široká and others).

Environs: 7 km NE of the town the Cistercian monastery called **Zlatá Koruna** (Golden Crown), founded by King Přemysl Otakar II in 1263; the area is walled-in; a Gothic church with valuable furnishings, a chapter hall. Main period of building activity 1300−1370. Baroque modifications in the 17th−18th century. Open to the public, museum expositions. − 6 km S one of the biggest paper works in Czechoslovakia at **Větřní**, which originated in 1870. − 7 km NW Mount **Kleť** (1,083 m) with an observatory. In 1825 one of the first observation towers in Bohemia was built here and on clear days even the Alps can be seen from it. Chair-lift from the N from Krasetín. − 6 km W, in the community of **Kájov,** a Gothic church of the late 15th century. − 10 km NE the ruins of the castle **Dívčí Kámen** (Maiden's Stone) of the mid-14th century.

ČESKÝ RÁJ   E 1−2
(Bohemian Paradise)

---

a region lying amid the towns of Mnichovo Hradiště, Turnov and Jičín in East Bohemia, highly frequented by tourists. The areas of **sandstone rocks** are broken up by a dense network of deeply cut valleys and in some places rock towns with fantastic scenery formed by rocks, towers, blocks, columns, battlements and needles, interwoven with deep, narrow passages and lanes, have originated. These rocky regions are very popular with tourists and mountain-climbers. There is a dense network of marked paths leading to the most attractive sights here. The striking landmarks of the Bohemian Paradise are the peaks Tábor (678 m, observation tower) and Kozákov (774 m, tourist chalet) and the ruins of Trosky and Kumburk Castles. Meadows and fields alternate with forests composed mainly of spruce and pine trees. Many ponds are used for recreation purposes. The Bohemian Paradise is the oldest protected landscape region in Czechoslovakia (proclaimed such in 1955).

Folk architecture forms an inseparable part of this region (Dolánky, Kacanovy). Particularly worthy of a visit among the numerous **castles** and **châteaux** are Kost, Humprecht near Sobotka, Mnichovo Hradiště, Hrubý Rohozec and Trosky. The town of Jičín is a historical town reserve. Železný Brod has a long-standing tradition in glass-making.

The core of the protected landscape region is **Hruboskalsko**, situated in the environs of Hrubá Skála Château 6 km SE of Turnov with a large rock town, an arboretum and the ruins of Valdštejn Castle. To the SW, in the direction of Mnichovo Hradiště, lies the region of rock formations called **Příhrazské skály**, overlooked by the basalt hill Mužský (463 m), which is visible from far and wide. Rising NE of Turnov, above the bank of the Jizera, are the sharply cut rock formations called Suché skály. The most frequented corner of the Bohemian Paradise are the rock formations called **Prachovské skály**.

Recommended car route: Mnichovo Hradiště — Příhrazy (on foot to the rocks and to Mužský) — Vyskeř — Hrubá Skála (a rock town) — Turnov — Malá Skála — Kozákov — Trosky — Prachovské skály — Sobotka — Kost — Mnichovo Hradiště. Total length approx. 100 km.

Recommended excursions of foot:
1. Hrubá Skála — Hlavatice — Turnov 7 km. Along the paths with red marks and the nature study paths. — 2. Sightseeing circuits at Prachovské skály: big circuit with green marks 3.5 km, with yellow marks 1.4 km and small circuit with green marks 2.2 km. — 3. Suché skály and the Besedický rock circuit at Malá Skála: network of variously marked paths, length 10—15 km.

ČESKÝ ŠTERNBERK   E 2

a community and castle of the same name in the recreation region by the River Sázava. The originally Gothic **castle** was founded about 1240 on the left bank of the Sázava. Later it was rebuilt in the Late Gothic and Early Baroque styles and finally gained its present appearance about the 18th century. Its interiors contain rich collections (arms, graphic sheets of the 17th century and period furniture).

Český
Šternberk

Typical sandstone rock town
in the Bohemian
Paradise

ČIČMANY   K 3

a village with original **folk architecture**.
The outer walls of the houses with galleries are painted with ornaments (e. g.
hearts, birds, suns, dolls). An ethnographical exposition is installed in one
of the houses (Radenov dom). Carved
crosses can be seen in the cemetery.
The Čičmany folk costume, covered
with the same ornaments as the
houses, was also very characteristic. —
Starting point for the Strážovské Hills.

DĚČÍN   D 1

a district town (pop. 56,000) situated on
the Elbe near the border with the German Democratic Republic. Railway
junction, the biggest inland port on the
Elbe, industrial centre. — A Slavonic
castle (Děčan tribe) stood here already
in the 10th century. A royal town was
founded here in 1283 whose further development in the 16th and especially the
19th century was connected mainly with
its advantageous position on the Elbe
water-way.
The landmark of the town is a **château**
on a headland 50 m above the confluence of the Elbe and the Ploučnice. It
originated as the result of a number of
reconstructions of the originally
Romanesque and Gothic castle of the
Přemyslids (first mentioned in 1128).
Last modified about 1790. Not open to
the public. Accessible by a 300 m long
path of access and the so-called Dlouhá
jízda (Long Ride), hewn in a rock after
1670. On the slopes below the château
there is the terraced Baroque **Rose Garden** with a sala terrena. Baroque
Church of the Holy Rood from
1687—1691. In the former hunting château at Podmokly on the right bank of
the Elbe the district museum with an interesting exposition devoted to navigation on the Elbe. Late Gothic stone
bridge over the Ploučnice with Baroque
statues by M. J. Brokof. — The composer F. Chopin stayed at the château in
1835. — Rising 150 m above the surface
of the Elbe through a steep rocky preci-
pice is the rocky wall **Pastýřská stěna**
(accessible by lift, observation restaurant, zoo on a nearby plateau).
Environs: the Elbe sandstone Rocks. —
8 km SE the town of **Benešov nad
Ploučnicí** with 2 Renaissance châteaux
(an exposition of Renaissance art and
samples of period furnishing are installed in the Lower Château). — 10 km
N the **Hřensko** summer resort (river
transport).

DEMÄNOVSKÁ DOLINA   L 3

a valley in the northern slopes of the
Low Tatras, 15 km long, S of Liptovský
Mikuláš. The most valuable **karst system** in Slovakia, including the Demänová Cave called Sloboda (Freedom), is situated here. Total length of the passages of the system 7,007 m, 1,887 m
accessible, exceptionally rich stalagmite and stalactite decoration. Also to
be found here is the Demänová Ice
Cave (sightseeing circuit 680 m, ice decoration, stalagmites and stalactites). In
the upper part of the valley lies the **Jasná recreation resort**, equipped with
several hotels and tourist chalets. The
biggest lake in this range — Vrbické
pleso — is also situated here. For skiers
the best downhill runs in Czechoslovakia, chair-lift on Chopok (2,025 m), another chair-lift and cabin funicular,
a number of ski-tows. Walking tours on
the ridges of the Low Tatras (highest
peak Ďumbier, 2,043 m, with a chalet
below it).

DOBRUŠKA   F 2

a town in the foothils of the Orlické (Eagle) Mountains. At the turn of the 18th and 19th centuries it was an important centre of the Czech national revival movement. In the square a Renaissance Town Hall of the latter half of the 16th century; a fine view can be obtained from the gallery of its tower. Preserved folk architecture. Starting point for the Orlické Mountains (Deštné 14 km).
Environs: 4 km SW Renaissance **Opočno** Château from 1560—1569 with a notable gallery and valuable furnishings; later Barocized. Near the château a Renaissance church, adapted in 1716, and a large park with a number of rare foreign trees.

DOBŘÍŠ   D 2

a town with glove industry. Local Rococo château used by the Union of Czech Writers, inaccessible. By the château a French park and large enclosure.
Environs: 3 km SE **Strž** Pond on whose bank stands a house of the same name in which Karel Čapek lived from 1935—1938 — exposition devoted to the life and work of this author, whose works are the most widely translated of all modern Czech writers.

DOBŠINSKÁ ĽADOVÁ JASKYŇA
(Dobšiná Ice Cave)   M 3

the biggest **ice cave** in Czechoslovakia, situated above the valley of the River Hnilec in East Slovakia. 475 m of the total length of 1,386 m of the passages of the cave are accessible — open to the public in the summer months only. Ľadová jaskyňa Hotel. — Starting point for the Slovak Paradise.

DOLNÝ KUBÍN   L 3

a district town (pop. 17,000) on the River Orava in a popular tourist region. Former office of the district adminstration — now a gallery of the late 17th century. Neo-Gothic church, Baroque wooden belfry.
Environs: 6 km S **Vyšný Kubín**, place of birth of the Slovak poet Pavol Országh Hviezdoslav (1849—1921). — 8 km N the dominant peak **Kubínská hoľa** (1,346 m), skiing grounds, ski-tows. — 10 km NE Orava Castle.

DOMAŽLICE   B 3

a district town (pop. 12,000) in the ethnically attractive Chod region. The original market village was raised to a royal town by Přemysl Otakar II about 1260. In 1431 an important battle took place near the town in which the Hussite troops defeated the Crusaders. The centre of the town is now a **historical town reserve.** Most of the historical buildings are situated in the long square náměstí Míru, which is lined with original Gothic and Renaissance houses with arcades. Their gables are mostly Baroque and Empire. The local landmark is the round tower of the archideaconal Church of the Nativity of Our Lady of the 13th century; it leans to the extent of 70 cm from its axis. The Town Hall standing opposite the church is Neo-Renaissance of 1891. Apart from remains of the walls and small gates, only the gate in the lower end of the square, dating in about 1270, has been preserved of the original

Dobruška

Gothic fortifications of the town. The **Chod Castle**, which lost its original Gothic appearance as the result of a number of reconstructions, is also a part of the former fortification system. Its round tower, in whose interiors the Museum of the Chod Region is installed, stands out well in the panorama of the town. — In the 19th and early 20th century several notable Czech writers stayed at Domažlice. They are brought to mind by memorial tablets situated on houses in the square. The ethnographical Chod Festival takes place in the town in August every year. — Rich ethnographical collections can be seen in the Jindřich Jindřich Museum (below the gate).
Environs: the ethnographical Chod region.

DOMICA   M 4

a stalagmite and stalactite **cave** in the Slovak Karst on the border with Hungary, 20 km SW of Rožňava. The cave system is 22 km long, 1,600 m of its passages being accessible on the Czechoslovak side. Boat trips along the underground River Styx. Archeological locality.

DUDINCE   K 4

a **spa** where diseases of the motory organs and nervous diseases are treated. Indoor and outdoor thermal bathing-pools. Protected natural formation Dudinské travertiny. Modern spa buildings.

DUCHCOV   C 1

an industrial town (pop. 10,000). Tradition connected with the workers' revolutionary movement. In 1931 4 participants in the hunger march of the unemployed were shot near the local viaduct. **Coal mining** from the first half of the 18th century; surface brown coal mines in the environs. — In the square a Baroque **château** with valuable sculptures by M. B. Braun. From 1785—1798 G. G.

Square
at Domažlice
with the Lower Gate

Casanova lived here as the librarian and also wrote his memoirs here. In the interiors collections of furniture, an exposition devoted to the Far East and a picture gallery. Frescoes by V. V. Reiner transferred to the modern garden pavilion.

Environs: 4 km NW **Osek**, where 142 miners lost their lives in the disaster which occurred at the Nelson mine in 1934. In the town a Cistercian monastery (of 1198) with a church, originally Romanesque of 1207, later Barocized (rich decoration and furnishings). Chapter hall of about 1240, cloister of the first half of the 14th century. The monastery is surrounded by a garden of the 18th century. The ruins of a Gothic castle overlook the town.

DUKLIANSKÝ PRIESMYK   O 2
(Dukla Pass)

a pass of the Carpathian ridge on the Polish border. From 8 September — 27 November, 1944 the scene of one of the toughest **military operations** of the Second World War. 300,000 soldiers took part in it on both sides, the Red Army losing 80,000 men. The 1st Czechoslovak Army Corps in the Soviet Union (loss of 6,500 men) also took part in the battles. On 21 September the first community on Czechoslovak territory (Kalinov) was liberated and on 6 October the Czechoslovak brigade crossed the border and liberated Vyšný and Nižný Komárnik. Below the saddle stands a **memorial** - a wedge-shaped pylon with a group of statues The Thanks of a Mother to a Soviet Soldier for the Liberation — surrounded by a cemetery. On the state border a 49 m high observation tower. Stretching to Krajná Poľana is an open-air museum of the Carpathian-Dukla operation: bunkers, un-

dergroud shelters, the command observation posts, aircraft, tanks, etc.

FRANTIŠKOVY LÁZNĚ   A 2

a notable **spa town** in the westernmost part of Bohemia. Its core forms a **historical town reserve.** Drinking cures employing the so-called Cheb water were taken here already from the 12th century and the water was supplied, for example, to practically the whole of Austria-Hungary in the 18th century. The spa was founded in 1793. It grew very quickly and consequently has a chessboard ground-plan. Nearly all the spa buildings are Empire. Treatment of gynecological diseases, circulatory diseases and metabolic disorders. The centre of the town is formed by the present square náměstí Míru in whose centre the biggest spring, called František's Spring, gushes forth in a pavilion of 1832. By it stands the popular statue of František, the symbol of the spa. The main street, Národní třída, with the old-

Dukliansky priesmyk

Memorial
to the liberation
at the Dukla Pass

166

est boarding-house, called U tří lilií (At the Three Lilies), runs off from the square. Other notable buildings in the town: the Gas Baths with the New Colonnade, the Court of the Glauber Springs, the Nižnětagil Colonnade of the Union of Czechoslovak-Soviet Friendship, Baths III and the Social House. Among others J. W. Goethe and L. van Beethoven stayed at the spa (memorial tablets).

Environs: 3 km S **Komorní hůrka** (500 m), an inconspicuous forested hill representing the youngest active volcano on Czechoslovak territory. J. W. Goethe gave the impulse for the research of its flue. — 5 km NE the **Hájek** (Soos) peat-bog on the site of a former lake with mineral springs and a European rarity in the form of gaseous exhalations of carbon dioxide. Nature study path.

a town (pop. 10,500) in the region of the Beskids. Linen production once thrived here and skis were also manufactured in the town, now known for its production of electric motors and textile goods. In the mid-nineties a new mining region (4 mines in construction at present) will be opened in the vicinity of Frenštát. — Neo-Renaissance Town Hall of 1890 housing a museum with expositions documenting linen and cloth production, an ethnographical exposition and a gallery.

Near the town the Horečky **recreation regions** with the Vlčina Interhotel, characteristic Wallachian inns and a skiing area with 3 ski-jump structures with a plastic surface.

Environs: 5 km SW **Velký Javorník** (918 m) with a tourist chalet. — 4 km SE the scattered community of **Trojano-vice,** folk architecture and recreation facilities. A part of it is Ráztoka, the lower station of the chair funicular to Pustevny.

Spa buildings
at Františkovy Lázně

FRÝDEK-MÍSTEK   J 2

a district town in the foothills of the Beskids (pop. 64,000) with a textile industry and sheet rolling mills (Karlova huť
at Lískovec with a rich revolutionary tradition). It lies on both banks of the Ostravice. Místek was founded on the
Moravian side in the 13th century and
Frýdek on the Silesian side during the
14th century. — Among other things,
Frýdek has a Baroque château of the
17th century and, in Hluboká Street, the
last old merchants' houses. — In the
square náměstí VŘSR (Great October
Socialist Revolution) at Místek there are
Renaissance and Baroque houses with
arcades, especially Nos. 1 and 2. Lively
construction. For motorists a suitable
starting point for the Beskids.

FRÝDLANT   E 1

a town on the northern promontory of
Bohemia whose name is connected
with the military commander **Albrecht
of Wallenstein** ("the Duke of
Frýdlant"). It originated as a market
community below the castle in the 13th
century. Its original Gothic ground-plan
and remains of its fortifications have
been preserved. — Gothic church with
the marble mausoleum of the Redern
family from 1605—1610. High above the
town an originally Early Gothic **castle**
with a round tower, 60 m, called Indica;
rebuilt in the 16th century. The Renaissance Lower Château was built in the
outer bailey about 1600. In its interiors
a Hall of Knights, salons, valuable collections (Czech Baroque paintings, furniture, gobelins, china, etc.).
Environs: the protected landscape region of the Jizerské Mountains.

FULNEK   J 2

a town lying SW of Ostrava. Mentioned
before 1293, a centre of the Czech
Brethren in the 15th and 16th centuries.
From 1618—1621 the pedagogue **Jan
Amos Komenský** (Comenius) taught at
the local school of the Czech Brethren;
the building has been converted into
a museum. The original chapel in which
Comenius preached forms a part of it.
Above the town a large château. The effective complex of the square: the Renaissance Town Hall tower of 1610, Baroque sculptures, Baroque Knur's
House, a Baroque church.

GERLACHOVSKÝ ŠTÍT
(Mount Gerlach)   M 3

the **highest mountain** in Czechoslovakia (2,655 m) — in the High Tatras. Its
rocky summit can be reached only with
a mountain guide, best of all from the
tourist chalet Sliezsky dom. For a long
time the peak Lomnický štit was considered to be the highest mountain, Gerlachovský štit having been regarded as
such since 1838. First ascent in 1868.

GOTTWALDOV   H 3

formerly Zlín (until 1949), a district town
(pop. 83,000) in Wallachia. Footwear industry (now Svit), rubber industry (Barum), precision engineering industry
and others. Mentioned in the early 14th
century. In 1894 Tomáš Baťa founded
a **footwear industry** (slipper production) here. It was not until the time of
the First World War that the town underwent rapid development (supplies of
boots from the Baťa factory for the ar-

Frýdek-Místek

my), which continued after the end of the war. The owners of the later concern adopted a number of elements of American industry, in particular flow production on conveyor belts and a boarding school for the training of young production specialists. They also established shops in Europe and overseas and various services for their employees. Le Corbusier was among those who designed the modern buildings of the town. Before the Second World War the Baťa concern became a world footwear enterprise. After the war it was nationalized.

The centre of the present town is round the squares náměstí Práce and náměstí Míru. To be seen in the historical part of the town is a Renaissance château, Barocized in the late 18th century. Now the Regional Museum of South East Moravia. English park. A footwear museum is installed in the multistoreyed building of the Svit National Corporation. Gallery of Czech painting and sculpture of the 20th century. Film studios which, under the management of Karel Zeman, have gained exceptional successes in the spheres of animated and trick films. Modern building of the Workers' Theatre.

In the Malenovice quarter a Gothic castle of the mid-14th century, reconstructed several times. Archeological collections can be seen in its interior. In the Kostelec-Štípa quarter a windmill of the Dutch type. In the **Lešná** quarter a romantic château of the late 19th century, adjoined by a large English park and a zoo.

Environs: 10 km NE the ruins of **Lukov** Castle of the 13th century. — 9 km E **Slušovice**, a modern agricultural complex run with the use of untraditional methods. It has rich associated production and a big horse — racing area (the Derby Centre). — 15 km E the small town of **Vizovice** with a Baroque châ-

teau from 1750—1766 — collections of furniture and china and a valuable picture gallery. French garden, large English park. Production of Jelínek slivovice (plum brandy) in the town. — 26 km E stood the village of **Ploština**, burned by the Nazis, who also shot its inhabitants, on 19 April, 1945. Now a memorial of the resistance movement.

HARRACHOV   E 1

---

a mountain resort (686 m) for summer and winter recreation in the western part of the Krkonoše Mountains. Road border crossing to Poland. Traditional glass production (export glassworks, small museum and shop). — Chair-lift affording access to Čertova hora (1,020 m) with 5 ski-jump structures on its slopes. The biggest of them is used for ski flights (critical point 165 m). Ski-tows at Rýžoviště, cross-country skiing track. Annual event in the form of the arrival of Krakonoš with a masked entourage.

Environs: at Mumlavský důl (2 km) the well-known **Mumlava Waterfall** (height 10 m). — Starting point for walking tours to the western part of the **Krkonoše Mountains**, especially to Vosecká bouda (chalet), the source of the Elbe, Labská bouda, the Kotel region and the group of chalets called Dvoračky. — From Harrachov a half-day excursion to **Rokytnice nad Jizerou** (520—620 m), a small mountain town with very good conditions for winter sports, particularly for downhill skiing — several ski-tows. In this respect it competes successfully with Špindlerův Mlýn and Pec pod Sněžkou. — Harrachov is a suitable starting point also for excursions to the eastern part of the Jizerské Mountains (Kořenov, Souš, Jizerka and other places).

HAVÍŘOV J 2

the youngest, newly founded town in Czechoslovakia (a town from 1955, pop. 95,000). It originated in 1947 as the housing estate of the Ostrava-Karviná industrial and mining agglomerate.
Environs: 6 km S the **Žermanice** dam reservoir.

HLUBOKÁ NAD VLTAVOU D 3

a town to the north of České Budějovice with one of the most highly visited and most picturesque Czechoslovak **châteaux**. It stands on a headland overlooking the Vltava on the site of a former royal castle, reconstructed on many occasions. It now has a Neo-Gothic appearance from 1841—1871, when the château was owned by the Schwarzenbergs. The two-storeyed building is lined with battlements above which several towers rise. As a whole the building has a very romantic, almost quaint appearance. Its interiors — some 140 rooms — are filled with rich collections of arms, gobelins, portraits, furniture, glass, china, etc. The riding-school of the château of the mid-19th century has been adapted to house the Aleš South Bohemian Gallery with very valuable collections of Gothic and modern art. The château park runs into an enclosure.
Environs: 1 km SW Baroque **Ohrada Castle** from 1708—1718, used on hunting occasions. A Museum of Forestry and Hunting, now a part of the Agricultural Museum with expositions of hunting, forestry, fishing, etc., was founded here already in 1842. Near the château there is a small zoo. Nearby the second biggest pond in Czechoslovakia, **Bezdrev** (520 hectares).

Havířov

Hluboká nad Vltavou
Château

HORŠOVSKÝ TÝN B 3

a town in the Chod region, founded in the mid-14th century from an old trading post. Even earlier, in the mid-13th century, a castle had been built here which, in the mid-16th century, was converted into a Renaissance château and lent a Neo-Renaissance appearance in the late 19th century. It has valuable interiors and on its northern side there is an English park. — A **historical town reserve.** In the square preserved houses of the 15th century. Town Hall of the late 17th century.

HRABYNĚ J 2

a community 12 km east of Opava. A modern memorial commemorating the **Ostrava Operation** forms the local landmark on the territory of which one of the most important battles of the Red Army in Czechoslovakia was fought under the command of Marshal A. Y. Yeremenko from 10 March — 4 May, 1945. In all 60 divisions took part in the battle. In the environs a number of memorials, an open-air exhibition of military technology at Štítina, small fortresses and a permanent museum exposition in Kravaře Château.

HRADEC KRÁLOVÉ F 2

a regional town (pop. 100,000) and the administrative, economic and cultural centre of the East Bohemian region on the confluence of the Elbe and Orlice. Mainly engineering industry (production of plants for sugar factories and distilleries and of oil engines), but also food industry, works producing Petrof pianos and other industrial branches. Modern construction (the local housing estates rank among the most successful in Czechoslovakia). Permament theatre. Seat of medical, pharmaceutical and pedagogical faculties.

Originally a Slavonic castle site was situated here, which from 1225 was a walled-in royal town. In the 14th century it was the dowry town of the Czech queens. In the 15th century it supported the Hussite revolutionary movement and the Hussite commander Jan Žižka was buried in the local church. From 1660 the town was the seat of the bishopric. In the latter half of the 18th century Hradec Králové was transformed into a huge Baroque fortress against Prussia; it was abolished in 1884. From the early 20th century extensive building activity was carried out in which leading Czech architects Jan Kotěra and Josef Gočár participated. The centre of the old town (a **historical town reserve**) is formed by the triangular square Žižkovo náměstí. Standing in its centre is a 19 m high plague column. The square is dominated by the twin-towered, brick, Gothic **Cathedral** of the Holy Ghost, founded in 1307 and adapted in Neo-Gothic style in the 19th century. In its neighbourhood stands the sandstone White Tower from 1574 — 1589 with the second biggest bell in Bohemia (of 1509, weight 10 tons). Behind the tower stands the small Baroque St. Clement's Chapel, an original building perhaps of the 11th century. The old Renaissance **Town Hall** is lent a characteristic appearance by two Late Baroque towers. Standing on the southern side of the square is the large bishop's residence from 1709 — 1716, built with the participation of G. B. Santini, now the seat of the Regional Gallery with paintings by Czech painters of the 20th century (B. Kubišta, E. Filla, J. Preisler and others). The neighbouring

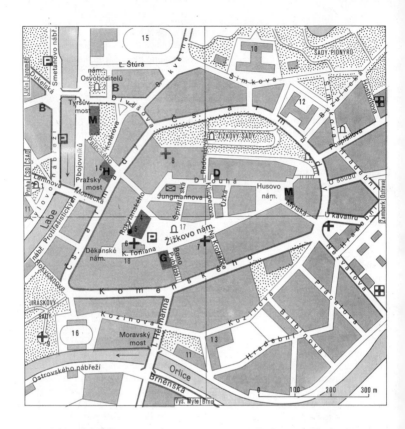

HRADEC KRÁLOVÉ

1. V. I. Lenin memorial (a). 2. Memorial Soviet tank No. 559 (a). 3. J. Žižka memorial (b). 4. Town Hall (a—c). 5. The White Tower and St. Clement's Chapel (c). 6. Cathedral of the Holy Ghost (c). 7. Church of the Assumption of Our Lady (c). 8. Group of buildings with Church of St. John of Nepomuk (a). 9. Little Greek-Catholic church (c). 10. Medical faculty (b). 11. Pedagogical faculty (c). 12. Regional National Committee (b). 13. House of Pioneers (d). 14. Bystrica Hotel (a). 15. Spartak Sports Stadium (a). 16. Winter Stadium (c). 17. Marian column (c). 18. Canons' houses (c).

house U Špuláků (At the Špuláks) is the most beautiful burgher's house in the square. Following it is the complex of Early Baroque Jesuit Church of the Assumption of Our Lady and a Jesuit college. The other side of the square is lined with houses with arcades. Outstanding among the buildings beyond the periphery of the former fortifications (their remains can be

seen particularly in the northern part in Žižka Park) are the building of the Regional Museum (J. Kotěra, 1909–1912) with expositions devoted to history and natural science and the Bystrica Hotel on the left bank of the Elbe. Kotěra's and Gočár's projects were realized mainly on the left bank of the Elbe in the direction towards the station (e. g. the complex of buildings in the square Gottwaldovo náměstí).

Environs: 8 km NW on **Chlum** Hill (336 m) a memorial to the Prussian-Austrian war in 1866 with museum expositions, an observation place and an ossuary. The decisive battles of this war took place on 3 July, 1866, the Austrian army suffering a heavy defeat, while Prussia gained the leading position in Germany. The battlefield is accessible along marked tourist paths and a number of memorials can be seen in the wide environs. — 9 km W the Neo-Gothic château of **Hrádek u Nechanic** whose interiors with valuable furnishings are open to the public. — 27 km W **Chlumec nad Cidlinou** with a Baroque château (1721–1723) called Karlova Koruna (Charles' Crown) on a hill in the centre of

the park; it was designed by G. Santini. Permanent exposition of the Baroque in Bohemia. In 1775 a peasant uprising was suppressed near the town and a memorial recalling the event stands by the roadside in the direction of Hradec Králové. — 12 km E **Třebechovice pod Orebem** with a museum containing rare folk carvings — the so-called Třebechovice Christmas Crib with 400 figurines.

HRADEC NAD MORAVICÍ   J 2

a town and **château** south of Opava. Originally a Slavonic castle site, later a Gothic castle converted into a Renaissance château, restyled in the Empire after 1795 and Neo-Gothicized from 1860–1887. Known in particular for the sojourns of L. van Beethoven (1806, 1811), Ferenc Liszt (1846, 1848) and Niccolo Paganini (1928). The large English park runs into the open countryside.

Environs: 6 km NE Empire **Raduň** Château where the collections of the château at Hradec are being exhibited dur-

Square at Hradec Králové
with cathedral
and Town Hall

ing the reconstruction of the latter. —
To the NW the deep, in places rocky
valley of the River **Moravice.**

HRONSKÝ BEŇADIK K 4

a monastery in the valley of the Hron.
Founded in the latter half of the 11th
century. Site of a Romanesque basilica
now occupied by a triple-naved Gothic
church of the 14th century. In the 16th
century, at the time of the Turkish
threat, the church and the monastery
were fortified. In the interiors numerous
Gothic sculptures and remainders of
frescoes.
Environs: below the community the
most beautiful sector of the Hron as regards scenery, the so-called **Slovenská
brána** (Slovak Gate) — a pass to the
lowlands of the Danube.

HRUBÁ SKÁLA E 1

a destination of excursions to the Bohemian Paradise. A château stands on
a forest rock plateau on the site of
a medieval **castle,** re-Gothicized in the
19th century; now a recreation centre.
Rock town with popular mountain-
climbing grounds: e. g. the rock tower
Kapelník (Bandmaster) and surrounding
group of rocks called Kapela (Band);
a narrow rock pass called Myší díra
(Mousehole) runs from the château to
the middle of the rock formations called
Dračí skály (Dragons' Rocks). Below
Mariánská vyhlídka (Marian observation
point) a small, symbolic cemetery of
mountain-climbers. Ruins of Valdštejn
Castle of the 13th century, adapted in
romantic style.

HŘENSKO D 1

an excursion destination on the right
bank of the Elbe, in the immediate vicinity of the border with the GDR. Lowest
height above sea level in Bohemia along
the flow of the Elbe — 117 m. After 1880
hotels and pensions were gradually built
in the rocky valley of the Kamenice and
by its mouth. 1 km SE entrance to **Tichá
soutěska** (Silent Pass) — a deep valley
with rock walls 50—150 m in height,
some of which are vertical; a part of the
valley is accessible by boat only —
length of boat trip 960 m. After 3 km the
2 km long **Divoká soutěska** (Wild Pass),
a part of which is also accessible by
boat only, links up with it at Mezní
můstek. — 3 km E **Pravčická brána**, the
biggest natural gate in Central Europe;
length of arch 26.5 m, height 16—21 m;
numerous observation points and the
Sokolí hnízdo (Falcon's Nest) Restaurant. A 14 km long nature study path
connects all the interesting localities in
the environs of Hřensko.

HUMENNÉ O 3

an East Slovak district town (pop.
30,000). Chemlon Works (production of
polyamide fibres). — Humenné was
mentioned in 1322. The originally Gothic
castle was converted into a Renaissance château in 1610 and adapted in
the latter half of the 19th century; now
a museum. In the nearby park an exposition of folk architecture (folk structures and small churches). Greek-Catholic Baroque-Classical church. Modern construction.
Environs: 35 km NE the protected landscape region of the East Carpathians,
an original area of primeval forests with
the occurrence of the bear and wolf. —

*Hronský
Beňadik*

16 km NW the **Domaša** valley dam reservoir (1,422 hectares) on the River Ondava, length 14 km; recreation at the waterside.

HUSINEC   C 3

a community in the region below the Šumava Mountains, the place of birth of John Huss (**Jan Hus**; c. 1372—1415), the Czech philosopher and leader of the social and religious reformatory movement. Among others, he followed in the ideas of J. Wycliff. At the Constance Council he was sentenced to death and burned at the stake on 6. 7. 1415. His death accelerated the development of the Hussite revolutionary movement (1419—1436), whose most outstanding military respresentative was Jan Žižka of Trocnov. In the community the house in which Master Jan Hus was born with the so-called Hus Chamber and a memorial to him by K. Lidický (1958).

JABLONEC NAD NISOU   E 1

a district town (pop. 42,000) in the foothills of the Jizerské (Jizera) Mountains. Development of the town from the 19th century in connection with the growth of **glass production** (the biggest world manufacturer and exporter of fashion jewellery), a town from 1866. Seat of the Bižuterie Concern Corporation and the Jablonex Foreign Trade Corporation, the LIAZ automobile works and other enterprises. Specialized Museum of Glass and Fashion Jewellery. The landmarks of the town are the new Town Hall from 1929—1933 and a constructivistic triple-naved church of 1930. Extensive housing construction. Dam reservoir. Starting point for the ridges of the Jizerské Mountains (8 km N Bedřichov, a winter sports resort).

Pravčická brána (gate)
rock formation
at Hřensko

JÁCHYMOV B 2

an old mining and later spa town in the Krušné (Ore) Mountains. **Radioactive springs,** treatment of diseases of the motory organs, nervous diseases, vascular diseases and others. Silver deposits; town founded in 1516 where **tolars** — the Joachimsthaler (hence the dollar) — were minted before 1520. In 1716 a mining school originated here. From the forties of the 19th century pitcheblend-uranium ore used in the production of dyes for glass and china was mined here. In 1903 Pierre and Maria Curie issolated radium from it. In the fifties Jáchymov was the third biggest producer of radium in the world. The spa began to develop after the exhaustion of the mines.
St. Joachim's Church from 1534—1540, Late Gothic Town Hall from 1540—1544, an old mint from 1534—1536. Spa buildings, the Radium Palace from 1910—1912 (now the M. Curie-Sklodowski Sanatorium), the new Dr. Běhounek Sanatorium of 1975. Museum of mining and balneology.
Environs: 5 km NE the highest peak in the Krušné Mountains, **Klínovec** (1,244 m, chair-lift from the local part Suchá), downhill runs, mountain chalet, observation tower. — 6 km N the mountain resort **Boží Dar** (1,028 m), formerly a mining town; characteristic architecture. W the Boží Dar Peat-bog and growths of dwarf pines and dwarf birches.

JANSKÉ LÁZNĚ F 1

a spa and recreation resort (630 m) in the eastern part of the Krkonoše Mountains. The **spa** was founded in 1677 and has 30 springs (radioactive, thermal, mineral), a modern Art Nouveau colonnade of 1893, the modern Vesna Sanatorium for children at Janův důl (conditions following operations and injuries, muscular diseases, neurological-disorders, etc.). Cabin funicular to **Černá hora** (1,299 m); below its peak 2 hotels and other recreation buildings; 80 m high TV transmitter. Černá hora peat-bog — a nature preserve. Nature study path.

JAROMĚŘICE NAD ROKYTNOU
F 3

a South Moravian town with a big Baroque **château,** built from 1700—1737. St. Margaret's Church with a huge dome and two steeples is connected with the two-storeyed château. Imposing entrance vestibule of the château and a main hall with portraits of ancestors. Château theatre and music hall with rich painted decoration. Sala terrena, French garden, natural park with sculptures portraying classical mythology. In the 18th century Jaroměřice was a centre of theatre and music culture.

JASOV N 3

a community on the outskirts of the Slovak Karst. Archeological locality, **cave** already settled in the younger Stone Age. Now accessible, rich sinter decoration, sightseeing circuit over 2 km in length. — In the mid-12th century a Premonstratensian **monastery** was founded at Jasov, now a Late Baroque building from 1750—1766. Wall paintings by J. L. Kracker.

Jáchymov

a town (pop. 14,000) and spa below the ridges of Hrubý Jeseník. — The **spa**, founded in 1822 (then called Gräfen-berg) by Vincenc Priessnitz, is situated on a hill overlooking the town; numerous mineral springs, favourable climatic conditions. Hydrotherapy of nervous, mental and metabolic diseases and diseases of the respiratory tracts. Main spa building of 1910. In the park a number of memorials erected as expressions of thanks of spa guests. In 1845 the Russian writer N. V. Gogol stayed at the spa. — In the town a Gothic **water castle**, later lent a Renaissance appearance, now a museum.

Environs: 4 km W **Lipová-Lázně,** a spa treating metabolic diseases, diseases of the alimentary tract and skin diseases. In 1931 8 participants in a demonstration against the sacking of people from work were shot on a cross-road here. Memorial to the victims. — 6 km NW the accessible **Na Pomezí** stalagmite and stalactite cave. — 24 km NW the town of **Javorník** with a Baroque château on the site of a Gothic castle. — 8 km E the **Rejvíz Peat-bog** (nature preserve) with a nature study path. — 10 km SW the community of **Ramzová** on the saddle Ramzovské sedlo (759 m); ascent to the ridgeway of Hrubý Jeseník, funicular on Šerák (1,351 m).

a big mountain region in the north-western part of Moravia whose highest peak is Praděd (1,492 m) at **Hrubý Jeseník.** Its ridge stretches from the saddle Ramzovské sedlo (759 m), accessible by road and rail, over the bare peaks of Šerák (1,351 m, tourist chalet, accessible by chair-lift from Ramzovské sedlo), Keprník (1,424 m, rocky summit) and Červená hora (1,333 m) to the saddle Červenohorské sedlo (1,013 m, the main road from Šumperk to Jeseník passes this way). From here the forested ridge rises to the Švýcárna Chalet and to the nearly bare summit of Praděd with a TV transmitter, visible from far and wide. Highly frequented by tourists are the environs of the chalets called Ovčárna, Barborka and Kurzovní (arrival by bus from Karlova Studánka). The deforested ridge, affording fine views, continues via Petrovy kameny (1,446 m, rocky summit) and Vysoká hole (1, 464 m) to the peaks Máj and Pecný (1,333 m) and then drops sharply to the saddle called Skřítek (877 m, the main Šumperk — Ostrava road). The summit parts drop through steep slopes to deeply cut valleys whose ends are characterized by hollows.

Practically the whole of the massif of Hrubý Jeseník is a **protected landscape region**. The mountain growths are all of the fir type (spruce monocultures) and the upper boundary of the forest lies at a height of 1,200 — 1,300 m.

The most important witness of the times when the high mountains were covered with ice is the botanically significant hollow called **Velká kotlina**. Preserves of **primeval forests** exist in the region: the primeval forest on the summit of Keprník, the submontane primeval forest at Františkova myslivna and others. The interesting sights of nature further include romantic valleys with **waterfalls** (Vysoký vodopád — High Waterfall — in the valley of the Studený potok river, the Rešovské Waterfalls, the waterfalls at Bílá Opava), protected peat-bogs, e. g. those at Rejvíz with Malé mechové jezírko (Small Moss Lake) and Velké mechové jezírko (Big Moss Lake). On the summit parts there are several outstanding rock formations and stone seas and in the slopes there is a number of **caves** (e. g., Na Pomezí). Rising north-west of Hrubý Jeseník, on the boundary between Bohemia, Moravia and Poland, is the relatively little frequented massif of **Králický Sněžník** (1,423 m) on whose slopes the River Morava springs.

Its south-eastern part is formed by **Nízký Jeseník** (Slunečná, 800 m), a range of hills of an average height of 600 m. There are several young volcanoes here (Uhlířský vrch overlooking Bruntál, Venušina sopka, Velký Roudný and Malý Roudný).

The whole region of the Jeseníks is very attractive from the aspect of tourism. The ridges of Hrubý Jeseník are the destination of tours on foot. A number of sought-after spa centres (Jeseník, Karlova Studánka, Lipová-Lázně, Bludov) have originated below the mountains. Extensive forests in the whole region afford the possibility of rest and of collecting forest fruits (mushrooms, raspberries, blueberries, cranberries), of which there is an abundance. Another attraction is the architecture of the local **châteaux** (Velké Losiny, Bruntál, Šternberk, Javorník, Hradec nad Moravicí). In the town of Fulnek there are memorials recalling the sojourn here of Jan Amos Komenský (Comenius). The environs of the town of Jeseník are sadly notorious for the witch trials of the 17th and 18th centuries.

Recommended tours on foot:
1. Ramzovské sedlo — Šerák — Keprník — Vřesová studánka — Červenohorské sedlo 14 km. Red-marked ridgeway with fine views.
2. Ovčárna — Kurzovní chalet — Praděd 3 km — Barborka — the Bílá Opava valley — Karlova Studánka 9 km. Along the green-, red- and blue-marked paths to the highest mountain in Moravia. — 3. Karlov — Velká kotlina — Vysoká hole — Jelení studánka — Alfrédka Chalet —

Karlov 21 km. To the most valuable nature preserve and to the main ridge with fine views.

Recommended car route:
Šumperk — Hanušovice — Ramzovské sedlo — Lipová-Lázně — Na Pomezí cave — Jeseník — Rejvíz — Vrbno pod Pradědem — Karlova Studánka — Domašov — Červenohorské sedlo — Velké Losiny — Šumperk. Tours on foot can be made from the mountain saddles. Total length of route 164 km.

Starting points: Šumperk, Jeseník, Bruntál, Ramzovské sedlo, Karlova Studánka, Malá Morávka.

JIČÍN   E 2

a district town (pop. 16, 000). Founded c. 1300. During the Thirty Years War the property of the military commander Albrecht of Wallestein, who chose Jičín as the seat of the so-called duchy of Frýdlant. In 1866 one of the biggest battles of the Prussian-Austrian war was fought here during which about 7,500 soldiers lost their lives. There are several small memorials in the environs. A **historical town reserve.** The square is surrounded by the continuous arcading of mostly Baroque and Empire houses. Set in the front of the houses is an originally Renaissance château which was enlarged in Early Baroque style. In its neighbourhood stands St. James's Church. Both buildings date in the period of rule of Albrecht of Wallenstein (d. 1634). Late Gothic **Valdická Gate** from 1568—1570 (height 52 m), a part of the town fortifications; from the gallery there is a view of the town and its surroundings.

Environs: starting point for the **Bohemian Paradise** (see items Český ráj, Prachovské skály, Kost, Trosky, Hrubá Skála).

a district town (pop. 50,000) and a centre of the Bohemian-Moravian Highlands. Extensive industry (engineering, textile). Theatre. Number of new housing estates.

The royal **mining town** originated after 1240 in the vicinity of deposits of silver. The local mining right became the model for other mining towns in Central Europe. In 1436 the compact enabling Czechs to take Holy Communion in both kinds was proclaimed here. The development of the town was halted by the Thirty Years War and it was finally the 19th century that brought new impulses (manufactories and the first factories). The historical centre of Jihlava is a **historical town reserve**. Its sloping square is one of the biggest in Czechoslovakia. Standing in its centre is the modern Prior department store and also a plague column and 2 fountains. Its sides are lined with medieval burghers' houses (one of the most valuable of them houses the Museum of the Bohemian-

Moravian Highlands) and on one side stands the Town Hall, originally Late Gothic in style with a Baroque turret of 1786. Baroque Jesuit church from 1680—1689. Gothic parish church with two steeples, founded before 1257. Preserved town fortifications and a Gothic gate, restyled in the Renaissance. The composer Gustav Mahler (1860—1911) spent his childhood in the town.

a district town (pop. 19,000) in the South Bohemian region of ponds. Textile industry (working of flax and cotton), production of gobelins.

Local castle mentioned in 1220, fortified town in the third quarter of the 13th century. In the 14th—16th century the lords of Hradec were one of the best-known Czech families. During their period of rule the town flourished and thanks to its advantageous position on the road from Bohemia to Austria and to Moravia it was one of the biggest

Jindřichův Hradec Château with Vajgar Pond

towns in Bohemia also in the 17th century. Frequent fires (in 1435, 1773, 1801). The local **château** is reflected in the surface of a pond. The building originated as the result of several reconstructions of a Gothic castle. Its present Renaissance appearance was lent it in the late 16th century. Next to the round tower stands the old castle palace with a chapel. In the Red Tower there is a so-called black kitchen; other buildings of the château complex are outstanding for their Renaissance arcades. In the château garden there is a rondel with rich sculptural decoration and a fountain. The château is undergoing reconstruction. Below it are the remains of medieval architecture.

The historical core of the town is a **historical town reserve**. In the square there are large Renaissance and Baroque burghers' houses and a Baroque column of the 18th century. Gothic provost's church of the 14th century, reconstructions after 1801. The meridian crosses the church 15° east of Greenwich and thus precise Central European time prevails here. Gothic frescoes can be seen in the former monastery church of the Minorites and the monastery itself has a cloister of the latter half of the 14th century. The District Museum is housed in the former seminary (also samples of Gothic and Baroque art, Christmas cribs).

Environs: numerous **ponds** suitable for bathing and water sports (8 km E Ratmírovský Pond, 14 km E Komornik, 16 km SE Osika near Albeř).

JIZERSKÉ HORY   E 1
(The Jizera Mountains)

---

a mountain complex in North Bohemia. Its summit parts have the character of highly situated plateaux with the gently raised, flat knolls of granite hills. Interesting rock formations can be seen in large numbers here. The mountains differ conspicuously from the environs. Particularly towards the north they fall as much as 500 m through high slopes. The highest peak is Smrk (1,124 m), situated in the immediate vicinity of the border, the second highest being Jizera (1,122 m) in the inland zone. Rivers and streams drain the mountains and, in the north, form deep gorges with rocks and boulders and often with waterfalls with cascades (Velký Štolpich, Smědá). Since the early 20th century 12 dams have gradually been built in the southern part of the range. The biggest of them are at Josefův Důl and Souš. The dams serve particularly for the supplying of drinking water.

A large part of these mountains is forested. The original mixed forests were mostly changed into pine monocultures, which in recent years have been damaged by the effect of industrial exhalations. Extensive felling activity is now taking place. The most valuable natural features are peat-bogs with peat-moss growths, peat lakes and, on the edges, dwarf pines. They are protected in nature preserves. The Jizerka and Na čihadle peat-bogs are accessible by means of nature study paths. In 1967 the Jizerské Mountains were proclaimed a **protected landscape region.**

The region of the Jizerské Mountains has a rich tradition in glass and fashion jewellery production (Železný Brod, Jablonec nad Nisou). In the 19th century textile production developed strongly in the foothills and Liberec became one of the biggest towns in Bohemia. Workers' associations, the first strikes (6 workers were shot at Svárov in 1870) and joint camps of Czech and German workers originated.

The southern part of the Jizerské Mountains in particular is a notable **tourist re-**

Jizerské hory

gion. It forms the background of the industrial towns of Liberec and Jablonec nad Nisou and the mountain ridges rise high above their outskirts. **Observation towers** and mountain chalets are situated on a number of peaks (e. g. Bramberk, Černá studnice, Špičák). Many mountain cottages now serve recreation purposes. — The most important skiing and tourist resort is **Bedřichov**, equipped with ski-tows and downhill runs. Marked tourist paths lead to Nová Louka (hunting château), Kristiánov (an isolated mountain locality with a small glass museum), Na čihadle (accessible peat-bogs) and Jizera (1,122 m, a peak affording far-reaching views, rocks). — **Josefův Důl** and neighbouring **Albrechtice** in the valley of the Kamenice are recreation resorts. Rising above them is Špičák (808 m), a skiing resort with a chalet and observation tower. — Spreading out below the south-eastern slopes of the mountain is the industrial town of **Tanvald** in whose immediate vicinity lies **Desná** with ski-jump structures (in 1916 a dam collapsed above the community in the valley of the Bílá Desná with the result that 62 persons lost their lives). — A road runs round **Souš** dam through the centre of the mountain range via **Smědava** Chalet (847 m) to Hejnice. — Situated on the border with the Krkonoše (Giant) Mountains is the popular summer resort of **Polubný-Kořenov**, overlooked by Hvězda (958 m) with an observation tower on its summit. — A mountain road leads to the former glass-making and wood-working community of **Jizerka** (860 m), now known for its recreation facilities, peat-bogs and the picturesque scenery along the River Jizerka (once a finding-place of semi-precious stones). Rising above Jizerka is the conspicuous basalt cone of the peak called Bukovec (1,005 m) with unique flora. The starting points for the Jizerské

Mountains from the north are Nové Město pod Smrkem, Bílý Potok and Hejnice. Rock formations (e. g., Ořešník above Hejnice, Frýdlantské cimbuří and Paličník above Bílý Potok) rise from the edges of steep precipices. The huge Baroque church in the small town of **Hejnice** dates in the 18th century. In the neighbourhood of **Lázně Libverda** there are mineral springs and peat is also used for therapeutical purposes. Restaurant situated in a huge barrel.

Recommended car route: In order to become quickly acquainted with the Jizerské Mountains it is possible to travel by car from Liberec to Rudolfov and Bedřichov (walking tours), to Josefův Důl, Albrechtice, Desná, Polubný and Jizerka (walking tour along a marked path) and then back to Polubný and via Smědava Chalet (ascent of Jizera) to Bílý Potok and Hejnice (excursion to the waterfalls and to Ořešník) and via Raspenava back to Liberec. Distance 100 km.

Recommended tours on foot:
1. The Jizerka nature study path — Bukovec, length 5 km. — **2.** From Bedřichov to the observation towers on Královka and Slovanka, length 5.5 km and perhaps to Bramberk 7.5 km. — **3.** From Hejnice to Ořešník and the Štolpišský Waterfall, circuit 10 km.

KADAŇ   B 2

a town (pop. 18,000) in the foothills of the Krušné (Ore) Mountains. The old community guarding the ford across the Ohře became a royal town in the mid-13th century. — Outstanding among the monuments in the **historical town reserve** concentrated round the trapezoidal square is the original Gothic **Town Hall** of the latter half of the 14th century with a huge tower dating in the

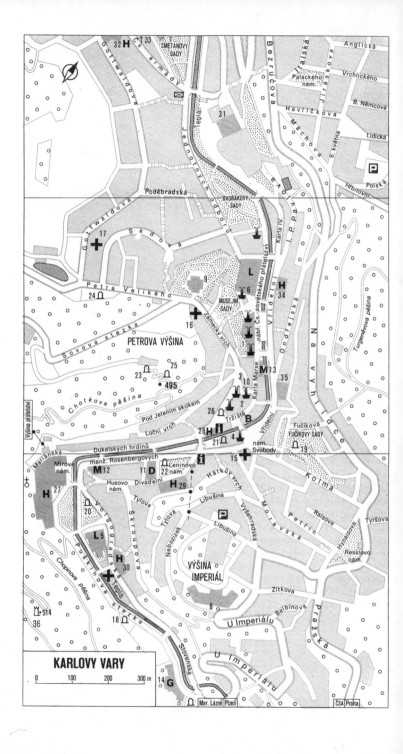

KARLOVY VARY

period before 1400, forming the landmark of the town. Certain Gothic, Renaissance and Baroque houses are also worthy of special note. The decanal church, originally Gothic, has undergone several reconstructions. The town fortifications with the Mikulovice Gate and the barbican of Žatec Gate of 1458 have partly been preserved. Plague column of the 18th century. In the western outskirts of the town a Franciscan monastery of the late 15th century with a church with a valuable interior, Baroque sculptures.

Environs: E the **Tušimice** power plant (brown coal). — 8 km N **Hasištejn**, the ruins of a Gothic castle (fine view). — 6 km NW **Klášterec nad Ohří**, a town with a china production tradition (since 1794). Romantically styled château with an exposition devoted to china production and a park with rare trees.

KARLOVA STUDÁNKA   H 2

---

a spa and summer resort (775 m) in Hrubý Jeseník. Treatment of diseases of the respiratory tract (e. g., silicosis). Spa buildings of the 19th century. Mineral spring.

Environs: W the valley of the Bílá Opava with **waterfalls** to the Ovčárna and Barborka Chalets and then to the highest peak of Hrubý Jeseník — **Praděd** (1,492 m), 6 km. — 6 km S **Malá Morávka**, a recreation resort on the Moravice, the seat of the administration of the Jeseníky protected landscape region, several recreation facilities, folk architecture. Part of the Karlov skiing resort, starting point for the Velká kotlina nature preserve (glacial hollows, rare flora).

KARLOVY VARY   B 2

---

a district town (pop. 58,000) and Czechoslovakia's **most important spa**. Situated in the valley of the River Teplá. Production of art glass of the **Moser** mark (e. g. giant snifters), china production (tradition from the 18th century, thin-walled and figural china), production of the **Becherovka** herb liqueur (from 1805), bottle-filling plant (Mlýnský Spring), production of curative spring salts. New construction. — Vítězslav Nezval Theatre (building from 1884—1886). Karlovy Vary spa orchestra. Every second year the scene of an **international film festival** and every year of the international Tourfilm film festival of tourist films. Annual music festival held under the name of Dvořák's Karlovy Vary Autumn.

The town was founded in the vicinity of thermal springs in the 14th century by the Emperor Charles IV. The springs were used for balneological purposes already at that time, although it was not until 1522 that a medical description of

---

1. Colonnade of Czechoslovak-Soviet Friendship (b). 2. Market Colonnade (b). 3. Château Springs Colonnade (b). 4. Sprudel Gagarin Colonnade (b). 5. Baths I (c). 6. Baths III (b). 7. Baths V (a). 8. Imperial Sanatorium (c). 9. State Sanatorium Bristol (b). 10. Château Tower (b). — 11. Vítězslav Nezval Theatre (c). — 12. Karlovy Vary Museum (b). 13. Karl Marx Museum (b). 14. Art Gallery (c). 15. Church of St. Mary Magdalene (b—c). 16. Anglican Church of St. Luke (b). 17. Orthodox Church of SS. Peter and Paul (b). 18. J. W. Goethe memorial (c). 19. Statue of Charles IV (b). 20. Charles IV memorial (c). 21. Y. A. Gagarin memorial (b). 22. V. I. Lenin memorial (c). 23. Peter the Great memorial (b). 24. K. Marx memorial (b). 25. Small statue of chamois on Jelení skok (b). 26. Group of statues of the Holy Trinity (plague column) (b). 27. Grand Hotel Moskva (Pupp) (c). 28. Atlantik Hotel (b). 29. Central Hotel (c). 30. Sevastopol Hotel (c). 31. Thermal Sanatorium (a). 32. Jizera Hotel (a). 33. Národní dům Hotel (a). 34. Otava Hotel (b). 35. Valencie Sanatorium with café (b). 36. Charles IV observation tower (c).

their properties was published. Some 200 spa institutions existed here already in the late 16th century. Rapid development in the 18th century. The spa gradually became known in a number of European countries. After a fire in 1759 a town built uniformly in Baroque style developed. Most of the monumental buildings originated in the latter half of the 19th century and at that time numerous outstanding personages from the whole world stayed at the spa. In 1938 Karlovy Vary was torn from Bohemia and became a hospital town. After 1945 the spa underwent extensive renovation.

The spa has some 60 **springs**, 12 of which are utilized (temperature approx. $42-72°$ C); the spring water is of surface origin and penetrates through fissures to a depth of 2,000 m, where it absorbs the heat of minerals and is enriched with dissolved minerals and drawn to the surface again by carbon dioxide. Drinking cure for diseases of the alimentary tract and metabolic diseases. The hottest spring is Vřídlo (Sprudel — $72°$ C) on the Sprudel Gagarin Colonnade. It has the form of a fountain.

A memorial to Yuri Gagarin stands in front of the colonnade. The Colonnade of Czechoslovak-Soviet Friendship from 1871—1881 (architect J. Zítek, Classical and Corinthian columns, coffered ceiling, 5 mineral springs) is of historical value. Further the Colonnade of Château Springs, the Colonnade of the Upper and the Lower Spring (Art Nouveau statue Protector of the Spring and a statue Hygie.). Nearby stands a Baroque group of statues of the Holy Trinity and the Market Colonnade (wooden structure, decorated with carvings).

The oldest part of Karlovy Vary is situated above the present locality called **Tržiště** (Market-place). The site of a former small hunting castle is now occupied by the Château Tower of 1608, accessible by lift; view of the spa. Třída Dukelských hrdinů, a street in the busiest part of the town with a promenade, runs in the upstream direction of the Teplá. It is closed by the **Moskva (formerly Pupp) Hotel.** Situated higher up is the Art Gallery (mainly Czech and Slovak painting and sculpture of the 20th century) and the Post Court of 1791, an old centre of Karlovy Vary's musical life. The main **sanatoria** (Baths I — formerly the Imperial Baths, Baths IV and Baths V) are also concentrated round the River Teplá. In the square Leninovo náměstí the **Vítězslav Nezval Theatre** (from 1884—1886). From the theatre a funicular runs to the hill with the **Imperial** Sanatorium (1910—1912), which forms the landmark of the town. The most outstanding historical building is the **Church of St. Mary Magdalene**, Barocized by K. I. Dienzenhofer. Of the town's other church buildings mention is deserved by the orthodox church of the late 19th century built after the model of the church at Ostankino in former Russia (in the 19th century the Russian aristocracy made up a considerable part of the visitors to Karlovy Vary). The Anglican Neo-Gothic church dates in 1877. A new landmark is the **Thermal Hotel** (16 floors) of 1976 with a thermal pool.

Numerous **outstanding personages** have stayed at the spa, most of them being recalled by memorial tablets and memorials: e. g. F. Schiller, A. Mickiewicz, N. V. Gogol, F. R. de Chateaubriand, J. W. Goethe (from 1785—1823 — 13 visits in all), K. Gottwald, A. Dvořák,

C. M. Weber, J. S. Bach, R. Wagner, F. Chopin, F. Liszt, J. Brahms, Z. Fibich and others.

Municipal museum (history, balneology, arts and crafts, workers' movement), Karl Marx Museum. There is a Casino in the town.

Walks along paths in park-like scenery above the slopes of the valley of the Teplá. A funicular runs from the Moskva Hotel to the top of the hill called Výšina přátelství (Friendship Hill) with the Diana observation tower. Above Tržiště Petrova výšina hill with Jelení skok (Stag's Jump — statue of a chamois). In the forests the Goethe observation tower (180 steps), the Charles IV observation tower and the Gottwald observation tower (636 m).

Environs: 10 km NE **Kyselka** spa with springs of Mattoni table acidulous water. — 17 km S **Bečov nad Teplou** with a Gothic castle and a Baroque château.

KARLŠTEJN   D 2

originally a Gothic **castle** on a rocky hill overlooking the valley of the Berounka. Built by the Emperor Charles IV from

Karlštejn
Castle

1348—1357 for the safe-keeping of the imperial coronation jewels and relics of the saints. In 1420 the imperial jewels were taken away byl King Sigismund and until 1619 the Czech coronation jewels were kept at the castle. After the Thirty Years War the castle lost its importance. A popular destination of excursions since the first half of the 19th century. Restored from 1887—1899. Standing on the highest elevation of the castle is a huge main tower containing the **Chapel of the Holy Rood,** whose walls are inlaid with semi-precious stones and bear a group of 127 paintings of saints by Master Theodoric

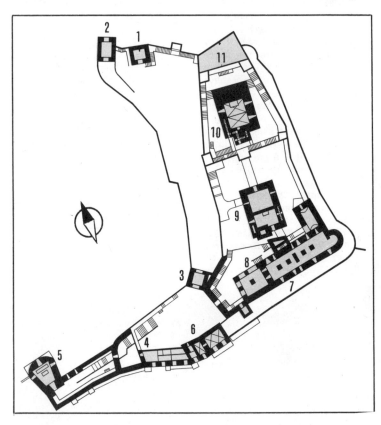

KARLŠTEJN
1. Original entrance tower, later called Voršilka. 2. First gate. 3. Second gate.
4. Staircase leading to the castle well; once the site of the old burgrave's house.
5. Tower with well. 6. Burgrave's house. 7. Imperial palace. 8. Third courtyard.
9. Small tower with the Church of Our Lady and St. Catherine's Chapel. 10. Main tower with the Chapel of the Holy Rood. 11. Bastion called Krchůvek.

Karlštejn

(1348—1367). A museum is now installed in the residential palace, where the Emperor Charles IV often stayed. Situated in the central part of the small tower is the Church of Our Lady with a group of Gothic paintings, including portraits of the founder of the castle. The adjoining Chapel of St. Catherine has walls decorated with semi-precious stones and paintings. It was the private oratory of the emperor.

Environs: attractive natural scenery of the protected landscape region of the **Bohemian Karst** — forests, limestone rocks and caves (the accessible Koněprusy Caves with rich stalagmite and stalactite decorations lie 7 km SW).

KEŽMAROK   M 3

a Slovak town (pop. 20,000) in the Poprad valley. Town rights from 1269, in the 19th century the first textile manufactories. — The historical core of the town is a **historical town reserve**. The original Gothic castle was converted into a Renaissance **château** and is now used for museum purposes. Late Gothic Church of the Holy Rood of 1444—1498, Spiš hall-type church in whose interior a Gothic altar and sculptures can be seen. Standing next to it is a Renaissance belfry of 1591 with graffito decoration and an attic. New Evangelic church from 1879—1892, built in Neo-Byzantine style. A number of historically valuable burghers' houses.

KLADNO   D 2

a district town (pop. 73,000) to the west of Prague. Centre of a **carboniferous basin**, big **metallurgical works** (steel production). Extensive new construc-

tion. — The small town grew considerably after the discovery of coal deposits (1842). Rich traditions in the sphere of the **workers' movement,** strikes and demonstrations (e. g. the so-called Corpus Christi demonstration in 1889, the general strikes in 1905 and 1920). In 1921 one of the oldest organizations of the Communist Party of Czechoslovakia, headed by the later president Antonín Zápotocký, was founded here. A memorial hall devoted to him is situated in the Workers' (now Culture) House. — Museum of the Kladno movement of United Steel Works (SONP) in Leninova Street.

Environs: 10 km N the industrial town of **Slaný** (pop. 15,000), partly preserved fortifications with the Velvary Gate and Gothic Church of St. Gotthard. Construction of new coal mines.

KLATOVY   B 3

a district town (pop. 23,000) in the foothills of the Šumava Mountains. A royal town already in the 13th century, in 1547 the seventh richest Czech town, from the 18th century an important cultural centre. — In the centre of the old town there is a quadratic square with a Renaissance **Town Hall** from 1557—1559 in whose neighbourhood stands the 76 m high Black Tower (wide view from its gallery) and a Baroque **Jesuit church** from 1655—1679 (valuable interior furnishings; below the church catacombs where members of the Jesuit Order were buried; entrance from the northern side of the church). In the square and also in the adjoining streets there is a number of Gothic, Renaissance and Baroque houses, outstanding among which is house No. 149, a pharmacy called At the White Unicorn — now a museum of pharmacy. In Krameriova

Street stands the Early Gothic Church of the Nativity of Our Lady (after 1260), rebuilt about 1400 and from 1550—1560, and next to it a Renaissance belfry called the White Tower (of 1581, rebuilt in 1758). Remains of the town fortifications, towers and bastions, have been preserved round the periphery of the historical core. — Tradition of Klatovy carnation cultivation.
Environs: Starting point for the Šumava Mountains. — 8 km SW the ruins of Gothic **Klenová** Castle with a gallery of creative art. — 12 km NW the community of **Chudenice** and Empire Lázeň Château with a valuable English park and the so-called American Garden (arboretum of American trees); on a small hill a tower called Bolfánek, converted into an observation tower.

A royal town founded already in 1257. Particularly outstanding among its numerous monuments is the Early Gothic **Church of St. Bartholomew.** Its nave dates in the latter half of the 13th century and the choir was built by Peter Parler from 1360—1378 (P. Parler was one of the architects who built St. Vitus's Cathedral in Prague); the belfry dates in 1504. The **Town Hall**, whose present appearance dates from 1887, was originally Gothic. Numerous Baroque houses. Old Jewish cemetery of the 15th century. In June every year the town is the scene of a brass band festival held under the name of Kmoch's Kolín.

KOKOŘÍN   D 2

---

a Gothic **castle** of the first half of the 14th century, situated picturesquely on a rock overlooking Kokořínský Důl valley 10 km N from Mělník. Adapted from 1911—1918. It has two dominating features in the form of a round tower with a cone-shaped helmet and the castle palace.
Environs: the **Kokořín protected landscape region** with interesting rock formations and sandstone valleys. — 2 km NE mushroom-shaped rock formations called **Pokličky.** — Folk architecture used for recreation purposes.

KOLÍN   E 2

---

a district town (pop. 31,000) in the fertile lowlands of the Elbe. Railway junction, extensive industry (chemical, engineering and food, printing works).

KOMÁRNO   J 5

---

a district town (pop. 36,000) on the confluence of the Váh and the Danube. Important port. Big **shipyards** (production of passenger and cargo boats, excavators). — From the 16th century a **fortress** against the Turks was built on the site of a castle of the 12th century; it is divided into the so-called Old Fortress of the 16th century, the New Fortress from 1663—1673 with a five-angled ground-plan with casemates, and the Palatinial Line — a system of bastions and walls from the times of the Napoleonic wars, surrounding the whole town. The fortress was never conquered by

---

Kokořín

Pokličky (lids)
sandstone formations
in the Kokořín region

the Turks. Bratislava Gate, built in Classical style in 1844. Numerous Classical houses. The former District Administration building and a Town Hall. — Museum devoted to the valley of the Danube. — Place of birth of the writer and poet Móric Jókai (1825—1904) and the composer Franz Lehár (1870—1948).

KONOPIŠTĚ   D 2

a **château** on the outskirts of the district town of Benešov. Original castle of the French type with 4 towers of about 1300, frequently reconstructed. Its present appearance dates from 1889—1894, when it was owned by the successor to the Austrian-Hungarian throne, Franz Ferdinand d'Este (in 1914 secret meetings with the German Emperor Wilhelm II took place here). In the interiors valuable collections, e. g., of arms (4,682 exemplars) and St. George (statues, pain-

tings, etc.). English park and rose garden (sculptures imported from Italy). *Environs:* in the district town of **Benešov** (pop. 16,000) the ruins of a Gothic Minorite church of the 14th century. — 6 km N, at **Poříčí nad Sázavou** two Romanesque churches, the cemetery Church of St. Peter with a lords' tribune of the late 11th century and St. Gall's Church of the early 13th century, later adapted.

KOPŘIVNICE   J 2

a town (pop. 21,000) in the foothills of the Beskids. In 1853 a factory for the production of coaches was founded here where the **first automobile** in then Austro-Hungary (President mark) was manufactured in 1897. Now the big **Tatra** automobile works for the production of lorries and passenger cars. Rich tradition in the workers' movement. —

Konopiště
Château

Technical museum oriented to the history of automobile production.
Environs: 2 km W Štramberk. — 8 km NE **Hukvaldy**, ruins of a big castle of the 13th century, surrounded by a large enclosure. The composer Leoš Janáček (1854—1928) was born in the community of the same name. Memorial hall in the house of his birth.

KOST E 1

a Gothic **castle** in the Bohemian Paradise. Picturesquely situated on a sandstone rock at the intersecting point of three valleys. Built at the turn of the 14th and 15th centuries, but frequently reconstructed. Rising from the highest elevation is a big tower on a trapezoidal ground-plan. Linking up with it are an old Gothic palace, the Late Gothic Šelmberk Palace and Bibrštejn Palace of the first half of the 16th century. To be seen in the castle is the original black kitchen and also the Gothic Chapel of St. Anne. An exposition of Late Gothic art from the collections of the National Gallery in Prague is now installed in the building.
Environs: SE of the castle the valley called **Plakánek**. It is lined with sandstone rocks and affords views of the castle. — 3 km SW a small château, **Humprecht**, built from 1666—1672 on an elliptical ground-plan. Museum expositions (e. g. children's books) are installed in its interior. — In the surrounding villages frame **folk architecture**.

KOŠICE N—O 3

a regional town (pop. 232,000) of the East Slovak region. The second most important political, economic and cultu-

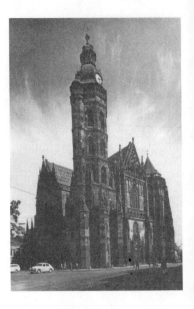

ral centre of Slovakia. The second most important **foundry complex** in Czechoslovakia, the East Slovak Ironworks, engineering and food industries. — On the slopes above the town a number of new housing estates, all situated in attractive landscape scenery. — Rich cultural life, a theatre with three ensembles, a state philharmonic orchestra, the seat of several universities. Annual scene in October of the International Peace Marathon.
The first mentions of the town date in 1230; its name was documented in 1248 and in 1347 it was made a free royal town. In the late 15th century the third biggest town in Hungary and in the 16th—18th century the centre of the anti-Hapsburg uprising. In the late 19th century building-up of industry and the development of the workers' movement. In 1919 the seat of the government of the Slovak Republic of Councils proclaimed in East Slovakia under the influence of the Great October Socialist

Kost

Cathedral
at Košice

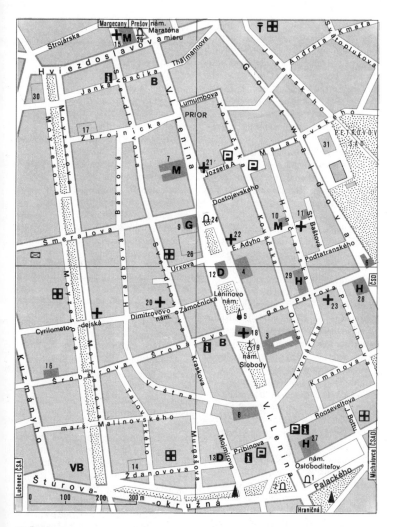

KOŠICE

1. Liberators' Memorial (d). 2. Unknown Warrior's Memorial (d). 3. House of the
Košice Governmental Programme (d). 4. Former Town Hall (Regional Library) (b—d).
5. Urban Tower (d). 6. Jakub's Palace (b). 7. Rákoczi Palace (Technical Museum) (a).
8. Forgách Palace (State Scientific Library) (d). 9. Dessewffy Palace (East Slovak
Gallery) (a). 10. Mikloš Prison (part of the East Slovak Museum) (b).
11. Executioner's Bastion (b). 12. State Theatre (d). 13. Thalia Theatre (Hungarian)
(d). 14. House of Art (c). 15. East Slovak Museum (a). 16. P. J. Šafárik University (c).
17. Technical University (a). 18. St. Elizabeth's Cathedral (d). 19. St. Michael's
Chapel (d). 20. Dominican church (c). 21. Franciscan church (b).
22. Premonstratensian church (b). 23. Evangelic church (d). 24. Group of statues
Immaculata (b). 25. International Peace Marathon memorial (a). 26. Municipal
National Committee (a). 27. Slovan Hotel (d). 28. Europa Hotel (d). 29. Imperiál Hotel
(d). 30. Sports Hall (a). 31. Indoor swimming-pool (b).

Revolution. During the Second World War Košice was occupied by Hungary. On 19 January, 1945 it was liberated and became the temporary seat of the president and government of Czechoslovakia and the Slovak National Council. On 5 April, 1945 the Košice governmental programme determining the post-war development of Czechoslovakia was approved.

The centre of the town is a **historical town reserve.** Standing here is **St. Elizabeth's Cathedral,** completed in 1506, the biggest church in Slovakia. F. Rákoczi II was buried in its crypt. Situated in its neighbourhood is the Gothico-Renaissance **Urban Tower** (belfry of 1628) and the Gothic Chapel of St. Michael. Opposite stands the building of the State Theatre from 1897—1899. Of the burghers' houses and palaces special mention is deserved by the **House of the Košice Governmental Programme** (of 1779, with modern museum — audiovisual programme), Rákoczi Palace (now the Technical Museum), the Renaissance building of the East Slovak Museum, Empire Forgách Palace (scientific library), Mikloš Prison — 2 Gothic buildings converted into a prison in the early 16th century, now a museum. The former Baroque-Classical Town Hall is now the Regional Library. *Environs:* 20 km E the **Dargov Pass,** in the winter of 1944—1945 the scene of tough battles for its conquering during which the Red Army lost 22,000 soldiers. Along the Košice-Michalovce road the Victory Memorial and the Rose Garden of Gratitude. — 18 km NE **Herľany** with a geyser which at intervals of 32—34 hours gushes to a height of 30—40 m. — W of the town the **Slovak Ore Mountains.** — 20 km NW the recreation region of the **Ružín** valley reservoir (water sports).

KOUŘIM   E 2

a town west of Kolín. SE of the town lies the Slavonic castle site called Stará Kouřim, the centre of the Zličan tribe. Three lines of ramparts have been preserved and excavations are revealing interesting finds. — The present town was founded c. 1260. On the periphery of the town fortification walls with the Prague Gate. Gothic parish church of the latter half of the 13th century. — A **museum of folk architecture** of Central Bohemian villages is originating on the outskirts of the town.

Environs: 4 km NW **Lipany,** where a barrow brings the fratricidal battle of the Hussite troops in 1434 to mind.

KREMNICA   K 4

a Central Slovak town where **gold** was mined already from the 11th century. Royal town from 1329. In 1329 silver groschens and from 1335 ducats were minted here. The local **mint** (in the square) is still in operation, but gold is no longer mined because this activity became unprofitable.

Historical town reserve. The former town castle dates in the 13th—15th century and its complex includes a Late Romanesque ossuary, a Gothic double-naved church with a steeple and fortifications with the Gothic Lower Gate. In the square houses of Gothic and Renaissance origin and a Baroque plague column. Museum of coins and medals.

KRKONOŠE   E—F 1
(The Giant Mountains)

the highest range of mountains in Bohemia whose main ridge stretches over

Kouřim

a length of 36 km along the border with Poland. The highest peak is Sněžka (1,602 m). Thanks to their diverse scenery, these mountains are the most frequented tourist region in Bohemia. Their relief bears clear traces of a former covering of ice. The biggest glaciers were at Labský důl and Obří důl through which the main rivers of the Krkonoše Mountains, the Elbe and the Úpa, flow. Huge granite rocks on a number of peaks (e. g. Dívčí kameny and Mužské kameny) are a characteristic feature.

Due to its exceptional natural wealth practically the whole territory of the Krkonoše Mountains was proclaimed a **national park** in 1963. The seat of its administration and the modernly installed museum is **Vrchlabí** (pop. 13,000). Information centres of the administration of the national park can be found at all big resorts in the Krkonoše Mountains. The greater part (80 %) of the national park is covered with a forest (mainly spruce trees). In the 19th century spruce growths were spread artificially at the cost of the original mixed and deciduous forests. At a height of 1,200 – 1,350 m above sea level the forests make way for dwarf pines or meadows (former pastures). In several places on the high plateaux there are mountain peat-bogs which have become the domain of plants which were a common occurrence in Central Europe in the Ice Age. The highest peaks in the Krkonoše Mountains are only sparsely covered with herbs and detritus. The most valuable mountain flora can be seen in the glacial hollows. The oldest reports concerning penetration into the Krkonoše Mountains date in the 15th – 16th century. Rapid development of **tourism** in the range came about in the latter half of the 19th century. Winter sports also underwent development (including skiing from 1894). The number of victims of the mountains also grew. Since 1934 a Mountain Rescue Service has been active in the Krkonoše Mountains for the safety of visitors.

Landscape in the Krkonoše Mountains, in the background Černá hora (1,299 m)

The western boundary of the Krkonoše Mountains is formed approximately by the valley of the River Jizera. The centre of the western part of the mountains, **Harrachov**, lies near the border crossing to Poland. The main ridge is reached via Mumlava valley with the well-known waterfall. The town of **Rokytnice nad Jizerou** (543 m) with a developed textile industry is a suitable starting point from the west. Its scattered buildings stretch from the valley of the Jizera to places below the slopes of **Lysá hora** (1,344 m) with skiing grounds. The summit parts of the western Krkonoše Mountains are also easily accessible from the recreation resort **Horní Mísečky** (1,100 m), to which a mountain road runs from Jilemnice. Buses transport visitors as far as Vrbatova bouda (chalet — 1,396 m). The **River Elbe springs** in a big summit plateau in the vicinity of the state border. Its spring called Labská studánka (1,386 m) is well-maintained and to be seen here are the emblems of the 24 towns through which the Elbe flows from its source to its mouth. Near the mountain hotel Labská bouda there is a 45 m high **waterfall** which falls into the Labský důl valley (a nature preserve). Situated nearby is the 130 m high Pančava Waterfall.

Situated in the close environs of Vrchlabí are the recreation resorts **Benecko** below the slopes of **Žalý** (1,019 m, observation tower, ski-tows) and **Strážné**. A road runs through the valley of the Elbe to the biggest resort in the Krkonoše Mountains, **Špindlerův Mlýn**, and continues (its use is limited especially in the winter season) to the chalet called Špindlerovka (1,198 m) on the main ridge. Enchanting **Sedmidolí** offers the possibility of making numerous atractive excursions. Ascent is facilitated by 2 chair-lifts.

Lying at a great distance SE of the main ridge is the huge fork of **Černá hora** (1,299 m), accessible by means of a cabin funicular from **Janské Lázně**. The valley of the Úpa connects Trutnov and other communities in the foothills with the centre of the eastern Krkonoše Mountains, **Pec pod Sněžkou.** It is just here that the highest peak in the Czech Socialist Republic, **Sněžka** (1,602 m) rises. The biggest mountain hotel in Czechoslovakia, Luční bouda (1,410 m, 316 beds), is situated in a mountain meadow near the sources of the Bílé Labe and the Úpa. Rising in its neighbourhood are Studniční (1,554 m) and Luční (1,547 m), the highest peaks in the Krkonoše Mountains after Sněžka. The chain of recreation resorts in the Krkonoše Mountains is brought to an end in the east by **Malá Úpa**.

The Krkonoše Mountains have excellent conditions for the development of **skiing**. Unfortunately, however, their funiculars and ski-tows are used to an enormous extent, frequent overburdening and long waiting periods being the result. They also have conditions for the development of **balneology** (Janské Lázně). Many buildings of private and works recreation are simultaneously interesting samples of folk architecture.

Recommended car route: Harrachov — Rokytnice nad Jizerou — Vítkovice — Horní Mísečky — Vítkovice — Hrabačov u Jilemnice — Vrchlabí — Černý Důl — Janské Lázně — Horní Maršov — Pec pod Sněžkou — Horní Maršov — Svoboda nad Úpou — Trutnov. Total length 150 km.

Recommended tours on foot:
1. The Fox route at Harrachov with fox symbols at important orientation points. It runs through the Mumlava valley to the slopes of Kotel (1,435 m), to the hut called Dvoračky and then back to Harrachov. Length 18.5 km. — **2.** The Eagle-Owl route at Špindlerův Mlýn with eagle-owl symbols. It runs from the chair-lift to Pláň below the peak of Luční

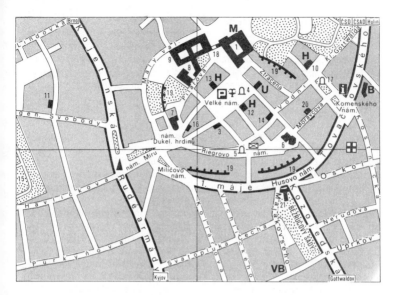

KROMĚŘÍŽ

1. Château (b). **2.** Podzámecká zahrada (Garden below the Château) (b). **3.** Town Hall (b). **4.** Marian plague column (b). **5.** Holy Trinity column (b—d). **6.** Parish Church of Our Lady (b). **7.** Piarist Church of St. John the Baptist (a). **8.** Chapter Church of St. Maurice (a). **9.** Former gymnasium (archbishop's seminary) (a). **10.** Straka Hotel (b). **11.** Old archbishop's granary (a). **12.** Haná Hotel (b). **13.** Central Hotel (b). **14.** Department store (b). **15.** Květná Garden (a). **16.** House of birth of M. Švabinský (a—b). **17.** J. Amos Komenský memorial (b). **18.** Mill Gate (b). **19.** Town fortifications (d). **20.** Town Hall of the former Jewish quarter (b). **21.** District National Committee (d).

hora and through the stony slopes of Kozí hřbety back to Špindlerův Mlýn. Length 14.5 km. — **3.** The Grouse route at Pec pod Sněžkou with grouse symbols. It runs to Lučiny (views of Sněžka) and to Černá hora. Length 6 km.

KROMĚŘÍŽ   H 3

a district town (pop. 26,000) in the fertile lowlands of the River Morava. Industry, research institute of corn cultivation.

An original castle site and community owned from 1107 by the bishopric of Olomouc; in 1266 a town. Considerably destroyed during the Thirty Years War, renewed in the latter half of the 17th century. In the 19th century an important and powerful centre of culture and education. From 1848—1849 the imperial constituent diet assembled here with the participation of Czech politicians. The assembly was dispersed by military troops.

Monumental Baroque **château** of the late 17th century on the site of an Early

Gothic castle. Château interiors with Baroque paintings and rich stucco decoration. Diet Hall, gallery (after Prague the most valuable collections of European painting of the 16th—17th century, e. g. Tizian, van Dyck, Brueghel the Younger, Bassano), sala terrena. Adjoining the château is **Podzámecká Garden** (the Garden Below the Château — English park) with Empire pavilions and the Pompeii Colonnade with classical statues of 1795. In the town the Early Baroque **Květná Garden** of the third quarter of the 17th century, area 485 × 300 m, a French park with a colonnade and a central pavilion. The centre of the town forms a **historical town reserve**. The square is lined with burghers' houses with arcades and a Renaissance **Town Hall** of 1611 stands in it. Most of the churches in Kroměříž were Barocized. Outstanding among them is St. Maurice's Church, built in Early Gothic style c. 1260. The tombstones of bishops can be seen in its interior. Remains of the former fortifications and Mill (Mlýnská) Gate of 1585. Baroque bishops' mint (1665) and granary (1711). On a hilltop Barbara's Chapel from which a Calvary with 14 Rococo halts (1762) runs. A Soviet tank brings the liberation of the town by the Red Army on 6 May, 1945 to mind.

KRUŠNÉ HORY   B—C 1—2
(The Ore Mountains)

---

a range whose 130 km long ridge forms a natural border with the German Democratic Republic in North West Bohemia. The ridge falls relatively steeply into Bohemia and considerably more gently into the German Democratic Republic on the other side. The highest peak is Klínovec (1,244 m). The greater part of this territory was mostly covered with spruce forests, but they have been substantially damaged due to the influence of exhalations from numerous industrial works (especially in the northeastern part); the pine forest is being replaced with deciduous and more resistant species of trees. Visitors to this region come across several peat-bogs, the most valuable of which is the Boží Dar Peat-bog. The interesting sights of nature also include radioactive springs at Jáchymov and Teplice.

The Krušné Mountains have a long-standing tradition in ore **mining** and traces of mining activity can be met practically everywhere (at Boží Dar, on Blatenský Hill, at Jáchymov and other places). The names of a number of communities were also derived from the local mining activity (Měděnec — měď = copper, Cínovec — cín = tin). Of the places of cultural and historical interest let us mention the château at Klášterec nad Ohří, the towns of Kadaň and Krupka (with Bohosudov), the ruins of Hasištejn Castle, the monastery at Osek, the château at Červený Hrádek and the town of Jáchymov.

The biggest concentration of tourist facilities can be found in the region of **Klínovec** (a chair-lift and mountain hotel), **Boží Dar** (1,028 m, interesting mountain architecture) and **Jáchymov**. Tourist facilities also exist in the environs of **Bouřňák** (ski-tows), Komáří vížka (chair-lift from Bohosudov and Teplice) and **Telnice** (skiing grounds near the town of Ústí nad Labem).

KŘIVOKLÁT   C 2

---

a **castle** in Central Bohemia which is picturesquely situated on a promontory overlooking the valley of the Křivoklátský potok (river). A wooden hunting castle of Czech princes stood here al-

Krušné hory

ready in the early 12th century, having been rebuilt as a stone castle after the mid-13th century. Numerous Gothic reconstructions were carried out particularly during the reign of Vladislav II (1471—1516). The later King Charles IV stayed here from 1319—1323 and in 1333. In the 16th century the castle served as a state prison. The dominating feature of the building is a round, 32 m high tower of the 13th century and standing between it and the square tower called Huderka is the castle palace (exposition documenting the development of the castle, the queen's chambers, a library, an exposition of Late Gothic sculptures and paintings). Château chapel with a valuable altar, a 40 m deep castle well, a collection of medieval intruments of torture in the prison. The castle also contains an exposition devoted to the **protected landscape region of Křivoklát** (a large territory covered with deciduous and mixed forests along the central flow of the Berounka, formerly a hunting-ground of Czech rulers.

Environs: 10 km NE **Lány** Château, the summer seat of Czechoslovakia's presidents with an enclosure with deer. — 12 km NW the district town of **Rakovník** (pop. 17,000), founded in the 13th century. It has two gates of the early 16th century (Pražská and Vysoká-High Gate) and a Gothic Church of St. Bartholomew with a wooden belfry.

KUKS   F 2

---

a complex of Baroque buildings in the Elbe valley, 18 km S of Trutnov. The uniform style of the buildings dates in 1694—1724. A château, a theatre, a summer palace and other structures were also erected here. Only the Baroque **hospital** with a church and the gallery of statues have been preserved in their original form. Inside the building there is a pharmacy with equipment from 1730—1740. On the façade of the Church of the Holy Trinity there are allegorical statues Virtues and Vices by M. B. Braun from 1715—1718 and in front of the axis of the church there are statues called Beatitude. Below them is the family grave of the Counts Sporck. *Environs:* 3 km W of Kuks a group of Braun's statues and sculptures Betlém (**Bethlehem**), carved in natural material in a forest environment.

KUTNÁ HORA   E 2

---

a district town in Central Bohemia (pop. 21,000). Engineering industry (ČKD Works), tobacco factory. — In the Middle Ages the second most important town in Bohemia, from time to time the seat of Czech kings. In the 13th century it underwent elemental development due to the rich deposits of silver ores in the locality. The profits from the local mines ranked Czech kings among the richest European sovereigns for a time. In 1300 a mint was founded in the town where Bohemian (Prague) groschens were minted. At the turn of the 14th and 15th centuries a favourite seat of King Václav IV. In the late 15th century uprisings of the miners, 10 of them were executed. The profits from the local mines dropped in the 16th century and the Bohemian groschen was minted for the last time in 1547. The mint was closed in 1726 and the decline of the town continued. Revival and extensive new construction as late as after 1945. The town has a rich cultural history, particularly in the 19th century. Place of work of many writers.

Historical town reserve. The town's landmark is **St. Barbara's Cathedral**

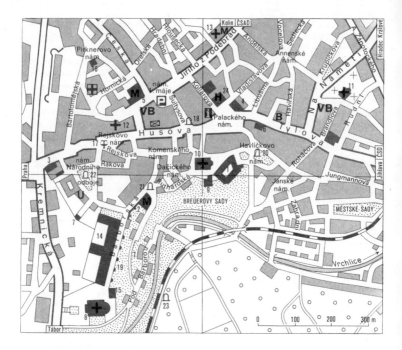

KUTNÁ HORA

1. Italian Court (b). **2.** Hrádek (museum) (c). **3.** Remainders of town fortifications (a).
4. Sankturin House (b). **5.** Stone House (museum) (a). **6.** J. K. Tyl monument (b).
7. Entrance to medieval shafts (c). **8.** St. Barbara's Cathedral (c). **9.** Archdeacon's
house (d). **10.** St. James's Church (a—b). **11.** Church of Our Lady "Na náměti" (b).
12. Church of St. John Nepomuk. **13.** Former Ursuline convent (b). **14.** Former Jesuit
college (c). **15.** Former Corpus Christi Chapel (c). **16.** Steeple of former St.
Bartholomew's Church (a). **17.** Stone fountain (a). **18.** Plague column (a). **19.** Gallery
of Baroque groups of statues (c). **20.** K. Havlíček Borovský memorial (b).
21. Memorial to victims of the First World War (c). **22.** Memorial to victims of the
Second World War (c). **23.** Relief of J. Vrchlický (in a rock) (c). **24.** Mědínek Hotel
(b).

(St. Barbara is the patron saint of miners), built from 1388—1565 by the most
outstanding architects of the Gothic period (P. Parler's workshop, M. Rejsek, B.
Ried). Magnificent net vault, emblems,
Gothic frescoes, paintings. The Gothic
Church of St. James from 1330—1420
stands out well due to its 82 m high
steeple. Paintings by P. Brandl and K.
Škréta can be seen in its interior. The
Italian Court, a Gothic building with
a chapel and tower from 1296—1299
was a royal seat and a mint. Valuable
Gothic interiors open to the public. **Hrá-**

dek, founded after 1300 and now Late Gothic in appearance (15th century) formed a part of the town's fortifications. Gothic frescoes can be seen in the Hall of Knights. The building is used as a museum (expositions documenting mining and minting). — Outstanding among the town houses are the Stone House of 1485 with oriels and a richly decorated façade, the Prince's House of about 1500 and Šultys's House. Several other churches and convents (interesting exposition of artistic crafts in the Ursuline convent, a Jesuit college with a gallery of sculptures in front of its main façade). Twelve-sided Late Gothic Stone Fountain from 1493—1495 (M. Rejsek), plague column from 1713—1715.

In the **Sedlec** locality a big **monastery** founded in 1142. Five-naved Gothic cathedral from 1290—1330, Barocized (paintings by P. Brandl). Nearby (400 m) a cemetery chapel with an ossuary (the bones of about 10,000 dead persons). 3 km from the centre **Kaňk Hill** (352 m) on which there are dumps and sunken galleries, remainders of medieval mining activity.

Environs: 5 km NE Empire **Kačina** Château from 1802—1822, remarkable library, agricultural museum, English park. — 10 km E **Žehušice** Château with an enclosure with white stags. — 9 km SE the historical town of **Čáslav** (pop. 11,000), remains of fortifications (the so-called Otakar Bastion), church of the 14th century.

LABSKÉ PÍSKOVCE D 1
(The Elbe Sandstone Rocks)

---

a **protected landscape region** to the north of Děčín near the border with the German Democratic Republic. Frequently, but geographically incorrectly called the Bohemian Switzerland (in combination with the immediately adjoining territory in the German Democratic Republic the Bohemian-Saxon Switzerland). This large territory is made up of quadratic **sandstone rocks** with rock towns on the edges of the rocky areas. The Elbe, whose most important tributary is the Kamenice, flows through the deep canyon from Děčín to Hřensko.

Gothic
St. Barbara's Cathedral
at Kutná Hora

A highly visited tourist region especially in the summer months. The biggest rock town is at **Tisá**, 12 km west of Děčín. Overlooking the community is **Děčínský Sněžník** (726 m) with an observation tower. Another starting point is **Hřensko**. Situated 3 km from the community is **Pravčická brána**, the biggest natural gateway in Central Europe. The river passes on the Kamenice are also a remarkable sight. — 15 km east of Hřensko lies **Jetřichovice**, the starting point for the Jetřichovice Rocks with a number of rock towers and rocks affording excellent views. Also to be seen here are the ruins of **Šaunštejn** Castle, a refuge of robbers in the 17th century. Well-preserved folk architecture can be seen in the whole region.

LEDNICE   G 4

---

a **château** near the River Dyje. It stands on the site of a castle and later Baroque château. It gained its present Neo-Gothic appearance in 1846—1856. Its interiors are outstanding for their richly carved ceilings and furnishings; collections of arms, china and hunting trophies. An agricultural, hunting and fishing museum is installed in a part of the building. Adjoining the château is an enormous greenhouse of 1845 with rich tropical vegetation. Well-maintained **French garden,** rich ornamental formations. The **English park** runs into the park-like open countryside with the River Dyje, its branches and ponds. A number of Empire **pavilions**, e. g. Apollo's Temple, the Temple of the Three Graces and Rybniční Château. The best-known structures in the park are the 60 m high **minaret** near Zámecký pond and the romantic ruins of Jan's Castle.

Environs: 6 km SW the town of **Valtice**, Early Baroque château on the site of a castle perhaps founded already in the late 12th century. Stucco decoration, wall paintings. English park with Empire pavilions. Wine production.

Lednice

Lednice
Château

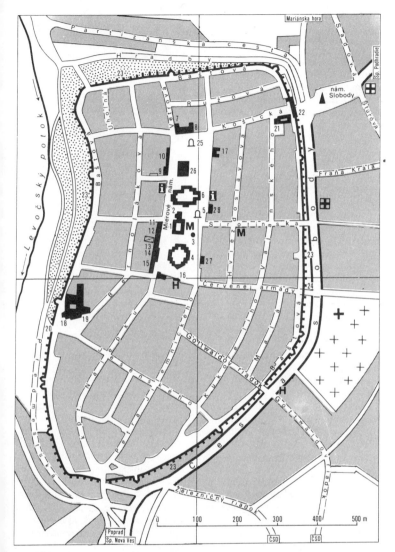

LEVOČA

1. Town Hall (Spiš Museum) (a). 2. Belfry (a). 3. Pillory (a). 4. Evangelic church (a).
5. Red Army memorial (a-b). 6. St. James's Church with altar by Master Pavol of
Levoča (a—b). 7. Former district administration building (a). 8. Former small district
administration building (a). 9. Former town inn (a). 10. Arcaded courtyard (a).
11. Okolicsányi-Zsedényi House (a). 12. Spillenberg House (a). 13. Mariássy House
(post-office) (a). 14. Old Thurz's House (a). 15. Hainovský House (Spiš Museum) (a).
16. Biela paní Hotel (a—c). 17. New Thurz's House (b). 18. Former Minorite
monastery (c). 19. Old Minorite church (c). 20. Polish Gate (c). 21. New Minorite
church (b). 22. Košice (Higher) Gate (b). 23. Town fortifications (a—b—c).
24. Menhard (Vrbov) Gate (d). 25. Ľ. Štúr memorial (a—b). 26. Merchant's house (a).
27. Brewer's Printing Works (b). 28. Master Pavol's House (b).

a town (pop. 13,000) founded in the mid-13th century. From 1271 the seat of the self-government bodies of 24 Spiš towns. A royal free town before 1323. Levoča stood on important trade routes and grew considerably rich in the 15th and 16th centuries. As the result of frequent fires a substantial part of the town was rebuilt in the Renaissance (apart from the main square over 200 Renaissance houses have been preserved to the present). At that time the town was an important cultural centre of the Slovak reformation (printing works of 1624) and from the forties of the 19th century it was the centre of the revival movement of Ľ. Štúr and his followers. Economic decline in the 19th century, construction of industrial works after 1945.

Historical town reserve. The most valuable monument is the Gothic parish **Church of St. James** of the late 14th century. Inside there is a carved Gothic high altar, the work of **Master Pavol of Levoča** (of the early 16th century). Its height is 18.6 m and its width 6 m and it has a scene of The Last Supper and sculptures of the Madonna and Child, St. James and St. John the Apostle. Standing in the neighbourhood of the church is the **Gothic Town Hall**, completed in the Renaissance, of 1615 (now a museum devoted to the development of Levoča).Nearby stand a belfry of 1656 and a pillory of 1600. In the centre of the square there is an Evangelic church with a dome. Fifty burghers' houses with Gothic stone portals line the square, whose present appearance dates from the 16th and 17th centuries. New Thurz's House (No. 7) with a Renaissance attic is particularly noteworthy. Well-preserved and gradually restored fortification wall, length approx. 2 km;

3 entrance gates (Košice, Polish and Menhardt Gates). In one of the bastions there is a museum devoted to the blind (there is a school for the blind in the town).

LIBEREC E 1

a district town (pop. 100,000) in North Bohemia. Development of textile industry from the late 16th century, now one of the biggest centres of Czechoslovakia's **textile industry**; seat of the University of Textile and Mechanical Engineering and research institutes. Production of lorries, plastics, etc. — From 1877—1880 the town was the seat of the central committee of the Austrian Social Democratic Party. At the time of the bourgeois democratic republic there was a strong workers' movement here. — The landmark of the centre of the town is the Neo-Renaissance **Town Hall** from 1888—1893 with a 65 m high tower. Another notable building is that of the theatre. Other older monuments include a Renaissance château of the late

Levoča

Town Hall
at Levoča

16th century with a chapel of the early 17th century. Small, framed houses of the mid-17th century in Větrná Street. Situated in the town is the oldest zoo in Czechoslovakia (of 1906) and also a botanical garden. Every second year Liberec is the scene of exhibition markets.

Environs: 6 km SW of the centre Mount **Ještěd** (1,012 m), accessible by means of a cabin funicular. On its summit a 92 m high TV transmitter with a hotel and restaurant; far-reaching views. Tourist and winter sports resort, skitows, ski-jump structures. — NE of Liberec the ridges of the Jizerské Mountains.

LIDICE   D 2

a community lying 6 km E of Kladno; a symbol of the struggle against fascism. On the pretence of the contact of two local families with the parachutists who assassinated R. Heydrich the **community was razed to the ground** by the German Gestapo on 10 June, 1942 and all the men (192) were mostly shot on the site of the Horák family's farm. 196 women and 105 children were dragged off to concentration camps. The whole area is now a national cultural monument. There is a museum here and also a Rose Garden of Friendship and Peace.

LIPNO   C—D 4

a valley reservoir (727 m) on the upper stream of the Vltava. The **dam** wall of only 25 m in height retains a lake of 40 km in length and about 16 km in width. Its area is 4,659 hectares. Underground power plant. Big **recreation region** on the banks of the lake: hotels, chalet communities, car camps, boat transport, bathing, water sports — advantageous position facing south below the ridges of the Šumava Mountains. **Tourist resorts** are situated on the banks of the lake in downstream direction: **Nová Pec** (the only resort on the right bank), **Horní Planá** (a small town, birth place of the Šumava writer Adalbert Stifter with a memorial hall and memorial to him), **Černá v Pošumaví, Frymburk** (a small town on a promontory surrounded by the waters of the lake, a Gothic church and a fountain of the 17th century), **Lipno nad Vltavou** (2 km from the community the Kramolín skiing resort). Below the dam wall lies the stony, usually empty bed of the Vltava, so-called **Čertovy proudy** (Devil's Currents) and overlooking it is the huge rock wall called **Čertova stěna** (Devil's Wall) with a stone sea (disintegrated granite). Below Devil's Currents Vyšší Brod monastery.

TV transmitter with hotel
on Mount Ještěd (1,012 m)
near Liberec

a town and a starting point for the Low, West and High Tatras. Ruins of an original Gothic water castle; in its neighbourhood a Renaissance château from 1600—1603 with period fortifications — inside an ethnographical museum devoted to the Liptov region. Baroque-Classical building of a weighbridge and a belfry near a former blast furnace for the working of iron ore — a technical monument (from 1792).

LIPTOVSKÝ MIKULÁŠ   L 3

a district town (pop. 29,000) in the Váh valley between the ridges of the Low and the West Tatras. A town from the latter half of the 13th century. From the 19th century an important centre of Slovak political life and the workers' movement. Tough battles during the liberation in 1945.

The town has several original Renaissance curias, one of which houses the Museum of the Revolutionary Poet Janko Kráľ. Originally Early Gothic St. Nicholas's Church with valuable interior, reconstructed on several occasions. Museum of the Slovak Karst in a former monastery. Numerous memorials and memorial tablets recalling functionaries of Slovak cultural and political life. Memorial to the May Day manifestation of 1918, marked by the demand for a joint national union of Czechs and Slovaks (the House at the Black Eagle). *Environs:* 3 km W the **Liptovská Mara** dam lake of an area of 21.6 sq. km and a max. depth of 43 m, power plant. Recreation resorts on the northern banks (Liptovský Trnovec), boat transport. — 17 km S the valley **Demänovská dolina.**

district town (pop. 25,000) on the River Elbe. Numerous orchards and vineyards in the surroundings (in September every year a traditional exhibition of fruit, vegetables and flowers held under the name of The Garden of Bohemia).
Already in the 9th century the castle site of the Slavonic Lutomiric tribe, from the 10th century one of the most important administrative centres of the Czech state and a royal town before 1234. Development of the town in the 16th century, considerably destroyed during the Thirty Years War. In 1655 a bishopric was founded here which gave the impulse for the Barocization of the town. **Historical town reserve.** In the square with a Gothic ground-plan can be seen the original Gothic **Town Hall** (now with a Renaissance appearance from 1537—1539, seat of the district museum nowadays). A number of Late Gothic, Renaissance, Baroque and Empire houses. The Renaissance building of the North Bohemian Gallery (Czech creative art from the 12th century up to the present and an exhibition of naive art). The decanal All Saints' Church (valuable interior furnishings). Standing on the site of a former prince's castle on a hill overlooking the Elbe (Dómský pahorek), in the place once occupied by a Romanesque basilica, is **St. Stephen's Cathedral,** a triple-naved Baroque building from 1663—1670 with rich furnishings (L. Cranach, K. Škréta); standing in its neighbourhood is a square tower of the late 19th century. Adjoining the cathedral is the bishop's residence of the late 17th century. — Cultural centre from the Middle Ages. The greatest Czech poet of the romantic period, Karel Hynek Mácha (1810—1836), lived and died here. *Environs:* W the hill **Radobýl** (390 m) of-

Liptovský
Hrádok

fering far-reaching views and the village of **Velké Žernoseky** with vineyards. The valley of the Elbe called Porta Bohemica with canyons and overlooking it the hill Lovoš (570 m). — 13 km SW **Třebenice**, museum of Bohemian garnets and the death chamber with relics of Ulrika von Lewetzow, J. W. Goethe's last love. — 4 km NE Baroque **Ploskovice** Château, converted from 1850—1853 into a summer seat for the ex-Emperor Ferdinand I.

LITOMYŠL   G 2

an East Bohemian town (pop. 10,000). Several industrial works, especially a factory for the production of glass fibres (Sklo Union Vertex).
In the 10th century mention was made of the Slavník family's castle here, before 1150 a Premonstratensian monastery was founded here, in 1260 the community became a town and in 1344 a bishopric; in 1421 the town was conquered by Jan Žižka and the bishopric ceased to exist.

Historical town reserve. Outstanding among the medieval monuments is a Renaissance **château** from 1568—1581, situated on a hilltop on the site of the castle and monastery. It is a four-winged building with loggias and graffito decoration and inside it there is a remarkable theatre from 1796—1797; exposition of the **Museum of Czech Music.** The Renaissance château brewery contained the family home of the Czech composer Bedřich Smetana (1824—1884) — now serving as a museum. Château garden with open-air theatre. — In the neighbourhood of the château a former Piarist college from 1641—1680 and a Baroque church. Gothic protestant church of the 14th century, repaired in 1604. — Elongated square by the former road from Bohemia to Moravia, lined with continuous arcading. Most of the gables were originally Renaissance, Baroque and Empire houses with attics from the 16th—19th century. Renaissance Town Hall with a tower (after 1546).
The town played an important cultural role at the time of the Czech national revival in the 19th century and also later.

Square
at Litoměřice

Every year in July an opera festival takes place here under the name of Smetana's Litomyšl and in September the Young Smetana's Litomyšl event is held here.
Environs: 13 km W Rococo **Nové Hrady** Château, effectively set in the landscape; valuable furnishings and a park.

LOKET   B 2

a town situated in a picturesque setting on a promontory overlooking the River Ohře. China production (tea and coffee services) since 1815. — An ancient centre of the western part of Bohemia with a castle and a town probably from 1240. On the highest elevation of the promontory stands a big Gothic **castle** with a square tower of the mid-13th century, later rebuilt. A **china museum** is installed in it. Valuable houses, an Early Baroque Town Hall (1682—1687) and a plague column (1718) in the square. Near the town a bridge of 1935, affording good views, spans the valley.
Environs: 5 km E the granite rock formations called **Svatošské skály,** above the canyon-type valley of the Ohře. According to a legend the rocks represent a fossilized wedding procession. This theme inspired the romantic writers Körner, Grimm, Goethe and others and Heinrich Marschner used this motif in his opera Hans Heiling. — 7 km SW the district town of **Sokolov** (pop. 29,000), the centre of a brown coal basin.

LOUNY   C 2

a district town (pop. 25,000) in North West Bohemia with railway workshops. — After 1260 a royal town with a bridge across the River Ohře. Preserved remains of the Late Gothic fortifications with Žatec Gate. Decanal **Church of St. Nicholas** from 1520—1538, the work of B. Ried's workshop, valuable interior furnishings.
Environs: diverse landscape of the **Bohemian Central Highlands.** — 18 km E the town of **Libochovice** with an Early Baroque château from 1683—1690. The place of birth of the outstanding scientist Jan Evangelista Purkyně (1787—1869). — 17 km NE the ruins of Gothic **Házmburk** Castle on a rocky basalt cliff (418 m), visible from far and wide.

LUHAČOVICE   J 3

a Wallachian town with a well-known **spa,** founded in the late 18th century. However, it began to develop as late as the early 20th century. Modern colonnade with the Vincentka and Amandka mineral springs. Treatment of diseases of the respiratory tracts, the alimentary tract, diabetes and obesity. — The first spa sanatoria were lent a unified appearance by the architect D. Jurkovič, whose house stands at the southern end of the spa colonnade. (Jurkovič

Loket

Vincentka Spring
at Luhačovice

based his projects on Wallachian folk architecture.)
Environs: 2 km NE a recreation region by a **dam** reservoir.

LUŽICKÉ HORY   D 1
(The Lusatian Mountains)

a picturesque range on the northern border between Czechoslovakia and the German Democratic Republic. The highest peaks are conspicuous basalt and phonolite mounds — Luž (791 m), Jedlová (770 m), Hvozd (750 m) with mixed forest growths. This range of mountains forms a **protected landscape region** with a number of nature preserves and protected natural formations, e.g. the Bílé kameny rock formations, the Naděje (Hope) Ice Cave, protected yew trees at Krompach (about 500 years old), the solitary basalt, column-shaped formation on the hill Zlatý vrch and others. Chamois live on the rocky slopes of Klíč (760 m) near Nový Bor, from where wide views can be obtained. Numerous frame folk buidlings can be seen in the whole region, e.g., at Horní Světlá, Kytlice and other places. The starting point for the Lusatian Mountains is **Jablonné v Podještědí,** 28 km W of Liberec, with a big monastery church of the 18th century (accessible crypt). — 3 km from here stands **Lemberk** Castle of the 13th century, rebuilt in the Renaissance and the Baroque. — **Starting points** are also the industrial towns of Hrádek nad Nisou, Varnsdorf, Cvikov, Česká Kamenice and Nový Bor.

MÁCHOVO JEZERO   D 1
(Mácha's Lake)

a big recreation pond (350 hectares) on the eastern outskirts of the Bohemian Central Highlands. Founded in 1366 by the Emperor Charles IV. It was originally called Big Pond, but was later renamed after the romantic poet Karel Hynek Mácha. Surrounded by pine forests, 2 rocky islands. Its banks are used for **recreation** purposes: sandy beaches, bathing, water sports, boat transport. — The town and summer resort of **Doksy** with hotels, chalet camps and a car camp lies on its southern bank. — **Staré Splavy** is situated on its north-western bank.
Environs: 8 km SE the ruins of **Bezděz** Castle on a conspicuous hill (604 m), founded by King Přemysl Otakar II. Early Gothic chapel, 40 m high Big Tower. — 11 km N Baroque **Zákupy** Château with valuable interiors with paintings by J. Navrátil. — 14 km NW the industrial district town of **Česká Lípa** (pop. 35,000).

MALÁ FATRA (The Little Fatra)   K 3

a range in the north-western part of Slovakia, near the big industrial centre and transport junction of Žilina. Approximately in the middle of the range the River Váh cuts its-way through the main ridge and creates the 12 km long Strečno Pass. In the Middle Ages the castles Starý hrad and **Strečno** guarded a trade route running through the valley.
The highest peak is **Veľký Fatranský Kriváň** (1,709 m) in the **northern part** of the range. It is relatively eeasily accessible from the upper station of the chairlift from the biggest tourist centre in the

Little Fatra, **Vrátna** valley. Several of the peaks in its environs are of a rocky nature and particularly outstanding is the rugged limestone peak called **Veľký Rozsutec** (1,610 m), one of the richest botanical localities in Czechoslovakia. Wild, rocky passes have also originated in the limestone rocks. At Šútovo there is a 38 m high waterfall. The whole of this part of the range has been proclaimed a **national park**.

The **southern part** of the Little Fatra is dominated by the valley Turčianská kotlina with the district town of Martin.

A chair funicular runs from here to the region called **Martinské hole**. The highest peak, Veľká lúka (1,476 m), is bare and it offers far-reaching views.

A red-marked **tourist path** runs along the whole of the main ridge; the crossing from Zázrivá (585 m) via Veľký Fatranský Kriváň, Strečno (360 m) and Veľká lúka to the saddle Fačkovské sedlo (802 m) is 72 km long (the most frequented parts are accessible by means of funiculars).

Recommended car route: Žilina — the Váh valley to Varín — Terchová — Rovná hora saddle — Zázrivá (numerous wooden folk buildings in the environs) — the Zázrivka valley — round the chair-lift to Magura (1,260 m) — the Orava valley — Kraľovany — Šútovo (the Šútovo Waterfall) — Martin (local part Priekopa) — the Váh Pass back to Žilina. Total length 100 km.

Starting points: Žilina, Martin, Terchová.

MARIÁNSKÉ LÁZNĚ   B 2

an important West Bohemian **spa** and big recreation resort of the Revolutionary Trade Union Movement, a garden town (pop. 18,000) on the southern edge of Slavkov Forest.

The local springs were known already in the 16th century. About 1809 spa sanatoria began to originate on plots of land belonging to the Premonstratensian

Mariánské Lázně

Ridges of the Little Fatra

monastery at Teplá. The founders of the spa were the abbot of the monastery, K. K. Reitenberger, and a physician by the name of J. J. Nehr. The spa has 40 cold **springs** (Křížový, Rudolfův, Ferdinandův, Lesní, Ambrožův and others) which are used for drinking cures, baths and mud therapy in the treatment of diseases of the kidneys and urinary tract, metabolic disorders, skin diseases, diseases of the joints and diseases of the respiratory tracts. The spa was raised to a town in 1866. It was built in accordance with the local terrain, transformed by generations of gardeners, whose first representative was Václav Skalník (d. 1861), into a kind of English park.

The historical centre of the town is concentrated round the cast iron **M. Gorký Colonnade** of 1889 and round the **Křížový Spring** (colonnade of 1818). Also situated in its neighbourhood is the Singing Fountain of a diameter of 18 m with hundreds of jets. On the stroke of every odd hour music is heard, in the evening with coloured illumination. Most of the spa and public buildings round the square Gottwaldovo náměstí and the street called ulice Odborářů date in the latter half of the 19th century. Other outstanding buildings: the Neo-Byzantine Church of Our Lady of the mid-19th century, an orthodox church of 1901 (a unique ceramic ikonostas produced by the china works at Loket), Rudolph's Spring Colonnade, the Casino social building of 1901 and others. Several memorials to and sculptures of eminent personages who took cures at the spa (Edward VII, Nicholas II, J. W. Goethe, F. Chopin, N. V. Gogol, M. Gorky and others) can be seen in the town. The Municipal Museum with expositions devoted to Goethe, Gorky and the development of the town is installed in the building in which J. W. Goethe was accommodated in 1823 (Gottwaldovo náměstí 11). — There is a memorial to F. Chopin in the town. *Environs:* 5 km NW **Lázně Kynžvart** with 6 springs of ferruginous acidulous water

Křížový Spring
at Mariánské Lázně

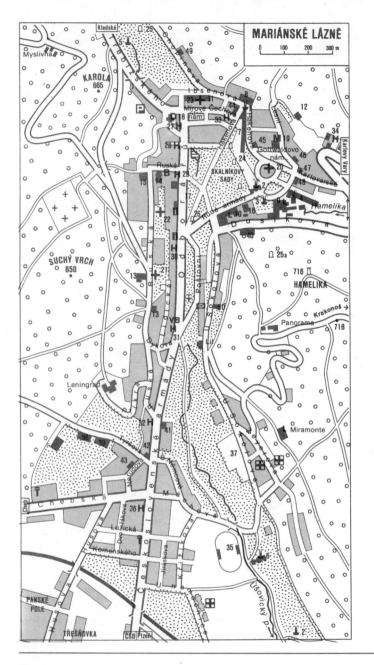

MARIÁNSKÉ LÁZNĚ

0   100   200   300 m

Myslivna

KAROLA
665

Kladská

Mírové Čechov
nám.

SUCHÝ VRCH
650

Ruská

SKALNÍKOVY
SADY

Rude armády

Gottwaldovo
nám.

Karlovarská

Hamelika

Karlovy Vary

HAMELIKA
716

Krakonoš
Panorama   718

Leningrad

Miramonte

Cheb

Chebská

Lužická

Komenského

PANSKÉ
POLE

TŘEŠŇOVKA   ČSD Plzeň

*Mariánské
Lázně*

210

and a children's sanatorium. Classical château from 1820—1833 in a big English park, a seat of Chancellor Metternich of Austria. — 12 km E **Teplá** monastery, founded in 1193. A fortified, originally Romanesque church reconstructed in the Gothic and the Baroque, a convent from 1685—1721, an old and a new library (80,000 volumes). — **Slavkov Forest**, a protected landscape region: Kladská hunting château with the nearby (SW) Kladská Peat-bog nature preserve with a nature study path.

MARTIN K 3

a district town (pop. 62,000) in the wide valley between the Big Fatra and the Little Fatra. Engineering and woodworking industries. — A town from 1340. In the 19th century a centre of the **cultural life** of the Slovaks; in 1863 the Matica slovenská cultural and educational organization was founded whose aim was to free the Slovak nation from Hungarian oppression. In 1867 one of the three Slovak gymnasia was founded. On 30 October, 1918 the Martin Declaration was proclaimed in which representatives of all Slovak political parties spoke in favour of the formation of one single Czechoslovak state. In 1944 one of the main centres of the Slovak National Uprising.
Modern Matica slovenská building. This old building from 1869—1875 has been declared a national cultural monument similarly as the National Cemetery in which well-known Slovak writers and cultural functionaries (e.g. J. Jesenský, J. Kráľ, M. Kukučín) are buried. A theatre, the Slovak National Museum and a medical faculty are situated in the town. The Museum of Slovak Villages (3 km from the centre) is gradually concentrating buildings of folk architecture from various parts of Slovakia.
Environs: The Big and the Little Fatra. — 20 km Renaissance **Diviaky** Château. — 22 km S **Turčianske Teplice** spa for the treatment of diseases of the motory organs; mineral water of a temperature of 42° C, thermal pools.

1. Cross Spring. 2. Rudolph Spring. 3. Ambrož Spring. 4. Maria Spring. 5. Forest Spring. 6. Ferdinand Spring. 7. Maxim Gorky Colonnade. 8. Management of the spa organization. 9. Central Spa. 10. New Spa. 11. Military Sanatorium. 12. Kremlin State Sanatorium. 13. Balneological Research Institute. 14. Municipal National Comittee. 15. Administration of the recreation houses of the Revolutionary Trade Unions Movement. 16. Casino Social House. 17. Cultural and Social Centre, Chopin House. 18. N. V. Gogol Theatre. 19. Municipal Museum (Goethe House). 20. Roman-Catholic church. 21. Orthodox church. 22. Anglican church. 23. Evangelist church. 24. Memorials in the spa: the Abbot Karel Kašpar Reitenberger memorial, the Frederik Chopin memorial, the Václav Skalník memorial. 25. J. W. Goethe memorials. 26. Liberation memorial. 27. Palace Praha Hotel. 28. Corso Hotel. 29. Atlantik Hotel. 30. Excelsior Hotel. 31. Cristal Hotel. 32. Slavonic House. 33. Sporthotel Slunce. 34. Esplanade Hotel. 35. Sports Stadium. 36. Haná Hotel. 37. Tennis courts. 38. Winter Stadium. 39. Sokolovna. 40. Sports Hall. 41. Municipal Popular Library. 42. Czech Savings Bank. 43. Slávie Cinema. 44. Dyleň shopping centre.

MĚLNÍK   D 2

a district town (pop. 20,000) in a fertile
agricultural region. Standing on a hill,
whose southern slopes are covered with
vineyards, in a dominant position on the
confluence of the two biggest Czech
rivers — the Elbe and the Vltava — is
a château. Important river port.
The beginnings of Mělník date in the
10th century, when a Slavonic castle of
the Pšovan tribe stood here. From 1274
it was a royal town in which the queens
often resided (till 1475). It was particularly the Emperor Charles IV, who
brought the Burgundian vine to Bohemia, that was responsible for the development of **wine production** here.
The **château** was built on the site of
a Romanesque and Gothic castle which
was supplemented with a Renaissance
wing and subjected to a number of Baroque adaptions. A museum (with an
exposition devoted to wine production),
a gallery (paintings by the outstanding
Baroque painters P. Brandl, K. Škréta,
V. V. Reiner) and a stylish restaurant are
housed in the interior of the château. In
the immediate vicinity of the building
stands the Gothic **Church of SS. Peter
and Paul** with a high steeple. Its present
appearance dates in the late 15th and
the early 16th century. Inside there are
valuable furnishings and an ossuary.
The square is surrounded by houses
with arcades and outstanding among
them is the Town Hall, Gothic in core,
but Barocized. Of the medieval fortifications the Prague Gate has been preserved.
Environs: 7 km N **Liběchov**, a small
town with an originally Renaissance
château, enlarged in the Baroque about
1730 (F. M. Kaňka). Wall paintings by J.
Navrátil. An exposition of Asian nations
(part of the Náprstek Museum) is now
installed in the buildings. — 14 km NW

Mount **Říp** (456 m), a forested basalt
mound with an important role in Czech
mythology (the legend about the arrival
of the first father Čech) which has inspired a number of artists. It is a place
of pilgrimage and of popular assemblies. On its summit stands a Romanesque rotunda consecrated to St.
George of the 11th—12th century.

MIKULČICE   H 4

the most important **archeological finding place** on the territory of Czechoslovakia. It lies on the right bank of the
River Morava 6 km SW of Hodonín. In
the 9th—10th century a rich town of the
Great Moravian Empire, a seat of
princes, stood here. It was revealed in
the course of archeological excavations
carried out from 1954. Remainders of 11
churches, the foundations of other
buildings and numerous adornments
and articles of every-day use have been
unearthed here. The area is accessible
and a memorial hall with expositions of
archeological finds is situated here.

MIKULOV   G 4

a picturesquely situated town on the
slopes of the Pavlovské Hills (on the
border with Austria); border crossing.
Vine-cultivation centre (especially for
white wine). The town was founded in
1322 in the outer bailey of a Gothic castle. Large Jewish population. In the 18th
century the Supreme Rabbi for the
whole of Moravia resided in the ghetto.
In the 16th century the ranks of the ana-
baptists spread here and about 1527
they founded a printing works at Mikulov.
Historical town reserve. The local châ-

Mělník

here in 1905 and their tradition is being continued by the **Škoda Works**. Modern construction. The old part of the town is situated on the promontory looking over the River Jizera. A castle, converted into a Renaissance château after 1555 and into a barracks in the 18th century, already stood here in the 10th century. The Town Hall is Renaissance from 1554—1559 and has undergone several reconstructions. The parish Church of Our Lady dates in the early 15th century. There is also a Renaissance building formerly used by the Czech Brethren (1544—1554) here. Old Jewish cemetery.

Environs: The Bohemian Paradise. — 13 km SE **Jabkenice** with a memorial hall commemorating the composer B. Smetana in the former Baroque gamekeeper's lodge, where he lived in the years 1875—1884.

teau (a Renaissance and Baroque building adapted in the early 18th century) with a preserved tower with a gallery from the original Romanesque castle is the most outstanding feature in the panorama of the town. Big wine cellars (a barrel with a capacity of 1,010 hl), a museum (also with an exposition devoted to viniculture).In the square a Baroque column of the Holy Trinity, the Late Gothic Church of St. Wenceslas, Renaissance and Baroque houses. In the former ghetto a synagogue and a Jewish cemetery.

On the hill Na kopečku overlooking the town stand an Early Baroque chapel and a Calvary with the Stations of the Cross. Starting point for the **protected landscape region of Pálava** (e.g., Mount Turold with caves, nature preserve of steppe flora, limestone rocks, vineyards, wine cellars).

MLADÁ BOLESLAV E 2

a district town (pop. 49,000). Laurin and Klement started the production of **cars**

MNICHOVO HRADIŠTĚ E 1

a town in the valley of the Jizera. Production of LIAZ lorries. — Baroque **château**, a three-winged building with accessible representative rooms, a rich library and a collection of Delft faience. English park, sala terrena of 1711. In the precinct of a former monastery of the Capuchins (in the Baroque Chapel of St. Anne) the tomb of Albrecht of Wallenstein, a military commander of the time of the Thirty Years War.

Environs: 7 km NE the group of rock blocks called **Drábské světničky** in which passages and rooms are hewn. Circular view from the neighbouring basalt hill called Mužský (463 m). At its foot the ruins of **Valečov** Castle.

Historical core
of Mikulov

a town with a textile industry (pop. 12,500). Its centre is a **historical town reserve** with a Late Renaissance château from 1612—1618. In the town, which has a medieval ground-plan, there are numerous Late Gothic and Renaissance houses, an originally Gothic Town Hall which was reconstructed in the Renaissance from 1550—1565 and a Baroque Piarist monastery of the 18th century.

MORAVSKOSLEZSKÉ BESKYDY
(The Moravian-Silesian Beskids)
       J—K 2—3

a long range on the historical border of Moravia, Silesia and Slovakia, in the north-eastern corner of the region of North Moravia. It culminates with the peak Lysá hora (1,323 m). The main river here is the Ostravice, the right tributary of the Odra. A valley reservoir containing drinking water for the Ostrava region has been built in the locality of Šance. Reservoirs used for recreation purposes can be found below the mountains at Horní Bečva, Olešná, Baška and Žermanice. The mountains are mainly covered with fir trees (spruces). Remainders of the original primeval forest growths can be seen on Mionší, at Salajka, on Smrk and on Kněhyně. The Moravian-Silesian Beskids are a part of the **protected landscape region of the Beskids.**
Above Rožnov pod Radhoštěm and Frenštát pod Radhoštěm rises the huge massif of **Radhošť** (1,129 m) with a tourist chalet and a chapel on its summit. The bare sector of the ridge, from which fine views can be obtained, ends on the mountain saddle at the tourist resort of **Pustevny**. Rising to the east

are the forested peaks called Kněhyně (1,257 m) and Smrk (1,276 m). At the end of the Second World War a strong **partisan movement** existed throughout the whole region. The starting points for this part of the Beskids (Čeladná, Horní Bečva) have been proclaimed partisan communities.
In the region of Třeštík and **Bumbalka** (859 m, hotel), at the place where an important road passes into Slovakia, the Moravian-Silesian Beskids are joined by the ridges of the **Javorníky** (Velký Javorník, 1,071 m) and the **Vsetínské Hills** (Vysoká 1,024 m) above the valleys of the Vsetínská and Rožnovská Bečva. To the north-east of Bumbalka the picturesque ridge of the Zadní Mountains with typical scattered mountain homesteads stretches along the Moravian-Slovak border. A big recreation resort is situated directly on the ridge on **Bílý Kříž**. Here the big ridge of Gruň links up with the inconspicuous peaks called Janikula (833 m) and Kozlena (886 m). On **Gruň** there are a small wooden church, a mountain hotel and also ski-tows. Approach by car from the community of Staré Hamry by the Šance valley reservoir. At neighbouring **Bílá** there is a small northern-type wooden church of 1875.
The highest peak in the Moravian-Silesian Beskids — **Lysá hora** (1,323 m) rises conspicuously above its environs. A TV transmitter is situated on its summit. The recreation community of **Ostravice** in the valley of the river of the same name is the biggest recreation locality in North Moravia (1,200 chalets and recreation cottages). Below the slopes of the mountain lie the recreation village Malenovice and the town **Frýdlant nad Ostravicí**. They are overlooked by the massif of Ondřejník (964 m).
The northernmost part of this range of mountains is formed by the recreation

region of Třinec (metallurgical industry) and Frýdek-Místek. There are several mountain chalets on the forested ridge. The highest of them is Velký Polom (1,067 m). A chair-lift runs to **Javorový** (1,032 m) and on Kozubová (982 m) there is an observation tower. The starting points are **Horní Lomná** and **Dolní Lomná** and **Jablunkov** from the east, **Morávka** (a dam, partisan community, memorial to partisans) from the west and **Komorní Lhotka** and **Řeka** from the north. Beyond the valley of the Olše the **Silesian Beskids**, still only little frequented by tourists, connects up on the border with Poland (Velká Čantoryje, 995 m).

Culturally and historically interesting sights are concentrated in the foothills: the town of Štramberk with frame houses, the ruins of Hukvaldy Castle and Nový Jičín, a historical town reserve.

Recommended car route: Nový Jičín — Štramberk — Frenštát pod Radhoštěm — Rožnov pod Radhoštěm — Bumbalka — Staré Hamry — Ostravice — Frýdlant nad Ostravicí — Frýdek-Místek. Total length 87 km.

Recommended tours on foot:
1. Pustevny — Radhošť, along the nature study path and then along the route marked with blue signs, 4 km. — **2.** Bumbalka — Konečná — Bílý Kříž. Marked with red signs, diverse route, 19.5 km. — **3.** Ostravice — Lysá hora, 9.5 km — Frýdlant nad Ostravicí, 19 km. Difficult ascent marked with red signs, fine views, descent along route marked with blue signs.

Starting points: Rožnov pod Radhoštěm, Frenštát pod Radhoštěm, Ostravice, Frýdlant nad Ostravicí, Morávka, Jablunkov.

MORAVSKÝ KRAS   G 3
(The Moravian Karst)

the most important **karst territory** in the Czech Socialist Republic; very interesting also from the archeological aspect. It consists of a limestone zone of a width of 6 km and a length of 25 km and lies to the north of Brno. The region is mostly covered with mixed forests. It has a number of karst canyons and various kinds of bizarre natural formations, bores, gorges and dry valleys, so-called glens, through which underground rivers flow. Visitors are mostly captivated by the local stalagmite and stalactite **caves**. The main starting point for this region is the town of **Blansko**. The underground River **Punkva** flows in the vicinity of the most attractive localities. The **Macocha Abyss** (138 m) is world-known. Views into the abyss can be gained from Upper Bridge near the tourist chalets and from Lower Bridge in the wall. The bottom of the abyss is connected with the sightseeing circuit in the Punkva Caves (the biggest acces-

Punkva Cave
in the Moravian Karst

sible cave system in the Moravian Karst).

The starting point for the circuit is the Skalní Mlýn hotel. This circuit, which is not very long, concentrates other accessible caves: Kateřinská (rich archeological finds, stick-type stalagmites), Balcarka (a 90 m long dome), the Sloupsko-šošůvská Cave (near the community of Sloup). There are several small caves known for archeological finds — Pekárna, Švédův stůl — in the southern part of the Moravian Karst nearer to Brno.

The Moravian Karst is a **protected landscape region.** It is richly forested (preserved and natural beech and pine trees and localities with red yew trees) and abounds in various kinds of flora. Various species of bats are represented among the remarkable fauna. Cultural monuments have also been preserved on the outskirts of the region, e.g. the town of **Boskovice** (pop. 13,000) with the ruins of a castle and a château, châteaux at **Rájec** (Baroque picture gallery) and nearby **Lysice** (valuable interiors and a park), a Baroque church at **Křtiny** and others. **Jedovnice** with a big pond is a popular recreation resort.

Recommended car route: Blansko — Skalní Mlýn — Punkva Cave — Sloupsko-šošůvská Cave — Sloup — Ostrov u Macochy — Balcarka — Macocha — Kateřinská Cave — Blansko. Total length 35 km, visit to the best-known caves.

MOST   C 1

a district industrial town (pop. 65,000). It lies in an area of big **brown coal** seams (coal has been mined here since the 17th century) and for this reason the old town was gradually demolished in the seventies of the present century and **replaced** with a new one situated several kilometres distant. In 1975 an architectonicaly valuable Late Gothic church of the first half of the 17th century was shifted over a distance of 841 m to another site. This was a unique and, from the technical aspect, an immensely difficult task. — New, modern town centre: a theatre, hotel and department store.

Environs: NW Záluží with a big chemical works and further N the industrial town of **Litvínov** (pop. 23,000) — 9 km NE the town of **Bílina** on the edge of the Bohemian Central Highlands with an Early Baroque château. **Kyselka** spa forms a part of the town, overlooked by the rocky phonolite hill called Bořeň (538 m, good views).

NÁCHOD   F 2

a district town (pop. 22,000) in North East Bohemia on the border with Poland (border crossing). Developed textile industry.

The town with a castle originated before 1254 on an old trade route running to Kladsko. The town is overlooked by a Baroque **château** (1650—1659, C. Lurago) standing on the site of an Early Gothic castle, later converted into a Renaissance château. Round tower, building covered with graffito, period interiors, valuable collections (gobelins). The château terraces afford far-reaching views. In the square a Gothic **church** rebuilt in the Renaissance in 1570—1578 with two steeples with wooden boarding. New Town Hall (1902—1904) with graffito by M. Aleš.

Environs: **Běloves** spa, a part of the town with an Empire sanatorium, Ida mineral table water. — 3 km SE the hill called **Dobrošov** (624 m) with a chalet and observation tower. Nearby the accessible structures of Czechoslovak for-

Most

the Renaissance up to the 19th century (24 pieces in all). — The River Oslava is spanned by a bridge with 20 Baroque statues from 1730—1740.

NELAHOZEVES D 2

a community 14 km SW of Mělník. Renaissance **château** from 1553—1593, built on a rock above the left bank of the Vltava. The Central Bohemian Gallery (collections of old European art) is now installed in it. Its interiors are equipped with supplementary furnishings from the 16th—17th century. Exposition of arms and other things. The house in which the composer Antonín Dvořák (1841—1904) was born is situated here similarly as a museum devoted to him. *Environs:* 2 km NE **Veltrusy**, Baroque château, English park, number of Empire romantic structures.

NITRA J 4

a district town (pop. 77,000) in a fertile agricultural region in SW Slovakia below the slopes of Zobor (588 m, chairlift). Important food and chemical industries. New building activity here ranks among the most successful in Slovakia (housing estates, the area of the Agricultural University, a department store). Theatre, Agricultural University, pedagogical faculty. In autumn national Slovak harvest-home celebrations in whose framework the Agrokomplex agricultural exhibition takes place. In the 8th and 9th centuries two big Slavonic castle sites were situated here. After 820 the centre of Pribina's principality with the first historically known church on the territory of Slovakia. From 880 the seat of a bishopric. At that

tifications built before the Second World War. — 7 km SW the **Rozkoš** reservoir, bathing, water sports. — 8 km SW **Česká Skalice** where the Czech woman writer B. Němcová (1820—1862) spent her childhood and youth. The oldest literary museum in Bohemia is devoted to her. — 8 km W **Babiččino údolí** (Grandmother's Valley), named after B. Němcová's best-known novel Grandmother (Babička). Standing here is a frame cottage called Staré Bělidlo, also a memorial to the Grandmother and Baroque **Ratibořice** Château, rebuilt in Empire style.

NÁMĚŠŤ NAD OSLAVOU F 3

a town in the Oslava valley. In the 16th century one of the centres of the Union of Brethren with a printing works (the first book of Czech grammar was published here in 1533). Tradition in carpet-weaving from the late 18th century. Renaissance **château** from 1565—1578, Barocized, with an exceptionally valuable collection of folk **tapestries** from

Staré bělidlo
in the valley Babiččino údolí
near Náchod

time Nitra was a part of the Great Moravian Empire. After it had ceased to exist it was the cultural centre of early feudal Slovakia and the seat of the apanage prince, successor to the Hungarian throne, up to the end of the 11th century. In the 16th and 17th centuries an important fortress in battles against the Turks who in 1663 conquered the town and castle and destroyed them.

On a rocky hill overlooking the town there is a **castle** with Baroque fortifications, accessible via a Gothic bridge leading to a Renaissance gateway. The local landmark is the **episcopal cathedral**. It is made up of 3 churches: the oldest is of Romanesque origin of the 11th century, neighbouring with it is the Gothic Upper Church (1333—1355) and below it the Early Baroque Lower Church. The episcopal palace from 1732—1739 stands on the summit of a hill. — From the plague column (of 1750, one of the most valuable in Slovakia) by the entrance to the castle a view can be gained of the upper part of the old town with numerous Baroque and Empire palaces (among other things an agricultural museum, an ethnographical museum and a gallery are installed in them) and also of the centre of modern Nitra.

Environs: 12 km NE the ruins of **Jelenec** Castle with a recreation region below it. — 16 km NE **Kostoľany pod Tríbečom,** Early Romanesque church of the first half of the 11th century with restored remains of wall paintings.

NÍZKE TATRY   L—M 3
(The Low Tatras)

---

a big range in the central part of Slovakia. The main ridge is 78 km long and it stretches from the tourist resort of Donovaly in westerly direction to the community of Vernár in the east. The range is demarcated by the valley of the River Váh in the north and the valley of the River Hron in the south. The most valuable natural parts of the Low Tatras form a part of the **national park** covering an area of 810 sq. km.

The central part of the ridge culminates with the highest mountain of the Low Tatras, rocky **Ďumbier** (2,043 m). Lying in its neighbourhood, in the environs of **Chopok** (2,024 m), is the most popular sector among tourists and skiers.

A chair-lift runs to the summit of Chopok from both the south and the north. Other conspicuous dominants are the long ridge called Prašivá (1,753 m), the huge peak Chabenec (1,953 m), rocky Dereše (2,003 m) and rugged Kráľova hoľa (1,948 m). The main ridge drops below 1,500 m only in a few places.

A road cuts through it on the saddle called **Čertovica** (1,238 m). Long, forested valleys penetrate deeply into the mountains (e.g. Revúcka, Demänovská, Janská, Bystrá and especially the valleys in the region of the basin of the Čierny Váh).

The mountains consist of granites and crystallic slates and on their periphery there are limestone layers (karst caves, a rock window on Ohnište). The lake Vrbické pleso (7 hectares) is of glacial origin. The spruce forests on the lower elevations (there are huge complexes in the basin of the Čierny Váh) make way for dwarf pines and the summits are covered with meadows or rocks. The forests are known for the biggest occurrence of the bear in Czechoslovakia.

At the time of the Slovak National Uprising the western part of the Low Tatras was the most important base of **partisan activity** in Slovakia. The battles and their victims are brought to mind by a number of memorials (e.g. Kalište and a memorial hall, Baláže, Švermovo, Nemecká).

The northern part of the Low Tatras is accessible from Liptovská kotlina from the valley of the Váh. The towns of Ružomberok, Liptovský Mikuláš and Liptovský Hrádok on the main road and railway stretch from Žilina to the High Tatras are starting points for excursions to it. The valley **Demänovská dolina** is the most important tourist centre in the Low Tatras. At nearby **Liptovský Ján** there is a thermal pool. There are other accommodation possibilities at the communities of Malužiná, Vyšná Boca and Nižná Boca along the road to Čertovica and at Magurka. Situated on a saddle by the road from Ružomberok to Banská Bystrica is the **Donovaly** tourist resort (960 m, hotel, recreation facilities, ski-tows, funicular) and Korytnica spa (curative springs) lies along a short side road.

The ascents to the main ridge from the south, from the valley of the Hron, are somewhat shorter than from the north. The natural starting point is Banská Bystrica, a centre of the Central Slovak region, at the western end of the range. The industrial town of **Brezno** is the centre of the charming region of **Horehronie** between the ridges of the Low Tatras and the Slovak Ore Mountains. The local population has preserved many characteristic features to the present, particularly as regards dialect, song, dance, clothings, customs, building activity and folk art production — folk costumes, embroidery, woven materials and wooden products are exhibited in the museum at Brezno. **Folk architecture** and folklore are best-preserved at the communities of Heľpa,

Kosodrevina Hotel
in the Low
Tatras

Sheep in a spring pasture
in the valley Bocká dolina
in the Low Tatras

Polomka, Závadka nad Hronom and Šumiac. Here the ridge of the Low Tatras terminates in the east with the conspicuous peak **Kráľova hoľa** (1,948 m) with a TV transmitter on its summit. The important Slovak Rivers Hron, Čierny Váh and Hnilec spring on its slopes.

The valley **Bystrá dolina** can be reached from Brezno and Podbrezová (metallurgy). A stalagmite and stalactite cave with a 600 m long sightseeing circuit is accessible at the community of Bystrá. Situated higher up in the valley is the resort of **Tále** with a hotel and car camp. From Srdiečko a chair-lift runs to the summit of Chopok and continues down the northern slope to Jasná. The southern slopes of Chopok are also used for winter sports.

Recommended car route: Ružomberok — Liptovský Mikuláš — Demänovská dolina — Jasná (chair-lift to Chopok) — Liptovský Mikuláš — Litpovský Hrádok — Čertovica (saddle) — Bystrá (cave) — Tále — Srdiečko (chair-lift) — Bystrá — Nemecká (memorial) — Banská Bystrica — Donovaly (saddle) — Korytnica (spa) — Ružomberok. Total length 200 km.
Recommended tours on foot:
1. Vrbické pleso — Jaskyňa Slobody (cave), or in the opposite direction (1 1/4 hours single journey). Blue tourist signs. A sightseeing tour of the cave lasts about 1 1/2 hours. — 2. Chopok — Ďumbier. Along the highest part of the main ridge and back (red tourist signs), 4 hours. — 3. Kosodrevina — Príslop — Pálenica — Tále, 4 hours. Blue tourist signs and then yellow ones. Descent route.

NOVÉ HRADY   D 4

a town 30 km SE of České Budějovice. Along the Vitorazská Path founded in 1279 a Gothic castle, rebuilt in the 15th and 16th centuries. Fortifications, gates and bastions have been preserved from the original building. An exposition of South Bohemian glass is installed in the castle.
Environs: 1 km SW the valley **Terčino údolí** and a park founded in 1756, protected territory. — 3 km NW **Cukenštejn** Stronghold. — 8 km NW **Žumberk**, a fortified medieval village whose castle was adapted for the Memorial of the Country People (with an exposition of painted furniture) in the seventies of the 20th century.

NOVÉ MĚSTO NAD METUJÍ   F 2

a town above the valley of the Metuje in the close vicinity of the Orlické Mountains. Founded as late as 1501 on a high promontory, it still forms a uniquely preserved complex of Renaissance buildings; **historical town reserve**. The oblong square is uniformly lined with Renaissance houses with arcades and gabled façades. The Town Hall dates in 1591, the Late Gothic parish church in the years 1513—1523 and the monastery church in 1767. With the exception of the gates, the town forfitications have been preserved. Standing in the neighbourhood of the square is a **château** with a striking round tower and a façade decorated with graffito. Originally a Renaissance building, it was reconstructed in the Early Baroque in 1655—1661 (C. Lurago) and for the last time in 1909—1911 by D. Jurkovič (its interiors are open to the public). Château park, likewise adapted in the early 20th century, Baroque sculptures.
Environs: attractive scenery in the deep, rocky valley of the Metuje. — 6 km NE the **Peklo** excursion destination and restaurant.

NOVÉ MĚSTO NA MORAVĚ F 3

a town (pop. 12,000) below the Žďárské Hills. The cradle of tourism and winter sports in the Bohemian-Moravian Highlands (museum expositions). Ski production. — Renaissance château with a gallery. — Mountain resort, cross-country skiing race tracks in the vicinity of the Ski Hotel (2 km NW, 660 m). *Environs:* the **protected landscape region of the Žďárské Hills**, big forest complexes, recreation ponds (5 km NW Sykovec and Medlov, 10 km N Milovský Pond), and on the summit parts conspicuous gneiss rock projections (Devět skal, 836 m).

NOVÝ BOR D 1

a town (pop. 15,000) N of Česká Lípa. Household and art **glass** (etched, cut and engraved) production. Baroque and Empire houses, a Baroque church. *Environs:* 3 km SE the romantic ruins of **Sloup** Castle hewn in a sandstone rock massif. — 5 km W a basalt, organ-like rock formation called **Panská skála** in the neighbourhood of the town Kamenický Šenov (glass industry). — 6 km N the community of **Kytlice** with numerous characteristic samples of folk architecture.

NOVÝ JIČÍN J 2

a district town (pop. 33,000). Founded at the turn of the 13th and 14th centuries, **hat** production from the late 18th century. — **Historical town reserve**. Ruins of the town fortifications of the 15th—17th century. In the square Renaissance and Baroque houses of the 16th—18th century with arcades (the Old Post Office of 1563), in the centre a plague column. Renaissance château, in its interior a hat museum. *Environs:* 5 km SW **Starý Jičín**, the ruins of a castle of the mid-13th century. — 8 km S the community of **Hodslavice** with a little wooden church of 1551 and the house where the historian and politician František Palacký (1798—1876) was born. — 12 km NE the town of **Příbor** with a square with mainly Barocized Renaissance houses and a Baroque church with a former Piarist college (now a museum and memorial to Sigmund Freud, a local citizen and the founder of psychoanalysis).

OLOMOUC H 3

a district town (pop. 106,000) in the fertile lowlands of the River Morava. The centre of the Haná agricultural region. Developed industry — the Moravské Ironworks, a factory for the production of pumps and irrigation equipment of the Sigma mark, the Zora chocolate factory, distillery, production of soaps and oils, etc. Important railway junction, three theatres, a symphony orchestra and the Palacký University.
In 1019 the Moravian apanage principality with its seat at Olomouc originated, in 1055 the first written records of the local castle appeared and in 1063 a bishopric was founded here. In 1306 the last member of the Přemyslid family, Václav III, was murdered at Olomouc Castle. Later King Charles IV, the Margrave of Moravia from 1333, often stayed at the castle. The town was run by the German patriciate, which resulted in its negative attitude towards the Hussite revolutionary movement. In 1469 King Matthias of Hungary had himself proclaimed Czech king here. The

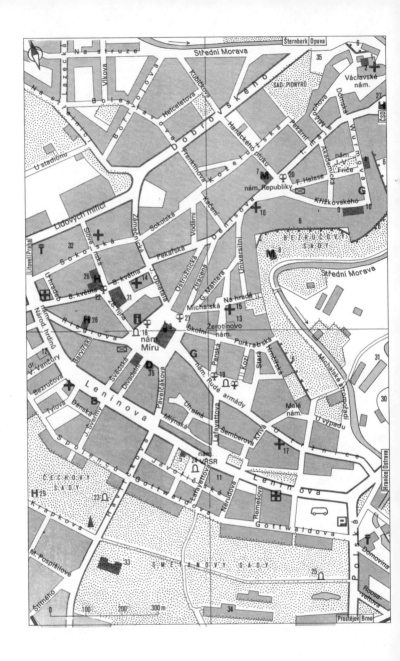

Olomouc

16th century was marked by economic and cultural development and a sharp struggle between the Lutherans and the Catholics. In 1573 the local Jesuit Academy was raised to a university. The town suffered great losses during the Thirty Years War. From 1641–1650 it was under the rule of the Swedes. The town was burned and demolished. New architectural development began in the first half of the 18th century, but it was halted in 1741 as the result of Olomouc being proclaimed a fortress town. All buildings within a distance of 1.5 km of the fortifications were liquidated. In the years 1848–1849 the imperial court fled to the town from the revolution and the Emperor Ferdinand I handed over his power to Franz Josef I. The town fortifications prevented industrial development for a long time and it was not until 1886 that the fortress was abolished. Industry developed in the surrounding communities.

Historical town reserve. On a hill overlooking the River Morava remainders of the masonry of the **Přemyslid palace**; compound Romanesque windows. Nearby the huge building of **St. Wen-**ceslas's Cathedral. The first Romanesque basilica was completed in 1131 and subjected to Gothic reconstructions in 1265 and in the latter half of the 14th century. Adaptations at the turn of the 16th and 17th centuries. Striking Neo-Gothic reconstruction from 1883–1890, two Neo-Gothic steeples above the façade, big 100 m high steeple, Neo-Gothic altar, several side chapels. — In the neighbourhood of the cathedral, in the so-called outer bailey, the archbishop's residence (Early Baroque palace with an 85 m long street façade), a number of Baroque canons' residences, university buildings (the rectorate), between the churches the conspicuous Cathedral of Our Lady of the Snows from 1712–1719, in the former convent of the Poor Clares the seat of the Regional Museum (nature, the primeval age, the history of the Olomouc region). The town originated to the west of the castle and its centre is formed by the square náměstí Míru with the building of the **Town Hall** in the middle. It has a Gothic and Renaissance appearance, a slender tower, a Gothic oriel with a chapel, a Renaissance loggia and ho-

OLOMOUC

1. Přemyslid Palace (b). 2. St. Wenceslas's Cathedral (b). 3. Town Hall with tower and horologe (a—c). 4. Archbishop's palace (b). 5. Theresa Gate (c). 6. Remainders of town fortifications (b—d). 7. Former convent of the Poor Clares (museum) (b). 8. South Slavonic Mausoleum (b). 9. Chancellor's office of Palacký University (b). 10. Philosophical faculty (b). 11. Faculty of natural science (a). 12. Medical faculty (c). 13. Pedagogical faculty (b). 14. St. Maurice's Church (a). 15. St. Michael's Church (b). 16. Church of Our Lady of the Snows (b). 17. St. Catherine's Church (d). 18. Holy Trinity column and Herculese's Fountain (a). 19. Neptune's Fountain, Marian plague column and Jupiter's Fountain (d). 20. Tritons' Fountain (b). 21. Caesar's Fountain (a). 22. Mercury's Fountain (a). 23. Liberation of Olomouc by the Red Army memorial (c). 24. Group of statues of V. I. Lenin and J. V. Stalin (c). 25. B. Smetana memorial (d). 26. Grandhotel Národní dům (a). 27. Palác Hotel (b). 28. Morava Hotel (c). 29. Flora Interhotel (c). 30. TJ Lokomotiva Stadium (d). 31. Prior department store (a). 32. Park of Culture and Rest (a). 33. Main pavilion of the Flora Olomouc exhibition ground (c—d). 34. Greenhouse with palm trees (d). 35. Summer cinema (b). 36. O. Stibor Theatre — Grand Theatre (c).

rologe which originated in the late 15th century. Its present appearance dates in 1955. Also to be seen here is the biggest Baroque group of statues in Czechoslovakia (**the Holy Trinity**). It originated in the years 1716—1754 and is 35 m high. Other features include Olomouc's oldest fountain, called Hercules's Fountain, of 1668 and Caesar's Fountain (representing the legendary founder of Olomouc, Gaius Julius Caesar). Of the two- and three-storeyed buildings on the periphery of the square Baroque Petráš Palace and the building of the Oldřich Stibor Theatre from 1829—1830. The most beautiful houses in the neighbouring square náměstí Rudé armády include Hauenschild's House of the late 16th century with a richly decorated Renaissance portal, the former butchers' shops and the house At the Golden Stag. Also situated here are a Marian column of 1715, built to commemorate the plague, Neptune's and Jupiter's fountains and a simple Baroque Capu-

chin church. The Olomouc parish **church** is consecrated to **St. Maurice**. It is a Gothic triple-naved building of the 15th and the early 16th century with two steeples, Baroque furnishings and the biggest **organ** in Moravia of 1745. On the periphery of the old town remains of the fortifications have been preserved in several places, most of them being built of bricks and dating in the 18th century. Dating in the same period are also the Theresa Gate and the Korunní (Crown) Fortress. **Parks** are laid out below the former fortifications, the main one in Olomouc being the Smetana Park in which the traditional **Flóra Olomouc** flower exhibitions traditionally take place. On the left bank of the Morava, north of the centre, lies the big area of the **Hradisko** monastery of 1078, rebuilt from its foundations from 1679—1739. — 8 km NE from the centre stands the pilgrimage church Kopeček from 1669—1679.

Olomouc

Square with Town Hall and group of statues The Holy Trinity at Olomouc

a district town (pop. 62,000) on the Polish border. An industrial and cultural centre of **Silesia**. Engineering (mining machines), chemical (dyes and paints), pharmaceutical and food (chocolate and sugar factories) industries. Extensive new construction.

The first written records of the town date in the late 12th century and it is documented in 1224. Part of the Opava principality, from the early 15th century the prince's seat. In 1742 the greater part of Silesia fell to Prussia and Opava became the metropolis of Czech Silesia (until 1928) and the seat of the provincial offices. Development of industry in the 19th century. In 1945 heavy battles were waged for the town, most of which was destroyed.

Historical core separated by park-lined streets on the site of the former fortifications from the newer quarters. The centre of Opava is the square náměstí 1. máje with the municipal tower (Hláska), completed in 1618. Standing in its neighbourhood is the **Town Hall** and opposite it the P. Bezruč Theatre. The typical building material of the town is red brick of which the nearby Gothic **Church of the Assumption of Our Lady** of the third quarter of the 14th century is also built. The second biggest area in the town is the square náměstí Velkého října with Baroque St. Adalbert's Church. — Numerous monumental buildings can be seen in the town: the Baroque palaces of the Blüchers and Sobeks, the Old Provincial House of the 17th century and the Classical New Provincial House. Building of the **Silesian Museum** from 1893—1895, one of the most outstanding and important institutions of its kind in Czechoslovakia; expositions devoted to nature, history, monuments, architecture and ethnography. In a park the biggest erratic boulder in Czechoslovakia — a relic of the Pleistocene ice cover. In the square náměstí Obránců míru the modern Kamyšin Hotel and a memorial to the soldiers of the Red Army.

The greatest Silesian poet, P. Bezruč (1867—1958) was born and buried in Opava. The founder of modern genetics, J.G. Mendel (1822—1884), studied at the local gymnasium.

Environs: 10 km W the arboretum at **Nový Dvůr** (2,000 species of home and foreign trees). — 13 km SE a windmill at **Choltice.** — 7 km E Baroque **Kravaře** Château with an exposition devoted to the Ostrava Operation. — 12 km SE Hrabyně.

ORAVA L 3

a region in the basin of one of the most beautiful Slovak rivers in the northwestern part of the country near the Polish border. The district town of Dolný Kubín forms its centre. Surrounded by mountain ridges: from Orava access to the most beautiful parts of the **West Tatras** — the Roháče Mountains (2,084 m); rising to the north of the dam reservoir is the peak **Babia hora**, 1,725 m (in 1912 V. I. Lenin made an ascent to its rocky summit from the Polish side); the Orava valley is lined with the ridge of the **Oravská Magura** Mountains (Kubínská hoľa, 1,346 m; good skiing grounds). The most valuable natural parts are included in the protected Horná Orava region.

Situated at the confluence of the Bielá Orava and the Čierna Orava is the **Orava dam reservoir** (35 sq. km, 603 m) on whose southern banks there are several recreation communities with hotels, hostels, car camps and restaurants over a distance of 11 km; bathing and water

sports; regular boat transport. The Slanica Island of Art — an island with a Baroque church (collections of folk sculptures in its interior), a remainder of the inundated village of Slanica.

Until the mid-20th century the characteristic forms and specific nature of local **folk culture** were preserved in the Orava region. Numerous frame buildings are still standing, the best examples having been preserved at Podbiel, Zuberec and, in particular, at the **Zuberec-Brestová skansen** on the road to the Roháče Mountains. **Orava Castle** is the most significant monument of medieval architecture.

Starting points: Tvrdošín, Trstená and Námestovo.

ORAVSKÝ HRAD (Orava Castle)　　L 3

---

a medieval castle on a steep, rocky cliff 112 m above the surface of the River Orava; 10 km NE of Dolný Kubín. It originated gradually from the 13th to the 17th century and its buildings are situated on three terraces of the castle rock. Access to the highest part, which is the oldest, is afforded by 880 steps. Historical interiors and a museum (13,000 exhibits) in a part of the castle. View of the river and surrounding mountain complexes.

ORLICKÉ HORY　　G 2
(The Eagle Mountains)

---

a range stretching along the north-eastern border between Bohemia and Poland. Conspicuous main ridge of a length of 30 km between Olešnice and Rokytnice. It has relatively small differences in height and it culminates with **Velká Deštná** (1,155 m). In its southern part the ridge is intersected in the narrow, rocky pass called Zemská brána by

Oravský hrad

Orava
Castle

the valley of the Divoká Orlice, over-looked by Suchý vrch (995 m) with a tourist chalet and an observation tower. It is accessible by car from the main Hradec Králové—Šumperk road.

The greater part of the range is covered with forests, the spruce growths having fallen victim to emissions in recent years. The original mixed growths of a **primeval forest** character can be found in the northern part in the Bukačka, Vrchmezí and Sedloňovský vrch nature preserves. In 1969 this range of mountains was proclaimed a **protected landscape region.**

The biggest recreation resort in the range is **Deštné,** 20 km north of Rychnov nad Kněžnou below the higest peak. Big Baroque church from 1723—1726. Numerous accommodation facilities owned by various enterprises, hotels, ski-tows. Šerlišský mlýn Hotel in a mountain valley 4 km to the north. Situated on the ridge above it the **Šerlich** tourist chalet (1,027 m). The saddle below it can be reached by motor vehicles.

Far-reaching view, starting point for ridge tours.

The mountain community of **Říčky** lies 7 km north of the small town of Rokytnice v Orlických horách. Here numerous charming, characteristic frame cottages serve mainly for family recreation. In winter excellent skiing grounds on the slopes of Zakletý, 2 ski-tows, scene of the international Skiinterkritérium junior skiing competitions.

The ridge between Říčky and Deštné is suitable for whole-day walking and skiing tours. It is relatively easily accessible.

A number of **folk buildings** lending character to the local countryside (Sedloňov, Uhřinov nad Bělou, Zdobnice) has been preserved in communities lying below the mountains. Town frame architecture is represented by houses at **Jablonné nad Orlicí,** 14 km SE of Žamberk. 6 km from Žamberk a recreation region in the immediate vicinity of the **Pastviny** dam reservoir.

The interior of the château
at Orlík nad Vltavou

a **château** now situated almost immediately next to the Orlík dam reservoir. Founded in the latter half of the 13th century as a royal castle. Frequently reconstructed. Its present appearance is the result of Neo-Gothic adaptations realized in 1849—1860. Access to the château via a bridge spanning a ditch. Standing on the left of the entrance a round tower of the 14th century. The oppositely situated wing above the river is the oldest part of the three-storeyed palace. Inside, for example, a hunting hall with trophies, a museum with relics pertaining to Prince Karel Filip Schwarzenberg, victor over Napoleon at the Battle of Leipzig in 1815, valuable coffered ceilings, an armoury, a library with 18,000 volumes, a Chinese salon. In the park (143 hectares) the Schwarzenberg tomb, circuits for tours on foot, view of the château and the lake.

Environs: 1.5 km SE **Žďákov Bridge**, length 540 m at a height of 50 m above the dam reservoir, built from 1957—1965. At its time it was the biggest bridge arch in Europe (span of 330 m). — 10 km N **Orlík dam** wall, the highest in Czechoslovakia (91 m), length on its crest 511 m. Built from 1954—1962, it retains a lake of an area of 2,732 hectares and is 68 km long. In summer boat transport, recreation resorts, car camps, camping sites, water sports.

OSTRAVA   J 2

the regional town (pop. 328,000) of the North Moravian region in the Ostrava-Karviná **coal basin** near the border with Poland. Czechoslovakia's biggest industrial centre, an administrative and cultural centre. **Metallurgical industry** (Vítkovice Ironworks of Klement Gottwald — VŽKG and NHKG — New Foundry of Klement Gottwald), mines, power plants, chemical industry, coking plants, seat of a mining university and pedagogical faculty. Theatre, philharmonic orchestra.

In the Middle Ages an unimportant town (from 1267) surrounded by walls. Discovery of coal deposits in 1763, mining activity from the eighties of the 18th century (participated in also by the Rothschilds and the Hapsburg Těšín archdukes — strong Germanization efforts). Foundation of the **Vítkovice Ironworks** in 1828, development of production especially after the building of a railway to Vienna in 1847. In 1875 the origin of the first workers' educational association, big strikes in 1896 and 1900 which were continued in 1918. Growth of the town through the attachment of originally separate communities. By means of the outflanking Ostrava Operation (see Hrabyně) the Red Army saved the town from destruction. It was liberated at the end of April 1945 (these war events are brought to mind by the big Red Army Memorial and the Liberation Memorial with the first tank). Several interesting samples of old architecture. — Centre of the town formed by the main square with the **Old Town Hall** (of 1556, rebuilt in 1859 — now the municipal museum); nearby the Gothic parish church with a Baroque steeple. Ruins of a château at Slezská Ostrava. In the square náměstí Říjnové revoluce the **New Town Hall** from 1924—1930 with an 85 m high tower. — In the town quarter of Hrabová a small wooden church from the latter half of the 16th century. — Museum of revolutionary struggles and the building-up of socialism, VŽKG Ironworks. Museum of the Ostrava Region, gallery.

Orlík nad Vltavou

a **protected landscape region** in the south of Moravia. Core formed by the hills Pavlovské vrchy. Their short ridge rises steeply from the Moravian lowlands and is demarcated in the north by the curve of the River Dyje (on it the Nové Mlýny system of reservoirs). The range of hills culminates with Děvín (550 m). The local **karst territory** is mainly composed of limestone; numerous small, shorter, sharp ridges, small rocks, tower-shaped rocks. Rich steppe and forest-steppe flora. On the summits the ruins of two castles Dívčí hrady and Sirotčí hrádek. Rich paleontological and archeological finding-places. — At **Dolní Věstonice** below the northern slopes of the hills Pavlovské vrchy, near the River Dyje, lies a former settlement of Man of the Older Stone Age (the mammoth hunter); local find of a small sculpture of a woman, the so-called Věstonice Venus (approx. 25,000 years old). At **Mušov**; now inundated, there was a Roman military post in the 2nd century. **Starting point for the region:** the town of Mikulov.

a district town (pop. 94,000) in a fertile plain of the Elbe. One of the most important centres of the chemical industry in Czechoslovakia (e.g. Synthesia), food (Pardubice gingerbread, brewery, mill) and electrical engineering (Tesla) industries. Chemico-technological university. Important railway junction. Numerous new housing estates.
A town from 1340 (the first archbishop of Prague was Arnošt of Pardubice), rebuilt in the Renaissance in 1507, 1521 and 1538. Further growth after the construction of a railway in 1845, industrial works, new suburbs. In 1942 the parachutists who took part in the assassination of Heydrich found refuge in the town. Inhabitants of the destroyed community of Ležáky were executed on the site "Na Zámečku".
The historical core of the town is a **historical town reserve** of a Renaissance character. Valuable **town houses** in the square Pernštejnské náměstí (e.g. the houses called At the Little White Horse, At Jonáš's, Werner's House and a pharmacy), Town Hall of 1894 with graffito by M. Aleš, in the centre a Marian group of statues (of 1680). Access through the gate Zelená brána of 1507. In the decanal church from 1507—1514 there is the tombstone of Vojtěch of Pernštejn.
Renaissance water fortifications and huge ramparts protected the four-winged **château**, originally a castle converted into a Gothic water castle. Present appearance from 1519—1543, arcades, entrance portal of 1529, regional museum and gallery in the interior. — The town also has an Art Nouveau theatre of the early 20th century and several outstanding modern buildings.
Since 1874 a well-known horse race — **the Grand Pardubice Steeplechase** — has taken place at Pardubice every year in October. The course of the steeplechase is one of the most difficult in Europe (length 6,900 m, 39 obstacles, the Taxis jump involving a leap of 9 m). Scene of the Golden Helmet of Czechoslovakia motorcycle race.
Environs: 6 km NE a conspicuously projecting hill on whose summit stands **Kunětická Hora** Castle, founded by the Hussites from 1421—1423, enlarged in 1491 by the Pernštejns and reconstructed in the 20th century. — 16 km E the town of **Holice** with a museum concentrating the African collections of the Czech traveller E. Holub (1847—1902).

PEC POD SNĚŽKOU   F 1

a **mountain resort** (769 m) for summer
and winter recreation in the eastern part
of the Krkonoše Mountains in the valley
of the Úpa and its tributaries. Originally
a mining and metallurgical community.
Hotels, works recreation centres, ski-
tows. Highly diverse terrain emphasized
with valleys, ridges, peaks and picturesquely set meadows with mountain
chalets, forests and dwarf pine growths.
Environs: starting point for the highest
mountain in the Czech Socialist Republic, **Sněžka** (1,602 m), accessible by
chair-lift or on foot (7.5 km). — Below
the slopes of Sněžka (steep walls up to
600 m in height) a high-mountain valley
of glacial origin, **Obří důl** with traces of
moraine and rare flora. — The biggest
mountain chalet in Czechoslovakia,
Luční bouda (1,410 m, 316 beds;
founded in the 16th century on an old
trade route running from Bohemia to
Silesia) ; access from Pec via Výrovka
— 7.5 km. — **Černá hora** (1,299 m),
a huge saddle running above Janské

Lázně, from where it is accessible by
means of a cabin funicular.

PELHŘIMOV   E 3

a district town (pop. 19,000) in the SW
part of the Bohemian-Moravian Highlands. A town from the mid-13th century, now a **historical town reserve.** Two
tower gates (Rynárecká and Jihlavská)
preserved of the fortifications. Gothic
parish church of the early 14th century.
In its neighbourhood a former château,
later a Town Hall and now a museum.
Environs: 16 km W **Kámen** — a Gothic
castle converted into an Early Baroque
château. Exposition of single-track motor vehicles in its interior.

PERNŠTEJN   G 3

one of the biggest and best-preserved
castles in Czechoslovakia, seat of the
powerful family of the lords of

Pernštejn. Its core dates in the latter half of the 13th century, considerably enlarged in the late 15th and the first half of the 16th century. The oldest parts are the tower called Barborka and the palace on to which other buildings and a Hall of Knights and chapels were gradually built, followed by peripheral fortifications with a turret watch-tower, etc. Interiors repaired in the 18th and 19th centuries, château installations, period collections.

over a distance of 9 km, marked path along the bank. Starting point of navigation at Červený Kláštor, numerous meanders, rocks reaching to the riverside, views of the dominant massif of Trzy korony in Poland, end of navigation below the community of Lesnica. Original forest growths, endemite species of flora and fauna. On the southern edge of the national park **Haligovské skály** — a richly articulated complex of limestone cliffs with cave formations.

PEZINOK   H 4

a town (pop. 19,000) at the foot of the Little Carpathians NE of Bratislava. **Vinicultural centre.** Wine-producing works and a stylish restaurant are housed in the original Gothico-Renaissance castle, converted into a Baroque château in 1818. A school, research institute and museum all devoted to viniculture are situated in the town. In September vintages traditionally take place here (alternately with neighbouring **Modra**). Production of popular ceramics, which has a long-standing tradition also at Modra.
Environs: starting point for excursions to the forested ridge of the Little Carpathians (13 km to the mountain hotel on Baba), skiing grounds.

PIENINY   M 3

a range of limestone mountains in East Slovakia along the border with Poland. Highest point Vysoké skalky (1,050 m). The part of the range belonging in the Pieniny **National Park** (2,125 hectares) is the most interesting from the tourist viewpoint. Deep, rocky valley of the border **River Dunajec**, raft navigation

PIEŠŤANY   J 4

a **spa** town (pop. 33,000) with a world reputation on the River Váh. Treatment of diseases of the motory organs — mineral springs of a temperature of up to 69.5° C, sulphurous mud. Centre of the balneological part on Spa Island (Kúpelný ostrov). Access to this island is gained by means of the **Colonnade Bridge** by which stands a statue of a man breaking crutches — the symbol of Piešťany. Two thermal pools and the Sĺňava dam reservoir (470 hectares) in and near the town respectively.
Environs: 14 km N the ruins of Gothico-Renaissance **Čachtice** Castle, whose perverted owner Elizabeth Nádasdy-Báthory bathed in the blood of young girls. In 1611 she was sentenced to life imprisonment for the murders she had committed.

PÍSEK   D 3

a district town (pop. 29,000) on the River Otava. Industrial centre (textile industry — Jitex, furniture production), rich cultural tradition (permanent theatre, developed education system already in the 19th century).

In the early Middle Ages a community and a washing-place of gold-bearing sand from the alluvia of the Otava were situated here (hence the name of the town — Písek = sand). Standing on the river is an original Early Gothic **castle** whose western wing (the royal palace) houses a museum (cross vault). The **stone bridge** of the late 13th century is the oldest documented structure of this type in Czechoslovakia. In the piers of the Bridge a Baroque group of statues of 1754—1757. Remains of the fortifications have been preserved — e.g. the gate Putimská brána. Visible from far and wide is the 74 m high steeple of the Early Gothic **decanal church** (founded in 1254, adaptations caried out particularly in the 15th and 16th centuries). The landmark of the square is the Baroque Town Hall from 1740—1765 with two towers, a clock and the emblem of the town. Numerous Gothic, Renaissance and Baroque houses.

Environs: the big forest complexes of the Písecké Mountains. — Several ponds. — 6 km SW **Kestřany** with a complex of 2 medieval castles and a château. — 5 km S **Putim**, a typical South Bohemian village with farms built in the style of the rustic Baroque. The village is known from J. Hašek's novel The Good Soldier Švejk.

9 km SE of the present centre of the town stood Plzeň Castle (above the present **Starý Plzenec**) already in the 10th century. It was the administrative and church centre of West Bohemia. Its rotunda of the late 10th century, adapted in the 16th century, has been preserved.

Plzeň was founded in 1295 on a regular ground-plan. In the Hussite period, in the 16th century and during the Thirty Years War it was on the side of the Catholics. In 1468 the oldest Czech printed book — the Trojan Chronicle — was published here. In the 19th century the town underwent considerable industrial development — in 1842 a brewery, in 1859 an ironworks which became the Škoda Works after 1869. In 1944 and 1945 local industry was the target of heavy bombing.

The centre of the town is formed by a big oblong square with the Gothic **Cathedral of St. Bartholomew** in the middle (built 1320—1470). It has the highest steeple in Czechoslovakia (103 m, view from the gallery). In its interior there are Gothic sculptures (a Madonna) and remains of wall paint-

PLZEŇ C 2

a regional town (pop. 175,000) and the centre of the West Bohemian region on the confluence of the Rivers Mže, Radbuza, Úhlava and Úslava. An important industrial centre — the **Škoda engineering** works, world-renowned **beer production** (Pilsner Urquell, Gambrinus). Railway junction. Theatre, seat of the Engineering University and medical and pedagogical faculties.

Plzeň

Gate to the
Pilsner Urquell brevery
at Plzeň

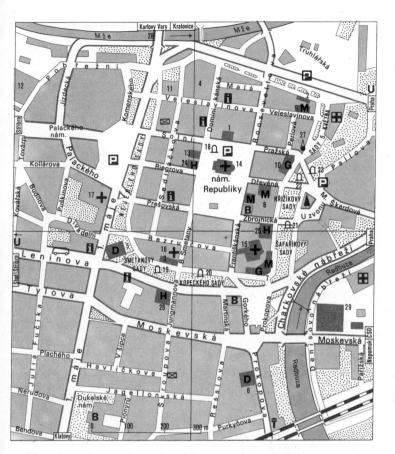

PLZEŇ

1. Town Hall (b). **2.** Accessible remains of fortifications (b). **3.** Former gymnasium (State Scientific Library) (c). **4.** Palace of Justice (a–b). **5.** J. K. Tyl Theatre (c). **6.** Chamber Theatre (d). **7.** West Bohemian Museum and West Bohemian Gallery (d). **8.** Gerlachovský House (now ethnographical museum) (b). **9.** Museum of Beer-brewing (b). **10.** Meat shops (West Bohemian Gallery and concert hall) (b). **11.** Pedagogical faculty (a). **12.** Exhibition ground (a). **13.** Archdeacon's house (a). **14.** St. Bartholomew's Cathedral (b). **15.** Franciscan monastery with church (d). **16.** Former Dominican convent with church (c). **17.** Synagogue (a). **18.** Marian plague column (b). **19.** J. F. Smetana memorial (c). **20.** Burgomaster M. Kopecký memorial (d). **21.** F. Křižík memorial (b). **22.** Statue of St. John Nepomuk (b). **23.** Pieta (on the bridge) (b). **24.** Ural Hotel (a–b). **25.** Continental Hotel (b–d). **26.** Slovan Hotel (c). **27.** Old waterworks tower (b). **28.** A. Zápotocký Bridge (a). **29.** House of Culture and a department store (d).

ings. On the periphery of the square there are several valuable houses with Gothic cores and Renaissance, Baroque or more recent façades. Imperial House, 1606, the archdeacon's residence, 1710, the Chotěšovský House, the Wallenstein House. Some of them are decorated with graffito after designs by M. Aleš. Renaissance **Town Hall** from 1554—1558 with a plague column of 1681 in front of it. — Also to be seen in the historical core are the buildings of meat shops (exhibition hall) and a waterworks tower. — The sites of the former fortifications are now occupied by parks and several monumental buildings — especially the J. K. Tyl Theatre and the West Bohemian Museum (exposition of arts and crafts, nature, etc.). — The Workers' House called Peklo, which was the first club building of the social democrats in former Austria-Hungary (1894), is a monument of the workers' movement. — Stylish restaurant by the entrance to the Pilsner Urquell brewery.

Environs: 10 km SE the ruins of **Radyně** Castle of the 14th century. — 14 km SE Classical **Kozel** Château with its original furnishings of the turn of the 13th and 14th centuries and an English park. — 16 km E the district town of **Rokycany** (pop. 16,000) with a tradition in iron production. — 22 km E a hammer-mill of the 19th century with a museum exposition at the community of **Dobřív**. — 20 km N the town of **Plasy** with a huge Baroque monastery complex, inside a museum. — 16 km W the recreation region in the immediate environs of the **Hracholusky valley reservoir** on the River Mže.

PODĚBRADY   E 2

a town (pop. 13,500) on the River Elbe. A **spa** (treatment of cardiovascular dis-

eases) from 1908, colonnade, spa park, 13 mineral springs (at depths of 86—105 m). Bohemia Glassworks (lead crystal glass). — On the bank of the Elbe a huge château with a round tower. The Czech king George of Poděbrady, an equestrian statue of whom stands in the middle of the square, came from here.

Environs: 8 km NW the district town of **Nymburk** with preserved fortifications and ditches from the 13th—14th century. — 21 km W **Přerov nad Labem**, museum of folk architecture of the Elbe valley.

POPRAD   M 3

a district town (672 m, pop. 47,000). Starting point for the High Tatras, important transport junction (modern railway station), airport. Industry (railway carriage works), extensive construction of new housing estates. — Elongated square with a Renaissance belfry of 1658 with a gabled attic, Gothic church and Classical, partly also Baroque houses.

Local part **Spišská Sobota**, historical town reserve. The square is lined with Renaissance two-storeyed burghers' houses with Baroque adaptations. In the centre an originally Romanesque church, rebuilt in the Gothic and adapted in the Baroque. The high altar is the work of Master Pavol of Levoča (1516). Renaissance belfry (1598), Barocized in 1728.

PRACHATICE   C 3

a district town (pop. 11,000) in the foothills of the Šumava Mountains. — Founded in 1323 on the Golden Path along which malt was exported and salt

Poděbrady

imported. In the period of flourish over 100 horses and mules passed this way daily.

The historical part of the town is a **historical town reserve** concentrated round the square with Late Gothic houses adapted in the Renaissance, richly decorated with **graffito** and ornaments (Rumpál's House, salt-house and others). Old **Town Hall** of about 1570, new Town Hall of the early 20th century, Neo-Renaissance (attic richly decorated with figural motifs). The landmark of the town is a Gothic triple-naved **church** of the 14th century with a conspicuous steeple; inside a Late Gothic altar. Part of the town fortifications of the 14th and 16th century has also been preserved (Písek Gate with graffito and Helvít Bastion), area by the fortifications laid out as a park.

Environs: 2 km SE the **Kandlův Mlýn** recreation resort with a bathing-pool. Overlooking the town in the SE is Mount **Libín** (1,096 m) with a 27 m high observation tower (from Prachatice a 6 km walk according to red tourist signs). — 5 km N **Husinec.** — 17 km N the small town of **Bavorov** with a peak work of the South Bohemian Gothic — a church from the latter half of the 14th century. — 13 km NE Renaissance **Kratochvíle** Château with valuable stucco decoration and an exposition of puppet and cartoon film.

PRACHOVSKÉ SKÁLY   E 1
(The Prachov Rocks)

a state nature preserve and popular destination of excursions in the Bohemian Paradise. Three marked circuits for tours on foot run through a **rock town** from Turistická chata (Tourist Chalet) with a car park. They afford numerous views of mountain-climbing terrains

(sandstone towers); considerable number of caves and narrow, deep gorges. The paths are made safe by means of railings and ladders. The Jinolice region of ponds lies below the rocks (bathing).

PREŠOV   N 3

an East Slovak district town (pop. 83,000). Developed industry — engineering, textile and food. Pedagogical and philosophical faculties, theatre. Slavonic settlement at the turn of the 8th and 9th centuries, first mention of the town in 1347, from 1374 a free royal town. Centre of the anti-Hapsburg uprisings in the 17th and 18th centuries, in 1831 an uprising of the town's poor. End of the 19th and beginning of the 20th century marked by widespread migration due to unemployment and want. On 16 June, 1919 the proclamation here of the **Slovak Republic of Councils** under the influence of the Great October Revolution.

The centre of the town is a **historical town reserve.** Along the elongated square a number of valuable burghers' houses (originally Gothic and Renaissance with Classical adaptations). Building of the Town Hall from 1511—1520 from whose balcony the Slovak Republic of Councils was proclaimed; in the nearby Rákoczi House a museum devoted to this event. A Gothic parish **church** with valuable interior furnishings.

Environs: 3 km E from the centre **Solivar**, salt mining from 1572, from 1752 the mining of brine from a depth of 150 m, used for the gaining of salt by means of evaporation. — 6 km NW, on a high hill (572 m), the ruins of big **Veľký Šariš** Castle of the 13th century. It ceased to exist after a fire in 1687. Far-reaching view.

PŘÍBRAM   C 2

an industrial district town (pop. 40,000).
SW of Prague. **Silver** was mined here
(to the greatest extent in the latter half
of the 19th century) already in the first
half of the 13th century, when the community gained town rights. — In the
square a church of the 13th century, rebuilt in pseudo-Romanesque style. —
On the hill **Svatá hora** (586 m) overlooking the town stands a church of pilgrimage, Barocized and enlarged after the
mid-17th century. By the church a former Jesuit residence. — In the part of
the town called Březové Hory there is
a mining museum. — Mining of uranium
ores in the surroundings.
Environs: 6 km S **Milín**, a memorial
commemorating the last shots of the
Second World War in Europe (11 May,
1945).

PUSTEVNY   J 3

a saddle (1,018 m) in the ridge of the
Moravian-Silesian Beskids, a notable
mountain resort, 8 km SE of Frenštát
pod Radhoštěm. The first hostel was
built here already in 1891. Libušín and
Maměnka Chalets built after designs by
Dušan Jurkovič — folk architecture influenced by the Art Nouveau. Approach
from the north by chair-lift from Ráztoka (approach by car from Trojanovice
restricted) and from the south from
Prostřední Bečva.
A highly frequented route for walking
tours runs round the **Cyrilka** observation pavilion (400 m W) to the statue of
the ancient Slavonic god of crops and
herds, Radegast (of 1930) and to the
summit of **Radhošť** (1,129 m, 3 km).
Standing here is a huge Baroque chapel
of 1848 with a group of statues of the

Slavonic missionaries Cyril (Constantine) and Method, who brought Christianity from the Byzantine empire to the
territory of the then Great Moravian Empire in 863, in front of it. A mountain
chalet and a TV transmitter are also situated here. Radhošť is a unique observation peak.

ROŽMBERK NAD VLTAVOU   D 4

a community in the southernmost part
of Bohemia. Standing on a promontory
around which the Vltava flows on three
sides is a **castle** founded in the 13th
century. Its oldest part is the slender
tower called Jakobínka. In the 14th century a two-storeyed palace with
a square tower was built which was later provided with Neo-Gothic battlements. In its interior an armoury, a Hall
of Fishermen with a coffered ceiling and
a picture gallery. In the mid-19th century the castle underwent an extensive
Neo-Gothic reconstruction and the New
Château was built on to it.

ROŽŇAVA   M 4

a district town (pop. 21,000) below the
southern headlands of the Slovak Ore
Mountains. Gold was mined here in the
Middle Ages. Baroque Classical **bishop's residence** from 1776—1778, originally Gothic church which was later
Barocized. In the square a Late Renaissance observation tower, the Town Hall,
valuable burghers' houses and remainders of the town fortifications with
a tower. Mining museum.
Environs: 6 km NW **Betliar** Château, rebuilt in 1880 after the model of French
Renaissance-Baroque châteaux, now
a museum of interior design, valuable

Příbram

English park. — 6 km E **Krásna Hôrka** Castle rising high above the community of Krásnohorské Podhradie. It originated about 1320, in the years 1578—1585 it was converted into a Renaissance fortress against the Turks, after 1676 it served as a representative seat and since 1910 it has been the family museum of the Andrássy family. By the roadside in the direction towards Košice the Art Nouveau mausoleum of the owners of the castle from 1902—1904.

a town (pop. 16,000) below the ridges of the Moravian-Silesian Beskids. Originally a small town with wooden buildings, now with modern construction and an electrical engineering industry (Tesla). In 1925 a **Wallachian open-air museum**, now concentrating over 90 buildings from the Wallachian region, was opened in the former spa park. Folk fur-

Wallachian open-air museum
at Rožnov pod Radhoštěm

niture, garments, vessels, utensils, tools and so on can be seen in their interiors. Standing here, for example, are a small wooden church, the former wooden Town Hall of Rožnov (of 1770), ale-houses, a belfry, courts, farmsteads, a forge, a bailiff's house, shepherds' huts, etc.
Environs: E in the valley of the Dolní (Rožnovská) Bečva the communities of Dolní Bečva, Prostřední Bečva and Horní Bečva, tourist and recreation resorts with accommodation facilities. At **Horní Bečva** there is a small dam reservoir (bathing). — 7 km NE Mount **Radhošť** (1,129 m), accessible on foot directly from Rožnov pod Radhoštěm, or along the ridge from Pustevny (1,018 m).

RYCHNOV NAD KNĚŽNOU   F 2

a district town (pop, 12,000) below the Orlické Mountains. Baroque **château** from 1676—1690 with the Kolovrat's big family collection of 500 paintings by Czech, Netherlandish and Italian painters and with a valuable library.
Environs: 8 km SW **Častolovice**, a Renaissance château with unique interiors, rich collections and an English park. — At nearby **Kostelec nad Orlicí** an Empire château. — 6 km S **Doudleby nad Orlicí**, a Renaissance château with graffito decoration. — 5 km SE the town of **Vamberk** with a tradition in lace production, museum expositions devoted to lace-making. Frame houses in the square. — 9 km SE **Potštejn** with the ruins of a castle of the late 13th century. In the outer bailey a Baroque château. — 8 km NE the village of **Liberk** with a wooden Baroque church and a frame belfry. Frame folk architecture in the surroundings.

SÁZAVA   E 2

a town and summer resort on the river of the same name. **Kavalier Glassworks** (laboratory and flameproof glass), whose tradition reaches back to the first half of the 19th century. — **Monastery** founded by Prince Oldřich about 1032. The monks used the Slavonic liturgy (the first abbot was Procopius). Preserved chapter hall from about 1350 with frescoes. Monastery church built throughout the 14th century, but not completed. In 1785 the monastery was abolished and later converted into a château. Now open to the public, exposition called Slavonic Sázava and a museum of technical glass.

SKALICA   H 3

a town (pop. 14,000) in the close vicinity of the Moravian-Slovak border. From 1372 a free royal town, in the 19th century an important centre of political and national life and a place of rapprochement of the Czechs and Slovaks. — Romanesque **rotunda** of the 12th century. Remains of the Gothic town fortifications.Several valuable churches. Slovak House of Culture built in 1905 after a design by D. Jurkovič. Museum with collections of Haban ceramics and Holíč majolica.

SLAVKOV U BRNA   G 3

a town with a Baroque château built about 1700. Valuable paintings and stucco decoration can be seen in its interiors. Museum devoted to the Napoleonic Wars.

Rychnov
nad Kněžnou

Environs: 9 km W the **Barrow of Peace**, a memorial commemorating the Battle of the Three Emperors which took place on 2 December, 1805 and in which 40,000 men lost their lives. The French Emperor Napoleon's troops gained victory here over the troops of the Russian Tsar Alexander I and the Austrian Emperor Franz I. Museum, view of the battlefield. — 9 km E **Bučovice**, a Renaissance château of the latter half of the 16th century with arcades; period garden.

SLAVONICE   E 3

a small town near the Austrian border, founded in 1277. Its ground-plan is a unique testimony to medieval building principles. Now a **historical town reserve.** In the 16th century a long road led this way from Prague to Vienna (post for changing of horses), at that time the biggest building work. A compact complex of Late Gothic and especially **Renaissance houses** of the 16th century with Lombardian and Venetian gables (many with figural graffito decoration) has been preserved in the squares (Lower) Dolní and (Upper) Horní náměstí. Gothic parish church with Renaissance steeple of 1549 and in its vicinity the Town Hall of 1599. Two fountains, Marian column. Numerous remains of Renaissance fortifications — especially Dačice and Jemnice Gates. *Environs:* 9 km E the ruins of Landštejn Castle.

SLOVÁCKO (Moravian Slovakia)   H 3

the south-east part of Moravia, a region running from the gently undulating White Carpathians (Velká Javořina, 970 m) to the fertile lowlands of the lower stream of the River Morava. In the west it is demarcated by the Chřiby Mountains (587 m). The present territory of Slovácko was formed by one of the important parts of the first union of Slavonic tribes (the Sámo empire, mid-7th century), but also by the far more important Great Moravian Empire (9th century). Its most important centre was probably Mikulčice (south-west of Hodonín).

The region is known for its **folklore**, songs and folk dances which often reflect the developed vinicultural activity of the region and its rich tradition. The local folk art production, national costumes, embroideries, painted Easter eggs, majolica, reed-mace products and other features are of a striking folklore character. The typical masonry-built, white and brightly painted houses with porches and heavy, thatched roofs have been preserved only in rare cases, complexes of **wine cellars** being more frequent. Well-known ethnographical **festivals** take place at **Strážnice** every year. A skansen of folk architecture is

Wine cellar at Petrov
in Moravian Slovakia

situated here. The colourful festival held under the name of **The Ride of Kings** (Vlčnov, Hluk) is a popular event. There are also attractive **architectonic monuments** in the Slovácko region — the landmark, visible from far and wide, is royal **Buchlov** Castle, situated 12 km NW of Uherské Hradiště, of the first half of the 13th century. Nearby is Baroque **Buchlovice** Château, with a large park, and **Velehrad** monastery. Valuable châteaux are also situated at **Milotice** near Kyjov (Baroque, rich collections) and at Strážnice. **Starting points:** Hodonín, Uherské Hradiště, Uherský Brod, Kyjov, Strážnice, Břeclav, Veselí nad Moravou.

SLOVENSKÉ RUDOHORIE L—N 3—4
(The Slovak Ore Mountains)

---

a 145 km long **mountain ridge** stretching in west-east direction from Brusno in the Hron valley as far as Košice in the valley of the Hornád. A considerable part of these mountains is forested and relatively little frequented. Good conditions for **walking tours**, dense network of marked paths, relatively unviolated landscape.

In the west, in the vicinity of Banská Bystrica, the ridge links up with the volcanic massif called **Poľana** (1,458 m). — 9 km SE of Brezno the community of **Čierny Balog**; preserved folk architecture; old forest railway; during the Second World War a centre of the partisan movement. Overlooking the community on the side of the ridge the oldest protected primeval forest in Slovakia (**Dobročský**) with pine, beech and spruce growths (up to 450 years of age). **Muránska planina** (plateau) to the east of Brezno is a huge limestone hollow (6 × 15 km) with numerous karst phenomena (104 caves, 35 small springs). The

highest peak is Kľak (1,409 m). **Protected landscape region** with rare flora and fauna (the bear). Overlooking the community of Muráň are the big ruins of the highest situated castle in Slovakia (938 m).

The range of hills called **Stolické vrchy** is practically wholly covered with forests and rising among them is the highest peak of the Slovak Ore Mountains, **Stolica** (1,476 m). Stretching out in the north-east is the national park Slovenský raj (the Slovak Paradise) and in the south-east the region of the Slovak Karst.

The eastern part of the range (the hills **Volovské vrchy**) is the most frequented by tourists. Tourist chalets are situated below the peaks Volovec (1,284 m) and **Kojšovská hoľa** (1,246 m) and there are good conditions here for ski tours and downhill skiing (ski-tows). On the River Hornád, 30 km NW of Košice, lies the **Ružín dam** reservoir (600 hectares), used for recreation purposes — water sports, accommodation. The Jahodná and Čermeľ region (pioneer railway) serves the regional town of Košice for recreation purposes.

Recommended car route: Brezno — Čierny Balog — Lom nad Rimavicou — Kokava nad Rimavicou — Hnúšťa — Tisovec — Muráň — Švermovo — Dobšinská ľadová jeskyňa (ice cave) — Dobšiná — Rožňava — Úhorná — Mníšek nad Hnilcom — Jaklovce — Košická Belá — Košice. Total length 255 km. The route crosses the main mountain ridge 5 times.

SLOVENSKÝ KRAS   M—N 4
(The Slovak Karst)

---

the biggest **karst territory** in Central Europe, forming a part of the Slovak Ore Mountains. It spreads out in southern

---

Slovenské
rudohorie

Slovakia along the border with Hungary in the environs of the town of Rožňava. Part of it is a **protected landscape region.** Here the layers of limestone attain a thickness of 400—500 m and are divided by deep canyons formed by rivers. There are many caves, gorges and springs on the karst territory. Rare warmth-loving flora.

Brázda Abyss, lying 10 km S of Rožňava, is one of the deepest in Czechoslovakia (180 m). — The gorge called **Silická ľadnica** is covered with ice and to be seen here, for example, is a 12 m high icefall. — The karst canyon **Zádielská dolina** 20 km E of Rožňava is 3 km long and 10 m wide in places and its vertical limestone walls rise to a height of 400 m. — The **Domica** and **Gombasecká Ice Cave** (10 km E of Rožňava, length of sightseeing circuit 45 min) are open to the public.

SLOVENSKÝ RAJ M 3
(The Slovak Paradise)

a very popular tourist region in East Slovakia, SE of Poprad, with a number of karst phenomena — gorges, caves, springs and karst plateaux with numerous waterfalls and rich flora and fauna. From the orological aspect the region is a part of the Slovak Ore Mountains — 600—1,000 m above sea level, highest point Havrania skala (1,153 m), predominant minerals limestone and dolomites. In 1988 the Slovak Paradise was proclaimed a **national park** (14,186 hectares).
Approach to the region from the north from Poprad to Hrabušice and to **Podlesok** (chalet communities, car camp), or from Spišská Nová Ves to **Čingov** (Flora Hotel, tourist hostels, chalet community). From here **Kláštorisko** (chalet community, restaurant) is accessible on foot

only. In the environs **passes** 150—300 m in depth whose bottom narrows down to as little as 1 m with waterfalls; accessible by marked tourist paths, ascents of necessity facilitated in certain places by ladders or secured by chains; passage through the gorges possible only from below in upward direction. The best-known gorges are Kyseľ, Suchá Belá, Veľký Sokol and Malý Sokol. Over a 16 km long sector the River Hornád forms a **canyoned valley** up to 300 m in depth; in many places the rocks fall directly into the water; passage made possible by a number of bridges, footpaths and steps; the most exposed places can be crossed with the aid of chains and climbing irons.
The starting point for the Slovak Paradise from the S is **Dedinky** (hotel, chalet community, railway station) near the reservoir on the River Hnilec (bathing). A chair-lift runs to the karst plateau called **Geravy** (hotel, cross-country skiing tracks). Higher upstream of the Hnilec lies the ice cave Dobšinská ľadová jaskyňa; the canyon Stratenský kaňon is accessible on foot.
Recommended car route: Poprad —

Waterfall
in the Suchá Belá Pass
in the Slovak Paradise

Hrabušice — Podlesok (on foot to the Suchá Belá Pass, to Kláštorisko and to the Hornád Pass) — Spišská Nová Ves (possibility of turning off to Čingov and making a tour to the Hornád Pass on foot) — the saddle Grajnár (1,069 m) — the Hnilec valley — Dedinky (chair-lift to Geravy) — the Dobšinská ľadová jaskyňa (ice cave) — Vernár — Poprad. Total length approx. 110 km.

SNĚŽKA   F 1

the highest mountain in the Czech Socialist Republic (1,602 m) in the main ridge of the Krkonoše Mountains on the Polish border. Its bare, rocky summit affords excellent **views** (on a very clear day it is even possible to see Prague from here). — The first attempt to reach its summit was made in 1456 by an unknown Venetian. Access by means of marked paths and a chair-lift from Pec pod Sněžkou. On the summit the Česká bouda restaurant, on the Polish side St. Lawrence's Chapel from 1665—1681, a meteorological station and a mountain hotel.

SOUTH BOHEMIA   C—E 3—4

a verry attractive tourist region with rich art and historical monuments and recreation possibilities on the banks of the local pónds. Lowland plains abounding in **ponds** are a typical element of the South Bohemian region. The biggest of them is **Rožmberk** near Třeboň (489 hectares), followed by Bezdrev near České Budějovice (450 hectares), Horusický rybník (415 hectares) and the longest and the deepest pond, Staňkovský rybník, on the border with Austria (6 km, 18 m, 241 hectares). They

are mainly used for **fish-breeding** purposes (the fishing-out of the ponds in autumn is a big tourist attraction), but some of them also serve **recreation** purposes (e.g., Svět at Třeboň). Velký Tisý is a bird sanctuary (342 hectares). The ponds are surrounded by extensive mixed forests in which pines prevail and their banks are usually grown with centuries old oaks. In the lowlands there are often marshes with rare flora. The most valuable part of this region forms a part of the **protected landscape region of Třeboň.**

The South Bohemian basins gradually rise to the peaks of the Šumava Mountains, the Novohradské Mountains, the Bohemian—Moravian Highlands and the Central Bohemian Hills, valleys having been cut in them by the local rivers, especially the Vltava, the Lužnice, the Otava and the Malše. — Czechoslovakia's longest river, the **Vltava,** flows from the Šumava Mountains to the České Budějovice basin and then cuts its way through the Central Bohemian Hills to Prague. Its valley is as much as 200—300 m deep in some places. **Castles** originated on high rocky promontories along its flow (Rožmberk, Český Krumlov, Hluboká, Zvikov, Orlík) similarly as monasteries (Vyšší Brod, Zlatá Koruna) and rich towns (Český Krumlov, České Budějovice). Nowadays the Vltava is bound by a cascade of **dams** (e.g. Orlík) which supply the national economy with electric energy and also serve recreation purposes. — The **Lužnice,** a tributary of the Vltava, is the most popular river among watermen, who navigate practically its whole length. Many places along the Lužnice were connected with the antifeudal Hussite revolutionary movement and the Hussite centre, Tábor, is situated on the river. — In past centuries the **Otava** was a gold-bearing river, proof of this lying in the gold-washing places which can still be seen on its banks. The town of Písek has the oldest stone bridge in Czechoslovakia and Strakonice (also a starting place for the Šumava Mountains), situated further upstream, has a magnificent medieval castle and a long-standing tradition in fez and motorcycle production.

In the Middle Ages the whole of South Bohemia (whith the exception of the royal towns of České Budějovice and Vodňany) belonged to the **Rožmberks** (the region of the five-petalled rose, which the family had in its coat-of-arms). Poverty and oppression led to the development of the Hussite revolutionary movement (Jan Žižka of Trocnov). From the 16th century ponds were founded here (the best-known of their builders was Jakub Krčín of Jelčany). In general economic development lagged behind that of the rest of the country and even the construction of the first **horse-drawn railway** from Linz to České Budějovice, the first on the European continent (1832), failed to improve the situation. Not until after the Second World War did a period of flourish set in, but the South Bohemian region is still the least populated in the Czech Socialist Republic.

Starting places: the regional town of České Budějovice, Písek, Tábor, Třeboň Jindřichův Hradec, Český Krumlov, Prachatice and Strakonice; Nové Hrady.
Recommended car route: České Budějovice — Zlatá Koruna — Český Krumlov — Rožmberk nad Vltavou — Vyšší Brod — Kaplice — Benešov nad Černou — Žumberk — Nové Hrady — Třeboň — Jindřichův Hradec — Červená Lhota — Tábor — Milevsko — Orlík — Zvíkov — Písek — Týn nad Vltavou — Hluboká nad Vltavou — České Budějovice. 3—4 days are necessary to cover this route, including sightseeing. Total length 350 km.

SPIŠ M—N 3

a region lying east of the High Tatras in East Slovakia. Varied landscape (the High and the Belianské Tatras, the Pieniny, the Slovak Paradise); settlement concentrated particularly in the valleys of the Poprad, Dunajec, Hornád and Hnilec. A number of rich **historical towns** originated in the valleys below the mountains (24). The richest as regards historical monuments are Levoča and Kežmarok; the administrative centre of the whole Spiš region is Spišská Nová Ves. Czechoslovakia's biggest castle — Spiš Castle — is also situated here. Rich folklore. Skansen below Stará Ľubovňa Castle. Notable spa of Vyšné Ružbachy.

SPIŠSKÁ NOVÁ VES M 3

a district town (pop. 37,000) in the valley of the River Hornád; a town before 1407, pledged to Poland from 1412 — 1772, Gothic church of the latter half of the 14th century with a 86 m high steeple. The Stations of the Cross are the work of Master Pavol of Levoča. — The cores of Renaissance houses can be seen in the elongated square. Ethnograpical museum.
Environs: 5 km SE Renaissance **Markušovce** Château of 1643, museum of historical furniture, ruins of a castle of the same name of the 13th— 14th century. — W the Slovak Paradise.

SPIŠSKÁ SOBOTA

See Poprad

SPIŠSKÝ HRAD   N 3
(Spiš Castle)

one of the biggest **castle ruins** in Central Europe, situated on a conspicuous hill (634 m) NE of Spišská Nová Ves. It originated in the 12th century, was gradually enlarged and resisted an attack by the Tartars in the 13th century. In the 16th century about 2,000 people lived here (the nobility, servants and men-at-arms). Destroyed by fire in 1780. Made accessible after the carrying out of repairs. In the oldest part of the castle there is a Romanesque tower, by it an old palace and huge fortifications. *Environs:* 2 km W **Spišská Kapitula,** a historical town reserve of the 13th century, then mainly inhabited by priests. Town walls, 2 entrance gates and Romanesque cathedral with twin steeples.

STARÁ BOLESLAV

See Brandýs nad Labem — Stará Boleslav

STARÝ SMOKOVEC   M 3

along with Nový, Horný and Dolný Smokovec (now also called Smokovec) the biggest **holiday resort** (1,010 m), with hotels, recreation houses of the trade unions and various corporations, in the High Tatras. Situated below the peak Slavkovský štít (2,452 m). It is the oldest community in the Tatras and was used as a summer resort already in 1797. Administrative centre of the High Tatras (Municipal National Committee for all the Tatra communities), cultural and social centre (summer music festivals, exhibitions). — Neighbouring **Nový Smokovec** and **Horný Smokovec** are known for their spa sanatoria (in particular treatment of diseases of the respiratory tracts). — Junction of the Tatra electric railway (Poprad, Štrbské Pleso, Tatranská Lomnica). Ground funicular to **Hrebienok** (1,285 m) with skiing grounds; starting point for excursions to the chalet **Zbojnícka chata** (2 1/2 hours, 1,960 m) and the chalet **Téryho chata** (2 1/2 hours, 2,015 m), also ascent to the red-marked arterial road (direc-

Spišský
hrad

Spiš
Castle

tion to Štrbské Pleso or Skalnaté Pleso), or along the blue-marked ascent to the peak Slavkovský štít (4 hours). The destinations of shorter walks are often the waterfalls of the Studený potok river and the Obrovský Waterfall.

STRAKONICE   C 3

a district town (pop. 24,000) in the foothills of the Šumava Mountains. In the 18th century developed stocking production and later cap production, from 1812 to the present fez production, extensive export. České závody motocyklové works (ČZ mark). — Castle founded in the 12th century, dominated by an Early Gothic tower with a gallery, in the former Romanesque palace a chapter hall, in the right courtyard St. Procopius's Church. A museum is installed in the castle (expositions, for example, of gold-washing and bagpipe production). International bagpipe festivals take place in the courtyard and the castle garden.
Environs: villages (e.g., Miloňovice, Sousedovice, Radošovice) with folk buildings in the style of the so-called rustic Baroque (19th century). — 13 km S the town of Volyně with a well-preserved stronghold of the early 14th century (museum expositions in its interior) and a Renaissance Town Hall with graffito decoration.

STRÁŽNICE   H 3

a town in the fertile South Moravian lowlands. Mentioned in 1302. Monuments in the form of a preserved château and two Renaissance town gates. Below the château a skansen of folk architecture of Moravian Slovakia.

In June every year an ethnographical festival takes place in the town. National costumes are still worn from time to time in the surrounding villages and certain old customs have survived to the present. White, masonry-built houses with brightly coloured porches can be seen here and the local wine cellars (e.g. those at Petrov) are an interesting sight.

STREČNO   K 3

the big ruins of a castle on the left bank of the Váh, SE of Žilina. The castle was mentioned in the 14th century and its present appearance dates from the turn of the 15th and 16th centuries; in the late 17th century it was demolished to prevent it from aiding the rebels during their uprising against the emperor. Below the castle the main road from Žilina to Poprad. In the immediate vicinity a memorial to the French partisans who heroically helped to defend the pass at the turn of September and October 1944 at the time of the Slovak National Uprising. Other tough battles took place in April 1945 (memorial on the summit of Polom, cemetery with the graves of 747 soldiers and partisans at Priekopa near Martin).

STŘÍBRO   B 2

a town W of Plzeň. Silver was mined in the local mines already in the latter half of the 12th century; in 1240 a royal town was founded near the mines. During the Thirty Years War it was devastated and deserted. — In the square houses with Renaissance portals and a Renaissance Town Hall with graffito (from 1883—1888). Barocized monastery and church. On the Gothic bridge spanning the Mže stands a gate of the mid-16th century.

Environs: 4 km S **Kladruby** — former Benedictine monastery with the Church of Our Lady of the 12th century, rebuilt in Baroque-Gothic style from 1712—1728 by G. B. Santini. Buildings of the Old and the New Convent and a prelature, likewise Baroque.

SUŠICE   C 3

a town (pop. 11,000) in the NW part of the region below the Šumava Mountains. From 1839 **match production,** later under the Solo mark; nowadays 80% of the total production is exported to 40 countries. The history of this production is documented in the museum installed in an old burgher's house in the square, where there are expositions of matchbox labels, etc. The originally Renaissance Town Hall stands in the centre of the square. Early Baroque Fialka House with graffito. Near the square stands a Gothic church. Remains of medieval fortifications.

Environs: 7 km E of the town **Annín,** a community with a glassworks whose tradition (crystal glass) goes back to the late 18th century. Above the community the hill called Mouřenec with a small church. A car camp is situated in the valley of the Otava. — 10 km NW **Velhartice** with a Gothic castle of the 14th century, whose tower is uniquely linked with the palace by means of a bridge. — 10 km NE, above the valley of the Otava, the ruins of **Rabí** Castle, ranking among the biggest in Bohemia. In 1421 it was besieged and conquered by the Hussite military commander Jan Žižka of Trocnov, who lost his second eye here. Valuable Late Gothic castle chapel.

SVIDNÍK   O 3

a district town (pop. 10,000) SW of the Dukla Pass. A town only since 1964, modern construction, garment and engineering industries. — During the Second World War (in September to November 1944) tough battles — the so-called Duklian Operations — took place NE of Svidník. In the town there is a 37 m high **memorial,** with a number of allegorical groups of statues. It commemorates the 84,000 Soviet soldiers who lost their lives or were wounded during the operations. The **Dukla Museum** documents the whole military operation of members of the Czechoslovak and the Red Army. Diorama of the battlefield. In the town there is also a museum of Ukrainian culture (Ukrainian national minority). Small **wooden churches** (national cultural monuments) e.g., in the communities of Potoky (8 km SE), Ladomírová (4 km NE), Hunkovce (7 km N), Bodružal (10 km NE), Mirola (12 km E).

ŠPINDLERŮV MLÝN   F 1

the biggest mountain **recreation resort** in the Krkonoše Mountains and Bohemia as a whole (714—860 m). From the 16th century the remote mountain valley was inhabited by wood-cutters and ore-diggers and in the mid-19th century it began to change into a summer resort. Biggest growth in the number of visitors after the Second World War and especially in the last 10—15 years. Starting point for tours to the most beautiful parts of the **Krkonoše National Park** (e.g., the valley of the Bílé Labe, Labský důl, Sedmidolí). Ascent to the ridges is facilitated by a road to the chalet **Špindlerovka** (1,198 m)

Sušice

and chair-lifts to **Pláň** (1,160 m) and **Medvědín** (1,230 m). The chalets Luční .bouda, Labská bouda (above Labský důl by the Labský Waterfall), Martinovka and Petrovka are popular destinations similarly as the mountain resort of Horní Mísečky and Vrbatova chalet on the ridge of the Krkonoš (bus). Very good conditions for **skiing sports** in winter: funiculars, ski-tows, downhill run tracks, ski-jump structures a cross-country skiing area at nearby **Horní Mísečky**, network of winter signposts and tourist marks. — 1.5 km below Špindlerův Mlýn there is a small **dam** reservoir on the Elbe.

tion in and by the **lakes** (so-called "tajchy") built in the the 18th century as reservoirs of water for mining purposes. The biggest is **Počúvalské jazero** (12 hectares, camping site, recreation). The highest peak is **Sitno** (1,009 m), situated 8 km S of Banská Štiavnica. Ascent on foot from the lake Počúvalské jazero (1 hour), botanical locality (roses), volcanic relief (rock wall on the summit), chalet below the summit. In the NW part of the range of hills lies the spa of **Sklené Teplice** for the treatment of diseases of the motory organs and nervous disorders, 12 springs (a cave pool by one of them) with water of a temperature of up to 52 °C.

ŠTERNBERK H 2

a town (pop. 17,000) at the foot of the Jeseníks. Production of Prim watches. — In the 13th century a **castle** was founded here and a town below it. The huge round tower of the original castle has been preserved. An exposition in the castle interiors affords an idea of creative art and furnishings from the Gothic to the Baroque. — In the neighbourhood a former Augustinian monastery, valuable Baroque architecture. — In the outer bailey buildings there is a clock museum.

ŠTIAVNICKE VRCHY K 4
(The Štiavnica Hills)

a volcanic range above the valley of the Hron in the central part of Slovakia. Exceedingly articulated relief, oak and beech forests. **Protected landscape region.** Situated in the centre of the range is the ancient mining town of **Banská Štiavnica,** the starting point for tours to the whole region. Bathing and recrea-

ŠTRAMBERK J 3

a small town picturesquely situated E of Nový Jičín. Its core is a **historical town reserve.** Below the round tower called

Štramberk
with the characteristic tower
called Trúba

Trúba (once part of a former castle) lies the square with Baroque houses and the parish church. Frame buildings of the Wallachian type have been preserved in the adjoining streets.
On the limestone hill **Kotouč** lying 1 km S of the centre there is a circuit for walking tours (observation tower, small chapel, memorials). In 1879—1883 a part of the skeleton and the jaws of a Neanderthal man were found in the cave called Šipka as well as the bones of a mammoth and rhinocerus, tools, a fireplace, etc.

ŠTRBSKÉ PLESO   M 3

the highest **recreation resort** and **lake** (19.8 hectares) in the High Tatras (1,355 m). Attractive high-mountain scenery with a landmark in the form of the peak called Vysoká (2,560 m). From the last quarter of the 19th century spa sanatoria were built here (treatment of diseases of the respiratory tract) as well as hotels. Extensive modern construction before 1970 in connection with the world skiing championships. A **skiing area** lies at the mouth of the valley Mlynická dolina: 2 ski-jump structures, the start and finish of cross-country skiing tracks, chair-lift (to Solisko, 1,830 m), ski-tows. Starting point for excursions to Popradské Pleso (1 1/4 hours) and ascents of Rysy (2,499 m, 4 1/2 hours) and Kriváň (2,494 m, 4 1/2 hours). The red-marked arterial road passes this way. The locality can be reached by means of the electric railway from Starý Smokovec or by the ground funicular from the Štrba railway station on the main Prague — Košice railway line.

ŠUMAVA   B—C 3—4
(The Šumava Mountains)

a big range in South West Bohemia near the borders with the Federal Republic of Germany and Austria. Approx. 120 km long, it stretches over a distance of as much as 45 km through the Šumava region to the inland part of Bohemia. It is highly frequented due to its beautiful natural scenery and cultural monuments. In 1963 the biggest Czech **protected landscape region** (1,630 sq. km) was proclaimed here.
The Šumava mountain range has not got a compact main ridge. Its most typical part is formed by the central region of upper plateaux situated at a height of 500—1,100 m above sea level above which the individual peaks project by as much as 300 m. It is just here that the Vltava, the longest Czech river, and the Otava, its left tributary, spring. The highest peak of the Šumava Mountains, Gross Arber (1,456 m), lies in the northern part of the range on the territory of the Federal Republic of Germany. From Železná Ruda the frequented tourist ridges of Pancíř (1,214 m) and Můstek (1,234 m) run inland. A number of higher peaks are situated in the inaccessible border zone. Another conspicuous group of mountains rises SE of the region of the upper plateaux — culminating with **Boubín** (1,362 m) with a well-known primeval forest. The highest peak in the Šumava Mountains on Czechoslovak territory is **Plechý** (1,378 m), situated on the border in the vicinity of the Lipno dam reservoir. There are several interesting peaks with **observation towers** also in the foothills: Libín (1,096 m) near Prachtice, Kleť (1,083 m) near Český Krumlov in the southernmost part of the range, Svatobor (845 m) near Sušice, Mařský vrch (907 m) near Vimperk, etc.

Štrbské
Pleso

In the Šumava Mountains there are 5 **lakes** which are the remains of glacial activity (the biggest is Černé with an area of 18 hectares and a depth of 39 m). The range is characterized by deep forest growths among which spruce trees predominate. A specific feature of the Šumava region are the local peat-bogs (situated particularly on the upper plateaus) with rare vegetation.

The biggest tourist centre in the Šumava Mountains is **Železná Ruda — Špičák** at the border crossing to the Federal Republic of Germany. 10 km NW, on the slopes of Můstek, lies **Hojsova Stráž** with skiing grounds and recreation buildings. Another recreation resort in this part of the Šumava Mountains is **Javorná** with a wooden church and typical Šumava farmsteads.

A road runs from Sušice in southerly direction to the core of the Šumava Mountains, passing through the valley of the River Otava. In the Middle Ages gold was mined in the environs of Rejštejn and Kašperské Hory. The Renaissance Town Hall and the Gothic church in the square at **Kašperské Hory** have been preserved from the time of flourish of the town. A museum devoted to the Šumava region (its natural features and the work of the local people) is situated in the town. 3 km N the ruins of **Kašperk** Castle in a dominant position 886 m above sea level, 2 characteristic towers with the remains of the castle palace between them. — 3 km S of Kašperské Hory, at Rejštejn, the confluence of the Vydra and the Křemelná give origin to the Otava. The romantic valley of the **Vydra** with a rocky bed has a 7 km long nature study path (a boulder sea, giants' cups, rock formations, etc.). At **Antýgl** there is a popular car camp by the former magistrate's house with a typical small belfry. — Lying on the edge of the region of the Šumava peat-

bogs (so-called "slatí") is the community of **Modrava**. The peat-bog called Třijezerní slať is accessible by means of a marked path. — Here the road leaves the valley of the Vydra and rises to the upper plateau of the Šumavské Pláně with scattered Šumava farmsteads (e.g. the villages of Filipova Huť and Horská Kvilda) and peat-bogs (Jezerní slať with an observation tower). The village of **Kvilda** lies in the vicinity of the sources of the Vltava. A church faced with shingle in the Šumava manner can be seen here.

Strakonice is a natural starting point for the central part of the Šumava Mountains. Lying below the slopes of **Javorník** (1,089 m, observation tower) are the small towns of **Vacov** and **Stachy** (folk architecture, mushroom preserve in the square). Stretching out on a break in the upper plateaux is the second biggest summer and winter recreation resort in the Šumava Mountains — **Zadov-Churáňov** with 2 modern hotels,

Wild valley
of the River Vydra
in the Šumava
Mountains

a chair-lift, ski-tows, ski-jump structures and especially excellent grounds for cross-country skiing and ski tours. A meteorological station is situated on the summit of Churáňov (1,119 m). A railway line also passes through the valley of the Volyňka from Strakonice to Vimperk as well as an important road. Situated at a height of 960 m on the saddle below Boubín is the mountain community of **Kubova Huť** with the highest situated railway station in Bohemia (995 m). There are also ski-tows here. The main communication here runs down to the valley of the Teplá Vltava. **Lenora**, a community with a glassworks whose products are exported to a number of countries, is a tourist resort. Its interesting sights include a roofed wooden bridge across the river of the 19th century and a public oven for the baking of bread. Lenora and nearby Soumarský Most rank among the most popular places with watermen in the Czechoslovak Socialist Republic. The community is the starting point for **Boubín** (1,362 m) on whose slopes there is a primeval forest (47 hectares) which has been protected territory since 1858. The forest is composed of natural Šumava growths which include in particular spruce, fir and beech trees, some of which are several hundred years old and have bizarre shapes (double trunks, tumours, stilt-like roots). A nature study path runs round the periphery of the forest. There is also a big stag enclosure on the massif of Boubín.

From Prachatice a road and railway line run to the Boubín region and the Lipno dam reservoir. The natural centre of this part of the Šumava Mountains is the town of **Volary** with a modern wood-working complex. The local 18th century wooden houses are an interesting sight. They resemble Alpine houses with a very wide saddle roof and a gallery running across the whole width of the building. To be seen at the community of Jelení, situated S of the town, is, apart from the tunnel of the **Schwarzenberg Canal**, Bear's Stone, a small memorial in the place where the last Šumava bear was shot in 1856, and on Bear's Path there are rocks affording attractive views.

Recommended car route: Železná Ruda — Špičák — Nýrsko — Klatovy — Sušice — Kašperské Hory — Modrava — Kvilda — Lenora — Volary — Horní Planá — Černá v Pošumaví — Lipno nad Vltavou — Vyšší Brod — Rožmberk nad Vltavou — Český Krumlov. Total length 236 km.

Recommended tours on foot: 1. From Špičák to the lakes Černé and Čertovo, along the green and yellow marks, accessible in daylight only, 11 km. — **2.** Through the valley of the Vltava from Čeňkova Pila via Antýgl to Modrava, red marks, 13 km. — **3.** From Churáňov to Horská Kvilda and Antýgl, blue marks, 11 km. — **4.** From Lenora to Boubín and Kubova Huť, blue marks, 17 km.

ŠUMPERK G 2

a district town (pop. 37,000) in the southern foothills of the Jeseníky. Production of textile and canvas from the 18th century and, later, of silk, corduroy, etc. In the square are Baroque burghers' houses, the conspicuous building of the Town Hall and a Marian column (1719). Barocized church of the 14th century, Renaissance château, later adapted. Remains of Gothic fortifications of the 15th century.

Environs: 8 km NE Renaissance **Velké Losiny** Château with a park, in the 17th century the scene of witch trials resulting in the putting to death of scores of innocent women. Local spa and paper works (from 1515) with traditional manual paper production. In the vicinity of Maršíkov and Žárová little wooden churches of the early 17th century. — 22 km NE the saddle **Červenohorské sedlo** (1013 m) dividing the ridge of Hrubý Jeseník into the Keprník and Praděd groups, ski-tows, hotel. — 12 km SW the saddle **Skřítek** (motorest) on the main road to Ostrava. — 4 km SW **Bludov** spa, mineral springs, children's rehabilitation sanatorium. Late Renaissance, later Barocized château.

ŠVIHOV   B 3

a Late Gothic **water castle** N of Klatovy. Built from 1480—1510, converted into a granary in the 18th century and renewed after 1952. In the core of the castle there are two palaces which run in parallel and enclose the courtyard. They are fortified with a parkan wall and in the corners there are round towers, one of which houses the castle chapel (valuable painting of St. George and the dragon of 1515 in its interior).

TÁBOR   D 3

a district town (pop. 34,000) in South Bohemia. Developed industry: PAL sparking plugs for cars, food (dairies, conserving works), garment factory. The town, which was built on the site of an older town and castle on a promontory in 1420 by the **Hussites,** was named after the biblical mountain Tabor. It played an important role in the Hussite revolutionary movement, all its buildings being designed to meet military purposes; irregular ground-plan. From 1437 a royal town, construction of stone houses and churches.

Historical town reserve. Its core is the square Žižkovo náměstí in which there stands the **Old Gothic Town Hall** with Renaissance gables. Inside a **museum** devoted to the Hussite revolutionary movement. Also situated in the square is a **Gothic Church** from 1440—1512; medieval town houses; in the centre of the square a Renaissance fountain and memorial to Jan Žižka. Below the square there is a dense network of underground passages accessible from the museum building. Preserved remains of the fortifications and bastion. **Kotnov Castle** of the 14th century, with which the Bechyně Gate (housing a museum expostion) is connected, also formed a part of the fortifications. Below the square **Jordán Pond,** the oldest valley reservoir on Czechoslovak territory, of 1492. It once supplied Tábor with water. Water sports.
Environs: 5 km SE **Kozí Hrádek,** the small ruins of a castle where John Huss sojourned in the years 1412—1414.

TACHOV   B 2

a district town (pop. 13,000) in West Bohemia. A prince's castle was founded here on a trade route to Germany already before 1126. The town was founded in the latter half of the 13th century. In the square burghers' houses

Square
with Town Hall
at Tábor

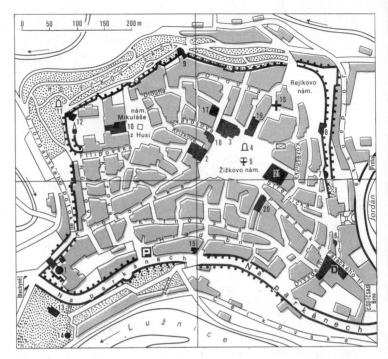

TÁBOR

1. Remainders of Kotnov Castle with tower (c). **2.** Old Town Hall (museum) (a—b).
3. Church of the Transfiguration of Our Lord on Mount Tabor (b). **4.** Jan Žižka of
Trocnov memorial (b). **5.** Renaissance fountain (b). **6.** Semicircular bastion (d).
7. Bastion (b). **8.** Waterworks tower (Upper Waterworks) (b). **9.** Soukenická Bastion
(a). **10.** Former Augustinian monastery with the Church of the Nativity of Our Lady
(a). **11.** J. Holeček memorial (a). **12.** Big (Žižka) Bastion (a). **13.** Cemetery Church of
St. James (c). **14.** The rock Granátová skála (c). **15.** Remains of a double parkan (c).
16. Hospital Chapel of St. Elizabeth (b). **17.** Dean's residence (b). **18.** New Town Hall
(b). **19.** Ale-house U Lichviců (b). **20.** House of Z. Nejedlý (d). **21.** District National
Committee (b).

most of which date in the 17th century.
Gothic church of the late 14th century,
adapted in Neo-Gothic style.
Environs: 1 km W a memorial to the victorious battle of the Hussites against
the Crusaders in 1427. — 13 km S the
ruins of Romanesque **Přimda** Castle,
mentioned for the first time in 1121. The
oldest documented castle of the nobility
built of stone on the territory of Czechoslovakia. Its core is formed by a huge
square tower (donjon). Observation
point. Access on foot (2 km) from the
small town of Přimda. At present the
castle is closed to the public.

Tábor

a big **recreation resort** (850 m) in the eastern part of the High Tatras below the peak Lomnický štít. A number of hotels, recreation houses of the Revolutionary Trade Unions Movement and works chalets. The oldest buildings date in the late 19th century, the local landmark being the Grandhotel Praha of 1905. Since 1940 a suspension cabin funicular to **Lomnický štít** (2,632 m, far-reaching views, astronomical and meteorological station) with a half-way station at **Skalnaté pleso** (1,751 m, excellent skiing grounds, chair-lift from here to the saddle Lomnické 2,189 m) has been in operation. — Seat of the Museum and Administration of the **Tatra National Park.** — Eurocamp, Czechoslovakia's biggest car camp.

Starting point for the highest part of the range. The route of the arterial road, marked with red tourist signs, runs to Skalnaté pleso, from where it turns off to Lomnické sedlo (2,189 m) and is marked with green tourist signs. The attractive route rises from the valley to the beginning of **Malá Studená dolina** and **Velká Studená dolina** (1 hour), while another runs along the water flow called Bielá Kežmarská voda to Brnčalova chata (chalet) u Zeleného plesa (lake) (3—3 1/2 hours). — 10 km N, above Tatranská Kotlina, **Belianská jaskyňa** (stalagmite and stalactite cave), access on foot 20 min, length of sightseeing circuit 1,000 m.

TATRY

see Nízke Tatry, Vysoké Tatry

TELČ   E 3

a town situated in the undulating landscape of the southern part of the Bohemian-Moravian Highlands. Men-

Historical town
of Telč

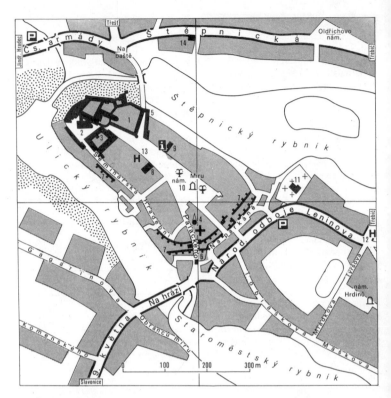

TELČ

1. Château (a). **2.** Parish Church of St. James (a). **3.** Former Jesuit college with church (a). **4.** Holy Ghost Tower (c—d). **5.** Small Gate (a). **6.** Big Gate (c—d). **7.** Town fortifications (a-b-c-d). **8.** Town Hall (a). **9.** Renaissance house (No. 61) (a). **10.** Marian column (a). **11.** Cemetery Church of St. Anne (b). **12.** Hotel U nádraží (d). **13.** Hotel Černý orel (a). **14.** Tourist hostel (a).

tioned already in the early 13th century, greatest period of flourish in the 16th century under the lords of Hradec. Unique **historical town reserve.** Gothic and Renaissance houses with arcades lining the elongated square, whose richly shaped gables are Baroque, however. A Marian column from 1716—1717 stands in the centre of the square. At the northern end of the square stands a Renaissance **château** of the 16th century, occupying the site of an original Gothic castle. Its interiors have rich Renaissance ceilings and period furnishings. In its neighbourhood stands the Gothic parish Church of St. **James** from whose steeple there is a view of the town core surrounded by Štěpnický and Ulický Ponds, which were parts of the fortifications. Opposite the château

Telč

stands a Baroque Jesuit church with a former college. — Two **gates** (the Big Gate and the Small Gate) and remains of the fortifications, in whose vicinity the oldest architectural monument at Telč, the Romanesque steeple of the Church of the Holy Ghost of the first quarter of the 13th century, have been preserved.
Environs: 8 km NW the highlands called Javořická vrchovina with the highest peak in the Bohemian-Moravian Highlands, **Javořice** (837 m). — 6 km W the community of **Mrákotín** with granite quarries. — 12 km S the town of **Dačice** with a Renaissance château adapted in Empire style.

TEPLICE   C 1

a district town (pop. 55,000) below the ridges of the Krušné Mountains. A **spa** (treatment of diseases of the motory organs and circulatory system, thermal spring Pravřídlo of a temperature of 42 °C), industrial centre (e. g. glass production). The local curative springs were already known to the Celts; new development from the 16th century, the spa of the Saxon electors and the court of Dresden; in the first half of the 19th century J. W. Goethe, L. van Beethoven, R. Wagner, F. Chopin, F. Liszt — to name a few examples — stayed here. Renaissance **château**, later adapted several times. Empire spa sanatoria, spa park laid out in English style. Numerous statues and fountains.
Environs: 4 km NW the small spa of **Dubí** (hydrotherapeutical institute). — 5 km N the old mining town of **Krupka,** founded in the 14th century near tin and copper mines. In the Bohosudov part a Baroque church of pilgrimage and a chair-lift to Komáří vížka (excellent view).

TEREZÍN   D 1

a town near Litoměřice on the River Ohře. Founded in 1780 on a chess-board ground-plan by the Emperor Joseph II as a Late Baroque **fortress** intended to defend Bohemia from the north-west. Named in honour of the Empress Maria Theresa. The Small Fortress was converted into a prison already in the 19th century and it was here that, in 1918, Gavrilo Princip, originator of the assassination of Ferdinand d'Este at Sarajevo, died. During the Second World War the town was changed into a **Jewish ghetto** (160,000 prisoners passed this way, 36,000 of whom died) and a concentration camp was established in the **Small Fortress.** The Small Fortress is now open to the public. In front of it is the National Cemetery with the graves of 29,172 victims of Nazism. Every year in May the scene of peace manifestations. Original fortifications preserved round the whole periphery of the town.
Environs: 6 km S **Doksany** with the complex of buildings of a former monastery founded in the years 1144—1145 whose present appearance dates from the turn of the 17th and 18th centuries. The Romanesque crypt of the original Romanesque church.

TOPOĽČIANKY   K 4

a **château** 26 km NE of Nitra. Originally a Gothic seat, it was rebuilt in the Renaissance and the Baroque and has Classical annexes. A former summer seat of the Hapsburgs and later of the Czechoslovak presidents. Now a recreation house of the Revolutionary Trade Unions Movement and a museum of period interior design. In the park there is a hunting château and 300 species of rare trees. An enclosure with a wealth of hunting game links up with the park. *Environs:* 10 km N a bison preserve in the Tríbeč Mountains.

TRENČÍN J 3

a district town (pop. 55,000) in the Váh valley. Garment and engineering industries. — The Roman military post Laugaricio (the northernmost in Central Europe) was built here. The **Roman inscription** hewn in a rock below the present castle to commemorate the victorious battle of the Romans against the German tribe of Kvads dates in the year 179. At the time of the Hungarian state the local castle was the seat of the district administrator already in the early 11th century. From 1412 Trenčín was a royal town. During the Slovak National Uprising it was the scene of the execution of antifascists and partisans (memorial).

The restored **castle** with a huge square tower is the landmark of the town and its environs and the seat of a museum. **Historical town reserve.** Preserved remains of the town fortifications, especially a gate of the 16th century. Renaissance and Baroque-Renaissance houses in the square.

Environs: 10 km NE **Trenčianské Teplice** spa. Mineral springs, treatment of diseases of the motory organs and nervous diseases. Hamman Baths from 1870—1888 with interiors in Arabian-Morish style. Modern spa sanatoria. Ideal position, possibility of walks in the park and to an observation hill (as high as 300 m above the spa). — 15 km SW, above the community of **Beckov** on a steep cliff, the ruins of a castle of the same name with a preserved Gothic core and Renaissance reconstructions. The castle was deserted from 1729, when it was the victim of a fire.

TRNAVA H 4

a district town (pop. 70,000) situated NE of Bratislava. Important industrial town with engineering and food industries. Theatre and pedagogical faculty.

It possessed the rights of a royal town already in 1238 — the first in Slovakia. In the years 1541—1820 the seat of the archbishop and from 1635—1777 a university town. A. Bernolák influenced the development of the literary Slovak language. Industrial development and a strong workers' movement from the mid-19th century. **Historical town reserve.**

Complex of Baroque **university** buildings of the 17th and 18th centuries. Parish church of 1380 on the site of a Romanesque church, remains of Gothic wall paintings. Preserved continuous line of town fortifications with bastions. West Slovak Museum.

Environs: 17 km W **Červený Kameň** Castle. — 18 km NW **Smolenice**, a picturesque, pseudo-historical castle building of the late 19th century, visible from a great distance. Now the House of Scientific Workers of the Slovak Academy of Sciences. — 12 km N Dolná Krupá, a Classical château of the years 1793—1795 in whose park there is a Rococo pavilion named after Beethoven (the composer visited its then owner).

TROSKY E 1

the remains of a Gothic **castle** on a basalt **rock** with two peaks (488 m). Conspicuous landscape landmark visible from all over the Bohemian Paradise. The castle was most likely built in the mid-14th century. Situated on the two volcanic peaks are towers called Panna and Baba with residential buildings below them. Views of the surrounding countryside.

TŘEBÍČ   F 3

a district town (pop. 37,000) in the SE part of the Bohemian-Moravian Highlands. Industrial centre — footwear production, engineering and other industries.
The town was founded in the vicinity of a Benedictine monastery (originated in 1101) on a trade route running through the valley of the Jihlava. In the 15th century it supported the Hussite movement in Moravia. Development of industry and the workers' movement after 1848.
— **Basilica of St. Procopius,** a unique monument preserved from an original Late Romanesque monastery complex. Rich Romanesque portal, Romanesque and Gothic windows, crypt with the tombs of the founders of the monastery. The West Moravian museum (e.g., interesting Christmas cribs — so-called Bethlehems — and collections of pipes) is installed in the former monastery, converted into a château from the 16th century. Large square, valuable burghers' houses. By the parish Church of St. Martin stands a square tower with a gallery and the biggest clock in Czechoslovakia (the diameter of its dial is 7.1 m).
Environs: 20 km SE of Třebíč the **Dukovany** nuclear power plant.

TŘEBOŇ   D 3

a town in the South Bohemian basin. Czechoslovakia's biggest **ponds** are situated in its environs (fish-breeding — the renowned **Třeboň carp,** recreation).

Balneological peat treatment of diseases of the motory organs, modern Aurora Sanatorium. Brewery producing Regent beer, founded in 1379.
In the 15th and 16th centuries, during the rule of the wealthiest family of the Czech nobility, the Rožmberks, the town underwent rapid development mainly in connection with the founding of ponds. The first pond, **Svět** (210 hectares), originated immediately beyond the fortifications. It is now used for recreation, bathing and motor boat trips. 3 km N the biggest Czech pond, **Rožmberk** (489 hectares, 2.4 km long bank), the work of the renowned pond-builder Jakub Krčín of Jelčany from 1584—1589. From 1602 Třeboň was the permanent seat of the last Rožmberk, Petr Vok (he died here in 1611).
Historical town reserve. Big Renaissance Rožmberk **château** of the mid-16th century, accessible interiors of the time of the last Rožmberks and an exposition of pond-building in the Třeboň region. Preserved remains of the town fortifications — 3 gates, 7 bastions, walls. Monastery with a cloister and double-naved Gothic church (valuable

Square
at Třeboň

paintings and murals of the late 14th century). In the square the **Town Hall** of 1566, the Renaissance house called At the Little White Horse, a fountain of 1569 and a Baroque Marian column. In the park of nearby Svět Pond the Neo-Gothic tomb of the Schwarzenbergs. *Environs:* the Třeboň protected landscape region; 15 km S the Červené blato preserve, big peat-bogs with small spruce growths, nature study path. — 5 km E Stará řeka, a meandering river of the original bed of the Lužnice. — 6 km N the ponds Velký Tisý and Malý Tisý, important bird sanctuary.

an industrial town (pop. 14,000) on the northern edge of the Bohemian Paradise. Founded in the 13th century. Known from the 17th century for the cutting of precious stones, now Bohemian garnet jewellery production. Gothic parish church, Barocized. Renaissance Town Hall adapted in 1894. Museum of the Bohemian Paradise with remarkable expositions devoted to mineralogy, geology, the technology of stone-cutting and ethnography.
Environs: 2 km N Renaissance **Hrubý Rohozec** Château with a collec-

Turnov

Fishing-out
of Svět Pond
in South Bohemia

tion of historical furniture. One km further on, likewise in the Jizera valley, **Dolánky** with Dlask's frame farmstead housing an exposition of the Turnov Museum. — SE the ruins of **Valdštejn** Castle and the region of sandstone rocks at Hrubá Skála. — 7 km NW romantic **Sychrov** Château of the mid-19th century — interiors with valuable furniture, coffered ceilings and a collection of French portraits. The composer A. Dvořák (memorial) often stayed at the château.

UHERSKÉ HRADIŠTĚ   H 3

a district town (pop. 38,000) in South East Moravia. Engineering and food industries and aircraft production in the locality called Kunovice.
A royal town founded in 1257 by Přemysl Otakar II. — Numerous archeological finds of the time of the **Great Moravian Empire** (churches and burial-ground at Staré Město, Sady, Špitálky) have been unearthed in the town and its environs. On the periphery of the town there are the remains of Gothic fortifications. Baroque armoury of the early 18th century (now a gallery). Late Gothic Town Hall, adapted in the 18th and 19th centuries. Late Gothic monastery church and Early Baroque Jesuit church. Numerous burghers' houses of the 17th—18th century, Baroque fountains, etc. — In the part of the town called Mařatice a continuous street front of wine cellars. — Moravian-Slovak Museum — exposition of folk art. *Environs:* 7 km NW **Velehrad,** an Ancient Slavonic site with a Cistercian monastery founded in 1202 and with a church; both buildings were of Romanesque origin, but were Barocized after a fire. Valuable frescoes and paintings decorate their interiors. — 10 km NW **Buchlovice** with a Baroque château of the early 18th century and an original Baroque park. — 13 km NW Buchlov Castle.

Buchlovice Château
near Uherské
Hradiště

UHERSKÝ BROD   H 3

a town (pop. 18,000) in Moravian-Slovakia. Founded as a royal town already
in 1272. Remains of fortifications of the
13th—16th century and originally Renaissance château adapted in the 17th
century. Several church buildings. In
the stable complex called Baraník of the
late 17th century there is now the
J. Amos Komenský (Comenius) Museum.
Environs: **folk buildings** in the nearby
communities of Vlčnov, Veletiny and
Havřice. — 10 km SW the community of
Hluk with a Gothico-Renaissance water
stronghold and folk buildings. In May
every year the folklore Ride of Kings
takes place here (similarly as at Vlčnov).
— 18 km S **Velká Javořina** (970 m), the
biggest mountain of the White Carpathians with a tourist chalet on its summit.

ÚSTÍ NAD LABEM   C 1

the regional town of the North Bohemian region (pop. 91,000) and an important industrial centre on the Elbe. One of
the biggest centres of Czechoslovakia's
chemical industry (chemicals, medical
remedies, oils, soaps, etc.). Important
transport junction, transloading of
goods of rail and river transport, 5 har-
bours on the Elbe. Theatre and pedagogical faculty.
The town was mentioned already in
1249. In 1426 one of the biggest battles
of the Hussite revolutionary movement
took place 5 km W of Ústí nad Labem
(Běhání). Rapid development of the
town from the second quarter of the
19th century, due in particular to its advantageous transport position. In April
1945 the centre of the town was destroyed during air raids. The centre with

administrative buildings is now undergoing **modern reconstruction**. Historical core in the environs of the square
náměstí Míru and the station. Preserved
Gothic decanal **church** whose steeple
leans 198 cm from its vertical axis. Baroque Church of St. Adalbert, now
a concert and exhibition hall. On the
right bank of the Elbe, on a phonolite
rock, **Střekov Castle** (round Gothic
tower, palace, fortifications, wine tavern
in the outer bailey). Popular with the romantic composer R. Wagner whom the
castle is said to have inspired to write
his opera Tannhäuser.

ÚŠTĚK   D 1

a town below the Bohemian Central
Highlands. Cultivation of hops and fruit
in its environs. — **Historical town reserve**. Ground-plan determined by
a narrow, rocky promontory. Part of fortifications preserved, including the bastion called Pikhartská. Gothic and Renaissance **houses** in the elongated
square. Late Baroque church
(1764—1772) with valuable interior furnishings (K. Škréta). So-called "Birds'
Cottages" built on rocky projections by
Italian workers who helped to construct
a railway in the mid-19th century. —
Chmelař Pond (70 hectares), used for
recreation and bathing.
Environs: the Kokořínsko and Bohemian
Central Highlands protected landscape
regions. — 3 km E **Hrádek**, the ruins of
a castle with a huge tower and an enclosure wall up to 12 m in height.

VALAŠSKÉ MEZIŘÍČÍ   J 3

an industrial town (pop. 27,500) on the
confluence of the Rožnovská Bečva and

the Vsetínská Bečva. Chemical, electrical engineering (Tesla) and glass (lighting glass) industries, gobelin and carpet production. — Founded at the turn of the 13th and 14th centuries, from the 16th century development of cloth production. After the mid-19th century an important cultural centre of Wallachia — above all specialized schools, from 1900, for example, a gobelin school. Valuable Renaissance and Baroque **houses** in the square and the adjoining streets. House No. 10 in the square once housed a pharmacy called At the Red Eagle with a Rococo façade. Renaissance building of the Town Hall of the early 17th century. Renaissance château, rebuilt in the 17th and 18th centuries. Gothic parish church of 1419, later adapted. Gothic, partly wooden cemetery church of the late 16th century. — In the quarter called Krásno, situated on the right bank of the Bečva (a separate town until 1923), there is a Renaissance Town Hall of 1580 and an Empire château with an English park and finally a Gothic cemetery church with Late Renaissance adaptations (1587). In the avenue between the church and the Town Hall there is a row of Baroque statues of the mid-18th century.
Environs: 8 km SE the **Bystřička** valley reservoir built in 1907—1912, serving recreation purposes (hotels, chalet communities, car camp). — 1 km N of it **Velká Lhota** with a wooden church of 1783; in the part called Malá Lhota there is a wooden belfry of the 17th century, restored.

VALAŠSKO J 3
(Wallachian Region)

a characteristic ethnographical region in East Moravia formed by the southern part of the Moravian-Silesian Beskids,

the Vsetínské and the Hostýnské Hills, the Javorníks, the Vizovická Highlands and a part of the White Carpathians. Among the conspicuous peaks are Radhošť (1,129 m), Velký Javorník (1,070 m) and Hostýn (730 m).
The region has large fir **forests.** Its main river is the Bečva (the Rožnovská Bečva and the Vsetínská Bečva). The Wallachian region offers very good possibilities for walking tours, camping and water recreation in both flowing water and in the richly frequented dam reservoirs at Bystřička and Luhačovice.
Mineral **springs** gave origin to the most popular Moravian spas — Luhačovice and Teplice nad Bečvou.
The region was settled in the course of the 16th century by herdsmen from the East Carpathians — from present-day Rumania. The villages were under the administration of a bailiff, who was endowed with numerous privileges.
Several localities with big complexes of **folk** frame buildings have been preserved, e.g. at Valašská Bystřice and Velké Karlovice (a Wallachian bailiff's house and a frame church) and in their wider environs (e.g. at Raťkov). At Rožnov pod Radhoštěm there is a notable skansen. Typical folk costumes can now be seen only in museums. Folk music and dances come to life at folklore festivals. Several elements of the Wallachian dialect have been preserved to the present.
Cultural and historical monuments can be seen in the towns of Valašské Meziříčí, Vsetín and Vizovice. Modern architecture is concentrated at Gottwaldov.
During the last war the region was the scene of a number of heavy battles between the strongest **partisan** unit on the territory of Bohemia and Moravia, the 1st Partisan Brigade of Jan Žižka of Trocnov, and the occupying forces, e.g., on Lemešná Saddle. On the order of the

Nazi command the community of Ploština was burned and its inhabitants burned or murdered.
Starting points: Rožnov pod Radhoštěm, Valašské Meziříčí, Gottwaldov, Velké Karlovice and Bystřice pod Hostýnem.

VEĽKÁ FATRA   K—L 3
(The Big Fatra)

a range of mountains in the central part of Slovakia between the towns of Ružomberok, Banská Bystrica and Martin. Its ridges stretch out in north-western direction and are bare in their highest parts. They culminate with the peak called **Ostredok** (1,592 m). Forests cover 90% of the mountains, their growths being mainly beeches and spruces. The biggest concentration of the original occurrence of yew trees in Europe can be seen here. There are about 50 pieces of bear in the mountains. The Big Fatra form a **protected landscape region.**
Access from the north is facilitated by a cabin funicular from Ružomberok to the winter sports centre, to the summit of **Málinô** (1,209 m). From Smrekovica (a recreation region) the ridges of the northern part of the range are mostly forested. The most conspicuous peaks of the bare central part of the range include Rakytov (1,567 m), Ploská (1,532 m) and **Borišov** (1,510 m), below whose summit there is a mountain chalet. The most frequented, southern part of the range is accessible by means of a chair-lift from Turecká in the vicinity of Banská Bystrica. Comfortable paths run through the valley Bystrická dolina from **Harmanec** (karst cave) to the hotel below **Kráľova studňa** (1,284 m). The whole ridge can be crossed along marked paths in 2—3 days.

The mountain **valleys** running below the ridges from the west are long and abound in striking **karst** phenomena (the most beautiful is the valley called Gaderská dolina with rare flora). Folk architecture has been preserved especially at **Vlkolinec** (south of Ružomberok , 40 wooden buildings) and at Liptovská Revúca. There are also small spas on the periphery of the range: **Ľubochňa** in the Váh valley and **Turčianske Teplice** to the south-west of the range. In 1921 the foundations were laid for the constitution of the Communist Party of Slovakia at Ľubochňa. The valley Ľubochnianska dolina is the longest in the Big Fatra (25 km).

VELKÉ KARLOVICE   J 3

a large community (510 m) in the valley of the Vsetínská Bečva. — Founded as late as the 18th century near the border of the Czech kingdom and Hungary (post of the border guards). During the Second World War there was a strong partisan movement here. — Frame church; a bailiff's house of 1793 in the Bzová valley, a number of frame cottages in the adjoining valleys and on the slopes of the mountain ridges. Museum.
Environs: Above the community, on the ridge of the range of the Vsetínské Hills, the Soláň peak (861 m). Scattered on its slopes are stylized cottages inhabited by Wallachian writers, painters and wood-carvers. Skiing centre.

VIMPERK   C 3

a town in the foothills of the Šumava Mountains. It originated on the Golden Path which passed through the Šumava

Veľká Fatra

forests in the Middle Ages. In 1484 a **book-printing** works was founded here where, for example, calendars as well as miniature Korans, etc. were printed. — Above the town a **château** on the site of a castle of the 13th century, last reconstruction carried out in the 19th century. In its western wing a museum with expositions documenting the Šumava protected landscape region, printing, glass-making and match production. A part of the town fortifications (walls, towers, the gate Černá brána) have been preserved. In the sloping square a valuable Early Gothic church with a belfry in its close proximity. *Environs:* 5 km NE **Mařský vrch** (907 m) with an observation tower, a chapel and a TV transmitter. A sea of boulders covers its slopes. Below it the village of Maří with a small Gothic church. — 4 km N the village of **Sudslavice** with a 600 years old lime tree with a circumference of nearly 12 m, one of the oldest in the Czechoslovak Socialist Republic.

VRANOV   F 3

a community and **château** on a steep rock overlooking the River Dyje by the dam of the same name. Mention was made of a castle here already in 1100. After 1655 it was converted into an ostentatious Baroque château by the architect Fischer of Erlach. Its most valuable interior is the Hall of Ancestors. Baroque paintings and sculptural decoration in the cupola. A château chapel with 2 steeples stands in the outer bailey.

2 km from the château a **dam** from 1930—1933, height 55 m, length at the crest 285 m; the dam lake is 30 km long. There are several **recreation facilities** on its banks; regular boat transport, bathing, water sports, fishing. Above the lake the ruins of a Gothic castle, **Cornštejn**, deserted from the 17th century; on a promontory above the River Želetavka stands **Bítov** Castle whose present Romantic Gothic appearance dates in the mid-19th century. The castle chapel has a Romanesque tower.

VRÁTNA   K 3

a tourist resort in the Little Fatra 25 km E of Žilina. Access only by following the road from the characteristic community of Terchová 2 km through the rocky Tiesňavy Pass. Magnificent scenery of the ridges of the Little Fatra (rocky Veľký Rozsutec 1,610 m, the highest peak Veľký Fatranský Kriváň 1,709 m). From Vrátna Chalet (720 m) a chair-lift runs to the saddle Smilovské sedlo (1,520 m), starting point for tours along the main ridge. Another chair-lift runs to Grúň (1,000 m, chalet). Boboty and Sokolie Hotels. Below rugged Veľký Rozsutec the small village of **Štefanová** with characteristic wooden folk architecture; accommodation in private homes. Starting point for tours to the rocky passes (Dolné Diery and Horné Diery), accessible by means of ladders and footpaths. At Vrátna there are excellent skiing grounds: ski-tows, downhill runs. The whole region forms a part of the Little Fatra National Park.

VRCHLABÍ   F 1

a town (pop. 13,500) in the Elbe valley, at the foot of the Krkonoše Mountains. Industry, especially textile and Škoda cars.

The original village was founded in the 13th century and in 1533 it was raised to a royal mining town. Iron, silver and

gold ores were mined north of the town, but mining activity ceased in the 18th century. — A number of characteristic **frame town houses** can be seen particularly along the main street. The former Town Hall is a Renaissance building of 1591. — Renaissance **château** with an oblong ground-plan, four octagonal towers in the corners. Seat of the Administration of the Krkonoše National Park. The château is surrounded by an English park with an arboretum, a small botanical garden with mountain flora and a mini zoo with voliéres and runs for certain species of Krkonoše fauna. A modernly conceived exposition of the **Krkonoše Museum**, oriented mainly to problems of the protection of the natural and living environment of the Krkonoše Mountains, is installed in the former monastery of the Augustinian Order on the outskirts of the park.
Environs: 4 km NW the forested peak **Přední Žalý** (1,019 m) with an observation tower; panoramatic view of the whole of the Krkonoše Mountains and the foothills. Ski-tow from Herlíkovice. — 6 km NW the **Benecko** recreation resort (682 m), hotels, frame cottages,

ski-tows. — 5 km N **Strážné** (798 m), family and works recreation, plastic skiing slope (length 500 m).

VSETÍN   J 3

a district town (pop. 31,000) in Wallachia. Developed engineering and electrical engineering industries. — First mentioned in 1309. In the 17th century the centre of the resistance movement of Wallachia against re-Catholization and the increase of statutory labour. Since the events of the last war the town has borne the title of Partisan Town. — In the square Horní náměstí a Renaissance **château** with Baroque and Empire adaptations (now a museum), adjoined by a park. Also standing in the square are the Old Town Hall of 1721 and Maštaliska, a Baroque building of 1710 with battlements (originally stables of the nobility), adapted in Neo-Gothic style in 1894. A fountain with Baroque statues of 1770. Two Evangelic churches: the former Augsburg, so-called Lower Church

---

Vsetín

Boboty Hotel
and Veľký Rozsutec
at Vrátna

(1782—1783) and the Helvetian, so—called Upper Church of 1827, which recall the former religious struggles in the region.

Environs: 8 km N the peak **Vsacký Cáb** (841 m) with a tourist chalet. On the upper stream of the Vsetínská Bečva a picturesque valley with folk buildings.

VYSOKÉ TATRY   M 3
(The High Tatras)

the biggest range of **mountains** in Czechoslovakia in the northern part of the Slovak Socialist Republic, along the border with Poland. Their 26 km long main ridge has several conspicuous forks running to the south and the north. The highest Czechoslovak mountain, **Gerlachovský štít** (2,655 m), rises from one of them. Due to their exceptional natural values, the High Tatras have been a **national park** since 1949. The Belianské and Západné Tatras form a part of it.

The western part of the range is dominated by **Kriváň** (2,494 m), the symbolic peak of the freedom of the Slovaks and a frequent theme of Slovak poetry. The most striking peak in the eastern part is the triangular pyramid of **Lomnický štít** (2,632 m). **Rysy** (2,499 m), the highest mountain in Poland, rises on the main ridge, on the state border. Since 1957 the International Youth Ascent of Rysy has been organized every year to commemorate V. I. Lenin's ascents of the peak in 1913 and 1914. Slavkovský štít (2,452 m), Kriváň and Rysy are accessible by means of a tourist path.

The High Tatras are mostly composed of granite. Thirty-five valleys with a conspicuous **glacial relief** are a reminder of glacial activity. About 100 mountain **lakes** are concealed in them. The biggest of them is Veľké Hincovo (20 hectares). It is also the deepest (53 m) and lies at a height of 1,946 m above sea level. Considerably better-known is the slightly smaller lake Štrbské pleso (19.8 hectares, depth 20 m, 1,346 m). There are also **caves** (Belianská), mountain waterfalls (Skok) and other natural features in the mountains.

The limestone **Belianske Tatras** culminating with Havran (2,152 m) link up

Štrbské Pleso
and peaks
of the High Tatras

closely in the east with the ridge of the High Tatras. The ridge parts are closed to visitors (strictly guarded nature preserve). The second highest mountain range in Czechoslovakia is formed by the **West Tatras** (Západné Tatry). Their main ridge is 37 km long and their most attractive part is the Roháče group with a striking high-mountain relief and lakes (see also Orava).

Continuous forest growths, mainly spruce, grow in the Tatras up to a height of 1,550 m above sea level, where the forest runs into knee pines. On elevations above 1,800 m Alpine meadows with highly varied high-mountain flora begin. The last belt of vegetation (above 2,300 m) is characterized by unique, scattered growths of grasses and plants between the rock ribs, in cuttings, hollows, etc. Chamoix, marmots, bears, lynxes, wild cats , wolves, grouse, black grouse and rock eagles rank among the rare representatives of the local animal kingdom.

Tourism in the High Tatras began already in the late 18th century. In 1841 the first national pilgrimage to Kriváň took place, incited by national and political aims. During the struggle against fascism partisans fought the enemy also in the Tatras.

The exceptional development of tourism which has marked the last 20 years in particular has made it necessary to enforce certain restrictions concerning sojourns of tourists in the interest of preserving the great natural values of the High Tatras. These include the prohibition of movement beyond the marked paths, the temporary closing of a number of marked tourist paths and an order banning the use of the main arterial road (Cesta slobody) by motor vehicles. A network of car parks has been established in the foothills between the mountains resorts of the Tatras, transport here being secured by an electric railway and buses. Access to the mountains is also facilitated by **funiculars** (a suspension cabin funicular to Lomnický štít, a chair-lift to Predné Solisko and Lomnický hrebeň, a ground funicular to Hrebienok and Štrbské Pleso). The **red-marked route** of the so-called **Magistrála** (arterial road), 46 km in length, runs along the whole southern side of the High Tatras. Difficult mountain-climbing grounds are accessible only to organized mountain-climbers. The favourable climatic conditions and high-mountain position of the Tatra region afforded good conditions for the origin of **balneology** — diseases of the respiratory tracts, allergies, TB, metabolic diseases and diseases of glands with inner secretion (e.g., Štrbské Pleso, Nový Smokovec, Vyšné Hágy, Tatranská Polianka).

Valuable historical monuments can be seen in localities in the foothills (Kežmarok, Spišská Sobota, Poprad) and folk architecture has been preserved in a number of communities below the Tatras (Východná, Važec, Ždiar). The main **starting point** for the High Tatras is the district industrial town of **Poprad,** an important railway and road junction with an airport. From here the local electric railway runs to Starý Smokovec and Štrbské Pleso and a railway to Tatranská Lomnica. The road border crossing Javorina — Lysa Poľana to Poland is situated on the northern outskirts of the High Tatras.

The High Tatras, small in area and easily accessible, rank among the most frequented regions in the Czechoslovak Socialist Republic. It is therefore recommended to secure accommodation at one of the mountain resorts from where one-day excursions can be made to the whole range. It is advisable to avoid a sojourn in the main holiday months (July, August). September and the first half of October are ideal for

Vysoké
Tatry

mountain tourism. The winter **skiing season** lasts from December to March. There are also several mountain **chalets,** open in the summer months only, Téryho Chalet (2,015 m) in the valley Malá Studená dolina, the Sliezsky dom Hotel (1,670 m) below the peak Gerlachovský štít and Zbojnická Chalet (1,960 m) in the valley Veľká Studená dolina.

Recommended tours on foot:
1. From Štrbské Pleso to Popradské Pleso, steep ascent to Ostrva (1,926 m) and then to the Sliezsky dom mountain hotel (1,670 m) below Gerlachovský štít and to Hrebienok (6 1/2 hours), ground funicular to Starý Smokovec. Red-marked Magistrála (arterial road). — **2.** From Štrbské Pleso to Kriváň (2,499 m), ascent along red- and blue-marked paths (4 1/2 hours). — **3.** From Starý Smokovec by funicular to Hrebienok and then along the red- and green-marked paths through Malá Studená dolina to Téryho Chalet (3 hours), or along the red- and blue-marked paths through the valley Veľká Studená dolina to Zbojnická chalet (3 hours). — **4.** From Tatranská Lomnica by funicular to Skalnaté pleso and to Svišťovka (1 1/2 hours).
Starting points: Štrbské Pleso, Starý Smokovec, Tatranská Lomnica, Poprad.

VYŠKOV   H 3

a district town (pop. 20,000) NE of Brno, industrial centre. The town flourished especially in the Renaissance period. Strong workers' movement. In the square stands the Renaissance Town Hall from 1569—1613. A part of the town is **Dědice,** the place of birth of the first working-class president of the Czechoslovak Republic, Klement Gottwald (1896—1953). In the house of his birth there is a memorial hall and in the square the Gottwald memorial.

VYŠŠÍ BROD   D 4

a **monastery** in the community of the same name in the southernmost corner of Bohemia. Founded in 1259. Its oldest part is its eastern wing with the chapter hall of 1285. The cloister dates in the 14th and 15th centuries, the refectory in the late 14th century and the monastery church in the early 14th century. Tombstone of the last member of the Rožmberk family, Petr Vok (1539—1611). The library contains numerous manuscripts and incunables. The gallery with works of Dutch masters from the 17th-18th century, etc. A postal museum is installed in the building. The whole area of the monastery is surrounded by fortification walls.

WEST BOHEMIAN SPAS   A—B 2
(Západočeské lázně)

one of the most important tourist regions in the westernmost part of Czechoslovakia near the border with the German Democratic Republic and the Federal Republic of Germany. Three well-known spa towns originated in the vicinity of the local **mineral springs** — Karlovy Vary, Mariánské Lázně and Františkovy Lázně. These towns have a long-standing tradition in balneology. The therapeutical effect of the so-called Cheb water (gushing forth in the locality of present-day Františkovy Lázně) was known already from the 12th century. The beginning of the use of the Karlovy Vary mountain springs dates in the period of rule of Charles IV in the 14th century. The West Bohemian spa towns underwent rapid architectonic development in the 18th and especially in the 19th century, when a number of famous personalities of European politics,

science and culture stayed at them in order to take cures. In all there are now some 230 springs with many-sided therapeutical effects in the region. Their waters gush forth from underground lakes situated on the territory of the Slavkovský Forest. The hot springs (those at Karlovy Vary of a temperature of 41−72 °C) spurt from a depth of 2,000 or more metres, while the cold ones, those at Mariánské Lázně, gush from a depth of hardly 100 metres. Big forest complexes with a number of nature preserves (peat-bogs) exist in the adjoining **protected landscape region of the Slavkovský Forest** (the highest peak is Lesný, 983 m). Stretching along the border with the German Democratic Republic is the ridge of the **Krušné Mountains** with the highest peak Klínovec (1,244 m). A mountain chalet and an observation tower are situated on one of its peaks and there is a number of ski-tows and a chair-lift on the slopes. Spreading out at the foot of the ridge is the former mining town of **Jáchymov.** The local deposits are now exhausted. − Nowadays a spa exists here where the local radioactive springs are exploited for therapeutical purposes. The region can also boast of numerous historical monuments − the towns of **Cheb** and **Loket** are historical town reserves and the popular destinations of tourism include **Kynžvart** Château and the monastery at **Teplá.** Samples of folk architecture have also been preserved in some places, represented by so-called frame houses. Important recreation regions have originated in the immediate vicinity of the Skalka and Jesenice **valley reservoirs.**
Recommended car route: Karlovy Vary − Bečov nad Teplou − Teplá − Mariánské Lázně − Lázně Kynžvart − the Jesenice valley reservoir − Cheb − Františkovy Lázně. Total length 100 km.

ZEMPLÍNSKA ŠÍRAVA   O−P 3

a big reservoir (area 13,350 hectares, length 11 km, width 3 km) below the Vihorlat Mountains in East Slovakia. **Recreation resorts** and hotels, restaurants and car camps on the northern bank. Good possibilities for bathing, motor boat trips.
Environs: 2 km N **Vinné,** the ruins of a Gothic castle, Vinianské Lake (8 hectares), bathing. − 18 km NE the lake **Morské oko** (14 hectares) in the Vihorlat Mountains, below the peak Sninský kameň (1,005 m). It is surrounded by a high beech forest. − 3 km SW of the banks of the reservoir lies the district town of **Michalovce** (pop. 35,000) with developed industry.

ZNOJMO   F 3

a district town (pop. 38,000) on the River Dyje near the Austrian border. A centre of South West Moravia in a fertile agricultural region, important **food industry,** conserving factories (well-known Znojmo cucumbers − brought from Hungary in 1571), wine production.
In the 11th and 12th centuries the seat of the apanage princes of the Přemyslid dynasty, royal town founded about 1226. In 1437 the King and Emperor Sigismund died here and in 1628 the renewed provincial administration, which strengthened the position of the Hapsburg family on the Czech throne, was proclaimed here at the provincial diet. **Historical town reserve,** preserved fortifications of the 14th−16th century. Original Gothic castle converted into a château in the 17th and 18th centuries, now the South Moravian Museum. In the present outer bailey stands a **Romanesque rotunda** of the end of

Zemplínská
Šírava

the 11th century with paintings of the Přemyslid princes of 1134. The **Town Hall** was partly destroyed during the Second World War, Renaissance portal, arcaded courtyard and Late Gothic, 69 m high tower. A number of burghers' houses of the 15th—17th century whose cellerage is connected by passages (partly accessible — entrance opposite the tower of the Town Hall). Gothic parish **Church of St. Nicholas** and in its neighbourhood St. Wenceslas's Chapel. The Dominican church is adjoined by a former monastery with a cloister and chapter hall of the 15th century. — In the locality **Louka**, a former monastery founded in 1190 and abolished in the period of rule of Joseph II in 1784. The monastery church has a preserved Romanesque crypt of the first half of the 13th century, reconstructed in the Gothic and the Baroque.

ZVÍKOV D 3

a Gothic **castle** on the confluence of the Vltava and the Otava. Founded in the first half of the 13th century. The kings Václav I and Přemysl Otakar II of the Přemyslid dynasty often stayed here. The building is one of the most valuable monuments of Czech castle architecture. Its dominant feature is the round defence tower standing on the narrow-

est part of the promontory and with a sharp corner facing the direction of possible access. The huge royal palace has arcaded galleries on its ground- and first floor and the 20 m high Hlízová Tower, faced with embossed granite cubes, forms a part of it. Inside the palace there is an exposition devoted to the history of the castle and a collection of documents pertaining to the history of the Czech state. The castle chapel is a summit structure of the Early Gothic with wall paintings of the late 15th and the 16th century. An iron gate affords access to the landing-stage for boats (regular trips to Orlík Château).

ZVOLEN L 4

a district town (pop. 40,000) in the Hron valley. Developed wood-working industry. University of Forestry and Wood-working. — The first mention of Zvolen dates in 1135. In the 12th century a castle was built here (SW of the present centre) and in the years 1370—1382 a hunting château of the type of Italian town castles originated here as the summer seat of King Louis the Great. A strong revolutionary workers' movement existed in the town in the first half of the 20th century. — The **château** has its original Gothic ground-plan, enlarged with fortifications against the

St. Nicholas's Church and St. Wenceslas's Chapel at Znojmo

Gothic vault at Zvíkov Castle

Turks in the 16th—18th century. Inside a gallery of medieval and modern art, exposition of the Slovak Gothic. Historically valuable town houses. Memorial to and cemetery of 17,000 fallen members of the Red Army and 11,000 fallen soldiers of the Rumanian army.
Environs: 5 km NW **Kováčová** spa (nervous diseases and diseases of the motory organs), springs of a temperature of 48 °C, thermal pools. — 5 km N **Sliač** spa, mineral springs, mentioned in 1244. The first sanatorium dates in 1812. Treatment of diseases of the motory organs.

ŽATEC   C 2

a town (pop. 23,000) on the River Ohře. The centre of a well-known **hops-growing region. Historical town reserve,** one of the oldest Czech towns. Preserved parts of the Gothic fortifications, including the gate Kněžská brána, a Gothic church on the site of a former castle, in the square a number of Gothic, Renaissance and Baroque houses, some with arcades. Hop-pickers' harvest-home every year in September. — *Environs:* 15 km SW the Baroque **Krásný Dvůr** Château from 1720—1724, where J. W. Goethe also stayed. Large château park with a number of Empire and Romantic structures.

ŽĎÁR NAD SÁZAVOU   F 3

a district town (pop. 26,000) in the central part of the Bohemian-Moravian Highlands. New industrial centre (engineering works and foundries). — In 1252 the Cistercians founded a **monastery** here and a small town originated in its vicinity. The monastery experienced its greastest period of flourish in the early 18th century. The prelature (now a **Book Museum**) dates in that period. An exposition devoted to the architect G. Santini is installed in the renovated stables. — Nearby the monastery cemetery with Baroque sculptures. Similarly as the church with a ground-plan in the shape of a five-pointed star on the hill **Zelená hora** (the most outstanding building of the Baroque Gothic in Czechoslovakia), it was built after a plan by G. Santini.
Environs: 8 km N the pond **Velké Dářko** (206 hectares) at a height of 617 metres above sea level, bathing, yachting, water sports.

Zvolen
Château

Raw material for beer-brewing
— the hop — is cultivated
in the environs of Žatec

ŽDIAR   M 3

a characteristic community at the NE foot of the High Tatras. Its background is formed by the rocky, limestone peaks of the Belianské Tatras. Most beautiful views from the easily accessible ridge of the Spišská Magura Mountains. Remarkable structures of **folk architecture** (reserve of monuments), wooden houses with coloured decoration, one with an ethnographical museum in its interior. Folk art production (textiles, wooden products). Wearing of folk costumes on public holidays. Good skiing grounds in winter, numerous ski-tows, tracks for beginners and less efficient skiers.

Germany. Founded in the 14th century near a trade path. Mining of iron ore from the 16th century, glass production in the 19th century. **Church** from 1727–1732 with a big, onion-shaped cupola. The building has a ground-plan with 12 angles. Museum with samples of Šumava glass.

Environs: 3 km N the saddle **Špičácké sedlo** (1,000 m), starting point for the glacial lake **Černé jezero** (another 4 km, area 18 hectares, the biggest in Bohemia, depth 39 m), to the lake **Čertovo jezero** (2 km, area 10 hectares) and to the peak **Pancíř** (1,214 m, observation tower, chair-lift). Both lakes are accessible along marked paths only and in daylight. Hotels, skiing grounds, ski-tows, downhill run tracks (especially from Špičák).

ŽELEZNÁ RUDA   B 3

one of the biggest **recreation resorts** in the Šumava Mountains (790 m) on the border with the Federal Republic of

ŽELEZNÝ BROD   E 1

a submontane town on the River Jizera. Long-standing tradition in **glass** production (off-hand shaped, drawn and

Ždiar village
below the Belianské Tatras

blown glass), school of glass-making and glass museum. Numerous frame buildings in the centre and on the outskirts of the town (in the square the building called Klemencovsko, now incorporated in the modern building of the savings bank).

Environs: 6 km W the **Malá Skála** summer resort. Ruins of a Gothic castle called Skála, converted into a rock Pantheon to commemorate well-known personalities, below it a view of the Jizera valley. — 1.5 km E of Malá Skála sharply forked rocks called Suché skály. — 2.5 km NW the ruins of **Frýdštejn** Castle of the 14th century with a conspicuous round tower. On nearby Kopanina (1.5 km N) an observation tower, view of the Bohemian Paradise, the Jizera Mountains and Ještěd.

ŽILINA   K 3

---

a district town (pop. 92,000) in the Váh valley — NW Slovakia. Industrial centre (engineering industry, chemistry, woodworking, food industry), one of the most important **railway junctions** in the Czechoslovak Socialist Republic. Seat of the University of Transport and Communications. New housing construction.

Oldest written reports date in 1208, in 1312 a town and in the 15th century strong influence of the Hussite revolutionary movement from Bohemia. In the early 19th century Žilina was an unimportant serf town. After the opening of the Košice-Bohumín (1871) and Váh valley railways (1883) industry and the workers' movement underwent rapid development. After the outbreak of the Slovak National Uprising the town was occupied by fascist units-terror and executions. Žilina was liberated on 30 April, 1945, after tough battles lasting three weeks, by the Red Army.

The town has not many art or historical monuments. Its quadratic square is surrounded by houses of the 16th-18th century with arcades. Parish church originally Gothic, fortified in 1540, often reconstructed. A belfry stands nearby. Historical town reserve. On the confluence of the Rivers Váh and Kysuca stands **Budatín** Château whose oldest part is the residential tower of the 13th century, Renaissance palace of 1551, now the seat of the Váh Valley Museum (e.g., an exposition devoted to the tinker's craft in Slovakia). On Borik, a hill near the town, a cemetery of the Red Army (1,782 burials).

Environs: Starting point for the mountains, especially to the **Little Fatra** (Vrátna).

Explanation to plans of towns:

B	Bank (currency exchange office)	L	Spa
D	Theatre	M	Museum
G	Gallery (exhibition hall)	U	Hostel (tourist)
H	Hotel	VB	Public Security (police)

Orientation cross

a	b
c	d

Note: Pedestrian zones are marked with hatching.

Žilina

INDEX

The index informs about the position of the localities on the map (the letters indicate vertical and the numbers horizontal co-ordinates; medium type face indicates that the locality is shown on the map of Czechoslovakia or in the plan of Prague). Also indicated is the place of mention of a locality in the text (medium type face indicates a more detailed description) and about photographs of localities (respective page indicated in italics).

Gothic diamond vault
at Slavonice

ZAHRANIČNÍ LITERATURA

státní podnik

GREAT ASSORTMENT
OF IMPORTED FOREIGN LANGUAGE BOOKS
IN OUR SHOPS

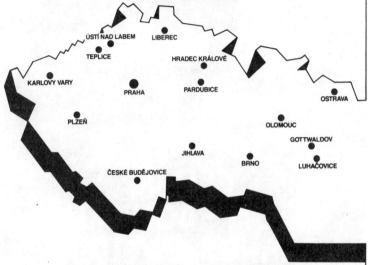

ZAHRANIČNÍ LITERATURA
PRAHA 1, Vodičkova 41 (vchod z pasáže ALFA) ● PRAHA 1, Na poříčí 28
ČESKÉ BUDĚJOVICE, Žižkovo nám. 35 ● PLZEŇ, nám. Republiky 19
KARLOVY VARY, Marxova 1 ● ÚSTÍ NAD LABEM, Fučíkova 47
TEPLICE, Leninova 21 ● LIBEREC, Gottwaldovo nám. 8
HRADEC KRÁLOVÉ, Leninova 30 ● PARDUBICE, tř. Míru 97
JIHLAVA, 9. května 16 ● BRNO, nám Svobody 18
OLOMOUC, nám. Míru 17 ● GOTTWALDOV, Revoluční 5
LUHAČOVICE, kolonáda ● OSTRAVA, Janáčkova 6

SOVĚTSKÁ KNIHA
PRAHA 1, Vodičkova 41 ● BRNO, nám. Svobody 7
OSTRAVA, Dimitrovova 1

KNIHY
КНИГИ
LIVRES
BÜCHER
BOOKS

GRANÁT,
Art Production Cooperative,
TURNOV

CLASSIC
BEAUTY – BOHEMIAN
GARNET JEWELLERY

Available
from the GRANÁT shops at TURNOV

and in the ALFA Passage,
Václavské náměstí 28, PRAHA 1

TAKE ADVANTAGE OF OUR SERVICES

HOTEL **CEDRON** — Hrabačov
PSČ 514 01   Hrabačov u Jilemnice

RESTAURANT **DIANA** — Znojmo
Městský lesík   PSČ 669 00   Znojmo

WE WAIT FOR YOU

Čedok, Travel and Hotel Corp.,
Na příkopě 18, 110 00 Praha 1
phone: 2127 111   telex: 12 11 09

**FOR ANY REASON
IN EVERY SEASON
TO CZECHOSLOVAKIA WITH ČEDOK**

OLYMPIA GUIDE

CZECHOSLOVAKIA
PRAGUE

MARCEL LUDVÍK

OTAKAR MOHYLA

Translation by Joy Turner-Kadečková
Read by Vladimír Adamec, Jarmila Davidová,
Michal Flegl, Jiří Hosnedl, Mária Jakubičková,
Josef Rubín, Jan Novotný
Cover by Zbyněk Zajíček, graphic design by Jan Zoul
after graphic design by Miloslav Fulín
Photographs by František Maleček, Jiří Morávek, František Přeučil
and from the archives of Olympia
Plans by Jiří Linhart and Zdeněk Stehlík
Map: Geodetický a kartografický podnik v Praze
Published by the Olympia Publishing House,
Prague 1989, as its 2 487th publication
1st edition, 282 pages
Responsible editor: Marcel Ludvík
Assistant editor: Dagmar Eisenmannová
Technical editor: Jan Zoul
Printed by Severografia
Thematic group 11/6
Author's sheets 24,69
Printed sheets 28,77
505/21/826   27—079—89
Printed in 30 000 copies
Price Kčs 40.00